Forever Changes

ARTHUR LEE
and the Book of Love

by **JOHN EINARSON**

Forever Changes
ARTHUR LEE AND THE BOOK OF LOVE
John Einarson

THE AUTHORIZED
BIOGRAPHY OF
ARTHUR LEE

A GENUINE JAWBONE BOOK
First Edition 2010
Published in the UK and the USA by Jawbone Press
2a Union Court,
20–22 Union Road,
London SW4 6JP,
England

www.jawbonepress.com

ISBN 978-1-906002-31-2

DESIGN Paul Cooper Design
EDITOR David Sheppard

Printed by Wai Man Book Binding (China) Ltd

1 2 3 4 5 14 13 12 11 10

Contents

ABOVE LEFT: **Chester Taylor with Agnes and Arthur in Memphis, about 1950.** ABOVE RIGHT: **Agnes Lee at her Los Angeles home at 3215 West 27th Street in the early 60s.** BELOW: **Arthur, age 19, at home with his dog Flash and cousin Anthony Lee.** RIGHT: **Arthur, age 17, playing the organ at home.** OPPOSITE: **Johnny Echols (guitar) and Arthur onstage in early 1966, with Love, playing at the Hullabaloo in Los Angeles.**

OPPOSITE: **The *Da Capo* lineup of Love, September 1966, left to right: Tjay Cantrelli, Johnny Echols, Michael Stuart, Alban 'Snoopy' Pfisterer, Kenny Forssi, and Bryan MacLean, with Arthur perched above them.** TOP: **Arthur in London, England, in February 1970.** RIGHT: **The *Forever Changes* lineup of Love, left to right: Stuart, Forssi, Lee, MacLean (behind), and Echols.**

TOP: **Arthur playing guitar at the home of childhood friend Hank Lee (no relation).**
RIGHT: **Arthur with his Irish Wolfhound Screwbop, pictured at the Avenida del Sol property in the early 70s.**
OPPOSITE: **Love onstage on their first European tour, in March 1970, left to right: Gary Rowles, Arthur Lee, George Suranovich, and Frank Fayad.**

CENTRE: **Arthur onstage during the late 70s.** ABOVE: **The** *Black Beauty* **Love lineup, left to right: Joe Blocker, Melvan Whittington, Robert Rozelle, Arthur Lee.**

ABOVE: **Arthur onstage in the 80s.**
RIGHT: **Note by Arthur in prison revealing his early health concerns.**
OPPOSITE TOP: **A letter from Bryan MacLean to Arthur, January 1998.**
OPPOSITE BELOW: **Diane and Arthur in Los Angeles, August 2005, shortly before moving back to Memphis.**

Jan 12

Arthur
        Is it true that you won't
talk or correspond w/ anyone, is that
a rumor? Did you see the letter
I wrote to Mojo Magazine telling them
to stop picking on you?
        Do they let you play guitar,
your best songs well may not have
been written yet, you know! There is
no such thing "as too late"!
        Did you know I just finished
eighteen months in the most intense
Rehab program?
        Would you be interested in
participating in a written oral
history of the band "Love"?
        I still believe in you, and
I'm praying that this is all working together for the best (and
for your appeal!)
                        love
                            B.

Un Recuerdo De Mexico En El Corazon De Los Angeles
A Small Part Of Mexico In The Heart Of Los Angeles

OLVERA STREET
THE BIRTH PLACE OF LOS ANGELES
El Pueblo De Nuestra Señora La Reina De Los Angeles Founded in Sept 4th 1781

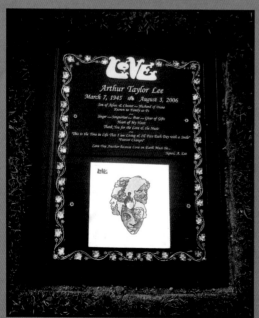

ABOVE: **Arthur (centre) with Memphis Love band, late 2005, with Greg Roberson and Alicja Trout on Arthur's right.**
LEFT: **Arthur's gravestone at the Forest Lawn Memorial Park, Hollywood Hills.**
RIGHT: **Arthur triumphant onstage in York, England, on the Forever Changes tour, June 28 2004.**

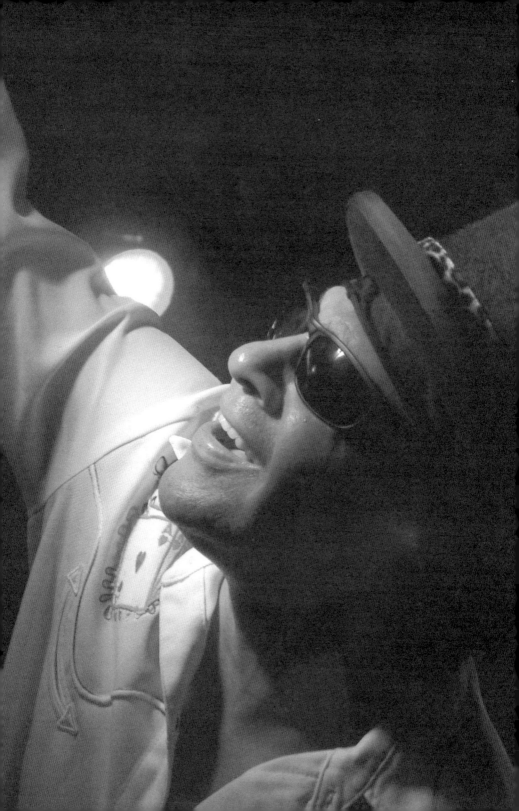

PREFACE

In 2003, following his release from prison and the acclaimed *Forever Changes* concert tour, Arthur Lee decided it was time he wrote his memoirs. Frustrated by what he considered flawed, exaggerated, and generally inaccurate published accounts of his life, Arthur was determined to set the record straight.

Entitled *Rainbow In The Storm: The Book Of Love (Part One)*, the manuscript was Arthur's life story in his own words, as dictated to a friend, Chris Boyle. Chock full of hitherto unrecorded personal reflections, insights, and anecdotes, the chronicle was nonetheless a flawed diamond in need of polishing and editing. There were also great gaps in Arthur's chronology that needed filling in, most notably the long, troubled period stretching from the early 70s to the beginning of the 90s. Memories of his final years of touring were also absent. As indicated by the title, this was to be the first instalment; a further volume was to follow.

On August 3 2006, Arthur passed away, his memoirs uncompleted and unpublished. In 2008, I contacted Arthur's widow, Diane Lee, with a proposal to write a full Arthur Lee biography based upon first-hand interviews with those closest to him. These would include family members, childhood friends, bandmates, associates, contemporaries, managers, and girlfriends – over 60 individuals in total. I would incorporate Arthur's 'voice' in the narrative, using edited portions of his original memoirs where appropriate. The result is the book you are holding. You will find Arthur's voice presented in italics throughout.

I would like to extend my sincere appreciation to everyone who agreed to be interviewed and whose names appear in the book. Special thanks go to my friend Dennis Kelley for being the facilitator of this project from the outset, and to Johnny Echols, Jac Holzman, Rick Williams, Bill Wasserzieher, Neal Skok, Chris Hall, Russ Danell, Chris Moise, Johnny Rogan, Barry Ballard, Rob Hughes, Mike Randle, Riley Racer, Andria Lisle, Pete Kurtz, Larry Marks, David Dunton, David Housden (publisher of Love fanzine *The Castle*), and Torben Skott (and his wonderfully helpful and resourceful Love website: http://love.torbenskott.dk), for keeping the Love flag flying. Thanks to Maria Johnson for her typing skills and also to David Fairweather, Mark Linn, Marc Skobac, Kara Wright, the one and only Harvey Kubernik, and Scott 'Lemonade Kid' Earle for his positive vibes and encouragement.

Additional thanks go to Tony Bacon, Mark Brend, my editor, David Sheppard, and the entire Jawbone crew for their enthusiastic support of this project.

I'd like to express my sincerest gratitude to Diane Lee for allowing and encouraging me to write Arthur's story frankly and sincerely. You are a very special person.

John Einarson
Winnipeg, Canada 2010

INTRODUCTION
LOVE ON EARTH MUST BE

It seemed only fitting that the audio and video recording of Arthur Lee's January 2003 *Forever Changes* concert – the rejuvenated singer essaying Love's magnum opus in its entirety, backed by a full electric band and a mini-orchestra – should take place before a UK audience. Long revered on these shores, Arthur's star had hardly dimmed in Britain after more than 35 years on, but more often off, the music scene. The UK music press, Love fanzine *The Castle*, miscellaneous websites, even Honourable Members of Parliament, had kept Arthur's freak flag flying during his incarceration in the latter 90s. While his homeland had ostensibly shunned him, on the European side of the pond Arthur's loyal fanbase remained both adoring and forgiving. Now here he was, at London's stately Royal Festival Hall, about to perform Love's iconic masterpiece in the flesh – a prospect which would have once been only a dream nurtured in the hearts of his most diehard devotees. On the night, you could have cut the anticipation with a knife.

Over the years, the absence of substantive information about Arthur Lee and his legendary band has merely propagated myth and misinformation. The rumors were as persistent as they were improbable. Had Love really murdered their roadie as punishment for stealing their drugs? Had two band-members actually been imprisoned for robbing LA donut shops? Had Arthur shot himself on stage at the end of the song "7 & 7 Is," fried his brain on a daily dose of acid, or died in a prison knife fight? However farfetched the stories, there was little doubt that Arthur had been to hell and back. Yet, somehow, the legend, the man, and the music had prevailed. "People have taken this group to heart and it's gone beyond the music," observes Love's original guitarist, and Arthur's childhood friend, Johnny Echols. "Part of the story was missing. When you don't have the facts, you make them up to fill the void. That's where all the myths about Arthur came from."

The undisputed prince of the Sunset Strip in the 60s, holding court in his expansive Los Feliz mansion; written off as a drug-addled recluse in the 70s and

80s; imprisoned in the 90s only to resurface stronger than ever in the new millennium; if nothing else, Arthur Lee was a survivor. Having outlived peers and partners-in-excess such as Jim Morrison, Janis Joplin, and Jimi Hendrix, his had become one of rock'n'roll's great redemptive stories. "If cats have nine lives," says veteran LA music journalist Harvey Kubernik, "then Arthur Lee had 18."

Arthur was released from Pleasant Valley State Penitentiary in Coalinga, California, on December 12 2001, having served five-and-a-half years of an excessively harsh 12-year sentence (courtesy of the state's controversial 'three strikes' law) for negligent discharge, illegal possession, and being a felon in possession of a firearm. In March 2002, Arthur pleaded 'no contest' to the final indictment rather than endure another trial. The two other charges were dismissed on appeal. Although he was free, the question remained: would the world of music still remember Arthur Lee?

"I think Arthur's popularity and worth increased while he was in prison in a way that he couldn't have made happen if he hadn't been in there," suggests Len Fagan, a close friend of Arthur's. "I remember him expressing his surprise and gratitude that the worldwide music community was embracing him, after being in prison. He said to me, very seriously, 'They didn't have to do that.' It proved to me that he knew how lucky he was to be so well-received."

The liberated Arthur hit the road running, undertaking the most extensive and demanding touring regimen of his career. "I was wondering if, after six years, he could still sing," says another of Arthur's friends, David Fairweather. "I was totally unprepared for his voice being stronger than I'd ever heard it before. He was like a lion and totally blew everyone away."

A 26-date European tour, beginning in Odense, Denmark, saw Arthur hooked up with Swedish arranger Gunnar Norden and an orchestral octet to perform the intricate *Forever Changes* material. "The concert tour was Gene Kraut's idea, not Arthur's," says David Fairweather. An American working in the Swedish music industry, Gene was a staunch Love and Arthur Lee fan who had taken a chance by booking Arthur on a European tour in the mid 90s, prior to his imprisonment. Arthur's dubious reputation for inconsistent performances had labeled him a risky bet, one which few promoters wanted to touch. Nonetheless, Gene recognized Arthur's enormous stature in Europe and believed the shows were worth chancing. His faith was rewarded by a successful nine-date tour, although additional concert plans would be scuttled by Arthur's incarceration. Post-captivity, Gene was determined to resurrect his client's career; performing a fully augmented *Forever Changes* would be the means to that end.

"Gene found this guy guy in Sweden, Gunnar, who had to write out all the parts [to the album's songs] because the original sheet music was long gone," says *Forever Changes* band guitarist Mike Randle. "We had to learn it by ear. Arthur couldn't really read music, but if he didn't like something he'd let us know and we'd play something different until he'd say, 'That's it. Do that.' We were able to inject ourselves into the performances and give it the energy which he loved."

Never one to wallow in his past, Arthur was initially reluctant to revisit *Forever Changes*. He ultimately acquiesced under Gene's unyielding conviction that mounting his crowning artistic achievement as a live concert would be the key to putting Arthur's misbegotten career on a sustainable upward curve. "Prior to this tour, Arthur was not at all interested in resurrecting the 60s or reliving all that," notes David Fairweather. "He'd say he didn't like *Forever Changes*, or that the band couldn't play it. That was just an excuse, because they *could* play it. He just didn't want to."

Forever Changes was recorded between June and September 1967, at the height of flower power and the Summer of Love and against a backdrop of the Vietnam War, draft resistance, civil rights marches, and student unrest. Even Love's local hedonist playground, Hollywood's Sunset Strip, had been the scene of youthful insurrection. Yet while it was undoubtedly conjured within this pervading countercultural milieu, *Forever Changes*, then as now, stands at one remove from the time and place of its conception and presents few, if any, of the psychedelic hallmarks of contemporaneous hit albums. Listen to The Doors' *Strange Days*, Jefferson Airplane's *After Bathing At Baxter's*, or even The Beatles' *Sgt. Pepper's Lonely Hearts Club Band*; all bear indelible hallmarks of 1967 whether in choice of instrumentation, arrangements, or lyrics. While label-mates and acolytes The Doors sold truckloads more records than Love, their music is forever preserved in the amber of that psychedelic summer and now sounds somewhat dated and perhaps a little pretentious. Not so *Forever Changes*. Love's third album is a uniquely homogenous body of work that transcends the confines of context and era. It continues to resonate with a timeless appeal that requires no prior connection to the era or cultural circumstances of its making. *Forever Changes* speaks a multi-generational language. It remains a consistent and cohesive set piece; the product, according to innumerable fans and critics, of genius and vision.

"When you think back on 1967, whether it's The Beach Boys, The Byrds, Jefferson Airplane, or Love, it was an era when there was a lot of room for experimentation," observes veteran writer, critic, and longtime observer of the LA music scene, Jim Bickhart. "People were open to it. I had heard strings and horns in rock before but never as thoroughly integrated into the arrangements as they were on *Forever Changes*. In my review in *Rolling Stone*, in early 1968, I didn't try to pass the album off as a commercial masterpiece, but I *did* try to talk about the artistry of it. That was obvious, even to a relative novice like me; and that's the thing that has proven most enduring. Listening to it more recently, my impression is that *Forever Changes* holds up in the same way that The Beach Boys' *Smile* album does. While *Forever Changes* got finished and could be enjoyed in real time, unlike [the long-shelved] *Smile*, it makes more sense over time, too. That's certainly true of the lyrics. A great artist has the ability to see into the future; that was Arthur. When he came out of prison and started doing those *Forever Changes* tours I remember thinking, 'at least he remembers that he did something great.'"

As the *Los Angeles Times* recently pointed out, *Forever Changes* crystallizes the unique atmosphere of LA better than any other album of its period. Its shades of color, much like those of the city itself, are both dark and light, and present "a seamless summation of the town's fun-house angles and myriad complexities." The article went on: "*Forever Changes* captures the way the city feels, the cadences of its sunny stuttering locomotion. Its timelessness stems from the notion that as much as LA changes, it will always retain certain immutable qualities that Love's music captures."

Over and above those "immutable" evocations, its bountiful melodic hooks, sonorous symphonic arrangements, and opaque yet always curiously topical lyrics, what is remarkable about *Forever Changes* is that it was a commercial failure on release, falling on deaf ears everywhere except the group's southern Californian heartland and in the UK. Indeed, its reputation as one of the greatest albums of all time has been built almost exclusively by rediscovery and word of mouth. What was for so long the quintessential cult classic is now universally hailed for its artistic brilliance. Yet its 1967 target audience missed it almost completely, dealing a crushing blow to its creator and contributing to the inevitable break up of the original nucleus of Love.

In the intervening decades, Arthur would consistently badmouth the album, largely as a defense mechanism knowing he could never reproduce it on stage nor better it in the studio. For Arthur, *Forever Changes* became a blessing and a curse, a milestone and a millstone. In the 70s, when fans would call out for songs from the album, he would retort: "I don't play that shit any more." He informed beleaguered journalists that he loathed the album. Every subsequent record Arthur released, whether as Love or under his own name, would be measured against *Forever Changes* and would invariably come up short.

All of which simply added to the emotional spectacle of a reinvigorated, 21st century Arthur Lee finally giving his fans what they had despaired of ever seeing or hearing: Love's tour de force album being performed on stage, just as it was originally conceived and recorded. Most commentators acknowledge that Love could have been big league contenders had Arthur been more willing to tour and promote their albums back in the day. Now in his mid fifties, he had a lot of catching up to do and much to prove. Between 2002 and 2004 he would tour more extensively than at any other time in his career. The demand for *Forever Changes* appeared insatiable. Arthur wrote about it in this first extract from his memoirs.

People have been asking me all the time how it feels to be touring on an album that I recorded 35 years ago. All I can say is that it feels good. First of all, God has truly blessed me by making all this possible and, secondly, the album is still as good today as when I wrote it. Maybe, just maybe, now is the time I'm supposed to be touring and playing it. Had I done it back then, of course, I might not even be here to tell you this story.

It really feels good to be back on the road again and to be received so well by people around the world. There are people in other countries who I wasn't aware even knew my music. In Spain, these people knew the lyrics to every song I wrote. I found out they knew no English except my lyrics. Talk about a warm reception; theirs was unforgettable. One night, in Manchester, the audience chanted "Arthur Lee" to the tune of the "Notre Dame Fight Song" for over ten minutes. What can you say when an audience does that? I was blown away. We played in Ireland and the crowd would not let the tour-bus leave. I went down and shook every hand and signed every autograph because I knew we'd never get out of there if I didn't.

Unlike the graying devotees who flock to shows by what are generally labeled 'vintage,' 'retro,' or 'dinosaur' acts from the 60s, Arthur's audience was largely comprised of younger fans, most not even born when *Forever Changes* was recorded. "There were people who came to these UK shows whose parents had turned them on to Love years ago, and now they're grown up and bringing *their* kids to the shows," marvels Mike Randle. "You would see three generations. That made Arthur really proud. He knew we were doing something special."

"London was almost like Arthur's home turf," says David Fairweather, recalling the rapturous response Arthur received in the UK capital. "He felt very at home there and even talked of wanting to live there. The red carpet was rolled out for him in London. In LA, he had become practically unknown but in London it seemed everyone knew who he was. One of the freakiest things took place when Arthur and I were walking back from a restaurant one evening. You don't see too many homeless street people in London but we saw one guy who looked straight off Jethro Tull's *Aqualung* album cover, with the long coat and the straggly hair. He was literally lying in the gutter, semi-conscious. As we walked by, this guy looked up and you could see the glimmer of recognition in his eyes. He slowly pointed up and cried, 'Arthur Lee!' I was so impressed. Arthur was surprised. It shook him up as much as it gratified him."

Life on the road with Arthur Lee was never easy or predictable. The longsuffering musicians in his backing band, Baby Lemonade, were prepared for anything. It was akin to riding a rollercoaster, blindfolded; they never knew quite when the ups and downs would come, only that they were inevitable somewhere along the way. It was impossible to know how it would end, whether a smooth stop or an abrupt crash and burn. "You never knew, day-by-day, what Arthur was going to be like. Sometimes it was minute-by-minute," says drummer David 'Daddyo' Green, whose job description also included looking after Arthur's everyday affairs on the road and making sure he was on an even keel for the concerts. "Everyone had to tolerate Arthur's behavior because of his great talent," confirms David Fairweather. "There were arguments, but the band loved him. Arthur had idiosyncrasies you had to deal with."

"He came out of jail a kinder, gentler Arthur," observes his former manager Mark Linn. "The fact that he played so many dates in a row ... the old Arthur could never have done that. Something would have blown up. He appreciated the band; they were kids who really had it together. They were rehearsed and dependable," says Linn. "He put them through hell, sure, but with the old Arthur it would have been much worse. Mostly, Arthur was appreciating the acclaim he was finally receiving."

On the evening of January 15 2003, everything was ready at the Royal Festival Hall. Having performed the album's complex tracks for six months, often accompanied by the Swedish string and horn sections, and with two gigs on the current tour already under their belts, the ensemble was becoming a well-oiled machine. Nonetheless, with the recording and film equipment poised to capture the concert, there was plenty to be anxious about. "Arthur was nervous at the recording because of all the cameras on him," recalls David Fairweather.

The atmosphere was palpably charged, but Arthur would be a match for it. "He was extremely focused," notes 70s Love drummer Joe Blocker, who attended the Royal Festival Hall concert at Arthur's request. "He wasn't drunk, he wasn't high. He knew the band was sounding good and he was on point. He knew what he had to do and he wasn't going to let it affect him. He put on his hat, walked on stage, and the crowd erupted." Indeed, Arthur's entrance, a little while after the band, would earn an extended standing ovation. "Those people had been waiting 35 years to hear this music," says Joe. "I can't describe to you how happy each and every one of them was to be there. I remember walking through the lobby beforehand and people were recognizing *me*, and I was in one of the later line-ups of Love. That's how into it they were. They gave Arthur a standing ovation that lasted a good five minutes, just for walking on stage."

"Arthur moved languidly, like a cat," recalls Tina Winter, a British Love fan who attended the Festival Hall show. "He wore a cowboy hat, bandana, shades, white fringed shirt, jeans, and boots ... as cool as they come. And his voice was incredibly strong and clear."

From the subtle, fingerpicking opening of "Alone Again Or," the evening would be an unmitigated Love-in, with the audience transfixed by every note, word, hook, and nuance. There was an audible gasp from the crowd during the opening song as its dramatic Spanish Corrida trumpet solo took flight, reaching a crescendo with the swelling strings. It was an uplifting confirmation for the audience that this was the *Forever Changes* they knew and loved from memory. "I was just completely choked with emotion from the first chords," admits Tina Winter. "The trumpet in 'Alone Again Or' just made me cry. This is something I never really thought that I'd see or hear. It's one of the most memorable experiences of my life."

"I was in heaven with every tune," wrote Graham Cole in a blog on Torben Skott's dedicated Love website. "I am so thankful that I saw and heard the songs performed so exquisitely. At the conclusion, I suspect mine were not the only eyes that had misted over," said Cole. "The entire theatre rose to its feet. The applause just went on and on. It had, I suspect, surpassed what many may have expected after all that time."

Good things come to those who wait, but for me, that ain't the half of it. When a girl at the Royal Festival Hall concert yelled out, "Arthur, you don't know how long we've waited for this," I replied, "But you know how long I've waited."

By the time the ensemble reached the triumphant closing song, "You Set The Scene," with its glorious violin and brass flourishes, there could be little doubt that its prophetic lyrics: "This is the time and life that I am living / And I'll face each day with a smile," now rang truer for Arthur than when he had originally conceived them in 1967.

Having endured nearly six years of prison, Arthur had indeed learned to embrace every day with a passion and give thanks to a higher power that he had been able to return to what he loved best: his music and performing for his fans. Arthur Lee had truly been blessed and he knew it.

When asked by interviewers to put into words the significance of the *Forever Changes* tour and his remarkable return to the spotlight, Arthur simply replied that he had received a direction from God: "Love on Earth must be."

CHAPTER 1

WHEN I WAS A
BOY I THOUGHT
ABOUT THE TIMES
I'D BE A MAN

Arthur Lee, age 11

There are those close to Arthur Lee who regarded him as a complex, multi-faceted individual who was difficult to assess or comprehend. Others claim the contrary: that he was the simplest of men once you stripped away all the trappings of adulation and celebrity that surrounded him. Both factions agree, however, that to understand Arthur Lee you need to know 'Po' – the boy who grew up to become the legend.

My mom, Agnes Porter, was born into a family with lots of brothers and sisters. She was the daughter of Ed Porter, my grandfather. He was white. He died before I was born. My mom was born and raised in Memphis, Tennessee and graduated from Manassas High School before going on to LeMoyne College and Tennessee State in Nashville. She then taught school at Manassas. She married Chester Taylor, a cornet player, and they lived in Memphis in a neighborhood known as New Chicago. I didn't come into this world by my own choice. My mom was in labor for a long time and I put up one hell of a fight before I was finally born on Wednesday, March 7 1945, in John Gaston Hospital, Memphis. I was named Arthur Porter Taylor.

As an only child, I felt like a loner right from the start. My mother was fair of complexion and looked white. My father was a brown-skinned black man. As I grew up, I was too light-skinned to be black and too dark-skinned to be white. It was kind of lonely. In those days, it was "Negroes," "niggers," or nothin'. Today, it's "Black" or "African American." I wasn't crying, "Oh God, what'll I do?" or anything like that, but I learned to be tough. People always looked at me as though my face was saying, "What are you looking at?" even when I wasn't actually looking at them at all.

I remember my mother telling me about her brother, Johnson, who was once asked by a surveyor if he was white or black. He looked almost exactly like Errol Flynn. As a little boy, he once said he was white and my grandmother, Mal Porter, heard him. She said, "Johnson, you better tell that man you are black." From a picture I've seen, Mal was light-skinned and looked white.

Born on February 17 1903, Agnes Porter was the eldest of five children parented by Ed and Malvise (Mal) Porter (nee Mosley). She had two sisters: Vera and Edwinor and two brothers: Johnson (John) and Marshall. Her father was white, her mother black. Agnes, as Arthur notes, had fair skin and white features.

The story goes that she and one of her sisters were once denied admittance at a black hospital because the staff did not believe they were of color. "Agnes looked white," confirms Lovey Joyner, the wife of Arthur's cousin, Joe Joyner. "A lot of people never knew she was black."

The extended Porter family lived along North Bellevue Boulevard in New Chicago, a predominantly black district of Shelby County, Memphis (more recently the location for hip hop movie *Hustle & Flow*). Joe Joyner's grandmother, Ella Mosley Crawford, was the sister of Agnes's mother, Malvise, Arthur's grandmother, and lived on Bellevue. "They all lived across the street from us in a big, two-storey house," Joe remembers. "My grandfather bought all these houses on Bellevue; ten lots, including the house my mother lived in and the house Agnes lived in. Bellevue was like a business district. They had maybe eight grocery stores and a funeral home. There was a railroad track kind of separating the blacks and the whites, although there were whites living throughout New Chicago; a lot of people didn't know that. It was a working class neighborhood. All the people in my family were either teachers or principals; that includes Arthur's family."

Despite the presence of white families in New Chicago, this was still the early postwar South; segregation was a part of life. Johnny Echols, Arthur's musical auxiliary in the original line-up of Love, grew up one street away on Leath. "Where we lived in Memphis, there were white people living behind us," Johnny explains. "My mother was friends with these people and would talk over the fence, yet they were never together on the *other* side of that fence. They were great friends at home but couldn't go to the same clubs or restaurants. It was a strange situation."

Little is known of Arthur's maternal grandparents. Joe Joyner recalls Mal Porter contracting diabetes and having to have her legs wrapped up every day. Arthur's grandfather died in 1936, before Joe's birth. The five Porter siblings remained close, even after marriage.

By the standards of the time, Agnes married late in life. A respected school teacher, she had already turned 40 when she was wooed by a local jazz musician – cornet player Chester A. Taylor. They were wed soon after meeting. "Arthur's mother was quite a bit older than my mother," says Johnny Echols. "When Arthur was born, Agnes was in her forties, so she was best friends with my grandmother. They were school teachers together and hell-raisers, too. They would follow Jimmie Lunceford's band and other orchestras. They were swingers, in the sense that they were very into music. That's how Agnes met Arthur's father; he was playing in Jimmie's band."

Memphis was a hub for the jazz and blues music that traveled between New Orleans and Chicago. The many clubs which lined the city's Beale Street, not to mention the chitlin' circuit which extended throughout the rural South, meant the region offered plenty of work for a good musician. Joe Joyner is uncertain whether Chester Taylor was, in fact, a member of the popular Jimmie Lunceford band, as Johnny Echols suggests, but he does recall that after he married Agnes, Chester took on a regular job to help support the family: "Jimmy Crawford, the son of my great aunt, Susie Mosley Crawford, was a drummer in Lunceford's band. Chester might have played in Jimmie's band, too, but he had a day job working downtown." Jimmie Lunceford died suddenly of a heart attack, in July 1947, which might be the reason Chester sought more orthodox employment, although the Lunceford band actually persisted until 1949.

Aged 42, Agnes gave birth to Arthur Porter Taylor (it is believed that Chester's middle name was Arthur) and brought the baby home from hospital to 1322 North Bellevue Boulevard – Edwinor Porter's house. Soon afterward, Chester, Agnes, and baby Arthur moved to 1361 North Bellevue Boulevard, a bungalow across the street from Edwinor's home.

A precocious child and a handful at the best of times, Po – short for Porter – was often looked after by one or other family member so that Agnes could resume her teaching career. Chester was either on the road or at work.

All I have is one picture of my father, Chester Taylor, with my mother, who looked white, and my aunt, who also looked white. Chester is in the middle: a handsome, brown-skinned man. He looks like he doesn't give a fuck about anything. He left me his house and his car when he died, but I never knew him. I think my mother loved him until the day she died, even though she remarried.

One early memory I have is of sitting on my Aunt Vera Porter's porch, in Memphis, when I was three. She was drinking beer, smoking cigarettes, and listening to the blues station on the radio – the only one she ever played. Vera was my mom's sister and she used to baby-sit me when my mother taught school. We had us some fun. She was the most soulful person I ever knew and a very important person in my life. She raised me. She used to curse a lot and I thought it was cool. She taught me how to cuss and she always used to say,

*"Don't take nothin' from nobody." Aunt Vera was a boozer. She died from
drinking rat poison.*

A free spirit, Vera Porter had one daughter, Edwinor, known to everyone as
'Peaches.' When Vera died, Peaches came to live with her aunt Edwinor (after
whom she was named) who had no offspring and so raised the child as her own.
Johnson Porter would move to California where, in 1980, he was killed in a
shooting incident. Arthur loved his uncle and was devastated on learning of his
murder. "Arthur was always very sentimental about family," notes his widow,
Diane Lee. Agnes's youngest brother, Marshall Porter, had two sons: Marshall Jr.,
or 'Bubba,' and Preston. The latter died in a car accident in Mexico in the 70s.
Arthur sent money to bring his body back to Tennessee for burial. "Arthur had a
big heart and helped out family members," acknowledges Joe Joyner. "If I had
wanted anything, he would have given me the shirt off his back."

Agnes returned to Memphis in the 80s and moved in with her sister, Edwinor.
The house was later bequeathed to Arthur who resided there for the last two years
of his life. The property remains in Diane Lee's possession.

*Vera would drink and smoke, drink and smoke; she was having parties almost
every day, downstairs. My mother didn't even know about it because she was too
busy teaching at Manassas High School. That's where my career actually began,
sitting on Vera's porch listening to the old blues guys on the radio, the spirituals
they sang at the Baptist Church every Sunday and hearing the Manassas High
School Band practice every school day. We lived close enough to the school that I
could hear them play, and I'd echo it back on the wash tubs. That's what got me
started playing music.*

*The first musician I came into contact with was my father. He played cornet.
I don't know if it rubbed off on me, but I was fascinated by music. It was born
right in me, I guess. I picked up on music faster than an ape can peel a banana –
faster than anything else I attempted to do, except for athletics, which I dug later.
It was easier for me to pick up on things I heard when I was a kid. I always sang
in the bathtub. I did the whole routine of singing and mimicking records on the
radio – old blues cats like Howlin' Wolf and Muddy Waters, spirituals, and all the
other songs they played. I would find myself singing and humming the songs and
just groovin' along with the radio.*

When I was four, I made my stage debut at the Baptist Church. It was on Easter Sunday. All the kids had to learn skits, so my mom taught me this poem about a red telephone. I was supposed to say this little poem, then pick up the phone and answer it. When I got up there, in front of all those people, I found the phone was broken and I froze. I couldn't remember a thing. I started crying 'cause I thought I was gonna get a whoopin' for that one.

I was smoking when I was three. I started a fire in Aunt Edwinor's chicken house and burned it all down, chickens and everything. I got my ass whooped for that one. I was rowdy alright. My mom used to beat my ass all the time when I got into trouble. I remember once being with my mom in the grocery store and there was this little kid lying on the floor kicking, screaming, and crying. My mother walked me over there and said, "Arthur, you see that? If you ever do that in front of me, I'll kill ya." I never did that, ever.

Arthur developed a very close bond with his mother that remained throughout his life. Although authoritarian and not afraid to mete out corporal punishment when she felt it necessary, Agnes doted on her only child. A follower of the Christian Science faith, she raised her son to believe in the power of prayer and in doing good deeds as a means of self-improvement. Even during Arthur's darkest years, she remained his most ardent supporter and would come to his house in the Hollywood Hills to do his laundry. Arthur was overwhelmed with grief when she passed away in the late 90s, while he was imprisoned. He knew his incarceration had brought shame to Agnes and being refused permission to attend her funeral broke his heart.

My mom was the best. I can remember her bathing me, way back. She would always say, "Goodness gracious" and "Mama's baby"— sweet things like that. My mother really had a hold on me. She was everything I thought authority could be. I think I was a good kid from age one to three, because I don't remember giving my mother that many problems. I loved my mother. She was my comfort, my security, and my connection with the world outside. She cooked for me, watched out for me, loved me, and always wanted the best for me. My mother and I eventually lived alone and I thought that's how it should be.

In a mid 90s interview, British journalist Barney Hoskyns asked Agnes to describe her son as a young child. She responded: "He was a spoiled brat but he had a good heart." Joe Joyner certainly remembers young Po being something of a mischief-maker: "Arthur played with my brother, Ray, who was two years younger than me but older than Arthur. One time, he and Arthur took a friend of my mother's car out of the yard. The two of them drove around the block. They could barely see over the steering wheel. Both of them got a scolding when they got back."

Agnes and Chester separated in the early 50s. Arthur often told a story about his father going out for milk and coming back two years later. In fact, the basis for the split was that, as the divorce petition stated: "The defendant has abandoned complainant and refused or neglected to provide for her." There may have been other reasons. The petition was signed by Agnes Porter Taylor, Edwinor Porter, and Vera Porter. Agnes was given exclusive care and custody of Arthur. Chester received visitation rights although he never exercised them. The court also gave Agnes the house on North Bellevue Boulevard, in lieu of alimony. "Agnes didn't talk much about Arthur's Dad," says Arthur's former girlfriend, Gaye Blair, "except to say that he was a great musician but no good."

I guess my father did what he had to do. He was his own man. I only recall seeing him three times in my whole life. One reason they separated was that my mom wanted to better my future, and to do that she needed to move to a nicer place. We lived on a street without sidewalks. This yellow bus used to come by to take everybody to go pick cotton.

Joe Joyner, then a teenager living two doors down from the Taylors, remembers another possible motivation for Agnes's move: "She came out to California on a visit, and while she was here she met Mr. Lee. Someone introduced them. Mr. Lee was in construction. I don't know what he told her, but I guess she thought he could give her the world. So she went back to Memphis, packed up all her stuff while Chester Taylor was gone to work, and then left. She and Arthur took the train to California. When Chester came home, they were gone. They later divorced and Mr. Lee adopted Arthur. He was no longer a Taylor, he was Arthur Lee. That's a true story. I was a little boy at the time, but I remember that for a fact. Everybody in the family knew. Arthur's story [about Chester Taylor walking out on the family] sounds good, but it didn't happen like that. Clinton Lee was a well-respected guy and was successful. He helped build a lot of beautiful buildings down on Wilshire Boulevard, so he was pulling in a lot of money. He owned several houses in other neighborhoods."

Agnes Taylor did indeed travel to California, but whether she met Clinton 'C.L.' Lee on that first trip is unconfirmed. She certainly returned to Los Angeles permanently in 1952, with seven-year-old Arthur in tow. "Agnes told me that when she came out to LA from Memphis, it was not easy for blacks," says Gaye Blair. "And she was alone with a little child. She admitted that she had to pass for white all the way."

Agnes's divorce from Chester Taylor was granted on January 1 of the following year. She would marry C.L. on April 23 1955. Arthur was still Arthur Porter Taylor until formally adopted by his stepfather on June 6 1960, C.L. having filed a notice of adoption in 1958. One of Arthur's early bank books reveals the name Arthur Porter Taylor scratched out and Arthur Taylor Lee written in. On marrying C.L., Agnes Porter Taylor formally dropped her given family name and became Agnes Taylor Lee.

"Arthur was *Po* to us, all his life," recalls his childhood friend Azell Taylor (no relation). "We also knew him as Arthur Taylor, but never Arthur Taylor Lee or Arthur Lee. I remember I was working at a place called The House Of Hides, around 1967 or '68, and this guy there says to me, 'You ever heard of Arthur Lee?' I said, 'No, I don't know any Arthur Lee.' We always knew him as Arthur Taylor. We used to tell people we were cousins, 'cause I'm a Taylor, too. Even when I looked at that *Love* album cover, I still didn't recognize him. Another time, I was walking through the parking lot at A&M Records and I heard someone say, 'Azell Taylor? Is that you?' I replied, 'Yeah. Who's that?' He said, 'Arthur. Arthur Lee!' I didn't recognize him or the name. Then he said, 'Arthur Taylor' and I got it. I said, 'Arthur Taylor! Man, how you been?'"

Chester Taylor eventually moved up to Detroit and lost contact with his son. Arthur never knew whether he had any half-siblings. "Arthur didn't have direct contact with his natural father," confirms Diane Lee, "but sometime in the early 1980s, when we were living together, Arthur was on the phone with Chester and he handed it to me to talk to him. I remember Chester saying, 'What's the matter with the boy?' because Arthur was all emotional. Chester passed away not long after that." Chester Taylor's thoughts about his son's musical career go unrecorded.

Originally hailing from Cotton Valley, Louisiana, Clinton Lee was the third of seven children. He served in the US army during World War II before settling in Los Angeles in 1946, taking a job in construction. Skilled at masonry, he prospered during LA's postwar construction boom. Arthur would often point to the sculptures which adorned several buildings along Wilshire Boulevard as evidence of his stepfather's handiwork. "Arthur was very proud of what Clinton did," says Diane. "He tried to show Arthur how to do that kind of stonework, but Arthur wasn't interested. He wanted to show Arthur a trade. He was a good man."

Agnes was able to pick up her teaching career in LA. The second income meant the Lees could afford to buy a modest home. They found one at 3215 West 27th Street, in the West Adams area of South Central LA, adjacent to the well-heeled Baldwin Hills neighborhood. Boasting clean streets lined with white stucco bungalows, the neighborhood was predominantly home to middleclass white and Asian residents.

I remember when we came to LA on the Rock Island Line from Memphis. It seemed like it took 30 years. My mom got a job at the 24th Street Child Care Center and got remarried to Clinton Lee. My stepfather didn't play any sports or music; all he knew was hard work. If you didn't work hard you were not a man, in his estimation. When he bought our home in South Los Angeles, he, his brother, and cousins were the only blacks on the street. My neighborhood was mostly white in the 50s, with a few Japanese. My neighbors, the Anchors, used to be involved in motion pictures. They made the layouts for different movies. I saw one of these layouts and it was King Kong, a little bitty ape not bigger than my hand.

It didn't take long for Po Taylor to establish himself in the neighborhood. Friends recall him as both a natural athlete and a spoiled bully who always had to get his way. Although exceptionally bright, quick-witted, and a good reader (a habit that remained lifelong), Arthur did not excel academically, much to his mother's dismay. Arthur's great aunt, Susie Mosley Crawford, a former school principal in Memphis, came to live with the Lees in the late 50s after being diagnosed with glaucoma. The pressure on Arthur to succeed in school was brought to bear by this two-pronged attack. Arthur once remarked that he'd come to loathe school because when he returned home each day it felt like he was still in class.

I was the toughest kid at Sixth Avenue Elementary School, West Jefferson Boulevard – which I jokingly refer to as my 'alma mater.' They used to put you on teams according to how good you were doing in your studies, so I always got put on the worst team. I remember playing softball, and when I walked up to the plate I'd say, "If you touch this ball after I hit it, I'm gonna kick your ass." I'd get a hit and, sure enough, Ron Talley would catch it and I'd have to go over and kick his ass. He went home and got his brother, Tito. He said, "I hear you been messin' with my brother. I'm gonna kick your butt." I blasted him straight off. From that moment on, I was known as the toughest kid in the neighborhood. They all got out of my way.

"As a kid, Arthur was really something," remembered his childhood friend Ann Stewart Denard, speaking at Arthur's LA funeral service in 2006. "He was the best athlete at Sixth Avenue Elementary School. Everybody wanted him on their team. He was also the school bully and beat everybody up. Nobody would challenge Arthur Taylor because he would be waiting for you after school. He was really good with his dukes. We girls used to say, 'Maybe we should marry a guy like Po, because he could protect us.' He taught me all the techniques to beat everyone in tetherball. His mother, Miss Agnes, was so beautiful. She looked like a movie star, she was so pretty. She gave him a solid home training. She made him go to Sunday school every Sunday."

Joe Joyner recalls visiting Arthur and Agnes in the late 50s: "They lived in a very nice neighborhood. Sugar Ray Robinson, the boxer, lived around the corner. It was a mixed area. The Lees might have been among the first blacks. Baldwin Hills, right nearby, was mostly Jewish. Their home was on a great street. C.L. was in construction and so he and his brother expanded the house."

A British writer once referred to Arthur as "a ghetto punk" while claiming, erroneously, that Agnes lived in deprived Watts. The reality of the Lees' domestic situation was very different: Arthur's hardworking stepfather always made sure of that. Later, the diligent C.L. would take responsibility for maintaining Arthur's homes. "At one point, when Arthur had a lot of dogs, C.L. put fences up separating them," recalls Joe Joyner. "When Arthur would go out of town, C.L. would go and check on his house." Joe remembers the young Arthur being impulsive: "He was kind of a hostile guy. He got into a lot of fights. He was arrogant and had an attitude about him. Being an only child and being spoiled had something to do with it. He had everything he wanted and got away with a lot of things that normal kids wouldn't have. That was just the personality he had."

"Arthur was a tough kid," confirms Douglas Prince who, like his brother, Leonard, was a neighborhood friend of Arthur's. "He had a reputation and street savvy. He was kind of spoiled; if he didn't get his way he'd get upset. He always had to be number one and have the most of things. He was competitive but he had a little more help than the rest of us. We had to earn our money; Arthur's parents gave him his. He always had money in his pocket. He could also do some mean things. If Arthur didn't get his way he used to set his dog, Sissy, on you."

Douglas and Leonard were really a trip. We used to have fun. We would have rock fights, the two of them against me. I made up this throwing technique where I would throw a rock high in the air and while they were looking at that one, I would throw another two or three rocks straight ahead at them. We used to play football and basketball, or wrestle, box, or run track, all on the sidewalks or in the street.

"We kind of had rival groups of friends," recalls another neighborhood character, Riley Racer, who also lived on 27th Street and would go on to become Arthur's personal assistant in the early 70s. "It wasn't like gangs. Arlington Avenue divided us. Arthur went to Sixth Avenue School, whereas most of the guys on the east side of Arlington went to 24th Street Elementary School. At first, we would have things like rock fights across the street, but then we just started blending in together. Doug Prince and his brother, Leonard, lived right around there. John Lucky was a friend, too. We all kind of gravitated towards each other. I knew Arthur's dogs, Sissy and Flash. Flash was the dog that 'lies hypnotized' in Love's song "7 & 7 Is." His eyes always had this eerie glow to them."

Arthur was fond of contradictions, Riley recalls: "He would name a mean dog Sissy because the dog was exactly the opposite of that. Whenever Arthur would make a hissing sound between his teeth, Sissy's ears would prick up and he would be ready to attack. A lot of Arthur's friends wouldn't go near Sissy. I was one of the few that could go in the backyard alone with the dog. I don't think there were many people who walked down Arthur's side of the street without Sissy trying to bite them. I think that's when Arthur and I kind of bonded, because he could see that Sissy trusted me. Arthur always loved dogs. He said he always wanted to own five dogs – and when he was successful, he did. I think Arthur understood animals. He had one of the largest number and the most variety of pigeons anywhere. He had Rollers, Tumblers, Muffs, Fantails ... he had them all. People used to come to see his pigeons. This was when he was about 15 or 16. He had a reputation for knowing just about everything about pigeons. Anything Arthur did, he wanted to be the best at it."

All my life I have raised pigeons. When I was a little boy, I was scared to death of anything that flew or had wings and claws. One day, I was visiting a friend of mine who had built a pigeon coop and he asked me to pet one of his birds. I was afraid at first, but he assured me that they didn't bite and he told me to put my hand up to its face. He said that if it did peck it wouldn't be hard. The flapping of the wings terrified me as much as the claws and beak, so he told me to hold one all by myself. The more I held them the more I got used to them. Pretty soon I was sticking my hand right into the nest, checking the eggs and babies.

I asked my mother if I could build a pigeon coop and raise a few of my own. She said "yes," just like she always did. I really had a great mom. The only thing was, whatever she and my stepfather let me have, I had to take care of. If I asked for a puppy, I had to clean up behind it and, when it was old enough, teach it how to bark when strangers came around and bite if they came on the property. I did real well with all the animals. Those pigeons became one of my favorite hobbies. I would go to the library and read books on them. I never would have guessed that there are so many different kinds of pigeons. One of my biggest joys was sending away for them and having to go to the train station to pick them up after they arrived from places like Pennsylvania, New York, Ohio, or wherever else people had the variety that I wanted.

I counted my birds one day and I think my parents had let me have at least 450 of them. I would cross-breed them all with Parlor pigeons. Parlors are the kind of birds that look just like ordinary pigeons but they can't fly. All they do is jump up and turn flips. If you mate a Parlor pigeon with a regular one you get a Flying Tumbler or a Parlor Roller. I had so many birds ... I started putting Easter egg dye on them. What a sight it was to see the sky covered with black, white, brown, red, blue, green, pink, and yellow pigeons - whatever color dye I could get my hands on. All 450 pigeons would come rushing out past me and then spread out all over the place. There is just nothing like the feeling I would get.

For all his sensitivity with animals, Arthur was still a belligerent youth. Riley Racer discovered that knowing the local tough guy had its benefits: "Arthur taught me to stand up for myself. There was a bully on the street named Nate who always used to pick on me. Arthur told me, 'If you don't stand up for yourself he's gonna keep picking on you the rest of your life.' He even taught me a left hook. One day, Nate and I had it out and the next day he was my best friend."

At one point in my life, I actually considered becoming a boxer. I was really good at it. To me, the object of being a good boxer is not to get hit. I studied that art by looking at the best that they had at the time on the Friday Night Fights, on TV. I saw Sugar Ray Robinson and Cassius Clay – alias Muhammad Ali. I had Ali's picture on the wall in my bedroom. I remember my stepfather taking me to see him fight Sonny Liston at the Olympic Auditorium in downtown LA. My father went to get some popcorn and when he came back the fight was over. He had paid $50. What a bummer.

I learned to shoot a gun in Boy Scouts. I took first place for the whole of Los Angeles County in shooting at targets, at Lake Arrowhead. My stepfather bought me a BB gun when I was 12 or 13. Douglas and Leonard Prince and I used to shoot birds almost every day. One day my stepfather said, "Enough. Any birds you shoot from now on, you've got to cook and eat." I was eating mockingbirds, blue jays, pigeons, doves ... you name it.

Around this time, another boy moved into the locality. "Arthur and his mother left Memphis when he was about seven and we moved out about a year or so later," remembers Johnny Echols, Arthur's junior by two years (he was born February 21 1947). "Unbeknown to my family, we moved almost adjacent to each other – two doors down on 27th Street. We didn't even realize it until I went out to meet the neighborhood and there was Po playing on the street. I recognized him immediately. Arthur was gregarious and always the center of attention, no matter where he was. He and a bunch of local kids were playing football. Someone had scored a touchdown over him and he was crying foul. That was Arthur. He had a strong personality; he had to be the leader of the bullies, so to speak. Then Mrs. Lee came out of the house. I talked rather loudly back then, and she recognized me. 'I might have known it was you,' she said, and gave me a big hug. Of course, she met up with my grandmother again and they remained friends from then on."

Reacquainted, the two boys noted a marked contrast in their respective experience of school. "We went to school together, although Arthur was a grade higher than me for a little while, until he started not wanting to go to high school and they kept him back a year. Back in the South, you would go to the same school from kindergarten, all the way through high school; so the teachers knew you and knew your family. If you got into trouble, they would all know. But in LA, it was more isolated and separate. You could get away with stuff. No one was going to give you up to your parents, and something that happened at home, the school could care less about. Also, it was a totally integrated society." A combination of these factors allowed some, most conspicuously Arthur, licence to get away with just about anything.

Having older parents who indulged his every wish, Arthur learned from a young age not to take responsibility for his actions, even if that was at the expense of others. "For Arthur, it was like having grandparents for parents," says Johnny. "Because they were older when he was born, they spoiled him. The rest of us kids would have to turn in bottles for pocket money; not Arthur. His Dad being his stepfather, he doted on him. His mother would try to corral him and punish him a bit by having him stay in his room, but Arthur had a television in there, and none of us had that. He also had his instruments in there; so what kind of punishment was that? That kind of upbringing sets up your character and the way you deal with life. I think that was, to a large extent, why Arthur only saw things from his own perspective without thinking of the consequences, or that the other person might have a point of view, too. He could get away with things none of us could."

Life was simple for me back in those days. All you had to do was wake up and do what somebody else told you. Sometimes I hated it. "Children are to be seen and not heard," that's what they said. I think it took me about ten ass-whoopings to find out what that meant.

Old sayings have always been a trip to me. Life can sometimes show you what they really mean. My great aunt Susie used to say: "A fool against his own will is the same opinion still." It took me a long time to figure out what that meant. It means a person that knows he's doing wrong, you can't tell that person to do right, because he already knows he's doing wrong. Going against yourself; man, I've had a lot of practice doing that.

"His mom being a school teacher, she wanted more out of Arthur, but he was not really that academically inclined," observes Johnny. "As a child, he was kind of introverted and withdrawn. The flamboyant Arthur that came out later was basically a façade; that wasn't really him. The Arthur that I knew was a quiet, introspective, romantic type of person. He was always looking for that perfect girl, that perfect love. He was always searching and getting his heart broken. I would tell him that he wore his heart on his sleeve. A lot of his songs alluded to that. Others, like '7 & 7 Is,' referred to his home life. I would go over to his house and there would be this homey, *Leave It To Beaver* scene. It's hard to picture Arthur Lee's domestic life like that, but that's the way it was."

Arthur moved on to Mount Vernon Junior High, at 4066 W 17th Street, where he excelled at athletics. Music would soon come to rival sports in his world, however. His house became the place to hang out and both make and listen to music. Throughout his life, wherever Arthur lived became the focal point for socializing and music. He rarely went in for clubbing or the social scene and remained very much a homebody. If you wanted to hang with Arthur, you came to him.

"He always liked to win," recalls Arthur's friend Curtis 'Smooth' Woods. "I remember in junior high, sitting on the bleachers with Po during a track meet and watching Calvin Elliot, who could outrun everybody at Mount Vernon. Calvin was strutting around, so the coach, Mr. Collins, who later became Arthur's uncle [he married his aunt], said to Arthur, 'Would you like to run against this guy?' Arthur jumped off the bleachers and said, 'Sure, coach. Just give me a chance.' I watched Arthur kick his shoes off. The starting pistol fired and they were off, running the 440 yards. Arthur outran everybody. He tore that track up. Afterwards, he came back up to me in the bleachers and made one comment, 'Shit, when they shot that pistol I thought they were shooting at me!'"

Sports weren't the only diversions at Mount Vernon. Jesse Kirkland was at school with Arthur and remembers its embryonic music groups: "At lunchtime, Azell, Allan Talbert, Arthur, and all these kids would get together and sing. The whole school was standing around listening. We had a group of five guys called The Valaquons. Arthur and I formed a relationship and, even though he wasn't in The Valaquons, we used to talk a lot about our music. He was in awe of us because we were getting all the girls. Then Arthur formed his own group. He still used to give me advice on The Valaquons, until we went on to different high schools."

"On Saturdays we did our chores so we could go to the movies," recalls Ann Stewart Denard. "Arthur and I would tell our parents we were going downtown to the movies, but this one time Arthur said we were going to the Paramount Theatre to see one of these rock'n'roll shows. We used to go to see The Spaniels, The Flamingos, or The Chantels. He was right into all that. One time, Arthur took me to the old Boulevard Theatre on Washington and we saw Jimmy Reed and Bobby 'Blue' Bland. Then we snuck into the 5-4 Ballroom when Wilson Pickett was there and Arthur said, 'I'm going to be like that one day, you'll see. I'm going to be famous.' I didn't doubt him."

As long as I can remember, I have been dancing by myself. I remember dancing on skates at the roller rink on Washington and Arlington. Boy, did they have some good dancers there. We used to dance to such songs as Richard Berry's "Have Gun, Will Travel," Elvis Presley's "Don't Be Cruel," and The Del Vikings' "Come Go With Me." When I heard Frankie Lymon sing "Why Do Fools Fall in Love?" I flipped, 'cause I could sing just like that cat.

I saw how they were dancing on those skates, so I tried to do like they were doing and, as time went on, I started making up steps of my own. You had to be cool to be in this place and I, of course, had no problem with that. What I did have a problem with was trying to put those skates into rhythm. After a while, it came to me like learning how to ride a bike. Once I learned how to rock, then I could roll.

Arthur's first instrument was neither guitar nor organ – instruments he would later be associated with – but the decidedly unhip accordion. While the instrument may have enjoyed a renaissance in recent years with the emergence of roots music and its adoption by everyone from John Mellencamp to Arcade Fire, it was, like the clarinet and ukulele, most definitely considered 'square' in the 50s and 60s. The hippest dude on the Sunset Strip in 1966 had begun his career on the least cool of all instruments.

Like the parents of many neighborhood kids, Agnes and C.L. had succumbed to a novel method of promotion in signing Arthur up for accordion lessons, as his friend and early bandmate Allan Talbert recalls. "This guy came down our street with a donkey. The kids would all be sitting on the donkey and the guy would pitch accordion lessons. My momma signed me up. Arthur also signed; a whole bunch of us did. There was this little tiny house on West U and Adams, just past the liquor store, and that's where we took accordion lessons. I didn't dig it, though. You had to learn how to read the notes. People say Arthur couldn't read music, but he learned how. You had to have some musical knowledge to play the accordion."

As Johnny Echols remembers it, the instruction did not last long. "If you bought the accordion you got two years of lessons. After a few months, Arthur convinced his parents to buy him an organ instead. The accordion and organ were kind of similar." An instinctively gifted musician, Arthur was possessed of a good ear and an innate musical sense that, while he was never formally schooled in music theory or composition, allowed him to pick out what others were playing, copy from records, and, crucially, write his own songs. He also added harmonica to his growing instrumental arsenal.

The Lee house on 27th Street became the focal point for budding after-school music sessions (sometimes during school hours, too), with Arthur holding court. His parents encouraged their son's musical endeavors. "Arthur used to have a lot of old records," recalls Riley Racer, "and his house sort of became the meeting place for listening to music. Sometimes we'd go over to John Lucky's house, but Arthur just seemed to have a better space for it. And he could sing. He would emulate Ray Charles and Johnny Mathis. He was very good at capturing someone else's voice. Arthur would entertain us in his living room. He had all the comedy records: Moms Mabley, Redd Foxx ... and we would all just crack up and roll on the floor laughing. He could really play the organ, too. I always wondered why he didn't play the organ in Love, but the guitar was the thing, back then. He could play like Ray Charles and sing like Johnny Mathis, Ray Charles, or Frank Sinatra. He also used to listen to Howlin' Wolf, John Lee Hooker ... all that blues stuff; and he liked playing harmonica even though he rarely used it on his records."

Arthur also owned a reel-to-reel tape recorder. "That was unheard of on our block," says Riley. "It was exciting, putting stuff down and then hearing it played back. I'm sure that was part of his evolution as an artist. We all kind of gravitated towards each other and were into this new vein of music. In that sense, we were all strongly influenced by Arthur."

The Lee house offered other inducements. "Arthur's mother, Miss Agnes, could really cook," says Curtis Woods, smiling at the memory. "She made 7 Up cake and hot water bread. She was a wonderful, very pretty lady. She always had something on the stove whenever you came over."

By this time, Johnny Echols was making his first stabs at guitar. "There was a show and tell one day at elementary school. You had to bring something in and explain to the class all about it. This kid brought in a big Harmony Sovereign acoustic guitar. For some reason, he was called to the nurse's office and he asked me to hold his guitar. I started strumming this thing and feeling the vibrations from the instrument in my chest; it was something I had never experienced before. I just fell in love with the guitar right there and then. I went home and asked my father for a guitar. He said 'no,' so I decided I would make a guitar for myself. When he saw how serious I was about making my own instrument he bought me an acoustic guitar. Just like Arthur with the accordion, a guy came around selling guitar lessons, so I was enrolled in a music school and my father was on the hook for $300, which was a whole lot of money. He made sure I practiced every single day. I had the guitar in my hands morning, noon, and night. I loved the guitar. It was meant to be. I later got a three-quarter size Guild electric, which was kind of a jazz guitar." Johnny was married to his guitar back then, confirms Riley Racer. "Everywhere he went, you'd see him carrying his guitar. It didn't matter what everyone else was doing, he'd say, 'I gotta go to my guitar lesson.'"

Having graduated to Susan Miller Dorsey High School (Dorsey High) at 3537 Farmdale Avenue and Rodeo Road, near Baldwin Village, Arthur's musical aspirations found fertile ground both among his classmates and in the local community. "Little Richard lived in our neighborhood, about three or four blocks from our school," recalls Azell Taylor. "He had retired from music at that point. His sister went to school with us. Bobby Day, who sang "Rockin' Robin," lived in the neighborhood and Kent Harris, the guy who wrote "Shopping For Clothes" for The Coasters, lived there, too. Kent used to manage our band. Ray Charles had a recording studio nearby and he signed The Valaquons. There was so much music in that area. Billy Preston went to Dorsey High and the guy from the Fifth Dimension, Ron Townson, was the janitor there." The Beach Boys' Mike Love was another contemporary Dorsey High alumnus (as was prominent criminal defense attorney Johnny Cochran).

Johnny Echols recalls there being plenty of opportunities to experience a variety of musical styles. "We were living in an apartment building, the Sherman Manor, just a couple of doors down from Arthur. They would have parties there, and they'd have all of the better jazz musicians come and play around the pool; so I got to hear a lot of them and meet them. Ella Fitzgerald and her husband, Ray

Brown, also moved in there for a while. Other jazz artists lived there, too. I was exposed to a lot of musicians just by being in the neighborhood. I went to school with Billy Preston. When we got to high school, it all changed. We got so involved in music, it's like nothing else mattered to us. We were always playing assemblies and talent shows." Johnny would serve as a catalyst in Arthur's decision to pursue music rather than a career in sports.

The idea of forming a band didn't really click until I saw William Crout, alias Crimson Crout, and Johnny Echols play at one of our high school assemblies. They had a five-piece band and played a song called "Johnny B. Goode." Not only did they bring the house down, they blew my mind, too. The idea of putting a band together of my own came from Johnny Echols, the man who would later be the lead guitar player of the group Love.

I set a school record for scoring in a single basketball game, 41 points, and it lasted for years and years. But I was a little too short for basketball. I got hit too hard in football games so that changed my mind about becoming a football player. I never planned on being a lawyer or anything. Singing came naturally to me. I found myself playing and writing music. The only thing I got out of school that did me any good in my career was learning to spell and read, so I could write these songs.

I was soon playing the organ in my first band, along with Johnny Echols on guitar, Roland Davis on drums, and Alan Goldman and Allan Talbert playing saxes. Crimson Crout played lead and rhythm guitar, Johnny used to alternate between bass and guitar, and I would sometimes play bass using the footpedals of the organ. After rehearsing at my house, or at Roland's, it finally came time for us to play at the high school assembly. We were on last, and I was as nervous as a snitch at a gangster party. The curtain was pulled back and there we were: "One, two, three, hit it!" We played "Last Night," a song by The Bar-Kays. The crowd went wild. I went wild. We played loud. The audience was loud. I think I was playing the right notes but all that mattered was that the feeling it gave me was better than breaking the high school scoring record in basketball and winning first place in the 50 yard dash, put together.

I made up my mind I was going to be a musician; not just a studio musician but a star. So much for Coach Bravo going around from class to class, asking the teachers to pass me so I could be on the high school basketball team. "Thanks,"

I told him, "but no thanks." You see, I had this problem: I didn't like school and you had to go to class to stay eligible. I didn't go to class enough, so I didn't get to play. Actually, I spent most of my time at Thrifty's, over by Dorsey High and Rancho Park, eating French fries. Coach Bravo said I was an up-and-coming prospect, but I had another idea and that was to make records.

"After we played our first concert at Dorsey High School, everybody in the school rushed the stage and chased us off, out the back of the auditorium and down the street," recalls Allan Talbert, who also served double-duty playing saxophone in Billy Preston's band. "We did three assemblies for all the grades. The 12th graders chased us. They'd never experienced anything like that – the magnetism of the group. It was like The Beatles or The Monkees, but way before them."

This fledgling group would soon evolve into Arthur Lee And The LAGs ('Los Angeles Group'), a spin on Booker T and the MGs ('Memphis Group'). His friend, Chester Shaw, remembers Arthur's fondness for the band: "Arthur was a big fan of the MGs. He loved 'Green Onions.' He was all over that one on the organ." The LAGs played their first professional gig at a golf course country club off Pico Boulevard – coincidentally, just across the street from where future Love member Bryan MacLean lived.

Following that, the group found themselves working fairly regularly, despite still being teenagers attending school (increasingly infrequently, in Arthur's case). Rehearsals were held in the Lees' garage. "Our parents did encourage us to play music, but they weren't encouraging us to go out and be professional musicians," stresses Johnny. "They just wanted us to be well-rounded human beings. They were all on the hook for these expensive instruments so they wanted us to be serious about it. They never put any roadblocks in our way when it came to pursuing music. Agnes wanted Arthur to finish school but she did encourage his music, even if she was a bit skeptical, thanks to what happened with her first husband."

Arthur would drop out of school in his graduating year, bent on pursuing his musical dreams. Although disappointed that he never completed high school, his parents continued to support him. On the occasions when he did attend school, classmates recall Arthur kibitzing around and getting into trouble as a result. He had a wicked sense of humor and loved practical jokes at the expense of others.

Azell Taylor: "Our science teacher used to say, 'Arthur, now you know you can't be doing things like that, boy. That's enough.' He was pretty smart but he liked to cut up with the teachers."

Although insubordinate, Arthur could be a source of empathy and encouragement to his friends, as Curtis Woods remembers: "At school, I was led to believe I would be nothing. There was no positive support for any of us. Arthur was the one who gave me that support. We were real rebel rousers in those days, but deep down inside, Arthur was a sweetheart. If he had a sugar roll, and you didn't, he'd share it with you." Arthur continued to be loyal to his childhood friends in later life, often employing them in his entourage. He never lost touch with his humble roots. "Even after he became successful, he still came back to the neighborhood," says Azell Taylor. "He'd visit his mother and go out for a drink with some of us. We would jam in my backyard and write songs. He was just one of the guys, you know? He never forgot about me."

"Arthur never lost touch with the people we grew up with from grade school onwards," confirms Johnny Echols. "He would always bring them up to where he was, so they were a part of it. And with all those people, he was the same as he was back then. He never lorded anything over them and he remained the perfect gentleman." In 1981, Azell Taylor was invited to sing on Arthur's self-titled solo record while Allan Talbert provided sax on his 1992 album, *Arthur Lee And Love*.

Curtis Woods remembers fondly the time Arthur invited him to play at one of his shows in 2004. "Arthur asked me to open up for him at Spaceland. He called the people up and got me on the bill. He said to me, 'Curtis, I'm not doing the gig without you. If they won't let you play, I'm not doing the gig.'"

Still in their teens, Arthur, Johnny, and the group found it necessary to look older than their tender years, as Johnny recalls. "When we first started, I was about 15 and Arthur was 17; we would pencil-in these little moustaches so we could play this place called The California Club. The manager there knew we were kids, but he would allow us to play as long as we stayed away from the bar. We ended up backing up all kinds of blues and R&B people. Arthur was listening to a lot of R&B, even though he didn't sing like that in Love. In The LAGs, we played rhythm & blues. We went out as The Coasters, The Drifters, whoever had a record out at the time. We had this shyster agent and he figured that all these guys looked the same and nobody knew what the groups really looked like, so he would book us as any of the groups who had a current hit. We could sound just like them and do their song so we got away with it. That was our introduction to the music business and getting paid."

Johnny and Crimson knew this agent, in Hollywood, who would get us gigs playing at parties and small clubs around the LA area. We played Cappy's in the Valley, the Red Onion, the Cinnamon Cinder, the Nite Life, and the California Club. We were sort of the house band at both the Nite Life and the California Club. We would back up bands such as The O'Jays and other R&B groups. People like Johnny Otis and Big Mama Thornton played there when they came to Los Angeles. All the big blues and jazz players played there. We were always the second band. It was a hell of a learning experience. We also played beach parties and rich people's house parties, in Beverly Hills.

Arthur and Johnny would quickly become musical comrades-in-arms, with Arthur as captain and Johnny as his trusted first lieutenant – a relationship that would be integral to their later success with Love. Often underestimated in Love's history, Johnny was a significant contributor to the band's musicality, arrangements, overall sound, and onstage appeal. Musically, he was Arthur's right hand man, often able to translate the singer's compositional vision into reality thanks to his facility with the guitar.

I was playing the organ at these gigs. Johnny Echols was playing the guitar and he was playing some of the best R&B guitar I ever heard. Not only was the playing the best but he was upstaging all the other guitar players in town, too. Johnny was playing behind his back, through his legs, behind his head, and even with his teeth. Talk about putting on a show ... and this was before Jimi Hendrix made it big doing all that shit. That was Mr. Echols, the man with the guitar. I really did admire him.

Rhythm & blues may have been The LAGs' staple but they soon realized that being versatile allowed them access to more gigs. At the time, surfing music was in vogue and the pop charts were dominated by guitar instrumentals by the likes of Dick Dale, The Surfaris, and The Ventures, then all big draws in southern California, along with the Beach Boys. However, that music made little impact amongst black Angelinos. Beatlemania was already in full swing in the UK and

Europe in 1963, but had yet to hit North America. US groups were, for the most part, still clean cut and sported crew cuts and matching striped shirts, mohair sweaters, or sharkskin suits. That year, The LAGs recorded a single for Capitol Records, the premier Los Angeles label, whose office tower headquarters, with its distinctive 'stack of wax' design, located just north of the intersection of Hollywood and Vine, was a beacon to aspiring young musicians. Arthur was among their number. He was determined to do whatever it took to make it.

In order to get my first record deal, I walked from Dorsey High School to Capitol Records. Not once, not twice, but as many times as it took to get someone to listen to my tapes. I just went up there and picked names off the wall, finding people to listen to my music. The walk from South LA to Hollywood was very interesting. I must have made that walk at least five times, but that was the faith I had in my talent. I just couldn't be held back. I had to cross Wilshire Boulevard to be in touch with people who I thought could help me. I found out later that Wilshire was the dividing line between the blacks and the whites. I used to walk by all these big mansions in Baldwin Hills and they must have wondered what this black kid was doing in their neighborhood.

I finally got Adam Ross and Jack Levy, publishers of Ardmore Beechwood Music, to listen to my songs. At the time, they had a group that was doing well called The Rivingtons. They had a song called "Pa-Pa-Oom-Mow-Mow," which was a hit on Billboard and Cash Box. Adam and Jack listened to a few of my songs. They decided to sign me up, along with Johnny, Roland, Goldman, and Talbert. They booked us at Gold Star Studios, where Phil Spector recorded all his hits. There, I made my first single, a 45 called "The Ninth Wave," with "Rumble-Still-Skins" on the reverse. That was a terrible record. The reason I did it was not only for the small percentage that was offered to me – I was still a minor at that time – but also because I'd decided not to give them my best music. I didn't trust them that much and I had no manager. My parents had to sign for me in order to get this record deal. I thought that if these guys put the song out and it did well I would then give them something really hot ... or maybe not.

As a kid, I listened to Nat "King" Cole records and they were on Capitol Records, so I wanted to be on Capitol, too. When I saw my name on that record label I was as happy as a sissy in prison. I must have played it until the groove came off. I played it for everybody in the neighborhood. But there was something missing. It just didn't move me like the performance we did at Dorsey High School. I never got paid for the record, anyway, so it was on to the next thing.

The single failed to make any impact on the charts and received little promotion from Capitol. Arthur remained undeterred. "Arthur always wanted to be somebody, even from the time he was a kid," says Johnny Echols. "He had this over-abiding faith that he was going to be somebody, someday, and make his mark. He had a strong sense of himself. One of the producers at Capitol Records used the word 'chutzpah' to describe Arthur. It was the first, but definitely not the last time I was to hear that word in reference to Arthur. He had chutzpah in spades. He always knew who he was and where he was going." Johnny does, however, quibble with Arthur's claim about walking to Capitol Records. "That's a bit of hyperbole. When he was 16, Arthur's dad bought him a little silver [Chevrolet] Corvair Monza. That was a couple of years before he started knocking on doors at Capitol Records. He would drive down there – it would have been an awfully long walk – but it sounds good, doesn't it?"

So I dropped out of high school and started playing music, full time. My father bought me a brand new Corvair Monza when I was 16. I didn't run away from home; I drove away.

Much like the earliest recordings which the pre-fame Neil Young made with his first band, The Squires, the pre-Love Arthur Lee recordings – including those by The LAGs, his subsequent band The American Four, and songs of his cut by Little Ray, and Ronnie & The Pomona Casuals (featuring Arthur on vocals) – offered little indication of the talent he would later reveal. They remain, for Arthur Lee aficionados and completists, fascinating artifacts but hardly portend the unique and distinctive genius so many would come to attribute to him. On the contrary, they are merely derivative of existing fads or styles – notably Booker T & The MGs – and never seek to create anything wholly original with those influences. Nonetheless, they represent Arthur's first tentative steps in the recording industry and, while they were unsuccessful, they certainly whetted his appetite and further motivated him. Ironically, these songs are in the rhythm & blues mold (with a little surf inclination), a style of music Arthur would not revisit again until the mid 70s. His career would be built not on emulating black music, but on his ability to understand and adapt white rock music. "There were very few black artists that have been able to come up with a white sound and cross over and be successful," concludes Allan Talbert. "Chuck Berry was one; Arthur was another, as was Jimi Hendrix."

A later recording session found (an uncredited) Arthur credited as a writer on a single on the tiny Revis label for singer Rosa Lee Brooks, a one-time member of Curtis Woods's band. Entitled "My Diary," the song was inspired by Arthur's clandestine relationship with neighborhood teen Anita 'Pretty' Billings. Born on the same date as Arthur, Anita would later inspire Love songs like "A Message To Pretty" and "7 & 7 Is." The session at Gold Star Studios was also significant in that it marked the recording debut of a guitarist called Jimi Hendrix.

"My Diary," that was the first time Jimi ever played in a studio. The first time I saw Jimi, I was walking in behind him at the California Club. He had that long hair, a hoodlum priest coat, silver gray with the neck cut off, and those boots with the run-over heels. He was playing in a band called The Furies, I think. I was writing a song for Rosa Lee Brooks called "My Diary." I wanted someone to play guitar like Curtis Mayfield did on his song "Gypsy Woman." Billy Revis, who owned Revis Records, said he knew just the guy. He brought in this left-handed guitar player, who turned out to be Hendrix. He could play with his left hand, right hand, one hand, upside down ... any which way. He had his amps turned up full blast. He would touch a string and the volume would cause feedback. He was living near the YMCA, over on Wilcox, and having a relationship with Rosa Lee. I remember that long hair. He had it all up in curlers. Billy got Jimi to play guitar on "My Diary" and it was a hit for Rosa Lee Brooks on KDAY, the black station, in 1964. I never received a penny.

That song was about my first girlfriend, Anita Billings. Rosa Lee Brooks says now that she wrote that song. I think she needs to get her brain checked. The song was written about me and my girlfriend who were born on the same date. We were ditching school and making love all over the place. One day, she called and told me her mother had found her diary and she said we couldn't see each other any more. I took it really hard. My love had been snatched away from me. It broke my heart and that's how I wrote the song.

On a break at The Fillmore, a few years later, I heard this song – a slow, bluesy kind of haunting song – and the people who were on the dancefloor were singing along. I noticed that some of them had their eyes closed, listening to this guy singing a song we had been doing in Love since '65 – but not this way – called "Hey Joe." I thought it was OK, so I asked someone, "Who is that guy?" They replied, "It's Jimi Hendrix. He's a black guy from England." I didn't realize it was the same guy who played on my session. He'd gone to England and become famous."

Like millions of other American teenagers, black or white, witnessing The Beatles' debut performance on *The Ed Sullivan Show* on February 9 1964 was an epiphany for Arthur. Overnight, playing rhythm & blues cover songs while sporting processed hair and mohair sweaters was out the window; long hair and Cuban-heeled boots suddenly became mandatory. Unlike the surfing music craze, The Beatles, The Rolling Stones, and other British Invasion artists united kids of all races. For young blacks, the rhythm & blues influence the British groups drew upon was unmistakable. "Billy Preston came by my house in late 1963," recalls Johnny Echols. "Arthur was there, and Billy starts telling us about the tour he had just been on to England, with Little Richard. They had met all these people over there and he told us about these guys who had funny hairdos and looked like little moppets. He said they were enamored of Little Richard and followed him around like puppy dogs. We didn't know who they were. We didn't hear about them for maybe a few months. The reason Billy had come by was to see if I wanted to put a group together to play behind him at the Nite Life club. It was Billy Preston and the Soul Brothers. Then, all of a sudden, while we were playing there, we heard The Beatles on the radio and Billy says, 'Those are the guys I met in England.' When The Beatles came to LA and played The Hollywood Bowl, in August 1964, they sent Billy tickets, so we went and saw them and saw the response they got from the audience. We played clubs that were relatively full and people would applaud, but it was nothing like what was happening to The Beatles. That's when we decided to do the whole long hair thing. Arthur didn't go with us to see The Beatles, but we told him all about it and then, later on, he saw all the chaos around them on television. Arthur couldn't wait to grow out his hair so he got this wig."

I don't think I would have had the wig idea at all if I hadn't turned my television on one night to watch the Ed Sullivan show and seen The Beatles. I can't put into words the feeling I had watching that TV show. There I was, sitting in South Los

Angeles, in front of my TV set, watching something that changed my way of thinking about playing music. The feeling I got was phenomenal ... the songs, the girls screaming. It blew me away as much as the first time I'd seen Elvis Presley play "Hound Dog." Those guys showed me what a four-piece band could really do. Their look, style, and music were a brand new thing.

Duly inspired, Arthur quickly broke up The LAGs and formed The American Four with Johnny. On bass, they recruited a friend who Johnny had met that summer at Hollywood High, John Fleckenstein, and they then added a drummer, John Jacobson. They were both white. The American Four would be among the first integrated rock'n'roll bands on the LA scene. "I met Johnny Echols when he was playing with The Chuck Daniels Band at the Sea Witch, on the Sunset Strip," recalls John Fleckenstein. "Johnny and I played there for a bit, and then he introduced me to Arthur. He asked me if I wanted to join a group with him and Johnny. That became The American Four, although we also played as The Weirdos. We played a lot of black clubs, places like Cappy's and the California Club, because we did a lot of soul music at the time: lots of blues and things like that, with Arthur on organ and, sometimes, piano. We did Booker T & The MGs type stuff. Then we moved over to play the Beverly Bowl. That was as both The American Four and The Weirdos. We all got wigs and it was just bizarre: two black guys and two white guys in long wigs. I liked Johnny Echols right away. I thought Arthur was kind of strange but he turned out to be a good guy. Arthur had definite ideas about what he wanted to do. It was his idea to get the wigs and all of that. He had a vision and he wanted to be successful right from the very beginning. He picked the songs and was really pushing the whole thing. He was getting all the bookings."

I'd asked Johnny, or one of the other guys, to let me play his guitar. They were having so much fun I wanted to play one myself. Guitar was the thing with The Beatles and those bands, not the organ. It took me a long time to even get a ring out of the thing. One day, Johnny said, "You'll never be able to play that thing." That was all I needed. I got together with a friend of mine, John Lucky, who also played guitar, and he showed me about six or seven chords. So I started singing and writing songs with the guitar as well as on the organ.
We got a gig at the Beverly Bowl in Montebello, a bowling alley with a club

in it. When we started playing, people were not only listening but dancing, too. We played there for about a year and a half, three or four days a week, sometimes three or even five sets a night. That was as The American Four. At the time, The Beatles were breaking with "I Want To Hold Your Hand." We were packing them in. In 1964, it wasn't every day you saw a black and white band. I'll never forget the look on the guys' faces when I told them to put on wigs, but they did it. We were not just having pictures taken with them on; we were playing jobs and wearing them around town. I wore my wig to the T.A.M.I. Show to see James Brown and The Rolling Stones. I remember the Stones had an image that you couldn't stop looking at. They weren't pretty, they weren't sexy, but they were very interesting. The Beatles wore suits, but these guys wore street clothes and had real long hair. In a way, they were completely different to The Beatles but just as charismatic. I thought Mick Jagger was something else. I thought he was gay, but that didn't matter.

The Beatles, the Stones and their ilk energized the teen scene in and around LA. Suddenly, more clubs and dance halls sprang up featuring longhaired rock bands, supplanting either staid supper club crooners or slick, rhythm & blues cover bands. Arthur recognized this youth culture sea change and decided to jump in, head first. His band seemed bound to be noticed. Being a mixed-race group was as much a novelty as a young black man singing like a white rock'n'roller.

Whoever heard of a black man trying to sound white, or pulling it off well enough that they were playing his music on the radio and thinking he was white? That's what I did, right in front of the whole world ... and they thought I was serious. I even read an article that said "Arthur Lee doesn't have a soulful bone in his body." So my idea paid off. I started out just putting them on. Even my band members weren't aware that I really didn't sing like that. And after doing that for a while, and listening to the voice I was using and my natural voice combined, I came out with a brand new voice of my own. I never would have thought of using it if I hadn't started hanging out and listening to what white folks were doing. I don't know if it's because my grandfather was white, or what, but it just came naturally to me, after a while. Not only was I singing like that, but I was writing like that, too. What started out as a put-on materialized as something real and positive. I created a whole new me – like a caterpillar turning into a butterfly. It was happening with each new song I wrote. Thank God I was gifted with the kind of voice where I can just about sing any style I choose.

"The American Four were kind of a Top 40 covers band," observes Johnny Echols. "We played everything that was a hit at the time. The Beverly Bowl management just wanted a young group in there and put no restrictions on what we played. So we played basically what was on the radio and popular at the time. We played songs like "Wooly Bully" and "Gloria," and we got a tremendous following there because we sounded very much like the records. We wore the wigs and were good. But it was a strange band because we were such an eclectic group of characters." Although pictured in a surviving publicity photo of The American Four, John Jacobson was soon replaced on drums by a local legend, Don Conka. "I remember Don at Hollywood High School, where I met Fleck," recalls Johnny. "Sometimes, I would walk through the quad and there would be Conka, with just a snare drum. He'd have a crowd of people around him listening to him play. He could do more with one snare drum than most drummers on an entire kit. He had his demons, as we all did, but he was gifted." Don Conka's intricate and lengthy drum solos, sometimes 30 minutes long, were renowned, and his playing was all part of The American Four's appeal. Don and Arthur would also develop a close relationship that would outlive their musical collaboration.

"At the beginning, when we were all really on it, Johnny, Don, Arthur, and I, we were all having a great time and Arthur was really pushing us to practice and do this and that," remembers John Fleckenstein. "It was Art's deal all the way. He was very concerned about moving the band forward. Arthur was a regular guy but he would take on this whole persona. He would sometimes do things I didn't understand. Nobody did. When we were at the Beverly Bowl, he came in wearing these weird, square glasses and said, 'I'm Professor Abifkin.' He was like an actor taking on a role. He could also be very guarded about his private life."

The American Four were drawing enough attention in the clubs to warrant the release of a 45. Borrowing stylistically from The Isley Brothers' "Twist & Shout," recently popularized by The Beatles, and cashing in on publicity surrounding new American president Lyndon Johnson's teenage daughter, Luci Baines Johnson, Arthur composed a song to launch what he hoped would become the next dance craze. The single, "Luci Baines," was released on the Selma label, a subsidiary of DelFi Records, in 1964. It boasts the saxophone of Allan Talbert, with Arthur on lead vocals. The flip side, "Soul Food," is credited to Lee and Echols and features some fine lead playing by Johnny, with Arthur on organ. The world wasn't ready to dance the Luci Baines, however, and the single sank without a trace.

Despite the popularity of The American Four in the dance clubs of South Los Angeles, by 1965, the local music scene was being transformed by an entirely novel sound. On March 26 that year, a new Los Angeles quintet, The Byrds, made their debut at a Hollywood club called Ciro's (originally Ciro's LeDisc), at 8433 Sunset Boulevard, just down the street from another soon-to-be-iconic Sunset Strip club, the Whisky A Go Go. Within days, The Byrds were drawing lines of fans around the block. Theirs was a distinctive sound that blended traditional folk music harmonies, melodies, and lyrical themes with a British Invasion backbeat indebted to The Beatles and The Searchers. Propelled by the characteristic jingle-jangle of a Rickenbacker 12-string electric guitar, The Byrds' sound was quickly dubbed folk-rock. It would become not only the sound of the Sunset Strip in 1965, but the sound of LA and, finally, the sound of the nation as the group was anointed America's answer to The Beatles.

As the Liverpudlian mop-tops had the previous year, so The Byrds changed everything. Theirs was music with a message. It was cerebral, offering poetry with a beat, and was unlike anything in pop music at the time. By turning Bob Dylan's surreal, acoustic folk song "Hey, Mr Tambourine Man," into an electrically shimmering hit, The Byrds had defined both the sound and substance of folk-rock. As musical chronicler Richie Unterberger says of The Byrds' ground-breaking new fusion in his book *Turn! Turn! Turn!: The '60s Folk-Rock Revolution*: "This was music with meaning, music to feed the body and the mind. Never had lyrics of such literary quality and ambiguous meaning been used on a rock record."

Ciro's had been one of the grand nightclubs on the Sunset Strip during an earlier heyday, back in the 40s and early 50s, but the club had fallen on hard times and had recently been sold to a restaurateur who decided to make it over as a rock'n'roll venue. One of the first groups hired was The Byrds, an event which signaled the changing of the guard on the Strip. As author Domenic Priore records in his book *Riot On Sunset Strip: Rock'n'roll's Last Stand In Hollywood*: "Nightclubs began booking longhaired, countercultural-type bands. Slicker, more predictable house bands, in the mode of Johnny Rivers, took a back seat." Indeed, Rivers, who had enjoyed a lengthy run at the Whisky A Go Go doing his quasi

Chuck Berry shtick, soon found himself out of a job, replaced by innumerable local folk-rock acts or imported British Invasion groups.

"The Byrds were different, arguably unique, at least for Los Angeles," asserts Billy James, publicist at the time for Columbia Records and a noteworthy LA scene-maker. "The Byrds' impact was truly extraordinary. They became an inspiration for all these other folk-rock groups. And there were the freaks like [eccentrically dressed, proto-hippie dancers] Carl Franzoni, Vito Paulekas, and all those folks. The Byrds didn't create those people but they encouraged them to be as outrageous as they were."

"On stage, The Byrds were very much trying to be like the early Beatles," recalls Morgan Cavett, who managed LA folk coffeehouse the New Balladeer. "Their music was so fresh and new." For music fans like Morgan, the scene at Ciro's was mind-blowing. "There were all these kind of leftovers from the beatnik generation, but not yet hippies. It was kind of a weird, eclectic combination of berets, beads, and bell-bottoms. Vito, Carl Franzoni, and their group were all dancing and just flailing away with wild abandon."

Originally known as The Beefeaters, The Byrds were formed by erstwhile folk musicians Jim (later Roger) McGuinn, Gene Clark, and David Crosby. They added Chris Hillman on bass and drummer Michael Clarke to mint a quintessential 60s folk-rock sound. Their "Mr. Tambourine Man" debut was already recorded but the frenzy surrounding their Ciro's stand prompted Columbia Records to rush release it that April. By June, it was #1 across North America. That summer, on a visit to LA, The Beatles declared The Byrds their favorite band.

They were also favorites of The American Four. "It wasn't just the music," Johnny emphasizes. "What impressed us when we saw The Byrds were the people in the audience – what *The Los Angeles Times* called the 'Sherwood Forest People' – because they looked like something out of Robin Hood. It was this huge, fascinating group of eclectic people, all dressed totally bizarrely, with long, long hair. These were the leftovers from the Beat era. They followed The Byrds around."

One night, we wound up at a place called Ciro's, on the Strip, and saw The Byrds playing. Their music sounded a lot like what I had been writing but had yet to record. After I heard them play, and saw the response of the people, I knew exactly what I was going to do. I was going to join in and help create a new kind of music called folk-rock. The Byrds blew me away. Their music went right to my heart. They played loud and they looked like barbarians with their long hair and freaky clothes. They were playing "I Feel A Whole Lot Better" and they were as hot as The Beatles or the Stones ever were. In fact, that night, I saw Brian Jones of the Stones there. He looked at me, I looked at him, and we looked at each other again.

Arthur was determined that this new music, folk-rock, born in the clubs of the Sunset Strip, would be his ticket to success. "I remember everybody was talking about The Byrds," remembers Riley Racer. "Arthur was convinced he could do that, too."

CHAPTER 2

BETWEEN CLARK
AND HILLDALE

The American Four – left to right: Johnny Echols,
John Jacobson, Arthur Lee, John Fleckenstein

B1965, the axis of the US music industry had shifted from the East Coast to the West. While New York City may have retained the corporate headquarters of many of the major record labels and booking agencies, the artistic and creative energy of American music was now largely emanating from southern California. The transfer was already underway by the time The Byrds emerged that spring with their distinctive folk-rock blend, a sound, then and forever, evocative of The Golden State. There had been stabs at combining the two genres by artists in other locales, but folk-rock was effectively a California invention. *American Bandstand*, Dick Clark's influential teen music television show, had recently made the move from Philadelphia to LA and found itself ideally positioned when the southern California music scene exploded.

If Los Angeles was the new focal point for American music, then the Sunset Strip was its epicenter. The approximately one-and-a-half-mile-long stretch, bounded by Crescent Heights to the east and Doheny Boulevard to the west, with its many clubs, restaurants, boutiques, and hangouts, became ground zero for the burgeoning youth culture erupting out of the city. This cultural explosion offered an overdue renaissance for the tired supper clubs and nighteries of a bygone Hollywood golden age. Given a new, youthful veneer, venues such as Ciro's, the Trip, the Whisky A Go Go, and Gazzarri's were reborn overnight as cool rock'n'roll clubs catering to the young longhairs. The latter quickly outnumbered the Strip's established Dean Martin and Sammy Davis Jr. crowd, just as rock musicians supplanted movie stars as the new celebrities.

Where folk music had been all about acoustic guitars in dank, bohemian Greenwich Village coffeehouses and college campus hootenannies, folk-rock offered the fast lane: chiming Rickenbacker electric guitars plugged into giant Fender Dual Showman amplifiers (the loudest on the market), pulsing stage lights, and dancefloors packed with gyrating teens garbed in the most bizarre 'anything goes' outfits. "The clubs in LA were really booming, then," recalls Mark Volman, singer with LA folk-rockers The Turtles. "It was very dynamic, and radio here was really happening and focusing on the local music scene."

The enthusiasm spread beyond the Strip, as enterprising entrepreneurs sought to tap the youth market by opening new clubs (or redecorating and renaming former nightspots or coffeehouses) such as the Haunted House on Hollywood Boulevard, Thee Experience and the Hullabaloo further down Sunset Boulevard – beyond what was designated as the Strip – and the Brave New World on Melrose

61

Avenue. In spite of Ciro's head start with The Byrds, the Strip's kingpin venue would ultimately be the Whisky A Go Go. Opened in January 1964 by former Chicago policeman Elmer Valentine, 'the Whisky,' located at 8901 Sunset Boulevard, between Clark and Hilldale, was one of the first venues to jump on the folk-rock bandwagon.

The Whisky, Ciro's, Bido Lito's, and the Brave New World – they were like second homes to me, back in those days. I and the group were always a big part of the scene on and around the Sunset Strip. After our shows, we would go down the street to Ben Frank's restaurant to eat, and large crowds would follow us. Later, the crowds followed us over to Canter's delicatessen. The Whisky became the catalyst where the whole scene came together. Elmer Valentine was not only a good friend, he was like a father figure to me. I know that all he wanted was the very best for me. I always respected him. Mario Maglieri, the manager, was another for whom I had a great deal of admiration. Mario and I shared some really good times together.

We opened the gate for The Doors, Buffalo Springfield, and all the rock groups that followed. We were the beginning of the longhair scene in LA, and I think we were the ones who spread the scene up to San Francisco. From the mid-to-late 60s, the Strip was a kaleidoscope of young hearts and music. The Whisky was the beacon, the shining light that drew the heaven and hell of our generation to the Strip.

I had some of the best times of my life during those dream-filled days when we were 'it.' By 'we' I mean my friends and I: people like David Crosby, Jim Morrison, Vito Paulekas, Carl Franzoni, Bryan MacLean, Sue Vito, Beatle Bob, James 'Scotty' Scott, The Byrds, Chris Mancini, Little Alan, Jiffy Jeffy, Neil Rappaport, Jimi Hendrix, Johnny Echols, and all their friends. It was a golden time. When I look back on those days, it's like a psychedelic movie in Technicolor that my mind rewinds and plays – an endless montage of beautiful people. Yes, we were the mood of the times. We were only a small spark on the Sunset Strip at first, but we became a wildfire.

The clubs catered to an ever-expanding teen audience – one that was, by and large, white. Even though many of Arthur's neighborhood friends had picked up on folk-rock as something new and exciting, few black musicians were out there playing it. "There were one or two black and Hispanic kids that were a part of that folk-rock scene," recalls Johnny, "but not a lot. They would dress in the same clothes as the hippie white kids. But the scene was predominantly middleclass white youth." He and Arthur were about to change that.

In our band, there we were, two black guys from Memphis, raised in LA, and three white guys from California. The more I thought about it, the more it seemed that this was the way the world should be, with everybody getting along with one another. I'm glad I tried to show unity in the world.

"There were a few rhythm & blues bands of mixed race in East Los Angeles, but Arthur had the first real interracial rock'n'roll band," notes veteran Love fan Paul Body, who saw the band often during the 60s. "That was cool because I was a black cat and I loved rock'n'roll. Love weren't playing "Mustang Sally" and all that kind of stuff. There were all these young black cats who were a little bit older than me but who knew Arthur from his neighborhood and followed him around to the clubs when he played, mainly because of the girls the band drew. They weren't a huge draw for many black kids, but there were a few of us. They broke down that barrier on the Sunset Strip. But it wasn't just Arthur, it was also Johnny Echols. Johnny was the guy. He was the coolest looking cat and he could play like nobody else could play: wild rock'n'roll as well as the little fills on songs like 'Softly To Me.' He could play that folk-rock Jim McGuinn thing, only better, and he could also play blues and jazz. Johnny was a great musician."

The abruptness of The Byrds ascent into the rock'n'roll stratosphere took everyone by surprise, but their contemporaries caught up fast. Within a matter of months, folk-rock had become part of the lexicon not only of the music business but of the wider popular culture. Respected mainstream magazines like *Time* and *Life* devoted major coverage to this new phenomenon. By late summer, the pop charts were overrun with folk-rock wannabes, most of them taking their cue from The Byrds by plundering Dylan's catalog. Dylan himself had recently struck an electrified nerve with his song "Subterranean Homesick Blues," before owning the pop charts in August '65 with a monumental folk-rock anthem, "Like A Rolling Stone."

What distinguished The Byrds from the pack was that they were also writing their own songs, most notably frontman Gene Clark, who Arthur admired for his moody, poetic compositions. Clark would inspire Arthur to explore more abstract lyrical ideas in his own fledgling songwriting. Overnight, The Byrds – individually and collectively – had become the hippest, most influential musicians on the West Coast.

In the wake of The Byrds phenomenon, The American Four redefined their sound – combining The Rolling Stones' swagger and raucous rhythms with Byrds-like guitars and poetic lyrics. They were ready to leave the bowling alley. In late April, they took up residency at the Brave New World, a tiny, formerly gay, bar on Melrose Avenue, two blocks west of LaBrea Avenue in Hollywood, not far from Canter's delicatessen. "When we started playing, the audience was about 50 per cent gay and 50 per cent straight," recalls Johnny. "After about a month, the gay people had been completely pushed out by the straights who came to see us. We kind of took away their scene."

The change of venue and sound would also prompt a name change. "When we moved to the Brave New World, we became The Grass Roots," confirms Johnny. "We had been listening to an album by Malcolm X called *Up From The Grass Roots* and we thought that would make a great name for the group. 'Grass' was a double entendre, and there was also the implication of coming up from the ground, from the streets. So we chose that as our name, and did the poor man's registration, which was to send ourselves a registered letter with the claim to the name in it. We thought that was enough." The band's repertoire was expanding, taking in a wider range of styles in addition to folk-rock. "We had become accustomed to listening to all kinds of music," says Johnny. "We liked everything, so we wanted to have a group that could play all types of music and not just be stuck playing rhythm & blues, which was expected if you were of a certain skin color."

Arthur was not yet skilled enough to play much guitar on stage, but the new sound required additional six-string rhythm. Bobby Beausoleil, from Santa Barbara, briefly filled the slot. An average guitarist at best, his main failing was a lack of commitment, something the increasingly focused and ambitious Arthur could not tolerate. "Bobby was just a sweet, innocent kid at the time," remembers Johnny, "although he became more notorious later." Indeed, 'Bummer Bob' as he was nicknamed, would achieve infamy through his association with mass murderer Charles Manson and his acolytes, 'The Family,' and would received a life sentence for his part in the 1969 murder of Gary Hinman, for which he is still incarcerated. "Bobby was always late," remembers Johnny. "We were trying to build something and needed people to show up on time and be ready to play. Bobby ended up pawning his instrument, so he didn't even have a guitar to play. It got to the point where we had to make a choice." Bummer Bob was given his walking papers in August after missing a gig at the Brave New World.

When we started playing at the Brave New World, only a few people came to see us. We started at $15 a night, but within two weeks we were packing the place. So much so, that we had to empty it out at least three times a night so that all those standing out on the sidewalk could get a chance to see us play. People were everywhere on Melrose, from one block to the next. After the gigs, we would all go to Ben Frank's, on Sunset Boulevard, to eat and hang out. I would meet all kinds of interesting people there, and things would be going on: smoking and joking in the parking lot until the wee hours of the morning, and picking up chick after chick. We were really close, my first Hollywood band and I. We shared a lot of good times together.

"One night, my girlfriend, Robin, and I were sitting at a table at Ben Frank's and we saw these two guys," recalls erstwhile Sunset Strip regular Annette Ferrel. "I had never seen a black person up close before and there were Arthur and Johnny at another table. They were still teenagers when I met them. I was about 17. They introduced themselves and I was immediately smitten with Arthur. They were very nice and told us they were in a band playing the next night at the Brave New World. We went to see them and I became an instant fan. We went just about every night, and then followed them to Bido Lito's and the Whisky. I had a thing for Arthur."

Hailing from Sherman Oaks, in the Valley, Annette and her girlfriends would hitchhike to Hollywood to see Love in the clubs there. For Annette, like many others, Arthur and Johnny were an anomaly on the white-dominated Sunset Strip scene, seemingly harbingers of an incipient, racially integrated society. "My eyes were not colorblind. Everyone seemed to accept Arthur, as far as I could tell. He wanted to stand out visually and would wear just the one moccasin or army boot, and those trademark triangular glasses of his. We were going out; I told him I loved him. He replied, 'You know, your father would never allow that,' and it was the first time I'd ever thought about it. No one I knew talked about him being a black guy; anyway, he had white features and his mother looked white."

Located at the eastern end of the Sunset Strip, Ben Frank's was one of the few local restaurants which were open all night. Dating from the 50s, and boasting a futuristic design, by 1965 its clientele so typified the local hip youth culture that when producers Bert Schneider and Bob Rafelson were casting for a television show based on The Beatles' film *A Hard Day's Night,* they specified "Spirited Ben Frank's types" in their *Variety* advertisement. The show in question, *The Monkees,* would hit the screens the following year.

On one of those late nights on the Strip, hanging out among their growing legion of fans, Arthur and Johnny met a strawberry-blond young man who looked like a beach boy or surfer. His name was Bryan MacLean. His would become a pivotal role in the story of Love. Obviously from the right side of the tracks but presently out of work, he had briefly been a roadie for The Byrds, an association which lent him considerable cachet on the Strip. When the LA heroes flew off for their first UK tour, in August, however, Bryan had been left behind.

Born September 25 1946 into a well-heeled Beverly Hills family, Bryan's architect father and artist/dancer mother split up when he was barely a toddler. Nonetheless, he enjoyed a privileged upbringing, shuttling between his parents' homes. "When I first met George, Bryan's father, I was 16," reflects Bryan's mother, Elizabeth McKee, who continues to keep her late son's memory and recorded legacy alive. "I had been a photographer's model. I'm sure my mother was manic depressive and, as a result, I was a miserable young girl. George was a way for me to get out of that situation. However, all the time we were married, he was with other women. The good thing, for me, was Bryan. He was about two or so when we split up, but I never kept him from his father. George bought a ranch down by the ocean and they had horses, so I used to let Bryan stay there for the whole summer."

When living with his mother, young Bryan was exposed to an artistic lifestyle – painting, dance, and music. From a young age, he showed an affinity for Broadway show tunes as well as operatic arias, both of which would inform his later songwriting. "There was always music in the house when Bryan was growing up," Elizabeth continues. "I had classical music and opera; for instance, Puccini's *La Bohème.* When Bryan was little and it was time for [the opera's tragic heroine] Mimi to die, he would come up to me and cry, 'Mama! Mimi!' He was very sensitive."

In a 1993 interview with Neal Skok, Bryan revealed more about his early musical influences. "My dad built homes for the rich and famous. I knew everyone in Hollywood. He was an architect for the jet set. My close friend, when I was a kid, was Liza Minnelli. She claims I was the first guy she ever kissed. We used to sit at the piano and sing her mom's stuff from *The Wizard Of Oz*. Next door was Fritz Loew, of [composers] Lerner and Loew fame; he wrote all the music. I came in and was sitting at the piano just doodling. Loew said, 'That's nice.' I replied, 'I'd love to be able to do what you do. Do you think I would need some type of training?' He said, 'Absolutely not. You're a melodic genius.'"

Despite an appreciation for this music, Bryan had no formal instrumental training and could not read sheet music. "Almost everything I do, even my straight blues, is more like Billie Holiday or George Gershwin than it is Robert Johnson," he told Neal Skok. "I was very much into show music records. I loved *Guys And Dolls, Oklahoma, South Pacific, New Faces Of 52,* and *West Side Story.* I wore those records out." Jack McKee, Bryan's stepfather, introduced him to cool jazz, notably the music of Miles Davis and Dave Brubeck.

Bryan and his natural father never developed a close relationship and this seems to have left a deep scar on Bryan's psyche. Throughout his life, he sought approval, largely to compensate for the lack of attention from his father. "Men who have never been validated by their fathers are never at peace," suggests Elizabeth McKee. "His father never told Bryan he loved him or that he approved of what he did. He never said, 'I'm proud of you as my son.' Bryan sought that, but never got it. Later, he tried to make father figures of others, like our pastors, but it never worked. He wanted so much to be approved. What he needed from his father he never got." Elizabeth also stresses that Bryan was bi-polar and that his condition would have a significant impact in later years. "It's typical when you have a certain genius that you are bi-polar as well. Both my children were bi-polar. Bryan's half sister, Maria [McKee, the singer and songwriter], is medicated. They gave Bryan lithium and it messed him up. It was a very heavy drug and was hard on him. Now they have things that are much better; back then, Bryan self-medicated with drugs and alcohol."

His eclectic artistic background notwithstanding, like so many teenagers in the early 60s, Bryan succumbed to the allure of popular music – especially folk and rock'n'roll – and began playing guitar. "I would have the guitar in my lap 18 hours a day; it drove my parents nuts," he later revealed. Bryan's musical tastes began to expand still further. "In the early 60s, there were places where young kids congregated and taught each other how to play guitar," recalls Elizabeth. "That happened with Bryan. Also, I was studying flamenco dancing and Bryan heard that music. I used to practice my castanets and he would come and put his finger between them because he got so sick of it. But the music sort of got into his blood. I had a Spanish guitar made for him and asked the guitarist from our dance class to give him lessons. But flamenco was too difficult for him. Instead, he would hang out at the Balladeer, where folk music was played." All these diverse influences would ultimately coalesce in the songs Bryan would compose for Love.

Located on West Sawtelle Boulevard, north of Santa Monica in West Los Angeles, the New Balladeer (or simply 'the Balladeer') was a coffeehouse owned by one Angelo DiFrenza and run, in the early to mid 1960s, by Morgan Cavett. Morgan was the son of two-time Academy Award-winning screenwriter Frank Cavett. "I managed the New Balladeer and several of the pre-fame Byrds – Gene Clark, Jim McGuinn, David Crosby, and Michael Clarke – used to hang there because it had a very loose atmosphere." In early 1964, Bryan Maclean was a Balladeer regular and mingled with the nascent folk-rock stars. Another Balladeer mainstay was John Kay, later to find fame fronting hard-rock band Steppenwolf. He recalls many of the regulars: "A number of people came through the doors who would go on to great things but who, at the time, were still scuffling, as I was. Taj Mahal was one. David Crosby played there a number of times and Jim McGuinn would come in frequently. There was a young kid, Bryan MacLean, kind of cocky but nonetheless a nice kid, who hung around Crosby and McGuinn. He wasn't their close friend but idolized them from a distance. Two of the nicest people I met there were the duo of Bob Kimmel and Kenny Edwards; they later hooked up with Linda Ronstadt in The Stone Poneys. Another young man who frequented the club was John Locke, a jazzer and piano player who became a founding member of the band Spirit."

For budding musicians, the Balladeer provided a comfortable place to hang out and hear different music, not the usual commercial folk fare. Drugs were also part of the scene. The likes of Locke and DiFrenza would turn Bryan on to marijuana. "I never saw Bryan performing at the Balladeer," notes Elizabeth McKee. "He was close-mouthed about that. I think he was doing grass then."

At 17, Bryan dropped out of high school, but not to pursue a music career. He was initially more inclined toward art. "Bryan was in the 12th grade when he quit school," says Elizabeth. "They wanted him to cut his hair but he wouldn't do it. His hair was very important to him. Jack kicked him out of the house because he wouldn't cut it. That was the saddest day of my life. He would crash at other people's houses."

Out on his own, Bryan briefly teamed up with singer Taj Mahal in a band called Summer's Children before landing the job as The Byrds' roadie (not their road manager, as is often cited).

"Bryan was the equipment guy on our first tour of the Midwest in the summer of '65," recalls Byrds' bassist Chris Hillman. "He was younger than the rest of The Byrds by two years or more. He was a pretty good kid but a wee bit cocky. He was a hard-working guy on our behalf. As I recall, he pretty much answered to Crosby and was David's assistant, to put it diplomatically – more like his gofer, in fact. He only worked that one tour. The next thing I knew he was off putting together the group Love." The Byrds completed the tour and, without pausing, jumped on a plane for their UK debut. "They went to England and didn't take Bryan," recalls Elizabeth. "That broke his heart."

An unsuccessful audition for *The Monkees* followed before Bryan's fateful meeting with Arthur and Johnny at Ben Frank's. The relationship that would develop between Arthur and Bryan over the next two years would become the central dynamic of Love and have a profound impact on the creativity and expression of both young men. Theirs would be a complex affiliation fueled by a competitive edge, both in terms of musical contributions and female attention. They were like sibling rivals who enjoyed each other's company, yet, when drawn too close, they could provoke bitter jealousies. Each brought out the best and the worst in the other. As Bryan's star began to rise on the back of Love's success, so Arthur grew to resent what he perceived as a challenge to his previously uncontested dominance of the band.

Initially, however, Bryan's appeal for Arthur was defined not only by his musicality but by his looks and the crowd he hung with. "A month or so after we saw The Byrds at Ciro's, we met Bryan at Ben Frank's," recalls Johnny. "He was this gadfly kind of character who knew everybody and was flitting from table to table. He wore striped pants and a scarf, and he had this long, strawberry hair. All the girls loved him. For whatever reason, he came and sat at our table. Of course, Arthur and I were the only two black people there at the time. Bryan was very open-minded. He sat down and asked who we were. We told him we were musicians, playing down at the Brave New World. We didn't know he played but a few days later he showed up at the club with five or six of these people we'd seen at Ciro's. Then he asked if he could sit in. At the time, our other guitar player was Bobby Beausoleil. So Bryan picked up Bobby's guitar and played a few songs with us. We liked the way he played. We wanted to sound more like the stuff we were hearing on the radio, and he fitted in. We'd noticed the people he brought in, too; so we asked him to join the group. Of course, he jumped at the chance. Bryan played along with Bobby for a while and we had two rhythm guitars and one lead guitar, but Bobby was jealous of Bryan because Bryan was getting more attention. Financially, we couldn't support another musician, because the owner of the club wasn't paying us any more money, so we had to let Bobby go." Thus, Bryan MacLean joined The Grass Roots.

At the Brave New World, I played guitar and sang but I thought I could do a better show if I mostly sang and sometimes played the harmonica. It would bring more intensity to the show. While watching The Byrds, I saw a guy in the crowd who really stood out. He was this redhead kid and he wore his hair shoulder length, with bangs and a ribbon. He seemed to be attracting as much attention as The Byrds themselves. He was always around the band, so I asked who he was and I found out he was Bryan MacLean. I would see him on and off at Vito's, and I heard him strum some notes a few times. Later, when The Byrds went on tour to England to promote their album, I decided to get the redhead kid in our band. He seemed to be the best man for the job. We were drawing a good crowd at the Brave New World but Bryan was like the new kid on the block and he brought a lot of Byrds groupies with him. Bryan had that baby face; he wore pin-striped pants, a red handkerchief around his neck, and was about as arrogant as they come. I might add that Fleck and Echols also had no problem with the ladies. If anything, the problem was keeping the girls off the stage and choosing which one we wanted.

I used to think of Bryan as The Byrds' reject, but he drew from The Byrds' crowd. Pretty soon the Brave New World was getting too small for us.

Up to this point, Arthur and Johnny were still living with their parents on 27th Street, and rehearsing in the Lees' garage. Meanwhile, Bryan had moved into a loft above Vito's sculpture studio, known as Vito Clay, at the corner of Laurel Avenue and Beverly Boulevard, just below Laurel Canyon. The Byrds had been using the lower studio as a rehearse space before they'd hit it big and moved out.

In the late summer, soon after joining The Grass Roots, Bryan acquired two new loft-mates: Arthur and Johnny. "It cost us $10 a week, each," recalls Johnny. "It was like this huge warehouse. You put a mattress on the floor and there was your space." The Grass Roots could also rehearse in the downstairs studio. They could finally move out of the garage.

I wrote at least half the songs for the first Love album when we were rehearsing in my parents' garage. I wrote "You I'll Be Following" there. I remember when we first recorded it at Buck Ram's house. He was the manager of The Platters and that was one stop among many that I made trying to get us a record deal. Anyway, I owe a lot to my parents for putting up with me and the band and all that noise.

"Most of the songs were written by both of us, at that time," remembers Johnny. "Arthur would write words and sing them to me and I would supply the chords. John Lucky showed Arthur how to play A, D, and G chords, but he didn't know many more at that point. Songs like 'Sherry Black,' 'I'm The Golden Boy,' and 'Stay Away' were Lee/Echols compositions. Arthur wrote 'You I'll Be Following' alone, and The American Four did record it at Buck Ram's home studio. That guy had an ego you wouldn't believe; he thought he was God's gift to the world."

By the later summer of 1965, the band was attracting its own colorful retinue. "Vito and those guys were like our groupies," recalls John Fleckenstein. "They trailed us everywhere we played and brought their whole scene with them. Bryan did help gain the band a huge following, no doubt about it. He was right into The Byrds and the whole folk-rock thing. He hadn't played the blues, rock'n'roll, or any of that kind of stuff, like we had. And he wrote some great songs. Bryan and Arthur had a pretty good relationship. Bryan was a little hard-headed at times and he wanted to get his songs done, too. But Arthur was very strong-willed. They were already starting to be competitive. When Bryan joined, we went all the way in that folk-rock direction. Everybody chipped in to create the sound. Arthur started writing in that style. It was folk-rock with this bluesy guitar from Johnny. Bryan and I did the pirate look, with the buccaneer boots and the little ponytails. Arthur had his little triangular glasses. We were an odd bunch. We had three white guys and two black guys; it was very different for a folk-rock band to look like that. People just started flocking to see us."

"Arthur was smart to get me in the band," Bryan told UK writer Barney Hoskyns in the mid 90s. "I think he let me join more for who I knew than for what I could do. I brought him the whole Byrds' scene, first at the Brave New World and, ultimately, at the Whisky A Go Go." Bryan conveyed something else from his former employers: the song "Hey Joe." Composed by obscure folksinger Billy Roberts (although often erroneously credited to songwriter Dino Valenti), it had been a staple of The Byrds' live repertoire. A stark tale of a man killing his woman before fleeing to Mexico, The Byrds' version had been sung by David Crosby whose driving, proto-punk arrangement ran counter to the group's contemplative, mid-tempo folk-rock. Bryan recognized the appeal of the song and brought Crosby's arrangement with him to The Grass Roots, making it, as Crosby had, his onstage showcase number.

Word about The Grass Roots spread among the hip Sunset Strip crowd, and the excitement generated by this racially integrated band with its edgy take on folk-rock meant they had soon outgrown the Brave New World. "They started blocking off areas in the parking lot for all these people and selling tickets for the overflow, but the owner didn't own the parking lot," remembers Johnny. "The fire marshal would come by every night and the club owner would get a ticket. He finally told us we had to move on, because he couldn't afford to keep paying the fines."

Success would necessitate another name change. Having built up a following as The Grass Roots, Arthur was stunned to discover another group using the same moniker. LA songwriters Phil 'P.F.' Sloan and Steve Barri had approached Lou Adler, owner of Dunhill Records, with the idea of recording some of their folk-rock songs under the name The Grass Roots. Sloan had some kudos, having recently penned "Eve Of Destruction," a #1 single for Barry McGuire. The two songwriters were apparently unaware of another group already using their chosen name. Sloan and Barri would cut one of their compositions, "Where Were You When I Needed You," backed by top LA session musicians, including drummer Hal Blaine and Don Randi on harpsichord, with Sloan on lead vocals. They then went in search of a group to 'become' The Grass Roots and be the onstage faces of their project. They found what they were looking for in a group from San Bruno, near San Francisco, called The Bedouins. They brought them down to LA in late summer 1965. "We didn't realize until we got here that a local band had already used the name," protests Bedouins/Grass Roots drummer Joel Larson.

"Sure, we got a little flack for that, but we soon established ourselves. Lou must have seen the name and thought it was really cool." Soon, people were coming to see Arthur's Grass Roots and asking them to play Sloan and Barri's cover of Bob Dylan's "Ballad Of A Thin Man" (known, in their version, as "Mr. Jones"), which was receiving local airplay. Arthur was infuriated and blamed Lou Adler for deliberately stealing his group's name, and with it the goodwill they had built up on the LA scene.

One day, when I was having lunch in Hollywood, a guy came up to me and said, "Hey, Arthur, I heard your record on the radio and I think it's cool." I didn't know what to say. At that time, all they had were reel-to-reel tape recorders and no one was allowed to record our shows; that was a rule of mine. But this record came out by The Grass Roots called "Mr. Jones." It freaked me out. Then I went up on the Strip and what do I see at the Trip but two names up in lights: 'Barry McGuire' and a group called 'The Grass Roots.' I heard they were from San Francisco. Someone had stolen my name! Suddenly, we were playing the Brave New World with no name, just because I didn't have it properly patented or registered. "I don't know what you're talking about," I said to the guy who came up to me. Then, the next day, I heard the song on the radio and it obviously wasn't me.

Whether or not Lou Adler intentionally pilfered the name remains a matter for speculation; however, Johnny Echols recalls an earlier encounter with Lou at the Brave New World which may have had some bearing on the matter. "Lou Adler had wanted to sign us but he came to the club really drunk. He was trying to impress this chick he was with. We really didn't know who Lou Adler was at the time, so we kind of fobbed him off and didn't pay him the respect he felt he deserved. Bryan and I were the ones talking to him and Lou got really angry, like we were totally disrespecting him. He had no intention of signing us; the whole thing was just to give the impression to this chick that he was a big shot." Johnny believes there was an ulterior motive for Lou Adler using the name. "We were pulling in loads of people as The Grass Roots; they would have assumed that a single that came out under that name was by us, so they went out and bought it in droves. It was devious but smart of Lou to do that."

When The Grass Roots' follow-up single, "Where Were You When I Needed You," became a major hit, the die was cast. Arthur's band was forced to look for a new name. Arthur never forgave Lou Adler for what he perceived as sabotage, and when Lou expressed interest in Love, two years later, Arthur turned him down flat. Johnny Echols: "Rather than fight for our name, we decided we'd change it. Everyone came up with suggestions. We considered Asylum Choir and several others which kind of sounded like the times. We hadn't really decided on a name yet, when one day we were driving down Melrose Avenue. Right after high school, Arthur had worked at this place called Luv Brassieres. We passed the billboard advertising this place and I told Bryan that Arthur used to work there. Of course, Bryan started laughing – we all did. Then Bryan said, 'You know, that'd make a hell of a name for the group.' We all agreed – and we went back and forth about how it should be spelled: not *Luv* or *The Luv* but simply *Love*. And that was it. It was serendipitous but that billboard changed everything."

Whether or not this opportune incident was actually the inspiration for the name Love remains moot. At one time or another, just about everyone in the original line-up, Arthur included, claimed he was the one who came up with the new name. Whatever the truth, The Grass Roots were reborn as Love by the fall of 1965. Arthur would retain the former identity when setting up a song publishing company the following year.

Having outgrown the Brave New World, Love moved over to another spot off the Sunset Strip, an erstwhile folk music club, the Unicorn, situated beside the Ivar Theatre at 1608 Cosmo Alley – a thoroughfare joining Hollywood Boulevard to Selma Avenue. The former Italian restaurant, run by the Thompson family – parents Bill and Dorothy and their children Linda and Tommy – had been transformed into a teen club in 1965. Incorporating the first two letters of each of the family-members' names into the club designation, Bido Lito's Backstage was born. Having been granted a cabaret license, the club could serve underage teens, as long as they purchased food.

With slightly more money on offer than at the Brave New World, Love would open at the club in October 1965. "When we moved to Bido Lito's, the audience followed us over there," recalls Johnny, "and we had the same problems with the crowds and overflow. But because Cosmo Alley was a semi-private street, they were able to block part of it off. They set up these huge speakers on the street. Even though people couldn't see the group they would pay to sit and listen to us, outside."

Bill Thompson administered a notorious sliding scale of admission fees, rising as the night went on and the crowds increased. "It was a small venue," remembers John Fleckenstein. "It reminded me of the place The Beatles started out – the Cavern Club – this little room with brick walls, kind of like a cave. When we were there it was packed. People there would call us 'Art's Orchestra.'"

When I started at Bido Lito's, I forget what fee Mr. Thompson offered me, but I think it was decent. If we drew this many people we would get this amount, and if we drew that many people we would get that amount. Well, anyway, that got to $25 for each of us. That was a lot of money. I can see Mr. Thompson now, with his little hat on, counting tickets. As the crowds grew bigger, the fee might have gone up to as much as $50, I don't recall exactly. Anyway, I was getting what I wanted out of the deal, and my band was happy. We were becoming even more popular than Mr. T ever thought we were going to be. The street was literally covered with people.

Bido Lito's was a trip. Like the Brave New World, it now seemed to me like we had to prove ourselves. That didn't take long. Within two weeks, we had them standing around the corner again. The club was too small for all the people but the music was loud enough that you could hear it from the sidewalks. There would be Johnny, with his big double-neck guitar – six and twelve strings. Love was the new name of the band, and did it fit, or what?

At Bido Lito's, we used to start the set off with "Smokestack Lightning," the Howlin' Wolf song. It always turned the crowd on. It would start off as that song but by the time it was over we were playing all kinds of different things in a sort of free style. Everyone would get a chance to show what he could do on his instrument. It would go into a lot of jazz feelings, like John Coltrane – it could get really far out, expressing what the person playing was feeling in the song. With a steady beat going, we used to improvise, everyone changing the music to what he wanted but somehow making it fit with what the others were playing. We'd play that song until it hypnotized the audience. I would go into all sorts of styles, taking the melody from blues to high-pitched screams and down to low-register, jazzy sounds, fading in and out of rock. I sometimes reminded myself of a snake charmer. I would close my eyes and play the sounds of making love on the harmonica, then open them and look out at the audience and see girls with their eyes closed and expressions of ecstasy on their faces. It was very interesting and quite a crowd pleaser, to say the least.

Bido Lito's looms large in Love lore. It was here, in the small, brick-walled enclave, that Love's sound – what Bryan MacLean later described as "a black version of folk-rock" – came together. The band's image, collectively and individually, took shape there, as did Arthur's unique persona. It was there that Elektra Records' president Jac Holzman caught the band's set, an event which would lead to him offering Love a recording contract. While The Doors are perhaps more generally associated with the club, it was Love who first put Bido Lito's on the musical map. "It was the right place at the right time," acknowledges Johnny. "The music was good, we were interesting, and we had all these people wanting to see us. Everything happened at the right time to bring us to the forefront: Bryan joining and bringing the Byrds' crowd, the Beatles phenomenon, the civil rights movement, and young people being more idealistic and open to an integrated group. We became a symbol for all this."

There were, however, a couple of the pieces yet to be added in order to complete the Love puzzle. Bass player John Fleckenstein would exit the group early in their Bido Lito's stand, opting for a more secure career in film. "While we were there, a friend whose father owned the optical house at Columbia Studios offered me the chance to get into the Cameraman's Guild, their union. So I left the group and didn't get the chance to play on their first album." John would receive a co-writing credit on the early Love song "Can't Explain." He later joined LA band The Standells before leaving the music business altogether and going on to become a respected cinematographer. "I've been associated with several very famous projects in my time," he reflects. "I worked on *ET* and *Close Encounters* with Steven Spielberg."

To replace Fleckenstein, the group tried out two or three bass players before settling on one Kenny Forssi. Born March 30 1943 in Cleveland, Ohio, Kenny and his family had moved to Sarasota, Florida, in 1956. A talented draftsman and illustrator, he had come out to Los Angeles in 1964 on a scholarship from the Arts Center School, and was living in Anaheim. Having been a semi-professional bass player with Floridian bands, Kenny placed his name on a bulletin board at Capitol Records, hoping to make some part-time money playing bass on weekends while attending art school. "Somehow, the manager of The Surfaris got a hold of this and the next thing I know I'm in The Surfaris," he recalled in a taped interview shortly before his death in 1998.

The Surfaris, a quartet from Glendora, California, were by this time on the downward slide after enjoying success with 1963 surfing instrumental "Wipe Out." Kenny joined in time to enjoy the last of the band's lingering fame. "We went to Japan and toured all over there, but by the time we got back the surfing thing was going down the tubes and here comes the hard-rock thing. I figured if surfing was dying I'd look for something else. I walked into Bido Lito's, on Cosmo's Alley in Hollywood, and there were Arthur Lee, Bryan MacLean, Don Conka, and Johnny Echols. I said to them, 'Sounds like you need a bass player,' and they said, 'Meet us here next Saturday,' and that was it. I never saw myself as an ace bass player, I just saw myself doing what I was doing."

Modesty notwithstanding, Kenny Forssi's distinctive melodic style suited Love's developing sound and would become a key ingredient in their later, more elaborate arrangements. His hollow-bodied Eko guitar also gave the group a distinctive bass sound. "Kenny was probably one of the most intelligent people I ever knew," remarks Johnny, "but you wouldn't know it from talking to him. He could look at an amplifier schematic and build it from scratch. And he actually did do that for us. He was like an engineer. He could do just about anything and could talk anyone into anything. He was a real Renaissance Man. His bass playing was the underpinning of our sound. He was perfect for us. He was able to pick up our stuff quickly and was able to fit in, so we hired him right on the spot. Fleck had already gone and we had a few other guys filling in: a guy named Mike Dowd and another guy named Doug. When Kenny joined we had the sound that we wanted."

Kenny Forssi's roommate at the time was a Swiss-born fellow art student and amateur drummer named Alban 'Snoopy' Pfisterer. Three years Kenny's junior, Snoopy fell under his elder friend's sway. "We met in art school and became friends. Kenny didn't have a place to live. He would invite himself over for dinner three or four times a week. He was very charming and liked being around my mother. Next thing, he asked if he could rent a room. It was his idea." This was during Kenny's stint in The Surfaris. "At first I was jealous because he was playing, being on television, getting fan letters, and going to Japan. He was buddies with The Beach Boys and others. He didn't want to be in art school. His mother sent him out to California to get a real job … he was already earning a living as a musician in Florida. Then, he started saying the guys in The Surfaris were too square in their matching shirts. Soon afterward, he was talking about seeing this band and meeting Johnny and Arthur." According to Snoopy, Kenny immediately recognized the potential benefits of hooking up with Love. "He saw the whole thing. He knew they were going to be big, I'll give him credit for that."

Having filled the vacant bass slot, the group now had to contend with their problematic drummer, Don Conka. A major draw at their group's shows and a dynamic contributor to their sound, Don was a drug addict and his habit often resulted in him being absent from gigs. Not seeking to ace him out of the band for good, the group nonetheless required some stability.

Lots of people came just to see Don Conka take a drum solo, which could sometimes last for an hour. He would hypnotize people with his different styles of drumming, from rock solos to Buddy Rich and real fast things, including those crossovers he did which were really a trip. People couldn't believe one person could hold an audience as long as he did, and on a regular basis. But every night, when he got paid, there were ten guys standing in line waiting for him. While he was playing people would yell, "Go Don Go! Go Don Go!" and he would play faster and faster until finally the solo ended with him sweating as hard as a government mule. He seemed to love it – and he sure had his share of lady friends. What he didn't know was that, while he was taking those long solos, we would be outside getting sky high. I don't think he would have played for so long if he'd known that!

Michael Stuart was the drummer with contemporaneous LA group, The Sons Of Adam. "We used to play Bido Lito's and, on an off night, I went there and saw Love playing for the first time, with Don Conka on drums. Don was just a blazing drummer, really on top of his game. The solos he took were incredible."

It all just seemed to fit in just fine until Don starting to miss more gigs than was called for. I had just about had it with him. I not only bent over backwards for him, I think I did a back flip. I thought he was going to play on our first album. I thought he was going to play at the Hollywood Bowl with us. I thought he was going to play the Trip, on Valentine's Day ... but he never showed. I had had it! Then, one night at Bido Lito's, this young kid shows up. It looked like he had brushed his bangs down in the front to make it seem like he had long hair. He told me his name was Snoopy. Against the better judgment of the band, I gave him a chance to sit in. I needed someone to fill the spot right there and then. The more

I thought about it, his youthful look and his innocence seemed to fit the band's
image; well enough, as it turned out, for him to be on the cover of the first Love
album. And so it was the five of us: Bryan, Johnny, Kenny, Snoopy, and me.

Kenny had suggested calling in his roommate on several occasions when it
appeared that Don wasn't going to make a gig. Snoopy readily obliged, knowing
he was merely filling in, not joining the group per se. "Don was one of *those*
drummers – he was like Ginger Baker – but he would take speed and sometimes
he'd show up, sometimes he'd be late, or not show at all," recalls John
Fleckenstein. "Snoopy couldn't do anything like Don could, but he could keep the
beat going." Snoopy would serve as a substitute until Don got himself together.
Those were the terms of his initial employment. "They never planned for me to be
the drummer," says Snoopy. "I had no experience before Love. I would just sit in
when Don couldn't make it. Then, when Don would say that he was straightening
out and going to be responsible, they'd fire me. A few weeks later they'd need me
again and ask me to sit in. They never rehearsed with me before I joined. I would
just get a call to come down and that was that.

"I remember we were playing Bido Lito's and Arthur warned me about
playing 'My Little Red Book.' That song is on the backbeat, on the opposite side
of the beat, and that always confused me. But I never had the chance to rehearse
with them to get it right. I was just a straight 4/4 drummer. I'd played with a
metronome since I was eight, so I had a real good sense of time. But I would
sometimes screw up coming back in at the right place on the right beat. This one
night, Arthur warned me that if I screwed it up I might as well pack up and go
home. Talk about intimidating. Sure enough, I screwed it up. Arthur was
obnoxious to me, but I stayed in the band. I took the shit. I don't know how many
drummers they tried but no one could deal with Arthur."

Snoopy's on-off role in Love carried through to the recording of their debut
album. "It just kept happening that way until they realized they needed a
drummer to record. I was around and available. I was reliable and Don wasn't, so
I did the album with them. Once I was on the first album, the record label decided
they should stick with me. Ironically, even though their actual drummer was
supposed to be better, they never had any more hits after my time on drums. So
much for the better drummer, is all I've got to say." Despite Arthur's domineering
and the tentative nature of Snoopy's employment, Love's lead singer and their

part-time drummer would eventually develop an elder brother/younger brother friendship. "Initially it wasn't like that: Arthur was totally intimidating," says Snoopy. "Musically, I was so inexperienced and the band was sort of down on me. Nobody really wanted me to be in the group."

Johnny Echols recalls the curious bond between lead singer and part-time drummer. "For some reason, Arthur liked having Snoopy around. Arthur never liked being on his own. He'd have nightmares, wake Snoopy up, and say, 'Let's smoke a joint,' just because Arthur didn't want to be alone."

While Snoopy bonded with Arthur, he could still find him dictatorial. "Arthur was definitely a megalomaniac; extremely authoritarian. Basically, the ultimate control [of the band] was Arthur's. It was Arthur's group, although I don't think he could have done it without Bryan." Snoopy and Bryan MacLean's relationship was always thorny. "I didn't like Bryan, and the feeling was mutual. He mistreated me more than any of them. He was really nasty to me. He thought I was square and he was hip – and I wasn't the drummer he wanted. Also, Arthur liked me … ." Bryan would later confirm his aversion to the young drummer. "I didn't get along with Snoopy," he told Neal Skok. "I didn't feel he was homogeneous with what we were doing. He seemed like this straight kid. He wasn't hip and didn't look right."

What Snoopy may have perceived as Arthur's authoritarianism might also have been interpreted as his tireless drive and determination to make the band a success. It was Arthur who wrote the bulk of the songs, made the bookings, dealt with the club managers and promoters, and, as front man, drew the most attention. There are those who insist that, from the get-go, Love *was* Arthur Lee. That is an oversimplification and negates the substantial contributions each member made to the group. However, in the eyes of the record-buying public, Arthur Lee was always the focal point of Love. "When we saw them live, it was obvious that Arthur Lee was the leader," recalls Paul Body. "He would be wearing those weird, triangle-shaped glasses and tight pants. But they all had their own image. Johnny Echols had the double-neck guitar, Bryan MacLean was a cross between Brian Jones and The Byrds' Michael Clarke, and Kenny Forssi reminded me of Prince Valiant. Snoopy was on drums, although Arthur also played them on a couple of songs, one for sure being 'Softly To Me.' They looked cool, wore the coolest clothes, and drew the most beautiful girls around them. They reminded me of The Rolling Stones, plus they had that sort of Byrds thing happening. At that point, The Byrds weren't a really good live band and Love was a *great* live band, as good as anybody else that was happening at that time."

LA music journalist Harvey Kubernik remembers Love's undeniable allure. "Chicks that I liked were glued to the stage when Love played. There were handsome guys in that group. Kim Fowley once said of Love that they attracted what he called 'surf pussy,' all these gorgeous blondes with pressed hair, in mini-skirts, grooving to the band. Love had a sexual energy but there was craftsmanship in that band, too. The blended sound and the conviction, especially in Arthur's voice and Johnny's playing, was incomparable. It was never lost on me that Arthur could sing like Mick Jagger, or sing like Johnny Mathis. Johnny Echols *looked* like Johnny Mathis. I'm sure there was more that Johnny contributed to their songs and sound than is generally assumed. I've always thought Johnny became the Keith Richards of the group. He was really essential, and some of that magic was denuded when he split the scene. It also didn't hurt that they had a guitarist who had hair like [The Yardbirds' singer] Keith Relf or Brian Jones. Back then, hair was important. Girls liked guys with rock'n'roll hair. And having Bryan MacLean there was an important visual element. He meant something to us, here in LA. When I got that first Love album I was so happy that they were from LA – we all felt that, way back then. I played their music a lot and went out of my way to write about them and Arthur. They were very cinematic characters."

I remember I asked my friend James Scott if I could borrow his soft leather, high-top boots. He said "OK" but there was a problem: he only had one boot. That's how another idea started. Everywhere I went – to the club, on stage, at home, anywhere – I wore that one, high-top boot. At the time, I was also playing the harmonica and people started talking about the guy who played the harp and wore only one boot. That idea really worked. I didn't have [Beatles manager] Brian Epstein for publicity or promotion, but I sure did attract a lot of attention. Rain or shine, I wore that one boot. A crowd of us would go to a restaurant in Hollywood and as I walked through the door the manager would say I couldn't come in because I didn't have both shoes on. The people I was with would say, "If he can't come in, none of us are coming in." Sometimes that worked and I got in. Sometimes it didn't.

"The original Love had a special magic to them. You could replace any one of them with a better musician but it wouldn't have sounded as great," contends

Arthur's friend Len Fagan. "When you walked into the room and heard the music, there was something incredible but inexplicable about them which made them better than the rest. That was what I experienced the first time I saw them at the Brave New World. I turned around to see who was making this amazing sound and I saw five guys up there that had as much charisma, mystery, and an element of dangerous unpredictability as I had ever witnessed. They had the same kind of aura about them as The Rolling Stones – even more so, in fact. With Love, there was something bigger than the five guys on stage together. They dressed like rock'n'roll stars when very few bands were doing so. There weren't many hip clothing stores, only certain shops you could go to, otherwise you were wearing Levi's. All the bands that were big and cool in LA were white bands with long, straight hair and a similar image. Love didn't fit that. They had this look about them that made you think, 'Do I really want to approach them after the show?' The whole package was very impressive."

To describe our show is easy. I was as wild as they came, singing, with one shoe on and one shoe off. I would jump from table to table, never thinking about falling. I just thought about entertaining. There were no cordless mics at that time. I also used to play guitar on top of the tables. Then there was Johnny Echols, creating all these sexy, intense sounds. The guy looked almost like Johnny Mathis; more masculine, but just as good-looking. We were driving those people crazy. Johnny just knew he was the best guitar player around. I would say, "Yeah, you're the best!" When he got his 12-string, we started putting it all together. We captured the sound that we needed for the band to be not only rock but also folk-rock.

When I first started, I had stage fright but I psyched myself out of it. If I thought for one second that I was standing up there singing a song in front of all those people, I'd probably have fainted. The way I overcame that stage fright was to say to myself, "There's nobody out there. All the faces in that crowd are nothing but a brick wall. There's nobody there." So I convinced myself that, no matter what happened, I would ignore it and concentrate only on what I was doing.

According to his sometime girlfriend Gaye Blair, Arthur was something special on stage: "He had a presence and there was a danger about him. He always reminded me of a thoroughbred race horse. As far as I was concerned, Arthur was the whole band. I never liked it when Bryan sang. Love was Arthur, and if some people didn't get it, too bad. He was always the creative force."

"When you saw Love, live, it was immediately clear that it was Arthur's band," concurs veteran southern California DJ Rick Williams, "and Johnny and Bryan, as wingmen, took their cues from Arthur. As much as the other guys in the band were cool-looking, Arthur was so much cooler than anyone on that stage. He knew all eyes were riveted on him. He had a real commanding stage presence. I also remember what a great harmonica player Arthur was; he was amazing, yet I don't think that was ever captured on any of the Love albums."

We had the perfect band. There was nothing else like it in the world. We had the sound, the look, the crowds, and the songs that the youth, and the Hollywood scene, wanted. What made us stand out most were our different races. We were so unique and sounded, and looked, so good, it didn't seem to matter what color we were; and that is as good as it gets in this life.

"Back in the day, we didn't see Love as a black and white band," says Harvey Kubernik. "I got my high school wardrobe off the cover of the first Love album. That's how influential the band was to all of us in LA. That, to us, was the *colored* aspect of that band, not their races. If someone was wearing whale cords and a thick belt on the cover, and shopped at [LA boutiques] Beau Gentry or deVoss, I would go there, too, and get the same clothes."

Despite the enlightened colorblindness of Love's audience, there can be no doubt, given the tenor of the times, with LA's Watts riot having just erupted and civil rights issues boiling over in other major urban centers across America, that Arthur was aware that he and his integrated folk-rock band were breaking new ground. With the notable exception of Taj Mahal and his band The Rising Sons, they were playing within an exclusively white musical genre and milieu. This was of no little significance, as LA music writer Jim Bickhart points out. "It seems unimaginable that Arthur's career was uninfluenced by the civil rights upheaval going on around him. In their own small way, he and Johnny Echols were pioneers. Their forays into the Hollywood music and recording scene – at the same time as The Byrds and other post-British Invasion LA performers were emerging – pretty much guaranteed they didn't have to be pigeonholed as black artists. They wanted to be able to do whatever they wanted – which is the epitome of equal opportunity. I think it's interesting that they followed in The Byrds' footsteps, stylistically and image-wise. In a way, Lee and Echols submerged much of what they could have been expected to know about music, from their upbringing and heritage, into what was really an adopted musical genre. But they did it so credibly, along with Bryan MacLean, who brought his own, very different, sensibility and a direct connection to the community around The Byrds. That allowed Love to step comfortably into their adopted milieu, with Arthur and Johnny as the 'psychedelic black men' who led a band that was a living, breathing monument to integration and the new social ethos."

"We were outlaws," claimed Johnny in an interview with Memphis journalist Andria Lisle, reflecting on Love's atypical presence on the Strip. Indeed, Arthur and Johnny, two black men from South Central LA, with their straightened hair and colorful clothes, were extreme anomalies in the clubs of Hollywood. "Arthur and I were interested in doing our own thing, and we were the only people of color right there, in the thick of it."

Harsh societal reality would sometimes creep back in once they left the cosseted environment of the Strip, however, as former Hollywood parking attendant Peter Piper – who worked across the street from the Whisky – recalls. "I remember seeing Love play on the Sunset Strip, then later that night seeing Johnny and Bryan with their hands up on their Volkswagen van, being frisked by the cops. A black guy and a white guy together was enough to get the police to pull them over. That was an automatic red flag to the cops, back then. They just figured there was something going on that shouldn't have been. Once he got off the Strip, Johnny was just another black guy."

A Love recording session was Arthur's next priority. Before the band could cut any tracks of their own, minus Arthur they contributed to a friend's recordings. Vince Flaherty was an actor who, as a child, had appeared on the silver screen in *The Texan,* starring Rory Calhoun. He had also been in the cast of *The Donna Reed Show* on television. Besides his acting career, Vince maintained a keen interest in music. A harmonica player and singer, he was a frequent visitor to the Brave New World and Bido Lito's whenever Love were playing. Vince had gone to school with Bido Lito's manager Tommy Thompson. "They didn't yet have a recording contract; I sat in with them at Bido Lito's," recalls Vince. "They had charisma, so I wanted to make music with them. If Arthur wanted a break, he'd let me take over. I just hit on the guys to come record with me. They didn't tell Arthur."

In the fall of 1965, Vince took Johnny, Bryan, Kenny, and Don Conka into LA's Gold Star Studios to cut four Flaherty originals: "Yes It's True," "Moth Child," "Dead From You," and "She." The intention was to land Vince a recording contract. However, while the band's accompaniments were robust, no contract was secured.

Vince maintained a cautious relationship with Arthur. "He could be a tough hombre and a force of nature. He was an asshole to me sometimes, but he could also be nice. Around that time, I saw him standing outside the Whisky, so I went up to him and told him I had been recording with the band. I just wanted to be upfront with him. He looked over the top of the little pince-nez glasses he wore, and mumbled, 'It's cool, man. It's OK.' He was there at the next sessions and [on the recordings] you can hear him talking in the booth and giving some directions to the band." Subsequent Flaherty recording sessions, some two years later, would also feature Johnny, Bryan, and Kenny, this time alongside Daryl Dragon (later the 'Captain' of Captain & Tennille fame) and Jimi Hendrix. "The influence of Johnny, Bryan, and Kenny is tremendous on Love's recordings," insists Vince. "But people don't seem to see that."

Despite the excitement and the standing-room-only crowds that Love were attracting, they still lacked a recording contract. They also lacked management. Journalist Jerry Hopkins, along with an associate named Doug Lyon, claimed to have managed the group for a brief period in the fall of 1965 and supervised a demo recording session at a studio, Original Sound, located at Sunset and Cahuenga. Hopkins is quoted in Barney Hoskyns' 2001 biography of Arthur, *Alone Again Or*, recalling his frustrating attempts to steer the band's fortunes while butting heads with Arthur. For his own part, Arthur always denied ever retaining the pair as managers. The alleged demo tape was supposedly rejected by all the major labels they approached. When Elektra Records' Jac Holzman signed Love in January 1966, it was on the strength of their live shows. No demos were ever offered or requested.

I read somewhere that Jerry Hopkins said he was once the manager of the group Love. I want to know where I was during that period.

Arthur did, however, have a signed personal management contract with Herb Cohen, dating from that same fall. Best known for managing Frank Zappa, Tim

Buckley, and, later, Tom Waits, Herb got his start working in the folk music community and was well-connected in the LA music business. His Third Story Music, co-owned with his brother, Martin, published the songs of a number of writers. The standard management contract was exclusive to Arthur only, not Love.

Shortly thereafter, the band's affairs would be handled by one Ronnie Haran. A sometime actress, hailing from New York City, Ronnie had come to Los Angeles to pursue a career on the screen. Between auditions, she worked as assistant publicist for Elmer Valentine, owner of the Whisky A Go Go and the Trip, before taking on the publicist role herself. Confident and feisty, Ronnie wasn't afraid to go to bat for her clients. "I remember being at the Trip with Elmer and Herbie Cohen, and Herbie saying to me, 'I have this band called Love and I need someone to run their fan club. Would you like to do it?' I said, 'Sure.' He gave me Arthur's phone number. I'd never met him and didn't know who he was, nor had I ever seen the band. I knew nothing about them.

"I called Arthur up and said, 'Hi Arthur, my name is Ronnie Haran; Herbie Cohen suggested I call you about running your fan club.' This was Arthur's response: 'Oh yeah, well, how'd you like to fire Herbie Cohen for me?' That was my introduction to Arthur Lee. I then went over and met him and it was instant friendship, as if we'd known each other forever. We got along like a house on fire from then on." Ronnie would subsequently act as Love's de facto manager, despite never signing a contract with the group.

"Ronnie was this little thing, about five feet two; she would wear short miniskirts and go-go boots, and she didn't take any crap from anyone," says Johnny. "She was spirited and dynamic, and we knew she was on our side. She acted as manager, publicity agent, mother hen … you name it. We would have done well to stay with Ronnie because she had our best interests at heart. We could trust her; she wasn't there to rip us off. But she was also a female, and women band managers were rare in those days. Being young guys, full of testosterone, we weren't going to listen to a female."

"I remember we were playing the Hollywood Bowl and we're in the limousine," recalls Ronnie. "We were at the backstage entrance, and the band went through in front of me. The security guard stopped me at the door and said, 'Sorry, no groupies allowed.' The band had gone in by then and he was locking me out. 'Excuse me,' I said. 'I'm their manager.' He replied, 'Yeah, right.' So I thought, 'How long will it take until the band realizes I'm not there?' This guy kept me there for 20 or 30 minutes. Finally, Bryan came out to get me, saying, 'Hey, she's with us.'"

The first order of business for Love's new management would be landing the group a decent recording contract. Enter Jac Holzman. Having established Elektra Records, one of the first successful independent record labels, in 1950, while still at college, Jac had been quick on the scene when the folk music boom hit in the mid 50s. Elektra had established its credentials by releasing roots and traditional folk recordings by the likes of Jean Ritchie, Theodore Bikel, and Shep Ginandes, as well as popular folk recordings. Among Jac's first major commercial successes had been folk singer Judy Collins, who helped elevate Elektra's profile in the marketplace. The label's reputation for artistic integrity was its calling card. Jac was always motivated by his own tastes and convictions, and was never afraid to take risks by signing artists which other labels may have shunned.

Ostensibly an acoustic music label, Elektra's first foray into electrified rock had come with The Paul Butterfield Blues Band, earlier in 1965. That same year, Jac had tried, unsuccessfully, to sign The Lovin' Spoonful. The acoustic folk boom was rapidly coming to an end and record labels were signing anybody with the slightest folk-rock inclination.

Looking westward, Jac recognized that the most exciting new sounds were coming from California. Having tried in vain to forge an LA beachhead for Elektra three years earlier, he returned to the West Coast to try again in December 1965. As recommended by Herb Cohen, one of Jac's first moves after touching down in LA was to check out Love at Bido Lito's. What he discovered was both shocking – he later described the club as "the Black Hole of Calcutta with a door charge" – and exhilarating. His wife, Nina, recalled the onstage spectacle: "Arthur Lee had these boots with the tongues hanging out, no laces, and his eyeglasses had one blue lens and one red, and were a funny shape. He was the most bizarre person I'd ever seen in my life, by far."

Jac had come to California specifically looking for new groups to sign. "I had a hunch that New York was not where I was going to find what I was looking for. I thought that the West Coast was going to be a very important contributor to music, for the first time. Music recorded in California did not tend to travel east, although music recorded in New York did travel west. I just thought that there was something different about music that was put together out here [in California]. As I always did, I picked up the papers, went through all the listings, and went to see all the groups I didn't know. I was looking for something different, something that didn't remind me of New York. I went to Bido Lito's and there were Arthur Lee and Love. It took me about three minutes to know. It was the energy and the audience. The scene off the stage was even better than the scene on the stage, but not by much. In New York, people watched bands; in California they were part of the band's performance. Some of the most gorgeous women I'd ever seen were there, that night. The band was playing well. They seemed to like being together. I asked myself the questions I always ask, 'Do I like this? Is it something I haven't heard before? Do I think this is going to be fun? Can I deal with these people?' I reasoned that the answer was probably 'yes' to all of them, so I made Arthur an immediate offer. It was instinctive, as these things often are. It's not about the deal, it's whether you like the group and whether you think it has staying power, because it's very rare that a first album happens right out of the box. It's generally around the third album that it takes off."

As for the band's racial mix, Jac saw it neither as an asset nor a liability. "To tell you the truth, I never noticed. I was so drawn to the sound, that the make up of the band never caught my attention. I was used to jazz bands, and there were a lot of integrated jazz groups, so this was nothing new. I saw no marketing advantage in it. Anyway, the marketing comes after the music; it's the music that tells you what to do." Jac intuited that Love was the band to break Elektra into the rock field. "I liked Arthur Lee; I liked what I saw on that stage. I had no idea what was going to happen down the line, but I was looking for a band and I thought this was my band. I thought I deserved them." Jac made his move that same night, approaching Arthur with a contract offer.

Johnny Echols recalls the band's introduction to Elektra Records. "Herb Cohen was this ex-military guy that we didn't really take to. He came to the club and told us he had this friend from New York, a record company executive, and would we mind talking to him. That's how we met Jac Holzman. We went to Canter's after the show, and Jac presented his case to us."

It's probable that Arthur knew little of Elektra's folk-based roster, given his own tastes in music. Nonetheless, it was an offer. Ever the Machiavellian, Arthur played it for all it was worth. "I developed a relationship with Arthur that had a hint of wariness to it," Jac confesses. "I knew he was a scoundrel. But there are scoundrels and there are charming scoundrels. [Greenwich Village folk singer] Fred Neil was a scoundrel but not a likeable one, and, although he was gifted, I didn't think he had Arthur's talent. But Arthur was still a scoundrel. You live with it, you see what happens. I let Arthur get away with a lot of stuff. On that first night he said to me, 'Before I sign, I need $5,000 in cash and I need it tomorrow.' He said he needed to buy something for the band to tour in. So we had a contract drawn over immediately.

"Ronnie Haran was on the fringes of this, somewhere," Jac conitnues. "The deal was made under the aegis of Al Schlesinger, a lawyer I had known, and a very honorable guy. So we made the deal, I gave Arthur the $5,000, and a couple of days later he rolls up in a gull-wing Mercedes. 'Is that for the band?' I asked. 'Well, I have to have something to drive around in,' he replied. At that point, I decided to let them sort it out. I later heard that he gave each of the guys $100."

Once again, myth overshadows reality. The often repeated story of how Arthur took Love's advance to buy a luxury car, paying the other band members just a paltry share, contains grains of truth and falsehood. The contract offered to the group (not to Arthur alone, as has often been written), commencing January 1966, was for one year with two further annual options (beginning January 1967 and January 1968, respectively) to be exercised at the exclusive discretion of Elektra. A minimum of 14 'sides' (recordings) were to be provided by the group in each of the contracted years. The contentiousness of the contract arose from a clause which stated that: "All checks shall be made to Arthur Lee on behalf of the group." It was a stipulation that effectively granted Arthur complete control of Love's advances and royalties. This would become a bone of contention and eventually precipitate a lawsuit.

As for the alleged $100 payments made to the band, the truth has been somewhat embroidered, explains Johnny. "For one thing, you couldn't buy a gull-wing Mercedes for $5,000, back then. I'll tell you exactly what happened. We got the money – Arthur, Bryan, Kenny, and I. Snoopy wasn't on the contract. We decided that Snoopy shouldn't have a full share, so the money was split between the remaining four of us. Arthur took Snoopy's cut and gave him $100 out of that. So Arthur got less than double what we got. Now, Lee Collins, the guy who owned the Brave New World club, had an aunt who kept this vintage Mercedes, one of those old Nazi cars, with the 'suicide seat.' She was an elderly lady, living in North Hollywood. Arthur and I went up to see her and he bought the car from her, for $1,100, I think. So that's another myth; someone took a little bit of truth and magnified it out of all proportion."

That 3000 S Mercedes was the icing on the cake. Even though I've had a lot in my life, I've never been a material freak. A musician's life, I knew when I chose it, was going to be a hard way to go. When you're up, you're really up, and when you're down, if you don't make your pennies last and save something for a rainy day, you're in bad shape, because trends in music change so fast.

The contract between Elektra Records and Love identified five band members: Messrs Lee, Echols (initially misspelled "Eckles" but later corrected by Johnny), MacLean (also misspelled and later corrected), Forssi, and Conka (misspelled Concha). The first four signed the contract, Don Conka did not. In January 1966, his four bandmates still believed that Don was very much a part of Love and were expecting him to be in the line-up for their recording sessions; thus, they wrote him into the contract. Despite expectations (and long-held rumors to the contrary), in the end Don would not play on Love's debut album. His sometime substitute, Snoopy, was still regarded as a temporary replacement and was excluded from the contract. He was not, by extension, an artist to whom royalties would be paid, even though when Jac first saw the group Snoopy was the drummer. In addition to his token $100 advance, Snoopy would receive session fees for the recording dates, as did all the band-members. "The relationship was affected by the fact that they always wanted somebody else on drums," says a rueful Snoopy. "Kenny, who was supposed to be my friend, went along with the general feeling of the group."

Another stipulation of Arthur's, before signing with Elektra, was that the group be given its own publishing company to administer the band's songs. This was a bold initiative given that, during this era, few recording artists controlled their own song publishing. Most record labels either had their own publishing house or had longstanding agreements with existing specialist companies. Either way, the label made money from publishing. It was an income stream that helped offset the cost of launching an artist, in addition to revenue from record sales. It also allowed a label to reap benefits long after an artist had left their roster or after an artist's career had crashed and burned.

For the uninitiated, and this included most musicians and songwriters before the mid 70s who unwittingly signed over the rights to their compositions, publishing accounts for 50 per cent of the income a song earns. It does so from four sources: performance royalties (from airings on radio, television, film, and in concert), synchronized licensing (for use on television or movie soundtracks), printed sheet music, and mechanicals (record sales, ostensibly). The term 'publishing' dates back to the days when sheet music was the principal source of revenue from songs. The Beatles' long and convoluted publishing history offers a sobering lesson in what not to do in the matter of song ownership. The fact that the late Michael Jackson was able to bid for and win (in 1984) the rights to The Beatles' publishing catalog would rankle with Paul McCartney for years. Some of the best-known songs of the last 50 years have been owned by someone other than the writer. Anyone can own a song, if they can make the deal and the paperwork is correctly filed. For many, it's the gift that keeps on giving.

While most of his contemporaries (including The Byrds) were uneducated in the ways of publishing, Arthur knew what was at stake. "Arthur was always hustling," says John Fleckenstein. "It was his band and he wanted the publishing and the credit on the songs. He wanted to get something going. Arthur knew how the business worked. He had this book called *The Business Of Music*. That had everything about publishing and record deals in it. He didn't trust people in the music business, and for good reason. A lot of people got ripped off. Arthur was a driven guy."

Arthur also benefited from the sound business advice of Ronnie Haran and Al Schlesinger. "I made sure that Love controlled their publishing," says Ronnie. "We were never unreasonable in what we asked from Elektra, but we weren't going to be fools. I felt like a sixth member of the band. We were all the same age and it felt like a family. I wasn't trying to rip them off."

Johnny Echols, however, bristles when the topic of Love's song publishing is raised. "I had been given some advice by Little Richard and Earl Grant: they insisted that you should always own your own music. They'd say, 'Don't let them take your songs.' So, when talking with Jac, we told him everything [in the contract] sounded good but that we had to have the publishing rights to our songs. That looked like being a non-starter for Jac. In those days, all the record labels controlled the publishing on songs. In the end, Elektra agreed – they were the only label to agree to that and so we signed with them."

Grass Roots Music was duly established to control Love's original compositions. This mostly meant Arthur's songs, along with a couple of co-writing credits to Johnny and John Fleckenstein and the handful of songs written by Bryan. However, having your own publishing and administering it are two different things. Many artists who control their publishing will licence the right to administer – in other words to monitor and collect monies owing – to an established publishing company. Most musicians have neither the time nor the expertise to track down publishing royalties. Arthur and Love were certainly not well-versed in these matters and later discovered that they had entered into a relationship the details of which they were not initially aware. "For years, our publishing royalties went through Third Story Music, which was Herb and Martin Cohen's company," explains Johnny. "Somehow, they had worked out a deal whereby they were administrators of our publishing, for a fee. Herb had worked with Jac. We assumed that the checks that were coming to us were from Elektra, not from Third Story Music. We just thought that Third Story Music was an adjunct of Elektra ... they had so many company names, like Nonesuch and so on. For years, Third Story Music was taking a percentage of the publishing money."

Jac Holzman is adamant that the label did nothing under a cloak of deception. "My recollection is that the writers got 100 per cent of their share and split the publishing with Third Story, who filed the copyrights, collected, and did the myriad things publishers do. It was a very professional operation."

Nonetheless, Johnny feels the group was misled. "We thought we had no relationship with Herb whatsoever; we had signed nothing with him. He'd introduced us to Jac Holzman, nothing more, as far I know. Here we were, thinking we were smarter than those guys that came before us, like Little Richard, who were all ripped off ... we thought we had all the i's dotted and t's crossed, when, in fact, we were just as naive and stupid as they were. We didn't have the savvy or the business sense to have somebody look at the contracts. That was our own naivety, but it was also because Arthur thought he knew everything. In the 90s, Arthur was looking to sell Grass Roots Music to Leiber and Stoller's Trio Music. That's when I found out that Third Story had been collecting part of the publishing on the songs for all those years. We thought we had all the bases covered and didn't see the signs."

Jac counters this view of events. "Arthur made the deal with Herb. He might not have told the band ... not right away, anyway."

Years later, Elizabeth McKee was able to wrest control of Bryan MacLean's publishing from Grass Roots Music. The four songs provide her with a modest income to this day. "When Arthur sold his song catalog to Leiber and Stoller, in the 90s, Bryan kept asking the music lawyer, who his half-sister, Maria, had employed, if he could get Bryan's songs back," Elizabeth explains. "Arthur had sold Bryan's four songs, along with the other Love songs in the Grass Roots Music catalog. The lawyer retrieved [Bryan's composition] "Alone Again Or," along with an advance of around $40,000. Later, I called up Leiber and Stoller and told them, 'You have four of my son's songs in Arthur Lee's catalog,' and they replied, 'So what are you going to do about it?' I said, 'I'll have my lawyer call you,' and I got those four songs back."

As one Love associate estimates: "That one song, "Alone Again Or," has probably earned over half-a-million dollars over the years."

Despite the administrative machinations, on January 24 1966 – three weeks after signing the contract with Elektra – Love entered Hollywood's Sunset Sound Recorders studio complex to begin cutting their debut album. Accompanying them were Jac Holzman, veteran Elektra producer Mark Abramson, and, behind the mixing console, engineer Bruce Botnick. The expectations of both band and record label ran high – and would ultimately be justified.

CHAPTER 3

MY FLASH
ON YOU

Love early 1966 – left to right: Johnny Echols, Bryan
MacLean, Kenny Forssi, Arthur, Snoopy

Although he was an experienced folk record producer, Jac Holzman was a neophyte when it came to recording a rock band, especially one as enigmatic as Love. Elektra staff producer Paul Rothchild was the logical choice for the job, having worked in the studio with The Lovin' Spoonful and The Butterfield Blues Band. He was indisposed, however, owing to a recent drug bust and a subsequent stint in prison; so the job fell to Jac, aided by fellow Elektra producer and filmmaker Mark Abramson. Jac had done his homework on Love. "I had watched enough of their performances to know what I wanted to do with them in the studio – which was very little. I saw them a number of times in the clubs before we recorded them. I didn't like going into a studio without knowing exactly what was going to be on the record and knowing the material. I'm a decent producer for bands that are totally self-contained. I know what's missing and I know if I'm not hearing something I heard live. When I went into the studio with Love, I knew what I wanted to hear."

Engineer for the sessions was Bruce Botnick, then a staffer at Sunset Sound, and soon to be a producer in his own right. The son of classically-trained musicians who worked in many of Hollywood's studios, Bruce was bitten by the recording bug as a teenager after attending his parents' recording sessions. In high school, he would record school orchestras and choirs. He had begun his professional career with Liberty Records before moving to Sunset Sound.

Located at 6650 Sunset Boulevard, the Sunset Sound facility began life in 1962. Opened by Walt Disney's director of recordings, Tutti Camarata, it was designed as a bespoke studio in which the company's movie soundtracks would be recorded. The studio supplemented its revenue with commercials and popular music sessions. Sunset Sound would go on to achieve renown in rock'n'roll circles, becoming the studio of choice for the likes of Love, Buffalo Springfield, and The Doors. The Rolling Stones used it for overdubbing – its isolation booth was renowned in the business. Bruce Botnick began working at the studio soon after it opened and gained his experience doing any recording task assigned to him. "I would do Midas Muffler commercials, children's albums, Annette Funicello sessions ... anything at all. In the evenings, I did rock'n'roll bands. I practically lived at the studio." It was Elektra singer-songwriter Tim Buckley who directed Jac to both Sunset Sound and Bruce.

"I had heard it had a good echo chamber," recalls Jac of the studio. "Not that I necessarily wanted a lot of echo, but it helps give a room dimension. And there was Bruce Botnick. That was the start of a friendship that has lasted for over 40 years. Our problem, at Elektra, was that we didn't have a lot of experience recording electric music. Bruce saw us through that first time with Love and I never made another album in California without him. When you find good people, you keep them."

"Jac was smart enough to know what had to be done," Bruce insists. "He knew the material, the keys, and what was happening in the songs. We blasted through that first Love album in four days. Jac knew I understood what was going on, otherwise he wouldn't have left the album in my hands to mix." As for the relationship between producer and artist: "There was a really terrific connection between Jac and Arthur. They got along so well on an intellectual level. I loved Arthur's use of words and how he played with the language, his visualizations and imagery. Arthur was very bright, one of the brightest people I ever met. But, then, I only knew him in the studio." Indeed, Arthur was determined to make his first major musical statement count. "He was phenomenally talented," says Jac. "Probably more talented than anybody in town, and he knew it. He hungered for success; he was always reaching for the brass ring."

Arthur's reputation for drug consumption, like much of the band's history, is shrouded in legend. This was a time of narcotic experimentation. Marijuana, hashish, and psychedelics such as LSD (acid) and mescaline were regarded as recreational drugs that also enhanced perspectives and stirred the creative juices. Although Arthur's drug of choice at that point was hashish (and in that regard he was considered a connoisseur), by 1966, he was already an acid user of some experience. As Bryan MacLean told Neal Skok, Arthur would take to the hallucinogen with characteristic gusto. "I never got on the LSD train but I did take it. I went along with the idea that my consciousness had opened up, but not for very long, and not like Arthur did. Arthur made it into a religious experience. Acid intensifies all your senses. It caused me to be very introspective and made me feel guilty a lot." Arthur took it upon himself to indoctrinate his buddies in the acid culture, as Riley Racer recalls. "Arthur came down to the neighborhood and picked a few of us up and introduced us to LSD. That was an eye-opener. ..."

"Arthur was stoned, 24 hours a day," insists Bruce Botnick. Perhaps owing as much to his natural demeanor as to any specific narcotic, Arthur seemed the epitome of the drugged, Sunset Strip hipster. He became the role model for others seeking the same cool quotient. "But like anyone who uses drugs consistently, they plateau," says Bruce. "Arthur functioned very well and could fully describe to the other guys in the band what he wanted them to play. He had the songs all conceived in his head." Indeed, to claim, as some have done, that Arthur's creativity was the result of an unremittingly drug-fueled lifestyle is a gross overstatement and does a disservice to his talent. At this point in his career, drugs may have been a means to an end but were they not the end themselves.

Despite being roughly the same age as the members of Love, Bruce had never heard, or even heard of, the band: "When they walked in that first day that was the first time I'd met them. I never saw Love perform on stage, only in the studio. They were the first Elektra artists I ever worked with. They didn't look that unusual to me, apart from Arthur with his little purple triangular sunglasses. He wore those incessantly. It was their music that spoke to me, so I didn't have a hard time relating to them. I had worked with Captain Beefheart by then and there were a lot of similarities."

Nowadays, when a band can take weeks just to get the right drum sound, it seems astonishing that Love were able to bang out the 14 tracks that constituted their self-titled debut album in a mere four days. However, what they were recording had been tried and tested on stage for several months already. They knew the songs, Jac knew what he wanted to hear, and Bruce made it all happen on tape. "They had been playing live every night at Bido Lito's," Bruce acknowledges, "and they knew their songs. In those days we didn't have multi-track tape, we had just four tracks. You had to put the bass and drums on one track, guitars on the other, leave one track for the vocals, and another for overdubs. We would sometimes bounce it all down to one track, which left us the remaining tracks to work with. You had to make decisions in those days as to what you wanted, then live with it. You couldn't fix it later."

Despite Arthur's previous recording experience, notably his time in Gold Star Studios (one of the locations in which Phil Spector had recently built his signature Wall of Sound), his input into the process itself had been minimal. This time it would be different, with the outcome reflecting Arthur's own vision of the songs and the sound of Love. "I don't remember the other guys, much," notes Bruce of those debut album sessions. "They were like hired hands, just the guys in the band. Bryan I remember the most. Snoopy wasn't that great a drummer and all the guys were very lazy. It got to the point where Arthur was choreographing every move they made. They weren't doing much beyond what he told them to do. Johnny did bring something to it. He and Arthur were buddies; that was obvious. But at the same time, Arthur had kind of beaten them all down. It was very much, 'I'm the man, don't forget it.' And they recognized that. They knew who was writing the songs and who was out front on the stage, singing and bringing in the girls."

According to Jac, Arthur could play everybody's instrument better than they could, with the exception of his gifted guitarist. "Johnny was a very good guitar player. Arthur would *suggest* things to Johnny, he would never scream at him. He respected Johnny and it showed in their relationship. As for the others, I think he felt he deserved better than he was getting. That original band would eventually become as good as Arthur ever had, but at the time of that first album they were a 'just out of the garage' band."

The sound of Love's debut album was rooted in the group's distinctive blending of edgy rhythm & blues with poetic lyrics and folk-rock instrumentation, harmonies, and arrangements. "Arthur was a poet and always turned a phrase in an interesting way," says his friend Ria Berkus. "He loved words. If you said a word that he didn't recognize he'd ask you what it meant and jot it down."

More than anything, the album offered a distinctive sound, one that had been crafted in the crowded confines of the Brave New World and Bido Lito's. Songs like "Can't Explain," "Gazing," "No Matter What You Do," "You I'll Be Following," and "Colored Balls Falling," with their chiming, jingle-jangle guitar chording and lush harmonies, showed how Arthur had absorbed all the characteristics and nuances of the folk-rock idiom. But it was the rawness that distinguished Love's brand of folk-rock, notable in Arthur's swaggering vocal delivery and Kenny Forssi's punchy bass. It was a sound quite distinct from the sweet, plangent signatures of The Byrds, The Leaves, or The Turtles. Love were more like the Rolling Stones of folk-rock. After the first album, it would be a style neither Arthur nor the band would ever comprehensively revisit.

There was also considerable musical sophistication to several of the songs on the album, notably "A Message To Pretty," "Softly To Me," "Mushroom Clouds," and "Signed D.C." The latter was like nothing any of Love's contemporaries had conjured. With its stark instrumentation, featuring just Arthur alone on acoustic guitar and harmonica, the song offered a harrowing anti-drug message drawn from the real life experience of drummer Don Conka – the titular 'D.C.'

Let me explain how I wrote the song "Signed D.C." We were playing at the Hullabaloo and some of the people that hung around the band were strung out, either on methadrine or heroin. They thought it was cool to be that way. After the show, I would see them sitting along the parking lot walls, all fixed up with their arms folded. So the song goes: "I can't unfold my arms / My soul belongs to the dealer / No one cares for me." As long as I stayed away from what they were doing, it was OK. It was all just writing down the words in a song, to me.

When I wrote the song, I had heard The Animals' "The House Of The Rising Sun" – that was a cool song, and I thought I would do something similar. The words were definitely not the same, however. The line: "Look out, Joe, I'm falling," was about one of Don's friends. I call it as I see it. No song I have ever written has been about something other than what I have experienced.

"Arthur's harmonica solo on 'Signed D.C.' is so haunting," says drummer Michael Stuart, who would later join the band. "It's like a freight train coming down the tracks. Nobody else could do anything like that. He took what the old blues harmonica players used to do, refined it, and gave it power. Those notes were so pure; there really was a high standard of excellence to everything Arthur did."

Contrary to Love mythology, Don Conka does not appear on any of the debut album's tracks. "It was all Snoopy, as far as I recall," confirms Bruce, who thought the drummer, despite his technical limitations, held his own on the sessions. "Snoopy was absolutely right for the band for that time. He supported them as far as he could. As the band progressed he just wasn't good enough. He didn't have the chops. He was the youngest emotionally and was wide-eyed and innocent."

I could have played all the drums myself but I wanted everyone who played an instrument in the group to play that instrument on the record. I heard later that Snoopy said the reason I didn't play drums on that album was because I couldn't. That's silly. I did play drums on several tracks. From the other things I've heard he said about me and the other band members, the only one he got right was about us not liking him. I remember that Kenny and I were about the only ones who got along with Snoopy. I don't think it was because he was the youngest but I do know he just cared too much about what other people felt about him. To say he was too paranoid would be an understatement. Snoopy used to live with me on Brier Avenue. We had some pretty way out times, but nothing you could tell to your mom.

Eleven of the album's 14 tracks were composed by Arthur, either exclusively or in collaboration with other band members. While Bryan Maclean shared co-credit with Arthur on "And More," and the other band members on "Mushroom Clouds," Bryan's solo contribution was the delicate, exquisite, "Softly To Me," a jazz-influenced pop confection that stood in sharp contrast to the darker edginess on the rest of the album. Although he supplied only four compositions to the trio of Love albums on which he appeared, Bryan's songs distinguish him as a unique talent, one that, while certainly not representative of the overall sound of the band, nonetheless lent Love a whole different color and texture. "I was always going after timelessness," Bryan told Neal Skok. "My goal was to write songs they could listen to 100 years from now and you wouldn't be able to place them in time. Arthur was more prolific than I was. I didn't have the confidence, then, that he did, but I spent more time on my songs. Arthur was kept abreast of what I was doing."

Much has been made of the creative tension that existed between the two songwriters. Love was always Arthur's group and he called the shots. If Bryan increased his prominence or profile within the group it was solely at Arthur's discretion. Theirs was the dynamic relationship that drove the group; a competitiveness both in music and in their personal lives. In many respects, their relationship paralleled that of two of their contemporaries, Neil Young and Stephen Stills, of Buffalo Springfield: two exceptionally creative individuals who prized one another yet found it difficult to co-exist within one group. As much as they were drawn together by centrifugal creative forces, clashing egos and power trips kept them apart.

"It was hard to define," says Johnny about the ambiguous relationship between Arthur the streetwise hustler and Bryan the hopeless romantic. "They were friends, but they were also rivals and were jealous of each other. Bryan thought that he should have more of his songs recorded. Arthur and I talked about that and we both felt that, while Bryan wrote very nice songs, you could only put maybe one or two on an album. He wrote these Lerner & Loew show-tune kind of songs. As part of a whole album they can work, but not on their own. They would never have been played on the radio. Nowadays they might, but back then you had to have something the kids could relate to. Bryan's stuff was a bit too soft – too many chocolate-covered rainbows. He saw everything through rose-tinted glasses. There was always conflict about us doing more of his songs."

Certainly, while Bryan's songs offered a pleasant diversion from Love's main thrust, one that showcased the versatility of the group and their author's unique gift, they hardly suited the direction that Arthur wanted to follow. "I think Arthur might have been a tad jealous of Bryan's vocal abilities and songwriting style," suggests Harvey Kubernik. "It may be that Bryan brought out different elements in Arthur and that created jealousy, disruption, and posturing. I wanted to see more Bryan songs on Love albums, in the same way that I wanted to see more George Harrison songs on Beatle records." In his interview with Neal Skok, Bryan claimed that "Arthur was not fair-minded. He would say 'yes' every time I suggested a song, but it would not turn out that way. Arthur's songs would crowd out everybody else's. He was smart, business-wise. He knew that the money was in writing the songs. I didn't. Arthur made it sound like Love was a big happy collective effort. He would always say, 'you can have as many songs as you want on the album,' but he didn't really mean it."

The thing I really wanted to happen was for Bryan and me to write songs together. That's what turned me on about The Beatles. It was always Lennon and McCartney on their records. I wanted that kind of unity with Bryan, but somehow it just never happened. I also wanted it with Johnny, Kenny, and the rest – so much so, that I even put their names on songs that they hadn't really written, merely contributed to.

According to Johnny, Bryan's songs were most often rough diamonds requiring polish from the other band members. "We had to work hard just to arrange Bryan's songs, to make them as presentable as they ended up being. We had to add an edge to them to make them fit in. There were constant disagreements between Arthur and Bryan over the songs. There was also a rivalry over girls. Arthur and Bryan seemed to end up liking the same chicks. For a short while, they lived together in a house that Elmer Valentine owned. Arthur rented the top part of the duplex and Bryan the lower part, so they were constantly forced to be together. I think they liked each other sometimes, but not all the time. It was like sibling rivalry."

It's perhaps noteworthy that both Arthur and Bryan were brought up as only children (Bryan's half-sister, Maria McKee, is 18 years his junior), both lost fathers to divorce, and both were indulged by their mothers. "I came to believe that everything pretty much started and ended with Arthur," observes Jac, "although I did appreciate Bryan's talent and what he brought to the group – the gentler aspect. That Arthur was willing to surrender to that softer part made it worthy of attention, I thought. The two of them had a strange history, and I never did quite understand the relationship. I think Arthur brought out in Bryan what he couldn't bring out of himself. It was complementary, but it was more than that. They were creative irritants for one another, in the best sense. I don't think either could do what the other could, but there was a context big enough to hold them both, and that was Love."

"They had a Mick Jagger and Keith Richards thing," insists Bruce. "Bryan added a different sensibility. Keith brought that other thing [to The Rolling Stones], the funk, while Mick was the intellectual side. There was this competition between Arthur and Bryan, but Arthur would always win because he was the leader. The band benefited from that tug of war between them. That said, Arthur had to give Bryan something, had to throw him a bone, because Arthur knew how important Bryan was as a color to their sound."

According to manager Ronnie Haran: "Bryan was like the baby of the group – adorable and sweet, easy and lovable – and Arthur was aloof, mysterious, and into himself. There would be occasional flare-ups but Bryan couldn't really stand up to Arthur. Arthur was a genius. Bryan would come in with his songs: they'd be lovely and sweet but only some of them were right for the band. But who decided that? Arthur. Who resented the decision? Bryan. He would accept what Arthur had to say up to a point then bitch about him behind his back."

Bryan once claimed that if he had been stronger and more assertive, he would have thrown Arthur against the wall and punched him out. "Yeah, right!" says an incredulous Ronnie in response. "But I can understand that feeling. Bryan would come in and suggest something and Arthur would say, 'Oh man, are you fucking crazy?' and Bryan would walk out of the room. Then he'd be saying, 'Fuck Arthur!' but never to his face. Arthur knew that Bryan was an asset. He knew Bryan had a certain charm and contributed a certain element to the band."

Two cover songs would become the hits that motivated sales of the album and, in the process, come to define Love in the minds of the record-buying public. While Bryan had brought "Hey Joe" with him from The Byrds and turned it not only into his own live showcase but also an album centerpiece, it would be "My Little Red Book" that propelled the group into the world beyond the Sunset Strip. The song was a cover of a Burt Bacharach and Hal David number written for the soundtrack of the 1965 feature film comedy *What's New Pussycat*, starring Peter Sellers. The original track was recorded by the British blues-influenced pop group Manfred Mann and included on their US album *My Little Red Book Of Winners,* released in late '65. Bryan MacLean remembered Arthur playing him Manfred Mann's version and telling him the band was going to cover it.

"Arthur and I went to see the movie *What's New Pussycat* and we heard 'My Little Red Book,' which was much slower than we later did it, and in a minor key," recalls Johnny. "We sped it up, put it in a major key, and gave it an edge. It was serendipitous because I forgot some of the chords after seeing the movie. When we went back and tried it at Arthur's house, I was missing certain parts, but that came to be the arrangement that we stuck with. We weren't intentionally trying to do it differently."

The appeal of the track was enhanced by the way in which it was recorded, with the instruments mixed high and loud. Right from the opening tambourine hit, the track practically leapt out of the speakers with a dynamic presence and immediacy. "That was Botnick," says Jac. "That came more in the mix. The signature Elektra approach was that I miked very, very closely and made the instruments sound bigger. If we had miked at a distance there would be no intimacy with the listener. They were playing 'My Little Red Book' that first night I saw them and I thought that was the single. It was searing energy applied to what was basically a mediocre song. Arthur made it his own. It was fun to see that happen."

The song would be chosen as Love's debut single. "When I hear that track now," says Bruce, "the tambourine seems so loud … but we were mixing for AM radio, back then. It's all bright, screamy, and punchy. That's how we mixed, because that's how we felt about the music. It's indicative of the times. It does leap out of the radio at you. I mix totally differently now." The recording would win many admirers, not least Sterling Morrison, guitarist with influential New York City avant-garde band, and Love's contemporaries, The Velvet Underground. Morrison always rated "My Little Red Book" among his favorite songs and once remarked that the VU (whose ranks boasted Lou Reed and John Cale, a pair of idiosyncratic rock enigmas to rival Arthur Lee) used to listen to that song repeatedly, trying to unlock Love's sound.

With so many strong, original songs at their disposal, why was a cover version selected for the first single? "Back then, it was normal for bands to do cover songs in their set," explains Bruce Botnick. "Even The Doors used to do [Bo Diddley's] "Who Do You Love" and other covers. It was important for bands to do songs that people already knew. No one knew Love's songs at that point. In those days, everybody listened to everybody else and everything around them and did their own interpretation of it. That's what Arthur did with "My Little Red Book," and Bryan with "Hey Joe." Back then, radio wasn't narrowcasting like it does today, so you could hear Frank Sinatra back-to-back with Jefferson Airplane, Simon & Garfunkel, and Love, for example."

To secure an appropriately eye-catching photograph for the record jacket, the band took Elektra art director William Harvey to a burnt-out house in Laurel Canyon (it was not, as has been rumored, actor Bela Lugosi's former home) where they posed around what was left of a stone fireplace. It was a striking image, the five band-members looking sullen, mysterious, and dangerous. "I remember my main thing on the first album cover was trying to look tough," Bryan MacLean once recalled.

The classic, curvilinear 'Love' logo, incorporating stylized male and female symbols, was commissioned by Jac Holzman and designed by William Harvey. It added further allure to a jacket that was itself somewhat revolutionary, Jac explains. "Love were the first artists to have an album printed directly onto the cardboard sleeve. If you watched people look at that album cover when it came out, they would go 'ooh' because it had a two-color presentation. I was able to have a double cover," meaning an image printed in color on both back and front. "Love was the first group to have the benefit of that."

Both the self-titled debut album and the "My Little Red Book" single (backed by Arthur's ballad "A Message To Pretty") were released in March. Elektra kicked the promotional efforts into gear with advertisements in various trade and teen publications. Although only a small independent label, lacking national clout and wider distribution, Elektra was nonetheless committed to making Love happen. By June, the album had reached #57 on the *Billboard* album charts, while the single peaked at #52, the highest chart placing for any Elektra artist up to that point (the song lodged even higher on LA charts). DJs beyond southern California began playing the single. "When I heard 'My Little Red Book' on the radio it was a very special moment," recalls a wistful Jac. "I despaired of ever hearing an Elektra single, or any Elektra track, on the radio." He was driving when he heard the single broadcast for the first time. Overcome, he pulled over onto the shoulder and cried. It was a pivotal moment for the label, one Jac still credits to Arthur.

Wallach's Music City was the music store on the corner of Sunset and Vine where everyone who was anyone would be. I remember how proud I was when our first record came out, and the way people would look at us when we walked into the store. You would have thought that Bryan was Elvis Presley himself. He would give them the kind of look that assured them that he was a star all right.

"I had never heard of Love when I arrived in LA," says writer Jim Bickhart, "but I recall looking at their first album when it came out and thinking they looked interesting. They delivered 1,000 per cent on that album. I couldn't resist because they looked like a band I would like. I didn't know what to expect from a band that was black and white, but it was perfect. I think The Byrds would have been lucky to have written some of those songs, they were that good. Looking back, it was almost like Arthur was adopting a persona: it was as if he was saying, 'OK, I see what's going on around me; that's what I'm going to do this week,' and cranked out his version of it."

Of the instant acclaim which the hit single brought the group, Bryan MacLean told Neal Skok: "We were little deities in our own sphere. I could walk through the door of any club and people would wave. They wouldn't quite bow, but from my point of view I thought I was hot."

Johnny also relished the new-found adulation. "It was kind of overwhelming to walk into any restaurant in Hollywood and be given the best table. We were living in fantasy land. We went from playing the Brave New World and Bido Lito's to dating *Playboy* bunnies. It started to go to our heads. The five simple guys who loved playing music were beginning to change."

By this time, we had moved up the Strip to the Whisky A Go Go. Like Ciro's before The Byrds played there, the club was on the slide. Ronnie Haran booked us there and for the first few gigs I could hear the owners, Elmer Valentine, Phil Tanzini, and Mario Maglieri, talking about closing the place down. But "My Little Red Book" was climbing the charts and our crowd followed us up the Sunset Strip. Once again, we were packing the place night after night and, because we were doing so well, other rock groups started playing there. I think we might have saved the Whisky.

We had our set down to a fine art. Our show was getting really tight – so tight, in fact, that the former drummer of The Knack, Bruce Gary, told me he saw one of our shows there and he thought they were playing a tape and we were faking it on stage, it was that good. After a set, we would stand out in front of the Whisky and I would hear someone playing the tambourine, sounding like the beginning of "My Little Red Book." It really made me feel good. We got a standing ovation every time we played at the Whisky ... encore after encore. We must have played there for at least three years, off and on. I carried on long after that with other versions of Love. I must admit that, although the musicians might have gotten better, there was really nothing to compare with the original band. When we first started hanging out at the Whisky, the place was just like a home away from home. It was just the place I loved to be.

I saw a lot of bands starting out, there. I remember seeing Van Morrison with his Irish group Them, when they first came to town. Someone slipped Van some acid, I think. I was in the audience when they started playing and I knew something was wrong with him but I couldn't figure it out. He opened his shirt and then he held it up over his head and ran across the stage, like he was flying but he just couldn't get off the ground. It seemed like he was going nuts. I felt sorry for the guy.

Love fan Paul Body recalls Them being admirers of Arthur and the band. "We saw Love at Bido Lito's and at the end of the night we looked around and there was Them's Ray Elliott, watching the band. Them were playing the Whisky at the time, but the whole band was there at Bido Lito's afterwards to see Love. Ray Elliott told us he really dug Love."

Elizabeth McKee was unaware that her son was in a rock band, drawing huge crowds at the Whisky A Go Go. "When Maria [McKee] was still just a baby, Bryan had a girlfriend whose mother came to baby-sit, so I could go see him at the Whisky, playing with Love. I got right up under Bryan's nose and he told me later that it was so odd to see me in the crowd in front of him. He was right next to Arthur, and Arthur kept telling Bryan, 'Don't play out of tune.' Bryan just kept playing. He never gave in. During the set, the band carried on playing while Arthur ran off to the side of the stage and smoked grass. You can imagine my reaction. I didn't know about all that stuff."

With the band's popularity on a steep rise, by early 1966 Arthur was effectively installed as prince of the Sunset Strip. "I remember we were standing outside at the back of the Whisky," says Paul Body, "and Arthur pulled up in his cool, purple Porsche. He opened the door and as he got out, this pot aroma wafted from the car. He said to us, 'Hey man, what's happening?' There he was, Arthur Lee, the coolest guy on the Strip. He also had a gorgeous blonde girl with him.'"

By this time, Arthur was renting one floor of a large, modern, multi-story house at 8563 Brier Drive, just north of Kirkwood in Hollywood. The house was owned by Elmer Valentine and, at one time or other, Bryan, Johnny, and Snoopy all lived there, occupying different floors.

None of the band members were lacking in attention from beautiful women and it was here that Gaye Blair first met Arthur. In common with several other women, Gaye would remain a friend and lover throughout Arthur's life. "I was a very Beverly Hills girl, from a different social stratosphere, and I was always well dressed in designer clothes," says Gaye. "When I met Arthur, at Elmer's house, it was love at first site. He stood in the doorway in a black shirt and black jeans, and it was all over. It was as if we'd known each other in previous lives. I hadn't even spoken to him at that point, but I had the thought in my head, 'My mother and my family will kill me.' My mother would never have accepted Arthur." Nonetheless, an affair would ensue and would last, on and off, for decades. "There were other girls with Arthur, but I had other guys, too. He was the big love of my life. We never married but, then, I always wanted a more normal life. I never did drugs, I never drank. If someone offered me a beer, he'd grab it away from them. I never smoked grass. Can you imagine being around all that? I'd be knocking down the bathroom door yelling, 'What are you doing in there?'"

One idiosyncrasy which Gaye remembers about Arthur was his fixation with hair. "You could never touch Arthur's hair. I remember him and Johnny, back in the early days, running around the house with pink rollers in. Arthur hated the fact that Johnny had better hair. Arthur's hair was never thick, even when he was young. I liked it better when he shaved it off." Arthur's friend Annette Ferrel confirms the hair obsession. "He had it processed and one time he left it on too long and it burned all the hair. He had a thing about it. I would tell him, 'Can't you just leave it alone? Just cut it, or let it grow,' but it would be horrible. He would do the strangest things to it. He wanted to have straight hair, like everybody else, but it would just look terrible." Arthur's sensitivity would manifest in other ways, Annette explains. "We would have these long conversations about life, how the world should be, and how life should be. He was very spiritual. He was very much a perfectionist and could get angry, once in a while, if someone wasn't doing something right. He also had a great sense of humor. He and I used to walk for miles up and down Sunset Strip, talking and laughing."

The Strip would be packed with people, back then. A lot of them drove by just to see the styles we were wearing. We sure didn't disappoint them. We were as freaked-out looking as you would want to see. To me, it was just a way of expressing freedom. I never liked suits and still don't. There we were, the talk of the town, and all from an idea I had about how and what I thought it could be. I'd see a lot of straight people just coming by to look at what they called 'the freaks.'

The crowds congregating after gigs every night at Ben Frank's grew so large that the cops were always there. What kind of hangout is it when you're getting harassed all the time? So we took the crowd somewhere else, a place called Canter's, on Fairfax, and did we start something or what? Everyone who was anyone would come to Canter's, after hours. Just about everyone that was in the audience when we played followed us to the place. I didn't know a sidewalk could fit that many people. We definitely started what was called the Hippie movement and it spread from there up to Haight-Ashbury and the Fillmore in San Francisco, and then all across the nation. By 1967, the same people who came to see the freaks turned out to be freaks themselves. It was still nice to see Carl and Vito and their friends, like Harvey, who would do his 'dance' which consisted of standing in one spot and then jumping up and down to the music. And then there would be 'Scotty' – James Scott – the other black guy in the crowd, all the time with a book full of girls' phone numbers like I've never seen before in my life.

In April, riding the crest of their growing reputation as Sunset Strip royalty, Love headed north to San Francisco and the Fillmore auditorium, which was fast becoming *the* gig in the Bay Area. The psychedelic scene there was still in its infancy and, despite its well known disdain for LA bands, especially those from the Sunset Strip, Love quickly became favorites with San Francisco music fans. The recognition of discerning local audiences would lead to frequent bookings over the next two years at venues in the city such as the Winterland Ballroom, the Avalon, the Rock Garden, and the Longshoreman's Hall.

It's safe to say we were the number one group on the West Coast when we went to play the Fillmore in San Francisco. I met [legendary impresario] Bill Graham at the Fillmore. I remember him sweeping the floor with one hand and counting tickets with the other. We helped put his place on the map. He used to introduce our band by saying, 'And now, here they are, Love: a nice four-letter word.'

We headlined at the Fillmore and I remember I had to stand and listen to Janis Joplin scream. She was the great white hope for the blues, but all she did was scream. You see, people think that when white people scream that it's soul. But that isn't soul, it's just screaming. I remember being in Washington, D.C. once, and the security guard asked me, when I walked on stage, "Hey Arthur, you gonna go up there and do some more screamin'?" Man, that really hit my heart and I haven't written a screaming song since.

We were the biggest group on the West Coast, bigger, I thought, than all the other groups of that era such as The Doors, Buffalo Springfield, Jefferson Airplane, Big Brother And The Holding Company, Moby Grape. ... When we played the Fillmore, we headlined over all these other bands. I remember playing the Hullabaloo in LA, right across the street from the Hollywood Palladium, on Sunset, where Buffalo Springfield were playing, with Stephen Stills and Neil Young in the band. Our side of the street was packed from corner to corner but their side was practically bare.

The previous month, four of the band members had moved home once more and taken up residence in a secluded mansion at 4320 Cedarhurst Circle, in the Rancho Los Feliz neighborhood of LA, south of Griffith Park, between Silver Lake and Hollywood. A throwback to the golden age of Hollywood extravagance, the spacious, 20s-era villa, with its Spanish accoutrements and wrought iron gates, had been built by movie director Maurice Tourneur and was originally named Talmadge House after silent movie star Norma Talmadge. By the early 60s, the house, then know as The Cedars, had fallen into disrepair with its owners living elsewhere. Nonetheless, for the new prince of the Sunset Strip and his regal entourage, this was a most fitting abode. The sprawling, distinctive residence, appropriately renamed 'The Castle' by the group, would play a central role in Love mythology.

In Start Productions' superb Arthur Lee and Love documentary *Love Story*, released in 2007, The Castle is revealed in its current incarnation: a finely-appointed, tastefully decorated, multi-million dollar mansion suitable for movie star, real estate tycoon, or banking baron. The surrounding Los Feliz neighborhood has always been exclusive and, over the decades, has housed an impressive inventory of cinematic and musical stars – everyone from Al Jolson and Cecil B. DeMille to Eddie Van Halen, Slash, Gwen Stefani, Beck, Leonardo DiCaprio, Brad Pitt, Adrian Grenier, and the late Heath Ledger. The likes of reclusive billionaire Howard Hughes once called Los Feliz home, as did notorious Hollywood madam Heidi Fleiss.

The *Love Story* documentary finds Arthur taking us on a guided room-by-room, tour of the lavishly refurbished mansion, pointing out where each of the four band-members – himself, Bryan, Johnny, and Kenny (along with a sometime fifth, drummer Don Conka) – would have once crashed. He stresses that the mansion has undergone a major transformation since he and the band were in residence, and that the 'palace' was considerably more disheveled when Love held court there in 1966.

According to Ronnie Haran, a real-estate-agent friend of hers named Jack Simmons had told her about the property. Arthur had wanted the band-members to live together and the mansion offered that opportunity. "They had all been living in various rented places and would get evicted all the time. So I showed them The Castle. It was a magical moment in their history and a great time." Johnny elaborates: "Bryan knew a guy who was the caretaker of this mansion. He didn't live in it. There had been squatters breaking in and living in the empty house. We were told that if we took over the upkeep and paid the taxes, we could live there. I think the total cost was about $600 a month. So we each paid $100 or so and the owners were happy, because they didn't have to worry about squatters. After we moved in, it became the hangout for everybody. Jefferson Airplane, Big Brother And The Holding Company ... all these bands, when they came to town, would stay there rather than at a hotel and we would all party." He is quick to point out, however, that contrary to an often repeated story, Bob Dylan never visited The Castle. "When you went over [to The Castle] you would see The Doors or Buffalo Springfield or Frank Zappa's band there," recalls later Love bassist, Robert Rozelle. "It was the social beehive of the music scene, back then."

"It wasn't like a party every night," says Ronnie, recalling The Castle's halcyon days, "but each guy had their own hangers-on and friends. People crashed on the floor in the living room. Arthur had his own little suite and he would go in there and lock the door. That was his place where he could be private. He always liked his privacy." The band could also make a lot of noise there, Johnny recalls.

"We were kind of arrogant toward the neighbors around us, because we would rehearse in the house, and the people who lived nearby – on property that had once been part of the estate grounds – would complain and call the police. To them, we were hippies living in this mansion. They didn't know what to make of us." Still, the grand residence had much to offer its young occupants. "There was a solarium with glass walls all around; that was our roller-skating room. I would skate in there for hours on end."

Elizabeth McKee visited her son Bryan at The Castle in the summer of 1966 and still has vivid memories of the place. "The first thing I saw was Johnny, roller-skating all over the hardwood floors. Kenny had his room to the left of the main living room. The kitchen was near there. To the right was a big room with a gorgeous oriental rug and in the middle was this huge hookah pipe, from India, sitting there like a glorious god of the universe. Bryan's room was near that, off the living room. Beside that was the bathroom that he and Arthur shared. Bryan said that was a big mistake."

Despite an opulent façade, the interior offered squalid hippie living. "They didn't have any furniture," confirms Robert Rozelle. "Each guy just picked a room and put a mattress down. But the ceiling was that of a theatre or a cathedral, with a huge chandelier hanging down."

"The living room had a gigantic fireplace down at one end," says drummer Michael Stuart, another frequent visitor. "I remember Kenny standing upright in that fireplace. He would stand inside it and shoot the breeze. When the ash on his cigarette became long enough, he would just flick it on the floor. Because he was standing in the fireplace it was OK. He was standing in an ashtray. The first time I walked in, Arthur was roller-skating round and round. He gave us a big wave, then whipped around and started skating backwards, showing off."

In keeping with his feeling of alienation within the band, Snoopy chose not to take up residence at The Castle. It's entirely possible that, given the prevailing sentiment of several band members, he may not have been invited to move in. "I'm the only one who did not live in The Castle. I didn't want to live with them. I didn't like those guys, and the feeling was mutual. The only person I got along with was Arthur." A frequent visitor, nonetheless, Snoopy pulls no punches when describing the scene at the crumbling Los Feliz mansion. "It was a total shit-hole. The place was dilapidated. The toilets were always plugged up and overflowing and the bathtub was filthy. When they lived there, that house didn't look anything like it does in the *Love Story* documentary. I couldn't believe it when I saw that film. In those days, they were like a bunch of poor guys living in a mansion they couldn't afford and didn't merit living in."

Ah, The Castle. What a trip. I'd never seen a house that big. It was the spookiest place I have ever lived in. It was so big that when I woke up in the middle of the night, I would meet two or three people I didn't even know on the way to the kitchen and back. The property covered a whole block and went around in a circle. What went on there was more than an experience. I would sometimes go to bed with one girl and wake up with another. It's a funny thing, I don't ever remember playing with the whole band together, there, but I do remember some of what went on, although the people that came and went were too many to remember every one. Night after night, day after day, for months, it was just like one big party, with no maid. That big kitchen was where the trash was dumped and it smelled like every filthy thing you could think of. The plumbing wasn't the best either. The place was old and the toilets were stopped up. Once, I flushed the toilet and the water, which had been standing in there for years, shot right up between my legs, right up to the ceiling.

The place reminded me of the house in the television show The Munsters. When we first moved in, a good friend of mine named David Biali came over – on acid – to feel the vibes in the place: if they were good or bad. He and his girlfriend, Carol Green, came by and David went to search things out. There was a place upstairs that we called the Porthole Room, and David headed that way. Carol and some others were walking around, tripping on how big the place was, and after about 20 minutes she asked, 'Where's David?' I said I didn't know, so she went looking for him. She found him in the Porthole Room. When they came back downstairs, she had him by the hand. He was as white as a sheet. I asked him how the vibes were and he gave me a look that I can't explain. His mouth moved but he didn't say anything. He just shook his head as if to say, 'No good.' Talk about a haunted house!

Love Story documentary producer/director Chris Hall recalls Arthur's belated return to The Castle. "When we met the owners of the house, Arthur was charming to them until they walked away. Then he said, 'I could have had this place for $50,000. I wouldn't pay $50 for it now!' Even though it wasn't anything remotely like it is now when they lived there, it was obviously a brilliant place for a band to inhabit. It didn't get much better than being the best band in LA and living in this place. Regardless of the state it was in at the time, it must have been pretty impressive. I think it was Robert Rozelle who said you'd come up there, ring the doorbell, and it'd take something like five minutes for someone to answer the door because of the size of the place."

Much of the Arthur Lee mystique is derived from his residency in The Castle. Although he and his bandmates lived in the house for less than a year, The Castle nonetheless remains crucial to the image of Love and of Arthur as a rock potentate, holding court to all who were deemed worthy of passing through its gothic entrance gate. At The Castle, Arthur was monarch and visitors were obliged to pay him due deference. "Arthur never liked going out," explains Gaye Blair, "but I didn't want to always sit around the house. I'm an introvert, too, but I also liked to get dressed up and go out. He was not into the social scene at all. Even Jim Morrison was more social. With Arthur, if we went to a nice place for dinner and people would be looking at us, he'd say, 'What are you looking at?' We were an odd pairing."

"If you wanted to see Arthur, you came to him," confirms his old friend, Len Fagan. "That was the way he was, no matter where he lived. A lot of that attitude came from not wanting to risk going out, being a black man in a nice car in a white neighborhood, perhaps being high. ... When Arthur *did* venture out to take in the nightlife, he was a celebrity of the highest magnitude. Women would approach him. It wasn't like he was wining and dining them. They would make themselves available to him." Arthur was happy to reciprocate, Ria Berkus recalls. "He liked the action. There were always women in and out of his life. His girlfriends were always upscale people, intelligent, with good values. And he liked being around people he trusted. He always surrounded himself with good, smart people who adored him."

Ria also remembers Arthur's characteristic reluctance to go out and socialize. "He liked people to come to him. He was an 'at home' kind of guy. And he loved to cook: he could whip up great food for anybody that was around. He had a very old fashioned personality. He liked very normal, traditional things. He was a guy who really needed the comfort of his own surroundings and didn't feel relaxed being on other people's turf. He liked being the boss." Johnny Echols concurs: "Arthur loved being *Arthur Lee*. He was totally happy in his skin, happy being who he was. By the same token, he was very, very insecure. He needed to be loved and lionized and he hated being alone."

In the few short months that had seen Love ascend from selling out tiny clubs like Bido Lito's to packing substantial venues like the Whisky and the Hullabaloo, so Arthur's stock rose accordingly. He was fast becoming an LA legend. Certainly a gothic mansion was a befitting domicile for an artist who projected such a uniquely dark and dangerous persona. "Back in the 60s, when you went somewhere with Arthur it was a big deal," recalls Annette Ferrel. "It was like the sea would part when we walked in."

Sixties Love fan Tim Martin remembers that Arthur had a contrastingly common touch. "The coolest thing about Arthur was that he would mingle with the patrons during a show at the Hullabaloo. He would come by your table and say hello. The man had charisma like no other."

"Arthur was mysterious, like [the rock star] Prince, or a black James Dean," observes infamous LA scene-maker Kim Fowley. "He was like a cross between those two guys. Arthur was always quiet, not screaming, yelling, or going crazy on a Rick James level. He was more of a lone wolf guy. Arthur had a mystique and worked it 25 hours a day."

That spring, LA radio station KRLA sent cub reporter Rochelle Reed to The Castle to interview Love for the station's music magazine, *The Beat*. A band on the rise, despite their local fame, they were still relatively unknown to the wider audience. When Rochelle met Love, she encountered a group of musicians very much enamored of themselves and of their success, and reluctant to partake in the inanities of a teen fan's questions. In the resulting July 9 feature, entitled *Is Love Lost?*, she lambasted the group for being arrogant after Arthur, Johnny, and Bryan gave her "monosyllables and giggles" in reply to her earnest queries. Describing the band as weird, rude and "in a world of their own," Rochelle concluded by stating that: "Their offstage manners leave them in the venerable [sic] position of being just another group to fall by the wayside. Only when a group reaches the top can their careers withstand what they may suffer from being continually rude and uncaring to fans and reporters alike." For Arthur and the others, such froideur simply ensured that their mystique remained intact.

Ria Berkus's first encounter with the group would actually occur a few months later, and would have a more positive outcome. Portraying herself as a reporter (from *The Daily Planet,* no less) she managed to get to the group's dressing room before a show, where she was met with their typical insouciance. "They were all stoned and there were all these beautiful women with them. Arthur was in the middle of the room, lying down on a chaise lounge-like beach chair, with a beautiful blonde girl standing over him, rubbing his shoulders and kissing him. I immediately went into my spiel about being a reporter doing a story on the band. I could tell Arthur was amused by the whole thing. I didn't realize I had neglected to bring a pencil. He said, 'Aren't you a reporter?' I said I was. 'Then, why don't you have a pencil?' he asked, and at that point everyone started laughing at me. I was just mortified by the whole experience. I was way out of my league. As the band came out to play their set, Arthur spotted me, flashed a big smile and sang every song directly to me. After the concert, I was walking up the aisle to leave and Arthur came up to me, all six foot one of him, in crushed velvet and boots, saying, 'I knew you weren't a writer because I've seen you at all our concerts.' He asked me what I was doing the next day and would I like to go for a ride with him."

Ria gave Arthur her address and the next day, true to his word, he arrived to pick her up. She was understandably impressed by him: "He drove over in a maroon, hardtop Porsche and was wearing a suede shirt unbuttoned to his waist. He got out of the car and looked like God himself, to me. I had anticipated this cool guy but what I didn't expect was his great sense of humor. I was a budding comedy writer and every time I said something funny he would fall on the floor laughing. He told me I was the funniest girl he knew. Then he said, 'I want you to meet my mom.' So we drove down to the Crenshaw area, and his mom was outside, doing some gardening. Here was this little, adorable, very little light-skinned woman, in an apron. Arthur said, 'Mom, this is my friend Ria.' She looked at me, looked back at him, and then said, 'Arthur Lee, you are robbing the cradle this time.' He just fell down laughing."

On June 18, Love made the first of their career's meager two television appearances, miming to their hit single on Dick Clark's *American Bandstand*. For Arthur, it was a dream come true, having watched the show since his youth. It was quite a different matter for Bryan, however. "I didn't care for Dick Clark," he later revealed. "There was something about him that scared me. I remember we went into his dressing room while he was getting his make-up, to be introduced to him. I felt he was phony. We also appeared on [Clark's daily television music showcase] *Where The Action Is* and I remember they had to shoot me above the waist because there was some problem with my pants which they thought were too tight."

"We did *American Bandstand* alongside The Bobby Fuller Four," recalls Johnny. "Bobby's out front doing 'I Fought The Law' while Arthur and Bryan are backstage, horse-playing around. They knocked the set over in the middle of the song. I don't think Mr. Clark was very happy about that, so he assured us we wouldn't appear on his show again. He was kind of a stiff, wooden guy. He came and interviewed us about the fact that we lived in a castle. He wanted to bring his film crew but he never did."

Two days after the show aired, the band returned to Sunset Sound to lay down a follow-up single. The resulting track would be like nothing anyone had either conceived or heard before, and would put paid to Arthur's folk-rock fixations. "7 & 7 Is" wasn't merely a pop single; it was a small-scale cultural phenomenon and a musical milestone – a loud, aggressive, no-holds-barred, garage-style punk song, a decade before that musical term was current. Like a blast from a cannon, "7 & 7 Is" boasted a pounding bass figure sliding between notes, crashing guitar chords, and a thunderous, non-stop drum torrent supporting Arthur's most menacing vocal delivery yet. It culminated in the sound of an atomic explosion, followed by the aftermath, a bluesy denouement. There was no context, no reference point, and no equivalent for such a revolutionary creation. But the track's aural turbulence arrived after an equally tumultuous session that would see Jac Holzman relinquish the Love producer's chair. "We spent an entire goddamn day recording that bloody track," he says, still sounding exasperated. "That's all they came in prepared to do, so they did it until they got it right."

Johnny explains the genesis of the song and the collaborative nature of its arrangement. "Arthur had written this song about Anita Billings, his high school sweetheart. They both had the same birthdays, March 7. It was a folksy kind of love song. It didn't have the drive that it would later have. Kenny Forssi deserves a lot of credit for the sound on that recording. We had signed an endorsement contract to use Vox equipment and they gave us these Super Beatle amplifiers and other equipment. They had invented a bass fuzztone and gave it to Kenny. Kenny and I decided we would try to use it in a song. Arthur heard us and said, 'Why don't you try that on that song about Pretty?' That was "7 & 7 Is." We started playing [with the fuzztone] and at first it sounded strange, but Kenny started doing this sliding bass thing with it. As we played it we could hear that this was something different, something new. We put it on the back burner, and when we went to the studio to do something else, Arthur said, 'Let's do that 'Pretty' arrangement.' Everything then came together in the studio."

While Arthur had a vision for the song, the recording of the track was very much a collaborative effort. "What we were trying to capture on "7 & 7 Is" was the sound of controlled chaos," says Johnny, "with feedback that would be in tune. It took a long time for me to figure out where to stand in front of the amp in order for me to play the chord and actually have the harmonic be in key. Kenny did the same thing. The bass fuzz just didn't work, it overpowered everything. So Kenny did the same sounds with his fingers sliding down the strings. He played an Eko bass which was semi-acoustic and would feed back. He was able to emulate the sound of the fuzz box on his bass."

Michael Stuart noted the bassist's contribution to the track. "If you listen to what Kenny played on "7 &7 Is," it's very powerful. He's playing two notes at once, octaves, and sliding into them. It was very orchestral and symphonic. He was an incredible musician."

"In order to get the sound we wanted – overpowering and overwhelming – we needed to get the sound in the studio itself, not on the [mixing] board," says Johnny. "It wasn't a case of 'We'll fix it in the mix.' So I turned my amp reverb all the way up, which was a no-no in the studio, and I had the tremolo on. It gave us those overtones that you constantly hear. It's almost like surround sound, even in mono. But Bruce and Jac fought us every step of the way. They knew how it should normally be done and we were breaking all the rules. We kept telling them, 'It has to sound this way. If we do it the way *you* want, it won't be the same song.' We would have had the song done in fewer takes but they kept stopping us, saying, 'It's feeding back!' We'd say, 'It's *supposed* to feed back. ... '"

In the end, the track required more than 30 takes to get it right (although not all were complete run-throughs), with Arthur and Snoopy trading off on the drum kit. "The session was a nightmare," stresses Snoopy. "I had blisters on my fingers. I don't know how many times I tried to play that damn thing and it just wasn't coming out. Arthur would try it; then I'd try it. Finally I got it. He couldn't do it. By the 20th take I got it. Everything before that was basically rehearsal."

Although it's persistently rumored to be Arthur playing drums on the final take, Johnny is adamant that he is not. "That is Alban 'Snoopy' Pfisterer, and he did a hell of a job, too. He really played his little heart out on that song and he deserves credit for it. It's the best he ever played. It was a very physically demanding song. It took about four hours to get it down, and, back then, four hours for one song was a long time." As for the song's bluesy coda, Johnny explains: "That part at the end was a song I had written by myself, kind of my take on Santo & Johnny's "Sleepwalk," and it became a bone of contention between Arthur and me. I was playing that song and Arthur says, 'Why don't we do that?' But my name's not on it. Before he died, Arthur was supposed to straighten that [missing writing credit] out but it never happened."

"I put in the atomic bomb explosion sound at the end," says Bruce Botnick, who engineered the session. "I took it off a sound effects record. We added it in the mix. It might have been the sound of a gunshot slowed down, I'm not sure; but it was my idea. Having the little blues thing after that was so cool. "7 & 7 Is" was pure power-punk all the way, and very influential. I loved it."

When the band subsequently played the song live, Johnny would turn the reverb on his amp up to ten then kick his amplifier. "It would sound like an explosion if I put the mic right in there."

The single's B-side, the jug band flavored "No. Fourteen," recorded earlier, was a group effort, according to Johnny. "It was not written beforehand. We just sat in the studio: Arthur started strumming something and we all fell in together. We were like brothers who knew instinctively where each of us was going. That song was total spur of the moment."

Despite the manic nature of the "7 & 7 Is" recording session, Arthur still found enough time to have the group lay down a wordless, acoustic demo take of a work-in-progress song, tentatively titled "Hummingbirds." This would emerge, fully formed, more than a year later as "The Good Humor Man He Sees Everything Like This," on the album *Forever Changes*. The initial demo, featuring Johnny and Bryan on delicately picked acoustic guitars, was in marked contrast to the cacophonous "7 & 7 Is" and drew inspiration from the similar guitar pattern in the Buffalo Springfield song "Nowadays Clancy Can't Even Sing." The latter was still unrecorded at that time but was already a mainstay of the band's live shows. Buffalo Springfield had opened for Love at the Whisky, just prior to the "7 & 7 Is" session, and the two groups had become friendly.

Released in July, "7 & 7 Is" rocketed up the LA charts and by late summer had even scaled the national *Billboard* hit parade, reaching #33. It was Love's best national showing to date. "That single got a lot of airplay and was a southern Californian hit," Jac confirms. "It caught your ear because it was so outrageous."

The record further solidified Love's reputation as the leading LA group, and proved that Arthur was itching to explore brave new musical vistas and not be typecast.

By this time, Love's live performances were drawing huge crowds and local promoters vied with one another to book the group into their concert venues or clubs. Despite being the biggest draw at the 2,000-capacity Hullabaloo club, a favorite venue of the group's, Love became less reliant on club dates as arena shows beckoned. All potential gigs continued to be vetted by Arthur. Being very much a homebody, he did not like to travel far from his domicile and preferred to be in his own bed each night. Thus, Love worked fairly consistently in and around Los Angeles, venturing as far north as San Francisco where they were always assured of a positive reception. "In '66, the gigs seemed like they were every day," recalls Paul Body. Harvey Kubernik concurs: "Every day you could see Love somewhere in LA. They became a West Coast and a Hollywood phenomenon because they played the same local venues over and over again. They never went on those US torture tours that other bands did. Back then, you just didn't do one night at Bido Lito's or the Whisky, you played multiple nights, sometimes a week, or more. As a result Love, collectively and individually, were accessible."

In 1966, it was customary that when a band released a record – whether an album or single – they would tour heavily in its support. This was the tried and true method of breaking an artist nationally: gaining exposure in regional markets across the country. That method hasn't changed much over the ensuing decades, although modes of transport and the concert venues have improved significantly. Back in the mid 60s, touring meant hopscotching flights or grueling road tours. Rather than the luxurious tour-buses of today, furnished with all the comforts of a Hilton hotel, bands used utilitarian, chartered Greyhound or Trailways coaches, with basic facilities. The occupants would sleep in their seats, when they could, as they motored between clubs, concerts halls, and high schools – anywhere the record label felt the band might gain exposure. It wasn't always pleasant but it was regarded as a necessary evil if you wanted to turn a regional hit into national success. Those were the rules of the game, and Arthur chose not to play by them. As he would often say: "Why should I go on the road and have to eat shit, for no money?"

Arthur's reticence about touring was compounded by the fact that Love remained unrivaled kings of the Sunset Strip; there, they could do no wrong. "That was the problem and the reason for the lack of touring," says Ronnie Haran, who was still managing the band at the time. "On his own turf, Arthur was a god. He got his own sound system, his fair shake at the door, and recognition from his friends. He got everything he wanted, so why would he go somewhere else, stay in a fleabag motel, and play through a lousy sound system for some sleazy promoter who was going to rip him off? It just wasn't worth it. San Francisco was different. Bill Graham treated bands with respect and presented them at their best. But everywhere else we went, they were just creepy people. In LA, Love always insisted on top billing and got it. Why would they go to other cities and take third billing to The Strawberry Alarm Clock and The Seeds?

Even financial inducements wouldn't necessarily tempt Arthur away from his home patch, Ronnie reveals. "Let's say we got a call that a promoter wanted the band to play in Tempe, Arizona, was willing to pay $1,000 for a show, and cover their hotel rooms. "Arthur would say, 'Tempe, Arizona? It's so fucking hot there. Do we really want to go to Tempe, Arizona? What's the point?' Then I'd phone up the local record store in Tempe and they wouldn't have ever heard of Love. So I'd say to Arthur, 'Yeah, you're right. What's the point?' In a way, I allowed him to be as headstrong as he was because I agreed with him. Arthur loved being home – he had this big house with his birds, his dogs, and his dope. He just wanted to stay at home and didn't want to go out on the road. He liked to play places where people knew what he was all about, and not go experimenting in new places. He would always say, 'Man, I don't want to go through all these changes.'"

Years later, Bryan MacLean told UK journalist Barney Hoskyns that Love "broke covenant" with their record label by not touring and not doing what Elektra felt was in their best interests to further the band's career. "It kept us from being more successful," Bryan concluded in his interview with Neal Skok. Ronnie echoes those sentiments and goes further. "They also broke covenant with Elektra because they had no respect for the label. Elektra didn't have their act together; they had no experience with rock bands before Love. They didn't know what they were doing. It was all trip, stumble, and fall. It was pretty clear that Arthur and I knew more than they did about how things should happen. A lot of that came from people like Lou Adler and [Byrds press officer] Derek Taylor; people I knew in the industry who were having better experiences elsewhere. I knew from talking with them that we were not being treated right. There would be nobody from the label to meet the group if we went to another town, no records in the stores, no pre-publicity, nothing like that. Once they signed The Doors, Elektra became more hip to all that, and it began to work."

"Arthur was a smart guy and a terrific musician who kind of did himself in," reckons Jac Holzman, in reference to the frontman's reluctance to leave Southern California. "It's very tough to force an artist to do something, even if it's for their own good; it was like 'Arthur, take your medicine.' He just wouldn't leave town."

Arthur's aversion to touring was partly down to his own insecurity, "I was scared," he admitted in the *Love Story* documentary. He had already proven himself in LA and San Francisco, but there was never any guarantee he could do so in other regions. In addition, the interracial nature of the band limited their markets, as Johnny Echols acknowledges. "Being an integrated group made it difficult for us to play in some places. A black group could play the chitlin' circuit and places like that, in the South, and a white group could go anywhere in the South. But it was different for an integrated group. We could play the West or East Coasts but the Midwest and the South were never big markets for us. It wasn't that we were lazy; we needed to earn a living and we needed to play." Johnny also feels that a potential market for the band was ignored by their label. "Elektra would not sponsor a tour of Europe for us. We were dying to go to Europe but we needed Elektra to underwrite us. They did finally sponsor an East Coast tour in 1968, but by then it was too late."

There was another issue that kept the band from accepting some booking offers, Johnny explains. "We had a reputation for being kind of hard to deal with because Arthur always insisted we had top billing. The Doors would accept that because they had always been second banana to us, as would Iron Butterfly, Big Brother And The Holding Company, even The Grateful Dead would agree to that, but a lot of the other groups wouldn't. So that stopped us taking some gigs."

I've been asked many times over the years why my original Love band didn't tour more, and every time I'm asked that question I have to stop and think about it, because there are so many answers I could give. One reason is that I've never trusted anyone that I've ever done business with. I love singing and playing music, but when it gets to the business part, it just really turns me off. It did then and it still does. Why didn't we tour? I'd have to say it was because of me and the way I saw others treated, and what they had to do to get where they were. Another thing was that I didn't like going on the road and playing for pennies. We were earning a decent living, playing in Southern California. It was hard enough getting along with the guys in the band in one place, let alone going on the road with

them. Also, we were pioneers as far as being integrated; that they went for it in
LA and New York didn't mean they would accept it in the Southern states.
Anyway, I'm sorry we didn't tour more and a lot of that was down to me.

Our manager, Ronnie Haran, did everything but break our necks trying to get
things right for the shows. I can't see how she could have done anything more in
trying to help us achieve our goal to be #1 and the first successful integrated rock
band in history. I can still see her now trying to make sure everyone was ready for
a show; if this one had the right clothes and that one's hair was in place ... .

Ronnie ultimately managed to convince Arthur that a trip to Dallas, Texas, would be worth the effort. "I found out that Dallas airport was called Love Field," she explains. "So I got on Elektra's case and made sure they would have albums in the stores if we did a concert there. When we arrived, we had a police escort. There were hundreds of kids at the airport. I did a lot of pre-publicity and had phoned up all the radio stations to drum up a lot of excitement. I also thought that if this was a big success, maybe Arthur would tour more. So I really put a lot into the Love Field event and it was very successful, especially for a mixed race band in conservative Texas. They treated Arthur like a king: a black man, and in the city where the president had been shot. Now that was something. If you could be received like that, there, you could be received anywhere." Johnny also remembers the trip being successful. "Ronnie worked this thing out so they gave us this big welcome and the mayor gave us the key to the city. We went to the Neiman-Marcus department store and they basically gave us a free run. And there was an album signing. It was really well worked out and that was all Ronnie."

Despite the goodwill the band earned on the promotional junket, the aftermath soured Ronnie's relationship with the group and prompted her exit not long after. "On the plane home, I was dividing up the money between everybody and Bryan said [disparagingly], 'You're getting the same amount as me?' That remark weighed on me so heavily because I had never been paid for anything. I'd been spending my own money on the band, paying their bills, fronting them money ... all that. That remark really poisoned my relationship with the group; it seemed they did not see the value of what I was doing; and to come from Bryan, who was always hugging me, crying on my shoulder, or bitching to me about Arthur, made it worse. I was there for Bryan as much as anyone in the group. That was the beginning of the end for me. I started looking elsewhere." That 'elsewhere' turned out to be the band that would ultimately taint Arthur's relationship with Elektra Records and Jac Holzman – ironically a group that Arthur had brought to the label's attention: The Doors.

Formed in July 1965 in Venice, California, by UCLA film students Ray Manzarek and Jim Morrison, The Doors had been playing the Sunset Strip club London Fog in the spring of 1966 when Ronnie caught a set. Impressed with the distinctive sound made by organist Manzarek, guitarist Robbie Krieger, and drummer John Densmore, and smitten with vocalist Morrison's macho bravado and good looks, she booked them into the Whisky in May, opening for various headliners including Love, Them, and The Turtles. Arthur was also impressed enough to insist Jac Holzman check out The Doors during his West Coast visit in the last week of May. "I 'got' Arthur and Love in the first three minutes," says Jac. "I had to go back four nights before I really appreciated the songs that ended up on The Doors' first album. I had a very high regard for Arthur's opinion, so I persisted." The Doors impact on Jac would prove very different to that of Love. "My connection with Love was a very visceral one. I walked into this club and got it right away. But the connection with The Doors was much more intellectual. The Doors took work. But I knew how to put it together and I knew exactly who the right producer was: Paul Rothchild. He was out of jail by that time, although he didn't like The Doors. I had a horrible time getting him to produce them." Jac eventually brought Rothchild down to the Whisky in August and, after the producer finally gave his stamp of approval, Jac signed The Doors to Elektra.

"Jac has altered history," insists Ronnie, still bitter about the way the Doors deal went down, and how her role in the band's story has been minimized. "He says *he* discovered The Doors and he *made* Love. That's such a load of crap. I brought Jac to the Whisky to see The Doors. He said, 'This group just doesn't do it for me.' Then he heard the buzz on the street about them and he called me and said, 'Maybe I should see them again.'"

The Doors' sound eschewed folk-rock completely and was far more psychedelic than Love's signature. Their music was rooted in a keyboard-based approach and drew on extended Eastern-inspired raga improvisations to create an acid-trip effect, quite different from Love's elongated jams which were jazz and blues-derived. Jim Morrison was a charismatic frontman who took the role to the extreme edge of what was generally considered tolerable, and sometimes beyond (the band was fired from the Whisky later the same week they signed with Elektra after Jim Morrison's oedipal ranting in the song "The End" pushed Elmer Valentine's buttons). Where Arthur exuded a dark, enigmatic mystery, Jim was more of a pretty boy with an in-your-face presence. Jim's poetry became his lyrics; Arthur's lyrics became his poetry.

"Jim Morrison was an intellectual genius in the sense that he was well read – Voltaire, Camus, and all that stuff," notes Ronnie Haran. "Arthur never read any of those books, but he was a street-smart genius. He was a human perceiver of where people are coming from. That was one of Arthur's expressions, 'Where's he coming from?'"

"Love was *the* band in LA, better than The Doors in the period 1966 to '67," insists Paul Body. "But [The Doors' 1967 album] *Strange Days* had a picture inside of Jim Morrison with his shirt off. My buddy's sister had that picture up on her wall and my buddy pointed to it and said to me, 'That's why Love will never make it.' That was Jim Morrison; he had that kind of appeal that Arthur didn't have. You didn't have a pinup picture of Arthur Lee on your wall. After that, The Doors became the kings of the Sunset Strip."

The Doors in general, and Jim Morrison in particular, idolized Love, so to be signed to the same record label was a dream come true for them, as Ray Manzarek acknowledges. "During one of our breaks at the London Fog, Jim and I took a walk right up the street to the Whisky A Go Go to see Love playing. We stuck our heads in the door to see the place packed to the rafters. Arthur Lee and Love were on stage just smokin' the place. Morrison turned to me and said, 'You know, Ray, if we could be as big as Love, man, my life would be complete.' I thought Love was one of the hottest things I ever saw. They were the most influential band in Los Angeles at that time, and we all thought it was just a matter of time before Love conquered America. Johnny was the first guy I ever saw playing guitar behind his head, before Hendrix. Love was also the first band I ever saw playing long, improvisational songs. Out of that came Doors songs like 'The End,' 'When The Music's Over,' and the long instrumental parts in 'Light My Fire.' Arthur Lee and Love: they were in charge. We wanted to be like Love. Arthur himself was enigmatic, very intense, and sort of possessed by darker forces."

In contrast to his experience with Arthur and Love, what Jac found in The Doors was a group of young musicians ready, willing, and able to do whatever was required of them to achieve success. They would play by the rulebook. "Once they got The Doors, Elektra was hip and everything worked," says Ronnie Haran, who found herself aced out of any management situation with the group soon after the band signed with Elektra. "The Doors were much more cooperative because they were hungrier. They didn't have a pot to piss in at that point." Indeed, Jim Morrison had no fixed address and had been sleeping under a pier. The Doors were also a democracy: four guys each having a say, and sharing equally in the remuneration. With Love, it was a dictatorship. Arthur ran the show.

The Doors were playing down the street and sometimes, during our breaks, I would go down and check them out. The first time I went I thought they were OK, but nothing special. I went again and I found Jim Morrison to be very interesting, although the girls seemed to think a lot more of him than I did. After a while, with Ray playing the organ, I could see that they were doing something quite different. I think Ronnie Haran told me about them and I told Jac Holzman to go down and check them out, which he did. Afterward I asked him how he liked them and he said, "Not much." I told him to go back down there and this time look at the crowd reaction. So it was then that The Doors became the second [West Coast] group signed to Elektra Records.

Later, I would wake up in the morning and Jim Morrison would be sitting outside my house in Laurel Canyon. One time he was shaking so bad I felt sorry for him. I'd say "hi" but then get into my car and go driving down the hill. I guess he just wanted to hang out with me. It wasn't that I didn't like him; I just didn't really know him as a friend. I had enough people hanging around me at that time.

One time, I was at the Tropicana Hotel, on Santa Monica, and out of my window I saw Jim and Bryan MacLean standing, face to face. All of a sudden, Jim socked Bryan in the mouth, pretty hard. I actually thought that was the best thing I'd ever seen Jim Morrison do. Bryan said later that he was arguing with Jim about his drinking and Jim hit him square in the mouth. I said to myself, "Regardless of what I think, Jim Morrison's got a heart." Bryan could really get on your nerves and it didn't come off too good with Jim.

I looked outside one day and a bunch of people – Jim Morrison, a few people from The Byrds, and other, different, band-members – were all naked in my swimming pool. Jim thought I was so free that it would be fine for him to swim naked in my pool. I said, "What kind of trip are you on, man, swimming naked in my pool?" Morrison replied, "We're on acid." I said, "I don't care what you're on. Get the fuck outta my pool!"

When I lived in Laurel Canyon, I used to walk from Brier to the Country Store on Laurel Canyon Boulevard. On my way down the hill, it used to gas me out seeing all the colorful people with their long hair and beautiful clothes. It was fashionable to rent garages in the area as places to stay. I was coming up Kirkwood one day with my dog and I noticed a girl on the other side of the street. She had her garage door pulled up and I could see into her fixed-up garage home. She was a nice-looking young lady, with shoulder-length red hair, freckles, and a cute figure. I don't remember who made the first move, but we started talking. I probably told her about my group and asked her if she'd ever heard of us. Anyway, one thing led to another and I asked her if she would like to come up to my place and trip. She said she would, and that was my first date with Pam Courson. She told me she was from Laguna Beach. As I looked around her place, I noticed something was missing. I don't remember if there was a refrigerator or not but I didn't see any food around. When I asked if she would like me to get some groceries she smiled and said "yes." And so it became a routine; as I walked or drove up Kirkwood, I would stop by from time to time and drop off some food for her. Our relationship was cool. It sort of played out after a while, but we remained friends.

I would see Jim Morrison from time to time, and now Pam was with him. I thought nothing of it until Jim's death. Then I noticed that on a poster of Jim, he was standing with a black Labrador retriever just like my dog. Later, a book came out about The Doors in which Jim Morrison said that what he wanted to be was as big as Love. I thought that was such a nice compliment, but I couldn't help thinking that Pam had been my girlfriend, then she was his girlfriend; I had a black Labrador and then he had a black Labrador; I was on Elektra Records and so was he … . It seemed to me that not only did Jim Morrison want to be as big as Love; he also wanted to be like me. Jim never bothered me, but he did kind of copy me.

I thought Jim was a lonely person. He was searching. Now that I think about it and put it all together, it seemed like he didn't have a self. He only lived on what he was told was happening. He portrayed something that he thought was great but I don't think he got a chance to be his true, natural self – or perhaps he didn't like his natural self. He tried to become something else. It caught up with him. You finally catch up with yourself and look in the mirror. You have to face the judge, jury, yourself, everybody, and everything.

CHAPTER 4

¡QUE VIDA!

Da Capo Love playing the Whisky, October 1966

O n a musical manuscript the words 'da capo' instruct the performer to repeat playing the music from the beginning. With Love's so-named second album, recorded and released in the fall of 1966, Arthur was making a bold musical statement about the group's progress over a mere nine-month period. Taking inspiration from the music he and Johnny Echols had been drawn to, and performed, before The Grass Roots, according to Johnny, *Da Capo* would be Love's attempt at "going back to the time before we'd gotten to Hollywood and changed into a rock group; back to this kind of bluesy group with a Booker T & The MGs type sound. [In fact] as the album materialized, it didn't go back to anything and instead it kind of pushed the envelope."

Arthur was about to shake up the music world by audaciously integrating jazz elements into a rock context – and doing it some years before jazz-rock would become a widely accepted genre. Indeed, in an interview with *Hit Parader* published in the fall, Arthur tried to nip that incipient idiom in the bud as he explained Love's new direction. "People who listen to music today would probably call it 'jazz rock' but I don't call it that. It's free music. We have to choose material that will fit this group and that's free music. We don't want any patterns; we go completely against the book. I try to accept all kinds of good music because all kinds are good, no matter what label it is." Johnny Echols added his take: "Jazz expresses feelings more than, say, rock'n'roll. Jazz gives people more solos; there's more feeling for the artist. You can use other forms to express yourself."

When I started out, I wanted to be like Elvis Presley, The Beatles, or somebody like that – stars like James Brown, Little Richard, or Mick Jagger. As I got older, I found that people were more interested in my music and words, so I began concentrating more on what I was doing. Change is nothing to me; I'm a walking example of change. To adapt and be able to profit from some gift that God has given you is something to be taken advantage of. My trip, when I first started out, was to do different types of music and not be categorized and labeled. I wanted to accomplish my dream of playing all kinds of music. I fulfilled it enough by going from punk-rock and folk-rock to rock; from rock to classical; from classical to a jazz orientation and R&B. All of my albums are different, and I try to use the voice that goes with the music. The voice I used on "My Little Red Book" isn't the same voice I used on "Andmoreagain."

Paul Rothchild had been brought in to produce The Doors' debut album in August, and, immediately following completion of those sessions, on September 27, he commenced work on Love's sophomore album. "Rothchild went in and out of our lives for about a period of eight months before I could get him out of jail," recalls Jac Holzman. "He was fortunate to have a very good parole officer who signed off on Paul going out to California." Jac believes Paul was the right man for Love: "*Da Capo* was an artistic stretch, and I think a lot of the reach on that album was provided by Paul."

Sessions were convened at RCA's Hollywood studios, at 6363 Sunset Boulevard. The engineer was Dave Hassinger, who had done a superb job the previous year on The Rolling Stones' single "Satisfaction." Despite exerting a tight grip on proceedings, and being unafraid to challenge the band in the studio in order to get his way, Paul hit it off straight away with Love. Johnny Echols: "We respected Paul. When Jac first introduced us to him he told us, 'By the way, Paul just got out of jail for weed.' That was something we thought was cool. And we respected him because we could see he knew what he was talking about." There was another advantage to Paul's more commanding presence. "He was able to control Arthur. He could be like a kid, trying to get away with whatever he could. Jac let Arthur get away with that and let him run around. Rothchild wasn't like that. He expected us to pay attention to him, and we did."

A no-nonsense producer, Paul had little time to soothe egos or submit to posturing. "Things had to be done quickly in those days," maintains Bruce Botnick, who would enjoy a long and fruitful relationship with Rothchild working on subsequent albums for The Doors. "There was no messing around. Paul was a perfectionist. With him, it was like an army going on a campaign and there were rules to follow. That's the way he produced. But Arthur wasn't like that. Arthur had it organized in his head, but there was a flow to it, an energy. So there were clashes between them. Not that there wasn't respect on both sides. There were times when Paul could overproduce. Control was the word. There's a fair amount of Paul Rothchild on that album."

The change of studio prevented Bruce from engineering the sessions, although he did mix the completed tracks, at Jac's request. "Arthur got it into his head that he wanted to get that Rolling Stones sound, so they went to RCA studios. "7 & 7 Is" and "Revelation" were cut at Sunset Sound; the rest were recorded at RCA, with Dave Hassinger engineering. He made Love sound different than I did, but I mixed the whole album so there would be no differentiation between Dave's work and my work."

Prior to commencing the sessions, Arthur revised and expanded the group's line-up to better reflect the musical direction he had in mind for the second album. Snoopy's limited drumming abilities were no match for the sophisticated, jazz-infused arrangements Arthur had conceived. He already knew who he wanted behind the kit. Michael Stuart had been making a name for himself as a talented drummer with The Sons Of Adam, a popular club act on the Strip. The group had opened for Love on several occasions, notably at Bido Lito's in the spring of 1966, and had even recorded one of Arthur's more bizarre compositions, "Feathered Fish." Arthur approached Michael about joining Love but, initially, the drummer rebuffed his advances, as he recalls. "We were playing Bido Lito's. During a break, Arthur came and sat down beside me and introduced himself. Right off the bat he said, 'I like the way you play the drums, man, and I'd like to invite you to join my band.' I told him I was happy with The Sons Of Adam and turned him down. He took issue with that and said, 'The Sons Of Adam are a great band but they're never really gonna go anywhere, and my band Love is going to go right to the top. The offer's open to you to play drums.' Later on, our agents started booking us on a lot of shows with Love. Mike Port, our bass player and I were invited over to The Castle and we hung out with Bryan and Arthur and kind of got to know the guys in the band." Despite being snubbed, Arthur persisted, knowing that Michael was capable of handling the complex time signatures his new music demanded. "It took them about six months before they got me," says Michael. "They even assigned Ronnie Haran to sweet-talk me. She was really campaigning to get me into the band. [By then] The Sons Of Adam had started having personality conflicts and issues with our direction. We were starting to break up; so I called Arthur and I joined Love just before they began rehearsals for the *Da Capo* album. That was the late summer of 1966."

For Michael, Love represented the darker side of the LA music scene, and he had some anxieties about joining. "I knew what the negative aspects were. I wasn't into drugs – that wasn't me – but I knew those guys enjoyed doing them. I had to be able to reconcile that because I would be right in the middle of it. The Sons Of Adam were just getting into smoking a bit of weed from time to time, but everybody knew the guys in Love were into drugs." Michael's joining was the catalyst for Love to err toward jazz, his skills granting them licence to attempt a more sophisticated kind of music. "When Arthur saw me play, he realized that I was versatile enough to do anything. So he thought that I would be a perfect fit for the material he had in mind. The music on *Da Capo* was more complex than their previous album, but I was kind of worried that it wouldn't make it in the popular music category. I was actually a little disappointed when he showed me the material for *Da Capo* – I wondered who was going to buy these songs. I was hoping he would stick with what he had done on their first album."

For all that, Michael couldn't help but be impressed by Arthur's talent as a writer. "Nobody was writing words like that, then. And the way he did it, it couldn't have been done better by anyone else. Arthur had something special. He had intelligence, confidence, and he brought something a lot of other musicians didn't have to music, and that was an athlete's attitude. He was not going to lose, ever. Arthur was an incredibly tough, powerful, profound, and unique individual, and that translated to his music."

Reluctant to cast his buddy adrift, and aware that he had been classically trained as a child, rather than sack Snoopy, Arthur moved him over to keyboards – harpsichord in the studio, organ and piano on stage. Ironically, as late as May 2, the group was still listing Don Conka on their union contracts for engagements, either in the hope that he would return or to ensure that Snoopy did not receive a fifth share of gig money. "Snoopy was OK with moving over to harpsichord," says Michael. "In the beginning, there was a lot of animosity directed at him from the other guys in the band, from Johnny especially, because they thought he was too robotic, had no soul, and was too rigid. He didn't have a lot of musical instinct. By the time I joined up, he had become a pretty good drummer. However, I think they figured he would not be able to do what was necessary for the songs on *Da Capo*. By that time, I think Arthur had developed a soft spot for Snoopy. So he figured they'd add keyboard parts to the songs for him to play. Snoopy and I became good friends, but he was the longest running short-timer in any band that ever was. I didn't know of another LA band where it was well known that everybody else in the group didn't like one guy and were trying to replace him. It was always on a night-by-night basis for Snoopy. He knew that, so he was happy to move over to keyboards. He knew it meant he could stay in the group."

Arthur would then expand Love to a septet with the addition of jazz saxophonist and flautist Tjay Cantrelli, who would join at the same time as Michael Stuart, adding more colors to Arthur's musical palette. "Tjay was a part of that scene at the California Club, with me and Arthur," Johnny explains. "He was the sax player when Arthur was on organ. He was from our past. Tjay's real name was John Barbieri, he was originally from Compton. He allowed us to take that leap into jazz, so I was overjoyed when he joined. We would get really deep into the Coltrane-type sound, the free-form fusion. Fusion [as a genre] didn't exist – we called it free-form rock, which added jazz to rock. We put together a seven-piece group just days before we got to the studio." Indeed, both Tjay and Michael were introduced to the rest of the band at rehearsals for that second album. They were expected to contribute to arrangements for Arthur's latest batch of songs, which ran the gamut from jazz to flamenco.

Tjay Cantrelli was playing professionally a little before I was. I remember when Johnny took me out to a place called Cappy's. It was a club in the Valley, and Tjay had a band that played there. I don't know what the name of the band was; all I know is that Johnny used to get paid for playing and they would let me sit in on the organ, from time to time. I thought that Tjay was extremely talented and was just what we needed for the change from folk-rock into more jazz-rock type music. Just what the doctor ordered. Being familiar with the stage, he helped make our band more polished than when we first started out. I will remember him as one of the best things that ever happened to Love.

Michael's first day with his new band was marked by a startling initiation which occurred when he, Arthur, and Johnny paid a visit to Elektra's offices. Unbeknown to their new drummer, Arthur and Johnny were staging a coup, an attempt to sever their contract with the label. As Michael relates so vividly in his excellent 2003 autobiography, *Behind The Scenes On The Pegasus Carousel* (published by Helter Skelter), the three marched into the label's offices and confronted one of the label executives. Their demand was to be released from the label, based on poor distribution of their debut album and shoddy vinyl production. The ploy failed and the three were sent away to begin rehearsing for the impending recording sessions. "They didn't even tell me what they were going to do," says Michael. "They just said, 'Come on, Michael. We want you to come with us.' Johnny had a copy of the first album in his hand. We walked in [to the Elektra office] and Arthur said, 'I want to talk to you about releasing us from our commitment to Elektra. You really don't have the capacity to be able to handle our group. What do we have to do to get off the label?' And Johnny said, 'Yeah, and your records are made cheaply. Look, you can't do this with any other record,' and he took out the vinyl and snapped it in half, throwing it down on the desk. The guy laughed and told them they weren't getting out of their commitment. He said, 'You owe us three more albums.' We walked out. Arthur was pissed but philosophical. This was the period where Arthur and Bryan were most creative, and I just thought, 'Why are we wasting time trying to finagle contracts and get even? We should be recording songs.' That creative window is only opened for a short time; you can't ignore it."

For Elektra, such maneuvers from Arthur Lee were nothing new. Back in April, long before Michael joined the band, Arthur had tried a gambit on Jac Holzman. Sensing, after the success of their debut single and album, that there was interest from larger record labels with national distribution and heftier promotional budgets, Arthur played his trump card. Claiming the original contract was invalid, he revealed that he had been a minor, not yet 21 and therefore not legally of age, when he had signed it on January 4 1966, thus voiding the agreement. Jac was livid. "That was the point in my relationship with Arthur where he moved from being a scoundrel to being totally dishonest," the Elektra president admits. "He said he wasn't making a second album, which meant [if he'd carried out his threat] that *Da Capo* wouldn't have happened and, therefore, *Forever Changes* wouldn't have happened, either. His lawyer, Al Schlesinger, said, 'It wasn't me,' and I told him, 'Al, I know it wasn't you. It never occurred to me to ask.' So I sat down with Arthur, and he said, 'Jac, I'm going to have a ten-piece band and so I'm going to need a ten per cent royalty,' which was an unheard of rate in those days. So I said to him that, by that logic, CBS would be paying the [110-member-strong] Mormon Tabernacle Choir a 110 per cent royalty. Even Arthur realized that he was being a bit over the top. I said, 'Fine, I'll give you an increase in royalties,' but the trick with Arthur was to tell him you would give him some extra money on the day of the signing. Arthur always thought his psychology was unknown to anybody but himself. He always lived on the edge of extinction, so I knew cash was the key. But this time [to substantiate Arthur's age] I took his driver's licence, photocopied it, and attached it to the contract."

The addendum to Love's original contract dated April 25 1966, signed by the four core Love members (once again Snoopy was omitted), and notarized on May 6, provided an immediate cash payment of $2,500, recoupable from future royalties. It also added a clause which stated that Elektra was exercising its option for 20 more sides (recordings), thus safeguarding their own interests by binding the group to subsequent albums. The presence of a notary for each of the four band members' signatures ensured there would be no further shenanigans with respect to their age (each member was required to state their birth date on the addendum). None of this prevented Arthur and Johnny plotting their later revolt, with Michael in tow, but by this time the label had learned to expect anything.

By September, Arthur had left The Castle and moved into what became known as *The Trip* house, named after Roger Corman's 1966 cult movie *The Trip*, starring Peter Fonda, which had been filmed there. High atop Kirkwood, in Laurel Canyon, the house boasted a panoramic view of Los Angeles. It wasn't the only distinctive feature. "Arthur took me up to see his house," remembers his cousin, Joe Joyner. "When we got there, you couldn't really see the building fully: it was embedded into a hill. When you went into the house, there was a bridge over the living room and there was a pool running through this room to the outside of the house. I'd never seen anything like that in my life. It was gorgeous."

I've always had a thing about privacy. I don't like a lot of people around my house. At The Castle, I'd wake up in the middle of the night and meet three or four people, on the way to the kitchen. That was par for the course. But fans can be a trip. I remember once, after I'd played the Hullabaloo, I had just bought a brand new Porsche. I left it parked in front of my house on Brier in Laurel Canyon. When I got up the next morning, I looked out and my windshield was covered with white marshmallows. I looked to see who the culprits were but I could find no one in the area. I think I said to myself, "That's kind of cute," but getting those marshmallows off my window was a drag. I cleaned them off and thought no more about it. The next morning, I woke up to find white marshmallows on my car windows once more, front and back. Again, I couldn't find anyone responsible. What was I to do? When I woke up the third morning, I looked at my car and there were different-colored marshmallows: green, pink, white, orange, yellow ... and whatever else. The next day, I got up real early, when I thought I heard something outside, and I saw these little girls running away and trying to hide behind some bushes. I looked to see what was in their hands and they were carrying a few bags of marshmallows. I went out and said, "Please don't put any more marshmallows on my car." The next morning, when

I awoke to take my dog for a walk, I found a bullet hole through the front window of my car.

The marshmallow thing was cute, but this wasn't funny, as I told my friend Bill Clark, who was staying with me at the time. The bullet went through my front window and into the driver's seat. After I had the window replaced and the back of the front seat fixed, I hired Bill and his brother Mickey to stand watch for a few nights, to see if they could find anyone doing anything outside.

There was a woman I would see, named Sherry, who rode in this white limousine; she was older than the usual groupie types. I would see her after a gig, or in different places around town. She introduced herself one night and we sort of became friends. I found out she had very expensive tastes. If I wanted a bottle of wine, she would have cases delivered to my house in a catering van. I remember she used to give me all these watches and clocks. One day I asked her, "What's with all the watches and clocks?" She told me she was "interested in my time." This woman sort of spooked me out. I never made love to her. When my birthday rolled around, there came a knock on my front door and I opened it to find Sherry, along with a red carpet and a catering truck filled with wine and all sorts of different food.

She insisted that we go downstairs, where she handed me these two boxes and told me to put my arms around her and hold her real tight. So I did, but I couldn't help noticing she was trembling. She was shaking from head to toe. Anyway, after she kissed me on the cheek, she said she had to go. This chick had given me about $25,000 to $30,000 in watches for my birthday. Years later, I found out she was the one who had my car shot at.

After that bullet episode, I decided to move up the hill to Sunset Plaza Drive. My friend David Biali, my dog Self, and I were walking to the highest point of the hill one day and we saw this house. There was a guy there who seemed to be working on it, so I asked him if the place was for sale and he said it was. When he took us in to look around, the first thing I saw was a swimming pool, half in and half out of the house. To get from the living room to the bedroom you had to go over this little bridge. That was it. I had to have his house. I found out later this was the house where they made the movie The Trip. The first thing I did when I moved in was to build a pigeon cage. You can see some of my birds on the video for [1968 Love single] "Your Mind And We Belong Together;" that was filmed at this house.

It was in this setting that Arthur unveiled his new songs to the group and worked on the arrangements with them. Since the first album, Arthur's songwriting had matured beyond the folk-rock template to embrace an increasingly broad range of musical approaches.

One thing I tried to do was to change styles on each Love album, because I didn't want to be categorized. The more I played, the more this variety of styles became a sound that was all my own. I have heard Love remakes by other people but no one has ever captured that haunting quality of my original band, or the sincerity in the music. One thing I can say: when my band played, they gave it their all, at least on the first two albums.

"I wasn't surprised at Arthur's songs on the second album," says Bruce Botnick. "Nothing that Arthur did in the studio ever surprised me. I always thought he was capable of taking me to the next level, because he had all that creativity going on in his brain. Those first three Love albums represent a prodigious output." Bruce regards *Da Capo* as a turning point, not only for Love, but for the wider music scene. "Next thing I know, I'm doing jazz albums. Everyone's got the Love record and they're going, 'This is cool; maybe we should introduce some of these ideas into *our* music.' This was when jazz was first trying to find its footing in the rock world."

Arthur's method of teaching songs to his bandmates involved playing the chords on his black Gibson acoustic guitar and singing the words, allowing his colleagues to then conceive their own parts to fit his basic structure. He would sometimes hum suggestions for melodic parts. What he offered was often rudimentary, a basic outline or aural sketch that the others were then expected to add color to. Rarely did he, in fact, tell them specifically what to play on their respective instruments. Arthur's genius was in the genesis and conception of his songs – his vision; the band members provided the execution. Arthur's limited abilities on guitar meant that he sometimes felt frustrated in trying to put across what was in his head, mainly because his chord repertoire was too narrow. As the others formulated and added their parts, Arthur would either approve or tell them to try something else. However, the oft-told tale of how he taught everyone, note-for-note, what to play and how to play it, is an exaggeration perpetrated by Arthur years later, long after the original band had folded. Arthur was a truly gifted songwriter in terms of conception and the big picture, but he allowed the players he worked with to complete the canvas.

"In a rock group, no one does everything," stresses Johnny. "Nobody tells a person to play this or that. Everybody contributes to the arrangement, but nothing gets written down as to who contributed what. Arthur would come in and sing the songs, but he wasn't a guitar player. He wanted to play, but he never took the time to learn more than a few basic chords, and those were the chords he used when he was writing the songs. So he'd play us the song he'd written, strumming the guitar, and even if the chords didn't fit, we'd have an idea of what he was trying to do. Then Bryan and I would take that and put a chord structure to it, Kenny would create a bass part, and Michael would come up with his drum part. Everybody wrote the part you hear them playing on those albums. They were respected as musicians, and that's why they were there. People listen to the group and wonder why that sound didn't continue after those first three albums; why, when Arthur got these other guys together, he didn't continue with the sound. The reason is the people that were closest to Arthur, and understood where he was coming from musically, weren't there any more. He was left to put everything together himself, rather than with those who intuitively knew what to play."

Kenny Forssi was a fine bass player and also came up with some pretty good ideas for his instrument. When I would be writing a song, Kenny would always want to contribute something that would make the song better. He really loved his Paul McCartney-style violin-shaped bass. He kept that polished as much as his Jaguar XKE. In the beginning, he really cared about what he was doing, and he added a great feel to the music. I just can't help thinking about what Carl Franzoni once said, "Stay away from drugs!"

"I don't ever remember Arthur saying to any of us, 'Play this,'" confirms Michael. "He never made any suggestions like that as far as I can recall. Instead, he'd say, 'Play something along with it,' and that's what we did. For instance, on the song 'Stephanie Knows Who' there's a little jazz duet that Johnny and Tjay play together; they made that up themselves. None of that was Arthur. He just wrote the [basic] song – the words and chords – and everybody made up their own parts. That really says a lot about Arthur's musicality, the way he just needed a few chords to write those great songs." Arthur was more prescriptive when it came to the harpsichord parts, Snoopy reveals: "Arthur would say, 'Here's what I want you to play,' and he would hum or sing it to me."

According to standard practice, songwriting credit was, and is, assigned to the person or persons who create the basic chords, melody, and lyrics, not those who embellish or arrange. So, despite the band's palpable contributions, it was Arthur who, for the most part, claimed authorship of the new songs.

I try to be as free as I can with my music, but in order to be free you have to start with something, and I guess that would be the basics. If I don't try to space everything out, or get across a big message, I can do a lot of things. When I write, there's a spontaneous musical melody or words that come into my head. Maybe half a song will come into my head, and then what I do is tell the other people in the band, from the first thought, the way I heard it. You go through changes with musicians and sometimes it comes out differently. I write songs like a letter. If you take away the music and leave just the words on a piece of paper, they'll probably tell you something you already know. That's all I'm here to do, to remind you. If you took most of the songs I wrote and put them together it would be a book. They all tell a story. They are what I've seen and lived. They're honest lyrics from what I've seen in life.

Most of the songs I've written over the years came to me early in the morning, just before dawn, like at 4 or 5am. I started pinpointing things like that over the years. I would hear a song in a dream. I would be at a party, in the dream, and I'd start singing this song and then I'd wake up and realize it was a new one.

Johnny maintains that the second album was stronger because the group had gelled over the preceding nine months, allowing them to make the transition to a more mature sound. "We had become more comfortable with each other and had gotten to know each other better. On *Da Capo*, each player knew what he was playing because it was their part, unlike on the first album. Then, for example, Kenny was playing bass parts that John Fleckenstein had written. Even though the first album was much quicker to record, because we'd played those songs every night, it didn't have the kind of consistency that we had on the second album. By then, we had played together more and were able to play sophisticated music rather than just rocking out. It was 180 degrees from that first album to *Da Capo*. It doesn't even sound like the same group. Most of those songs were rewritten and rearranged right there in the studio – which is not always the best way to do it, but that's what we did." He points to a further differentiation. "On the first album, a lot of those songs were written for dancing. We were playing loud music for young kids at our shows. The second album was a bit more adult; it was for sitting down and listening to. We were real musicians who had honed our chops and could play, so we wanted to do something that would take us away from the pack and stretch us out. We were also getting a reputation with jazz musicians. Our tastes had matured."

Despite Arthur's satchel of new songs, the first track tackled on the sessions was a Bryan MacLean composition, "Orange Skies." It was a song Bryan claimed dated back to the previous year and was inspired by the Byrds song "The Bells Of Rhymney" (itself a version of a Pete Seeger folk interpretation of the eponymous Welsh poem). "I was going to sing 'Orange Skies' but it was too high for my voice," claims Johnny. "I was going to do a Johnny Mathis imitation kind of voice. I do a pretty good Johnny Mathis." Ultimately, Arthur would sing it. His voice leading Bryan's song is often cited as evidence of the former dominating the latter. Bruce Botnick disagrees. "Arthur's voice was able to project more than Bryan's, so he was more suited to that song." Johnny has a similar explanation. "Bryan couldn't use a capo, which we would have needed to play in these particular open chords. That meant we couldn't transpose the key; it had to stay in D, so Arthur sang it. It was more suited to his voice than Bryan's."

Whoever sung them, Bryan's songs impressed Harvey Kubernick. "When you heard songs like 'Softly To Me' and 'Orange Skies' you knew that here was a composer who had [integrated] elements of Broadway, Hollywood, Sunset Strip, and the beach." The latter song would also be a vehicle for Tjay Cantrelli's expressive flute playing.

When Bryan wrote the song "Orange Skies," I thought that Tjay was just the man for the job, although Bryan would say that's not the way he wanted the song to go. So Johnny, Tjay, and I arranged that song. I had been listening to Gary McFarland and Wes Montgomery, and sort of blended those two jazz styles together. With Tjay being excellent on the flute, it wasn't hard to get that sound. He and Johnny fitted together like a hand in a glove. Tjay's efforts on the songs "Stephanie Knows Who" and "Revelation" were also exactly what I needed for what I had written.

"Stephanie Knows Who" arose from the real life experience of Arthur and Bryan, who had been vying for the affections of the same girl, Stephanie Buffington. "She was about 17 or 18 years old, from the Valley," says Johnny. "They both were in love with her. And I think they both won. In the lyrics, 'A my love' is Arthur and 'B my love' is Bryan."

Michael Stuart: "Arthur explained the song to me in one sentence, 'This is a song about a girl that Bryan and I have a little history with.' So I gathered that this was a girl that both he and Bryan wanted to date. Somebody mentioned that she bounced back and forth between them, but since Arthur had written the song I figured she was with him. By the time we recorded it she had gone back to Bryan. Arthur was philosophical about it."

Nonetheless, Michael feels that the incident drove a wedge between the two songwriters. "It was like a little tiny cancer, and Arthur began to resent Bryan for having won that battle. The competitive athlete in him came out and he began to think of it like a game he had lost. He couldn't abide it. It was naive of Bryan to think he could take Arthur's girlfriend in a power play. Arthur was always looking to get even. Bryan was a wise guy and a practical joker. To him, I don't think it was that big a deal that he won that battle. Arthur began to see this as a humiliation, however, and he got to the point where he was just always pissed off with Bryan."

Stephanie was the girl who liked both Bryan and me. That used to bother me a lot. I couldn't figure it out, as we weren't exactly twins. I wrote "Stephanie Knows Who" and part of "The Castle" about Stephanie Buffington. It's a trip. I never made love to that girl. Once, I went over to her house in the Valley and she showed me these marks on her side. I asked her what they were and she said a tiger had clawed her. I didn't know that they were actually stretch marks from having a baby. I didn't think a tiger had actually done that, but then again, I didn't know. That's why the words in the song "Stephanie Knows Who" are: "A tiger did you, said he did." She was a very pretty lady. I heard she passed away, God rest her soul. I can say one thing: she sure brought some good music out of me. I saw her coming out of Bryan's house, when he lived below me, on Brier, one morning. I think I got a little upset. I really liked Stephanie. The line in The Castle: "Going back to mother / Leaving on the double / Guess I'll go to Mexico," was about going back to my parents. The line: "Forget going through this / Make up your mind," was about going to Mexico and forgetting about all these changes I was going through, with a woman choosing between Bryan and me.

Then, there was the way Bryan always reacted to any girl that was interested in both of us. I would be pissed off, but Bryan would say, "Oh, Arthur!" I was almost ready to fight but he would just say, "Oh, Arthur!" I wonder if I really knew Bryan.

According to Michael, the incident would ultimately impact on the band's fortunes. "In the beginning, Arthur and Bryan were great friends. They loved to be around each other and did things socially together. They were funny. After the Stephanie thing, that began to deteriorate; it got to the point where they didn't hang together at all. Arthur was trying to organize it so that Bryan was no longer in the group. They rest of us kind of vetoed that."

While much of the album features Arthur's new, softer voice, "Stephanie Knows Who" retains the raw delivery found on the first album. The opening build-up between Bryan's fingerpicking guitar and Snoopy's harpsichord, however, offered a marked contrast with their debut, as did the break, with its Dave Brubeck-style 5/4 time signature interplay between Johnny and Tjay.

Johnny deconstructs the song: "I played every guitar part except for the fingerpicking folk style. That's what Bryan was, a folk guitar player, so he does that, and everything else is me. That song was kind of a jazz waltz. It's not a very danceable song. We were interested in playing for the effect of the song and what we could get out of the music, not being just a dance group. We would play it live and notice people couldn't dance to it. They could maybe waltz to it. The sound of that came from the movie *What's New Pussycat* and [jazz drummer] Chico Hamilton's group, with guitarist Gabor Szabo and saxophonist Charles Lloyd. I was very influenced by them." Arthur would one day guest on a Chico Hamilton album.

"The Castle" was based around Bryan's delicate fingerpicking and flamenco flourishes, with Johnny adding a flat-picked counter-melody. "Dave Hassinger was able to blend the two of those together pretty well," says Johnny. "Flamenco was a staple around Elektra," suggests Jac Holzman. "Remember, we had [flamenco guitar virtuoso] Sabicas on the label. And it was possible for our artists to come in and help themselves to our catalog. So you had a room filled with all these records, and we had at least half-a-dozen flamenco albums. Arthur and some of the guys, I think, availed themselves of those."

"¡Que Vida!" (Spanish for 'what a life' – its original title was "With Pictures And Words") is a straightforward pop number boasting sound effects (a champagne cork popping and sleigh bells) culled from Elektra's extensive sound library. It also features Arthur's more mellow vocal tone. Bruce Botnick: "Arthur was a really good singer and he could croon, too; he could sing just about anything. I said to him once, and I probably shouldn't have said it, 'Arthur, you're a black man trying to sing like a white man who's trying to be black,' and he laughed. Arthur never sounded black. I never, ever heard him do a rhythm & blues lick. He didn't listen to that music."

Versatility is a big part of my music. Being able to use a different voice was not only the key to my music but I believe it was a gift. If you got it, you got it. Either you can do it or you can't. Versatility was the main reason for all the different personnel in my bands. I have a versatile style of music. Some people can play fingerpicking music really well, but they can't get down with a Jimi Hendrix or B.B. King type of guitar solo.

Despite persistent stories to the contrary, the song "She Comes In Colors" was actually inspired by a fan's garish outfits. "That one was about this girl named Annette [Arthur's friend, Annette Ferrel] who would come to all our shows wearing these outrageous gypsy clothes," explains Johnny, who also recalls the track being the most difficult for the group to arrange and record: "because of all the strange chords that were involved in it."

Arthur's lyrical reference to being in "England town" is purely fictional – he had yet to venture overseas. He always insisted that The Rolling Stones' 1967 song "She's A Rainbow," containing the line "She comes in colours everywhere," was stolen from him after the British group caught Love's set at the Whisky, that fall. "Arthur wouldn't stop talking about that," confirms Bruce. "It bothered him so much." It would not be the only accusation leveled at the Stones by Arthur.

Perhaps the most controversial decision on *Da Capo* was to devote the entire second side of the album to one long track, "Revelation." There has been much speculation over the years about the decision to pass over a potential six further songs from Arthur or Bryan in favor of what most fans and critics regard as an over-long, meandering jam. Was Arthur holding back his songs in a ploy to renegotiate his contract with Elektra? Was the jam a form of revenge against the label for not allowing the group to break their contract and free them up to sign with a major record label? Or was it merely an example of Arthur's stubborn streak? Needless to say, the reality was less titillating than the conjecture.

Since their days at the Brave New World, Love had always included lengthy, improvised songs in their live repertoire. Their onstage version of the old Howlin' Wolf blues number "Smokestack Lightning," also recently recorded by Manfred Mann and The Yardbirds, was always a lengthy flight of fancy. Another of Love's elongated numbers which had evolved on stage was assigned the title "John Lee Hooker" and was based on a blues guitar figure that would often segue into Them's "Gloria." Love was known for these extended improvisations which showcased each individual band member's abilities and were, in fact, showstoppers which anyone who experienced the group in concert between 1965 and 1967 recalls fondly. Record buyers only knew the group's more arranged material, not the live, spontaneous element of their sound. Arthur decided to use the second side of *Da Capo* to enlighten them. The decision was a conscious one, made for a positive reason; there was no vindictive or sinister ulterior motive. Unfortunately, the results left both band and fans disappointed and marred what was an otherwise exceptional album of well-crafted songs.

"I remember times when 'Revelation' would open their live shows," says Paul Body. "To see and hear them play it live was amazing. Those cats could really cook. Johnny Echols would start it off. When I saw them, early on, they were doing 'Smokestack Lightning' and 'Gloria' and it eventually became 'Revelation.' It didn't even have a name when I saw them. They would just go into it and say, 'We're going to do this song' and they'd just start into it. On the album, it was sort of a disappointment because experiencing it live was incredible. It was monstrous. That was the kind of song that could never be captured in the studio. It was totally a live song."

"We played it every night and it was one of the favorite songs with audiences," confirms Johnny. "We'd get standing ovations when we played it at the Fillmore [in San Francisco]. We called it 'John Lee Hooker.' It had a different rhythm and a cacophony of stuff that they ended up putting together in the studio. It was basically a blues jam where we could show off all our different influences. Live, I would start off singing for the first ten minutes; then Arthur would come in and play the rhythm part in the background. It would start out blues then go into jazz, then a little classical influence, and finally a primitive, freeform thing.

We were going through different genres of music. It sounded so different live compared to what we got on the album. What Paul Rothchild did was record 45 minutes of this jam, but instead of leaving it alone and just cutting the end off, he hacked the song up into this mishmash, so you can't get the feeling for what we were trying to do. If it had been done the way we performed it live, it would have been a whole different song, a whole different feel. He said he was trying to 'paint a picture.' I explained to him that it was up to us to paint the picture and him to put it down on canvas, or tape, and not do something on his own initiative, like that. Anyway, he just spliced everything to bits and changed us all around. It got kind of whacked up in the mix, so you don't know who's playing what. You can't really judge what guitar or which instrument is coming in."

As for the decision to devote an entire side to one song, Johnny regrets it, placing blame, in part, on their record label. "We had the songs but that was one of the numbers that got Jac interested in us in the first place. He had heard this jam. We should have done it on the first album. It would have been more apropos on that album. But time was also running out for us and we didn't have a lot more days to record. If we had been able to record more, we would have had a different album rather than a whole side of this *noise*. It was really down to Elektra not giving us enough time."

"Revelation" was recorded at Sunset Sound with Bruce Botnick engineering. He recalls: "It was very popular to do long songs at the time. It was the thing to do. The Doors had already recorded [their 12-minute Sophoclean epic] 'The End.' Paul Rothchild and I were working on The Doors' record and Love's album concurrently in late 1966. I don't believe that Arthur recorded that jam because he wanted out of his Elektra contract and didn't want to give Jac any more of his songs [as has been rumored]. He came into the studio and told Rothchild that he wanted to do this one long track. And we edited it down. If Arthur wanted out of his contract, why did we go back in and do a subsequent album?"

In the end, with the clock ticking and a release date already announced, Paul took the jam and spliced it together, in some cases taking parts out of context. For example, Snoopy's harpsichord intro and outro were edited in. "That's a fugue from a Bach Partita," Snoopy reveals. "Arthur didn't show me that. They knew I could play it, so they said, 'Why don't we put that on there to open it and close it.' I actually think 'Revelation' was a piece of shit. It was a waste of a side of an album."

When we played "Revelation" on stage, it was more up-tempo. I think that out of all the times we played it, the worst was the one we put on the album. Being a group effort, and a spontaneous thing, at a club we could express love through it. But in the studio, everyone was mad at each other about something – I mean steaming mad. As a matter of fact, I wanted to call it quits, but Jac Holzman had his money on the line and kept saying it would be OK. Because of rumors about the band sometimes saying "the hell with it," I tried to do the best I could, and so did everyone else in the band. But still, to me, it was the worst we ever played it.

According to Jac, "Revelation" was a favorite of late-night DJs. "They could put the track on and have nearly 19 minutes uninterrupted time for a bathroom break, or even to get laid. Arthur wanted to be first to devote a whole side to one song, and even though he wasn't actually first, he was close." On their 1966 album *Aftermath*, The Rolling Stones had featured an 11-minute blues jam entitled "Goin' Home" which resembled Love's efforts on "Revelation." Arthur always believed the Englishmen had copped the idea from seeing Love in LA; however, it's more likely that both bands arrived independently at the notion of recording a bluesy free-form jam.

With the tracks completed, Bruce mixed the album (adding the already recorded "7 & 7 Is") and presented it to Jac for his approval. With a cover photo taken at the same burnt-out Laurel Canyon site featured on their debut, featuring the new seven-man Love line-up (including Arthur captured, according to Michael, exhaling from a joint), *Da Capo* was released in late November. It rose to a disappointing #80 on the *Billboard* album charts. "She Comes In Colors," backed by "Orange Skies," was released as a single, but failed to make the Hot 100, despite local chart action and heavy airplay on LA stations. Arthur blamed Elektra for the album's meager chart showing. Bruce begs to differ: "Arthur wouldn't go out and promote it!" Jac Holzman saw *Da Capo* as a transitional album. "On that first Love album we had the garage band thing with an occasional punk overtone. Now we had jazz. When I listened to the first side of *Da Capo*, I was curious about what it was going to develop into next."

The question remained: had Arthur overestimated his own audience with a body of music perhaps too complex and esoteric for their tastes? Certainly the music on *Da Capo* had no other context or reference in rock'n'roll up to that point and was an undeniably groundbreaking release for 1966. "I think, by that point, Arthur had shown he was kind of oblivious to who his audience was and how to appeal to them," suggests Jim Bickhart. A keen observer of the Sunset Strip music scene, Jim had followed Love's progress carefully. "The steady evolution of The Byrds had sort of softened me up for groups that weren't always going to sound like the same thing on every album. So when Love jumped from folk-rock to flamenco-jazz-punk, or whatever it was on *Da Capo*, I was ready to accept it. Although I didn't necessarily think the writing was that great or consistently good, it was certainly interesting, so I continued to pay attention to them. Arthur was consciously eclectic, that's for sure. That makes sense when you listen to *Da Capo*. I think he was simply following his muse. My guess is that he was not thinking, 'I'm going to bring my audience along with me,' he was just thinking, 'I'm going to do what I'm going to do.' But exactly what his motivations were, or what statements he was trying to make, it was difficult to discern."

To debut the new line-up and sound, the band began a residency on familiar turf, the Whisky, from October 19 to 30. They were an instant sensation. "We were well-rehearsed because we had just recorded the album, so it sounded good," Michael remembers, with justifiable pride. "It was great. The crowd was used to the group playing folk-rock and rock; they weren't used to us playing jazz-rock. It's kind of hard to dance to 'Stephanie Knows Who,' but you can dance to 'My Flash On You' [the album's most direct, garage-rocker]."

DJ Rick Williams caught the group's show during their Whisky stand and was impressed. "To me, Tjay Cantrelli made a huge difference. They were the first rock band I had seen that had flute and sax. And he had them amplified, so you could really hear them. He added a whole different tone to their sound. All the songs on *Da Capo* were so unique and different. On the first album, you could hear the Byrds influence and the obvious folk-rock thing, but the jump to the songs on *Da Capo* was like nothing else at the time."

"I saw that line-up several times," says Sunset Strip habitué Peter Piper, "and they were taking rock a step further than anyone else at that time, fusing rock with jazz, using the sax and flute. It was so different from their first album and I worried that some of the diehard fans wouldn't like it."

Love raised the bar for their contemporaries, displaying a level of musical sophistication hitherto unknown in the rock clubs of the Sunset Strip. "Jazz was my first love so that was my favorite time to play," enthuses Johnny. "The expanded group really sounded good. People would stop dancing and listen because it sounded just like the record. By that point, we had become a really good live band. It was probably the most fun we had playing."

A November 11 *Los Angeles Times* review of Love's performance at the Whisky noted the band's new direction and how they'd drawn "a cream crop of Sunset Strip celebrities who came to judge the change." Their verdict, the reviewer suggested, would have to be "damned good." The piece continued, noting that, with their new jazz orientation: "Brian [sic], Kenny, Snoopy, and Michael provided a concrete launching platform for Arthur, Johnny, and Tjay. Everybody had a job to do and they did it with excellence. Their new material, mostly by Arthur Lee, was highly creative and delivered with precision. Short of Beatles records and the live Buffalo Springfield, I don't recall hearing a cleaner presentation or balance of instruments and roles. Every tune they did was alive with adventure and intrigue." The writer also noted that Arthur's performance was more subdued than in the past. "He has quieted down some, perhaps in keeping with the new jazz face of the group. Now it is Tjay who clutches at your heart. Whenever he soloed (all too few times!) he clearly reigned."

An earlier *LA Free Press* review singled out "Revelation" for particular mention as "a wild and improvised thing that you'll have to hear to believe," noting that the group played an all-ages Sunday-afternoon matinee, where they gave away free copies of the "She Comes In Colors" single. *Los Angeles Times* music critic Digby Diehl featured the band in an October 26 piece in which he used the term "jazz rock" to describe Love's new sound, citing the additions of Tjay and Michael as catalysts of their new direction, allowing the group to explore innovative musical territory within a rock context. The sound, he wrote: "... is a sonic ocean filled with new tone colors and violently pulsating rhythm that washes over the happily gyrating audience in waves of jazz-heightened crescendo. These sheets of sensation that are slammed against the audience remind one of John Coltrane playing with a vengeance." He continued, in similarly grandiloquent vein, describing Love's new direction as "a hypnotic mélange" and adding: "The flute and harpsichord jazz improvisations on numbers such as 'Stephanie Knows Who' and 'Orange Skies' lend a fresh lift to what might be an ordinary rock piece. The vocals are especially effective when flavored by the exotic weavings of an oriental-sounding guitar obligato or a jazz flute accompaniment that works so effectively in this setting. With jazz rock, Love has added a bit of spice to what was in danger of becoming a rather flavorless pudding of popular music. This new style of sound also requires the musicianship and imagination that will inject sophistication into the intuitive folk-based field of rock that will enhance the energetic excitement of groups such as Love."

Jim Bickhart's first opportunity to see the new-look Love came the following month. "They played the UCLA Homecoming Dance in late November 1966, in the grand ballroom. I had heard *Da Capo* and they were reproducing the record pretty well. I remember they looked pretty much like they did on their album covers, and the sound was well mixed and well performed. They did the things you would expect like '7 & 7 Is' and 'My Little Red Book,' and I remember when Arthur introduced 'My Flash On You' he called it 'Our Flash On You.' Arthur didn't gyrate around or anything, he just pretty much stood there and did his thing. He was into his own variation of the Byrds mode of standing still and being serious. They did a mix of songs from the first album and *Da Capo* and closed with 'Revelation.' That was the one where you could tell Snoopy was becoming expendable. They had him playing a regular piano and you couldn't really hear him. His part came at the end, and as that part approached and he started playing, Arthur just looked at him as if to say, 'Forget it; they can't hear you anyway,' and they left the stage. So I wasn't surprised that Snoopy didn't stay around much longer. But they sounded like their records, which I thought was pretty impressive, especially since, on *Da Capo*, they were trying something radically different from their first album."

Following a trip up to San Francisco to play three consecutive nights at the Fillmore, beginning December 2, the band returned to LA and to Santa Monica's Civic Auditorium on December 9, headlining a bill that included The Turtles, The Standells (featuring former Love bassist John Fleckenstein), The Leaves (who had enjoyed a minor chart hit with their version of "Hey Joe"), Count V, and a rare solo appearance by Gene Clark, who had recently exited The Byrds. It was an evening that would end abruptly. "I was at that show when Love was headlining," laughs Peter Piper, "and they were right in the middle of a song when the power went out. The entire place went totally silent, except for one voice that yelled out 'Fuck!' That was Arthur. That was the only thing you could hear throughout that whole auditorium. I don't think they came back on once the power was restored."

In the interim between Love's Whisky and Santa Monica Civic appearances, the scene along the Sunset Strip had undergone a radical transformation.

Responding to continuing complaints by Sunset Boulevard merchants, who regarded the longhaired youths inhabiting the Strip at all hours as undesirables who scared away potential customers, in early November, the Los Angeles Police Department cracked down on the scene. Through the auspices of LA's City Council, they enforced a 10pm curfew for anyone under the age of 18. The youths countered with a November 12 protest in front of Pandora's Box, a coffeehouse/nightclub at 8118 Sunset Boulevard, located on an 'island' where Crescent Heights intersects with Sunset Boulevard. Transit buses were halted by the throng of protestors who also threw bottles and rocks as riot police moved in to quell the disturbance. In the wake of what has become known as The Riot On Sunset Strip (its fame crystallized by a low-budget 1967 exploitation movie of that name, featuring musical appearances by The Standells and The Chocolate Watchband, among others), the LA authorities revoked dance permits for clubs along the Strip and moved to expropriate and demolish Pandora's Box to make way for a thruway joining Crescent Heights and Laurel Canyon.

Over the next two weeks, further demonstrations erupted, resulting in the arrest of over 350 protestors whose ranks included celebrities such as Sonny and Cher, Peter Fonda, and *Gilligan's Island* television star Bob Denver. Watching these events transpire on his television set, up in San Francisco, Stephen Stills was moved to write the song "For What It's Worth." It would go on to become an anthem for 60s protest. Stills later claimed to have been at the front of the marching protestors on the street.

In the wake of various ordinances which effectively shut out teens from the Sunset Strip, the club owners either brought in entertainment geared to an older crowd, particularly Motown and other soul acts, or took the 'topless entertainment' route. The changed circumstances proved only temporary, however, and, a few months later, clubs like the Whisky and the Hullabaloo were welcoming back rock bands catering to a returning teen crowd.

Never overtly political (aside from being a high profile, mixed race band – itself still a considerable political statement in late 1966), Love stayed out of the fray. Nonetheless, Arthur found that his usual gig circuit had temporarily dried up. In fact, the Sunset Strip never fully recovered and the golden age of that thriving and energetic scene had peaked by late 1967.

The temporary closing down of the Hollywood clubs offered the perfect opportunity for Elektra to put Love out on the road to promote their new album and single. Jac Holzman even flew Arthur to New York City in early 1967 to check out the club scene there, in the hope of convincing him to bring Love to the East Coast. "We had interviews set up for Arthur in New York, but he wouldn't show," Jac recalls. "He came to New York and then he went back, right away. He wouldn't stay and left a day early. The Doors were in town and they got the interview the next day."

"*Da Capo* didn't do as well as it should have," reflects Michael Stuart. "We should have toured behind it. But Love was never a touring band. Arthur really didn't enjoy the road; he didn't like staying in hotels or motels, eating bad food, or having to be somewhere at a certain time. None of us do, really; but for most of us it comes with the territory, and it's a worthwhile trade off. It's the only way you can sustain being a musician. Arthur thought he could make it without doing that stuff. His plan was to do what he enjoyed doing, without having to do the unpleasant part. I thought we should be playing more. Everybody knows that rock'n'roll bands are only popular for a short period of time, and then nobody wants you. I wanted to make the most of what we had. But I knew what I was getting into when I joined this group. It didn't shock me that they didn't tour. Arthur was different in every way, and prided himself on being different. If bands toured after releasing an album, he would do it differently. He thought we could be more individualistic, more interesting, more mysterious ... all these things that other bands were not, by doing things like turning down tours."

The lack of strong management made securing the group a fanbase beyond Southern California even tougher. Ronnie Haran had gradually bowed out (although she remained loosely involved with the group), turning over the managerial reins to Mike Gruber. "Mike was someone I brought the group to," Ronnie reveals. "He had a connection with The Rolling Stones."

"Everybody could see that we needed structure and an adult to supervise this thing – a strong manager – because we were totally undisciplined," admits Johnny. "We needed a strong figure to pull it all together. Mike Gruber came in after Ronnie and offered to take us to the next level."

Nonetheless, Arthur's aversion to touring remained a problem. "We had managers but they were always subject to Arthur," noted Bryan MacLean in his 1993 interview with Neal Skok. "I was always waiting for someone to take control of the band out of Arthur's hands but it never happened. You can't manage a person who won't do what you tell him to do. It kept us from being more successful. I thought we were going to be a much bigger success than we were. If I had been the leader, if I could have beaten Arthur up, things would have been done differently. But I was not a fighter; I was an artist. If I had been the leader, I would have found someone whom I considered decent and had integrity and turned the decisions over to him. I remember telling different managers to just take the decisions away from Arthur and we'll be fine. Every time, however, Arthur dominated them."

Michael Stuart broadly agrees with Bryan's assessment. "Arthur held the reins all the time. It's a hard thing for a performer to also be a manager. Arthur didn't like to be told what to do. But being in the band, he couldn't always see the forest for the trees. A manager has a much better vision of what's best for the performer. We should have been doing what we were told to do, but Arthur didn't like that. He wanted to be the boss." Johnny Echols goes further: "Arthur started getting this reputation for being difficult, and we had a reputation for not showing up, although, in fact, there was not one time that we didn't appear. So many things were just made up about this group. We might arrive late, but we'd be there. We needed the money because we were living lifestyles way beyond our means. We always needed money and you couldn't do that just by lying around all day."

Would Arthur have played ball and cooperated with another record label other than Elektra? "It depends," reflects Jac. "If it had been the right person, maybe something could have happened. But if the band wasn't willing to go out and work their records and do live performances outside of Southern California, they would have been dropped before the second album. We were crazier than that. I was willing to continue because the albums weren't that expensive to make and you never knew what you were going to get. I'd rather blow $5,000 or $10,000 on an album; if it didn't work it wasn't going to kill me. Arthur never had it as good with other labels. If he had told me the truth about why he wouldn't tour, I may not have been able to do anything about it, but at least I would have understood."

With fewer gigs and a seven-piece band to maintain, Arthur decided to jettison Snoopy and Tjay in early December and return Love to a quintet. Economically, it wasn't feasible to carry the two extra members. The jazz excursions of *Da Capo* would be regarded as a noble experiment, one Arthur would never return to on such a scale. Like folk-rock on their debut album, jazz-rock would be abandoned without looking back. None of Love's Elektra albums bore a stylistic resemblance to its predecessor, nor were the line-ups who made them ever consistent.

Michael remembers Tjay taking news of his dismissal in his stride. "Sometimes, Arthur would confer with us on decisions and explain what he was about to do, and other times he wouldn't. But I do remember we were at Kenny's house one day and Arthur said, 'I don't think we're gonna need Snoopy and Tjay on the next album. It's just going to be the five of us and strings and horns.' He asked me to go and talk with Tjay, who lived just around the corner. Tjay said, 'Yeah, I figured it might be just a one-album deal.'" As a veteran jazz musician, Tjay was used to gigs coming and going: it was all part of the scene. Besides, there are those who claim he never really fitted in with the other band members and was always an outsider. "I couldn't stand him," Ronnie Haran reveals. "He was a great sax player but he was like oil and water with the band. He was older, he was slimy, and he was a serious doper, as far as I could tell. I just think he introduced a whole other element to the band that never clicked, for me."

As for Snoopy, he had been expecting to be cut adrift right from the get-go. "My time on keyboards was very short-lived. I couldn't improvise. I just stood there behind the piano most of the time and I did my little parts. But it became pointless. A lot of the time, I didn't do anything at all. Some of the guys in the band resented that." Rick Williams remembers Snoopy's keyboards always being kept low down in the mix at gigs. "You only heard him a few times. It wasn't like he was fully contributing." Snoopy thinks the band convinced Arthur to get rid of him. "I went along with it; I was relieved to be out of the band because everyone was so unpleasant, and I wasn't being paid. I don't remember any pleasant gigs. I stayed friends with Arthur after that, though. He was like an older brother to me. My first acid trips were with him. He was a very streetwise person and I enjoyed his company – and he enjoyed mine, because I was a good listener."

Since his days in Love, Snoopy has given the occasional interview in which he appears profoundly bitter over his tenure with the group. He has also been the source of some of the misinformation surrounding the band. Johnny Echols remains circumspect about Snoopy's attitude. "Suppose you were a ballplayer and you had the chance to play with the New York Yankees. Even if it was for a short period of time, wouldn't you cherish that moment and remember it as 'Wow, I got to play with the Yankees'? However brief, you had your moment in the spotlight, and you would be grateful for that moment. Well, Snoopy has been bitter, nasty, and mad about his time in Love ever since he was fired. He knew he wasn't up to the task. He was younger than the rest of us and we had nothing in common. Instead of cherishing that time, he's bitter about being fired and resentful of me, because I was the guy who was given the task of letting him go. I let him down very nicely, but he just blew it when he was cut loose. He just was totally out of his depth and he knew it."

The decision to return to a quintet was not met with universal approval. Writing in the *Los Angeles Times*, Digby Diehl, who had been one of the most vocal boosters of the band's jazz direction, was particularly disappointed. In his review of Love's December 23 appearance at the Pasadena Folk-Rock Festival he regretted that their performance offered "an unhappy reversal of their highly listenable history" and mourned the absence of the harpsichord and saxophone. He went on: "All that remains of a previously intriguing mélange of jazz improvisation with 'hard rock' is a migraine electronic sound that has degenerated to coarseness. They sound like every other dull, noisy rock group that smashes in and out of Sunset Strip. The inexplicable collapse of a skilful group that pioneered jazz rock is lamentable."

On Wednesday, January 4 1967, The Doors' self-titled debut album was released by Elektra, its arrival heralded with a giant billboard advertisement on the Strip. Arthur was disgruntled, Jac remembers. "Arthur saw their billboard on Sunset Strip and flipped out. He felt he should have had the billboard. One of Arthur's biggest problems was The Doors. He resented their success, and I think he realized it might have happened for him had he been prepared to do what they had done."

While The Doors' debut single, "Break On Through (To The Other Side)," failed to burn up the charts, its follow up, "Light My Fire," had reached #1 by June, with the debut album going gold (and later platinum). "Things started to hit on all cylinders because The Doors were happening," says Bruce Botnick, "and Jac had to devote his energies somewhere else [other than to Love]."

Michael Stuart believes there was no reason for Arthur to resent The Doors. "We were an isolated band. We didn't hang out with any other groups. The only camaraderie was Bryan's budding relationship with Jim Morrison. Arthur intimidated Jim. The Doors looked at Love as the band they wanted to be like: successful, mysterious, and profound. But The Doors were hard workers, and the other guys in the band had more control over Jim Morrison than we had over Arthur. The guys in The Doors could tell Jim to do something or show up somewhere and, even if he was drunk, he'd appear. But Arthur would say, 'Don't even ask. I'm in charge here.' So, eventually, we gave up trying. I started sitting in with other bands and Bryan started writing more."

Arthur's girlfriend, Gaye Blair, thought his problem was that he was basically afraid. "When The Doors were out there touring, I said to Arthur, 'Look, Jim is out there playing the game. Why can't you?' He'd say, 'Fuck it.' He didn't want to go to the South. He didn't want to go to New York. He didn't want to fly. He'd get too comfortable. He'd always have a bunch of the guys over and an excuse to drink, do drugs, and kick back. Jim didn't have that. I used to pit Arthur and Jim against each other. Love and The Doors together was a great show. When they were on the same bill, I would say to Arthur, 'Jim's really gonna put on a show tonight. He's going to outdo you.' I would stir them up. Arthur would rise to the challenge, because he was so competitive. Love could have been as big as The Doors if Arthur had played the game, but he wouldn't do what was necessary. Arthur resisted it."

While Paul Rothchild was recording Da Capo, he was also recording The Doors' first album. Our first album didn't exactly sell a million. The reason was, I guessed, because Elektra didn't have enough money to push it that far. But with the money they made from our first two albums, they just might have had enough to push The Doors to the top.

Viewed in retrospect, there may have been other underlying forces, an unconscious subtext, at work on *Da Capo* that would bear further fruit with Love's next album. "They may have begun thinking that the music business and the audience weren't going to be all that accepting of an integrated folk-rock band," suggests Jim Bickhart, "so Love began to allow who they'd always been to come closer to the surface. Perhaps Arthur, who was the driving force behind all of it, needed to reconcile who he really was with the self he'd reinvented and which informed *Da Capo*. He was trying to push social and cultural boundaries, years ahead of the time when that kind of thing wouldn't raise eyebrows. There were other bands around doing interesting music that didn't make it even as big as Love, and one of the key differences was that they didn't have an Arthur Lee –

or a Johnny Echols, for that matter. Arthur was a young man who wanted to be able to play music, and he picked up on what was going on around him as part of his inspiration. That's not so unusual, but the fact that he happened to be a special talent and a mercurial personality made it all the more interesting."

I feel that I found myself, or planted a seed of who I am today, on the Da Capo album. I was born on Da Capo. It's just been the same trip since then. Once you see what you want to do, once you see what you want to be, or whatever, that's the way you are from then on. That was me, then, and here I am, now.

CHAPTER 5

YOU SET THE
SCENE

Arthur Lee, 1967

much has been made of 1967, the year of flower power, psychedelia, and tie-dyed peace and love imagery. Context is always important, however. While many were getting high and trekking to San Francisco wearing the proverbial flowers in their hair, the backdrop to the decade's most celebrated year was decidedly less pastoral and hardly hallucinogenic. Indeed, the reality was far more sobering, and any music from that year which had any significant staying power (as opposed to trite novelty artifacts typified by The Strawberry Alarm Clock's corny chart-topping hit "Incense And Peppermints") was influenced, directly or indirectly, by that somber setting. It was inescapable.

In 1967, the escalating Vietnam War spread a pall across America and was, for young men between the ages of 18 and 25 in particular, an ominously hovering presence. Unless you were able to secure a college deferment or a coveted 4-F ineligibility rejection, the draft (compulsory military service) was a cold, looming reality for every adolescent American male. Members of rock groups were no exception. "There was an undercurrent of fear," recalls Johnny Echols of the era. "The war was always present for us young men at that time. It permeated everything."

Being often less able to secure the all-important college deferment, black Americans found themselves drafted in disproportionate quantity, and were thus slain in greater numbers, too. Johnny Echols: "I'd go visit my mother and she'd have the newspapers with the names of the guys I went to school with who had been drafted and died in Vietnam. I hadn't registered and my mother was clamoring for me to do so. Crimson [Crout, Johnny and Arthur's musical associate from Dorsey High days] had decided he wasn't going to register and dropped out. The FBI would regularly come by Arthur's place and my mother's house, looking for him. I was afraid they were coming to get *me*. It was very frightening. Finally Arthur and I went down to register. They called us down and we were wearing these strange costumes and looking totally unfit for anything. We were probably stoned, too. They would ask me to do one thing and I would do something else and spout all this gibberish. They finally told me to get the hell out of there. Arthur did the same and pretended he was gay. We did whatever we had to do to get out of there. But it wasn't all finished. That was just a short reprieve, because they were still calling people back even after sending them home the first time. So we always had that hanging over our heads. We were living the life of Riley, but we could always be snatched away and sent over there to die."

Arthur had already coached Snoopy on how to beat the draft by loading him up on acid and keeping him awake and unwashed for several days prior to his induction appointment. The ploy worked and the drummer was quickly shown the door. The war touched close to home for everyone, however, including Arthur. "I saw him when I was going into the service," remembers Arthur's childhood friend Curtis 'Smooth' Woods. "I was in my uniform; I'd been drafted and was about to catch a flight. I went over to this bank on Western and Adams to cash a check. Just before I went in, I looked up and saw Arthur on Western, right beside the bank. He had those combat boots he used to wear with the laces dragging on the ground, and he had jeans on. I said, 'Arthur?' and he looked at me and said, 'Oh, are you in the army?' I said, 'Yeah. I'm leaving today. Where you going, man?' He laughed and said, 'I'm walking to Hollywood.' So we hugged and I said to him, 'God bless you,' and I left to be stationed near the Iron Curtain. One day in the barracks, they were passing albums around and one of the guys says, 'Hey Curtis, you know these guys? They're from Los Angeles.' I looked at the album cover and I said, 'Yeah, that's Arthur and there's Johnny Echols.' It was Love. I said, 'Man, I know these guys!' I couldn't believe it."

Across the nation, anti-war demonstrations, draft resistance, and student unrest on campuses turned increasingly into violent confrontation, making the previous year's teen-curfew riot on the Sunset Strip seem trivial by comparison. Nonetheless, that protest, and the authoritarian response of the police, was now part of the fabric of the times, as was the lingering civil rights residue of the 1965 Watts riot in LA and similar unrest in other major urban centers with substantial black populations. Added to this was the increasingly entrenched administration of President Lyndon Baines Johnson ("Hey, hey, LBJ / How many kids did you kill today?" would become a familiar, Vietnam referencing provocation at protest meetings of the era), escalating drug use, and the widening generation gap. Together, these ingredients made for a highly charged political and social landscape.

All these circumstances and conditions inevitably permeated Arthur's writing that spring, as he prepared to record Love's third album. "I think there's little doubt that the tenor of the times subtly impacted what was going on in Arthur's head," says Jim Bickhart. Certainly, the spring of 1967 provided Arthur with much to chew over, the changes going on in the wider world paralleling those he and Love had experienced over the remarkable preceding year. Indeed, while operating behind the flower power façade, Arthur had his finger firmly on the pulse of undercurrents in LA society. In early 1967, he would perceptively articulate what was, for most, the darker side of California dreaming. "There was a lot of depth to Arthur's songs and in his lyrics," notes Bruce Botnick, who would co-produce Love's next album, *Forever Changes*, with Arthur. "He did go to the dark side but he had a way of talking about it that was unusual. Back then, you couldn't say certain things or talk about certain things. But if you were a really good wordsmith you could say something and cloak it. Arthur was very good at that. So, yes, he was very dark, but you had to really listen hard, or read the words, to know where he was coming from."

From the relative sanctity of his hilltop eyrie, Arthur had been working on a new set of songs based on his colorful, sometimes shady, and often surreal LA existence. They were songs destined to secure a permanent place in the popular music canon.

At the time I wrote those songs, I thought this might be the last album I'd ever make. The words on Forever Changes represented the last words I would say about this planet. The album was made after I thought there was no hope left in the world. I thought I was going to die. I used to sit there in my house on the hillside and think of all the things that had happened, or were happening all around, in my life, as well as to others. I would write them the way I saw them. I like to think that I write things about the way life really is, because if these things were happening to me, chances are they were happening to others, too. That was the key. I never was an, 'I love you, I want you, I need you, ooh baby,' kind of writer.

The lyric to the song 'The Red Telephone' goes: "Sitting on a hillside / Watching all the people die / I'll feel much better on the other side." By which I meant leaving this life for the next. The line, "I'll thumb a ride," was about the hitchhiking fad that was happening when I wrote that song. "I believe in magic / Why, because it is so quick / I don't need power when I'm hypnotized." That was a message, in a sense, to all the power-seeking people who are here today and gone tomorrow. "How do you feel? / I feel real phony when my name is Phil." That was about Phil Tanzini and Bill Clark, although Bill and I had some real good times together – until he broke into my house. "And if you think I'm happy, paint me ..." and then that color word. I had each band member say a different color at the same time – all the colors of people in the world. One said "black," another "white," and so on. It had a great effect and sounded quite interesting. "Sometimes I deal with numbers / I don't know if the third, the fourth, or if the fifth's to fix."

That referred to joints, which at that time were sometimes called 'numbers.'

The song "Between Clark And Hilldale" was written about the experiences that I went through, on a daily basis, at the junction of those streets, where the Whisky A Go Go is. It was actually about talking to someone outside, or inside when the music had stopped. It goes: "What is happening and how've you been? / I gotta go but I'll see you again / And oh, the music is so loud," by which I meant the music at the club. "And then I fade into the crowd," was about being outside the venue, where all the people would be standing around. The gimmick in that song was to start the next verse with the last word from the previous line, in this case the word 'crowd,' as in: "Crowds of people standing everywhere." I would walk across the street from the Whisky to a restaurant I called the Slop Affair. They had a jukebox with my music on it; as the song goes: "And here they always played my songs." That restaurant was actually called the Eating Affair; it was on Sunset. "And me, I wonder if it's wrong," the song continues. 'Wrong' starts the next verse but 'wrong' also meant playing my song on the jukebox when I walked in. Sometimes it made me blush and get nervous. "Wrong or right, they come here just the same," was talking about the restaurant and its menu. "Telling everyone about their games," means the things the people were saying to each other, as was: "If you think it's obsolete / Then you go back across the street." If I thought they were talking about the news or something out of date, I would just turn around and go back across the street to the Whisky. "Moon's a common scene around my town / Here where everyone is painted brown," I just threw in because I'm brown. "And if with you that's not the way / Let's go paint everybody gray," meant if you were prejudiced.

'The Good Humor Man He Sees Everything Like This' starts off: "Hummingbirds hum why do they hum? / Little girls wearing pigtails in the morning in the morning / La la la ta ta ta / Merry go rounds are going round in and all over / The town in the morning, in the morning." The way I wrote this song is maybe how The Beatles wrote some of theirs. I got up one morning and drove over to my old school, Dorsey High, to watch the kids going to and fro. I wanted to see if any ideas would come into my head. Little girls wearing pigtails were the last thing I saw.

Besides those omnipresent societal circumstances, there were also internal upheavals driving a wedge into the core of Love. "Before we became famous and popular we were able to come together as friends and brothers and really have a good time," says Johnny. "We were totally united: living together, practicing together, and playing together. If it had stayed that way, we could have done some incredible work. But as more people started to recognize the group, there became these little factions. Arthur had his little clique, Bryan had his, and Kenny and I each had ours. They began to pull the group apart."

"I wasn't hanging with the same people Arthur was," Bryan MacLean told Neal Skok. "I was steering myself out of the rock music crowd. I started going to parties in the nice part of town. I became good friends with Dino, Dean Martin's son, who played with [Hollywood singing group] Dino Desi & Billy. It seems to me that Arthur kicked me out of the band a few times. I had it in my head that we didn't need to rehearse because we played at clubs quite a bit. I skipped a couple of rehearsals. I was a snob at heart and was known as a snob. I thought I was something. When you're not happy with yourself, you look down on other people."

Compounding an increasingly divisive situation was the specter of harder drugs. While certain band members were no strangers to cannabis and to psychedelics, the Summer of Love would find cocaine and heroin gradually becoming their drugs of choice. "There was the allure of jazz and blues musicians doing it," notes Johnny of the harder intoxicants. "Don Conka had done [heroin]. We knew it wasn't good. I had an uncle who was an addict and was in prison at the time, and I knew what it had done to my family."

For years, interviewers have been asking me about drugs. Do they think I'm a chemist? Whatever drugs I took, I took because I was trying to be in with the in-crowd at that time. That's why we were all doing it. I was easily influenced. I always think about kids and I wouldn't recommend drugs to anybody. I don't especially like the idea of somebody watching me act like a fool because I'm seeing something they don't see. What's the difference between a hallucination and what's really there? The fact is you saw it, whether you saw it in your subconscious or as if it was in a dream. If you saw people in that dream that you knew in the past and they come to you and talked to you, how then can you actually tell yourself that they didn't? A lot of us took drugs. Who put the wine here to drink and the grapes that made the wine? Who put the weed here to smoke? God did. That's who.

Through the late winter and into the spring of 1967, Love gigged sporadically, often up the coast in San Francisco. In March, they were at the city's Winterland Ballroom, headlining a show billed as The First Annual Love Circus, and returned to play the Rock Garden later that same month. Back in January, Kenny Forssi had subbed for Bruce Palmer at a Buffalo Springfield gig at Gazzarri's in West Hollywood after Bruce had been deported back to Canada. "That started a bunch of rumors that I'd quit Love," he recalled. Kenny lived a few doors from the band's singer, Richie Furay, and his guitarist, Neil Young. "Everybody had fun and I made 100 bucks that night," Kenny recalls of his one-off appearance. The fee for his efforts would have been appreciated, too, as Love's bookings were down on the previous year, even though the lifestyles of the individual band-members remained lavish. On May 22, following another trip to San Francisco to play the Winterland Ballroom's Rock Revolution show, Love returned to Bido Lito's for a six-night stand that packed the tiny club once again.

While the remainder of Love may have had more free time on their hands, Arthur was busy composing his ambitious yet introspective new set of songs, material that would see the light of day on *Forever Changes*. From the outset, the album was conceived with orchestration in mind. For Arthur, the progression from folk-rock to jazz-rock and onward to orchestral-rock seemed perfectly logical. As early as the "7 & 7 Is" sessions the previous June, he had been experimenting with a softer approach – using acoustic guitars on the demo song "Hummingbirds."

Jac Holzman sort of gave me the idea of using acoustic guitars instead of electric. I guess that after hearing "7 & 7 Is," with the atomic bomb explosion, he thought it was the end and the only thing left for us to do was to literally blow up the world. So I think he suggested the acoustic direction, and it wasn't a bad idea at all. Thank you, Jac.

Rehearsals for the album sessions had been held at Arthur's house but the complex arrangements he had in his head were not easily conveyed to the individual players, nor was there sufficient time to work on them thoroughly. In most instances, the songs were presented as sketches and each player was encouraged to create a suitable part to fit the overall arrangement. There were several additional issues which adversely affected the rehearsals and impacted on the first round of recording sessions. One was that Arthur had conceived many of the songs with specific parts for strings and horns. For someone unschooled in music theory, and with a limited range of chords at his disposal on guitar, explaining these arrangements proved difficult and frustrating. Johnny Echols: "Arthur was a true wordsmith but his musical talent left a lot to be desired. He wouldn't practice enough to be a musician. His reality was such that he was able to see things most of us don't."

Once again, Arthur's genius lay in his ability to imagine songs, with fully formed lyrics and melodies. He still relied on the others to flesh out the arrangements to fit his vision, however. "Basically, Arthur would come in and sing the song, or at least play some of its chords," explains Johnny. "He often wasn't able to do the whole song on the piano as he couldn't play all of the chords. While he could perhaps play some interactions and the counterpoint, he wasn't able to play seventh chords, or chords that would tend to embellish the song more. He only knew major and minor chords. A lot of times he would just give us the basics of the song and the rest of us would put the arrangement together. Often, it was just his voice and we would add sixths, sevenths, or minor ninths to his major chords. On the recordings, Arthur's sung melodies would have to change because of these chord voicings."

"The other guys in Love may have been bit players," says Jim Bickhart, of the subordinate role habitually ascribed to the other band-members in crafting Love's sound, "but I don't think they could have participated in a project as ambitious as *Forever Changes* without having *some* input or thoughts on the songs and arrangements. Johnny Echols can credibly claim that the guitar parts on *Forever Changes* are his. Arthur, I'm sure, didn't necessarily tell him what to play but supported what he played. The other guys, too."

"There was only one Love and that was us," Johnny insists. "Years later, Arthur would introduce me as the guy responsible for this and that and say that if it wasn't for Johnny Echols there would be no Love. He was really warm and gracious and I appreciated it, but it was a bit late. I can't say there was bitterness but there was some tension there. We all put our hearts and souls into those records, and if you're not going to get a lot of money at least you should get recognized for what you've done. I still hear people who think Arthur played everything on *Forever Changes,* and there was one British writer who claimed Arthur played all my guitar solos. Unfortunately, those myths have been carried on for decades and people still believe them."

Another issue arose over Bryan and Johnny's songwriting contributions. Arthur's dominance over the compositions had become a source of frustration for the others, and they plotted a work-to-rule campaign once the group entered Sunset Sound Recorders in June to begin cutting the album. "There were a few of my songs that Arthur told me he planned to use but later they were rejected," Bryan told Neal Skok. "So I was probably not into it as much as I would have been if more of my songs had been used. I thought that my songs had enough strength to be included."

There was a further situation that impacted on the sessions. Back on October 7 1966, following completion of the *Da Capo* sessions and just prior to the album's release, the members of Love had once again attempted to sever their contract with Elektra Records. This time they'd claimed that the label was in breach of the original contract, dated January 4 of that year, and insisted on an immediate release. Elektra, through their lawyer, Al Schlesinger, countered on May 9 1967 with their own accusation of breach of contract, citing the fact that, as of that date, Love had yet to return to the studio to record a contractually obligated third album. In order to rectify the legal stalemate between the two parties, the May 9 agreement set forth that Love would record at Sunset Sound between June 9 and 16 (excepting June 11) with a producer agreeable to both parties. In the event that a mutually-agreed upon producer could not be found, Jac Holzman would serve in that capacity. The band would undertake to record 12 tracks (the finished album would actually comprise 11 tracks, with one fully completed outtake) and, should Elektra fail to release the tracks within four months of receiving them, the label would then formally release the band from its contract without further obligations. Furthermore, all monies owing still held in trust and not as yet dispersed to Grass Roots Music, the band's publishing company, would be paid out upon signing the new agreement, the rate being one-and-a-half cents per composition, increasing to two cents for a 'pop single.' As principal songwriter, Arthur stood to gain more from this disbursement. The contract named the four original Love members and noted that the provisions would also apply to anyone employed by the band for the purpose of recording, which, it noted, included Michael Stuart. Arthur was identified as signatory for Grass Roots Music. For their signatures on this new agreement the band would be advanced $5,000. They all signed.

The effect of the agreement on the recording sessions for *Forever Changes* revolved around Article Two, which stated that if, following satisfactory completion of the recording sessions and submission of tapes (along with a tally of all related costs, including session musicians, equipment and studio rentals, tape, engineering expenses, and union scale payments), the total outgoings amounted to less than $25,000, the band would pocket the difference. The terms of this new agreement were mutually beneficial. If the band could bring the album in within a reasonable cost, somewhere below that total budget figure (an extremely generous one for 1967), the group could walk away with some instant cash, while Elektra were guaranteed to receive Love's third album. It was, in effect, a form of blackmail. Jac Holzman had learned that when it came to Arthur, money talked.

Rhino Records' 2008 deluxe reissue of *Forever Changes* includes an outtake track on which Johnny, Bryan, Kenny, and Michael are heard segueing from a studio goof-around into a rollicking, impromptu jam version of Sam The Sham & The Pharaohs' garage-rock hit "Wooly Bully." Stationed behind the control-booth glass, Arthur, in his role as co-producer (contrary to popular myth, the frontman did not play a single instrument on *Forever Changes*), can be heard over the studio talkback system exhorting his bandmates to stop the tomfoolery: "Money is time these days," he says. It was true enough, given the nature of the Elektra deal. If the band could keep the costs within reason, they would receive an immediate cash injection without having to wait until the label's costs were recouped to start accruing royalty payments. In fact, royalties would not be earned on *Forever Changes* until many years later, long after the original band had ceased to exist.

As for the sound of the album, according to Johnny: "Arthur had already talked about integrating orchestration on the album. It was not a last-minute decision or an afterthought. We went into the studio knowing we would use strings and horns. We were all recording with that in mind and integrating the orchestration into the songs, rather than as an added afterthought. It was intended as part of a cohesive whole." Achieving that goal required a skilled orchestrator. To that end, Bruce Botnick suggested Arthur work with a young arranger named David Angel.

There's a guy by the name of David Angel who wrote charts and arranged music. I was introduced to him as someone who would help me out with the horns and string parts for the album. I would play the song for him and hum the horn and

*string parts that I wanted in the songs and he would write the notes down on
paper. After a while, it was fitting together pretty good. The story about David
Angel writing all the horn and string parts on Forever Changes was just not true.
I wrote them, thank you! David did add and suggest things that were also used.*

A native of Los Angeles, David Angel had grown up around classical music.
His father, an astronomer, played violin in his spare time, and his mother's family,
originally Russian, were all musicians – aside from careers as doctors and lawyers
– who'd had their own orchestra back in the old country. David studied classical
composition from age 15, yet trod a parallel musical path as a jazz saxophone
player. "It wasn't so common for musicians to live in both worlds – classical and
jazz – back then," he points out in his soft-spoken, studious manner. "It was very
rare, but I was fortunate to have a teacher who was like that. So I benefited from
having both musical foundations, and it made a big difference in my career."
David began his professional life tutoring a television and film music editor at
Paramount Studios. "He needed to read music better, so I taught him every week.
I was 19. Once, he asked me if I wanted to attend a recording session for [long-
running television Western series] *Bonanza*. At the session [noted soundtrack
composer] David Rose walked over. He said he'd heard of me and asked if I
wanted to work with him. From then on, I was a film and TV composer. That
would have been around 1960 or so. The studio kept me in the classical vein, but
I also continued playing jazz with my own band in LA."

When Bruce Botnick asked his mother – a music copyist for the likes of Frank
Sinatra arranger Nelson Riddle – to suggest someone to assist with scoring Love's
songs, she recommended David, who had worked as an orchestrator on sessions
for Riddle. "I brought David in and we sat down with Arthur," Bruce recalls. "By
that point, Arthur had started hearing counter-melodies. So I had Arthur sing all
the string and brass lines to David, who would make notes, then go off and
translate Arthur's vision into arrangements. Then they'd get together again and
David would play the arrangements for Arthur. He did bring in a lot of own his
ideas, too. Arthur liked them. David did an extraordinary job. Arthur suggested
many of the arrangements and that's one of the reasons why it all sounds as one,
because it *was* Arthur, too."

Not much older than Arthur, David had the experience and imagination to
allow the untutored songwriter to bring his more elaborate ideas to fruition. "In

film-studio work, you're dealing with classical musicians, and often the background themes are classical. I spent my life in those backgrounds. No one, outside the film music community, knew my name, because I was a ghost writer, but people in the industry knew of me. Back in 1967, when I got the call, I had never heard of Love."

Working with Arthur was an extraordinary experience for David, one he still marvels at today. He would be adamant in refusing to take a credit for arranging the songs on *Forever Changes,* choosing to be listed on the record jacket as 'orchestrator' instead: "It was my idea to call Arthur the arranger on the album and me the orchestrator. With Bryan's songs, I was more of an arranger, although he arranged the guitars [David is listed as 'arranger' on both the Bryan McLean compositions that would grace *Forever Changes*]. The difference was that Arthur communicated with me without words and without instruction. He knew some things, but he didn't know how to express them and had no training. He would refer to a 'string instrument,' a cello or violin, say, and I got the idea finally that he was referring to *any* stringed instrument. He would use general words like 'strings' or 'brass.' Sometimes he'd play a note on the piano and look at me, so I would make a mental note to make sure that note got in there. It was a largely non-verbal communication."

David still regards his experience on *Forever Changes* as unique. "To be involved in that project was something special. Arthur and I sat together at the piano, at his house, every day for about three weeks. There was a kind of magic between us. I was an experienced composer but about the same age as Arthur. I think he picked up on the fact that I wasn't a fool and that he didn't have to explain a lot to me. He just kept playing his songs over, and I would take notes: very rough transcripts. At first, his songs seemed a little different. He wasn't a piano player, so he was limited and would find the chord like someone would on the guitar. Then I began to feel the movement and the unique chord progressions of his, that inimitable music that influenced so many others. I'd never worked like that before. Usually, I got an assignment the day before and would work on it overnight. It would be ready for the next day. Then, I'd move on to the next project. With Arthur, I don't remember hearing any tracks or demo recordings. I just wrote the scores, working with him directly."

The orchestration of rock music had previously tended toward after-the-fact additions to finished tracks, typically without the artist's direct input. Arthur's vision was different; a seamless integration of band and orchestra within the superstructure of the songs. Even though the horns and strings would be overdubbed later on *Forever Changes,* when the band went into the studio to lay down the basic tracks it was with the knowledge of the larger arrangements in mind. It was this distinctive approach, with songs conceived and crafted in an alliance between songwriter and orchestrator before committing them to tape, that set *Forever Changes* apart from contemporary albums. Arthur heard the elaborate arrangements in his head, his band gave structure and substance to his ideas, and David brought Arthur's orchestral visions to reality.

"The normal way is that an arranger listens to the tracks after they're completed, writes an arrangement at home, then overdubs it onto the tracks," explains David. "That's not what happened with songs on *Forever Changes.* That's what made it different. One of the few things Arthur told me when we started working together was that he didn't want it to sound like overdubs, like normal rock bands. He wanted the music to be organic, with the orchestration within the groove, within the songs. Back then, arrangers who were doing overdubs simply listened to the tracks and had someone make a lead sheet [basic music notation]. If there was a problem, they'd just hold a G, or whatever, over to the next bar. It was just background. It wasn't serious. With Love, everything was integral. Every detail had its point and its place; it was a kind of magnetism, drawing the orchestra into the group and the song as opposed to merely being coloration in the background."

It was to prove a symbiotic marriage of minds. In Arthur, David Angel encountered a remarkably gifted and imaginative musician, a cut above the customary three-chord rock'n'roll composer. "I found Arthur to be an extraordinarily serious and deep individual who was stuck in this very superficial idiom. I know not everyone sees rock'n'roll as superficial, but I see it as that. The flexibility of guitar, bass, drums, and perhaps a keyboard is limited. Arthur was in this environment but he had the mind of someone who saw beyond it. He was extraordinarily serious in his attitude toward the work. Even though he had never had any experience of composing, he had the inner quality that could have applied itself, along with those skills and that knowledge. He took his own work seriously and he wanted me to also take it seriously."

David doesn't blanch when the term 'genius' is applied to Arthur. "It's hard to find another word to describe him. He had the depth to understand what he was working with. My impression of Arthur's songs was that this wasn't just pop music. He had the authority of someone who really knew that what they're doing is from down deep. That seriousness, in a rock'n'roll context, might seem like he's presenting himself as the boss but, actually, in the classical world someone like Arthur would be regarded as having a certainty about them. I saw it like that. I began to separate him from the idiom that we were working in [and regard him] as someone who really had a seriousness to him. That was something I had never experienced in pop music. One word to describe Arthur would be 'deep.' He was as straight as he could be with me. He wasn't stoned. He kind of held his head high when the other guys would make noise or talk. He was trying to rise above this stuff going on around the house that seemed irrelevant to what we were doing. He had a desire to focus on the work and not be distracted by anything. If the other guys got noisy, he'd just give them a look or say, 'Take it outside.' It wasn't apologetic or angry. He just didn't want to waste time on it. The other guys seemed to be hanging around with nothing on their minds."

The depth and insight of Arthur's words also impressed David. "I thought that lyrics like this don't come from a fool. They come from someone who is genuinely poetic. A lot of poetry is about the fear of death. I had the impression that these were not merely some words but an internal story about himself and his view of life. I had a similar impression with Bryan's lyrics, even though his words weren't quite as deep as Arthur's. I think of Arthur as being more surrealistic than Bryan, but in both cases, I thought their lyrics were exceptional within the idiom of rock'n'roll."

David also feels that Arthur's talents were such that they might have found other musical outlets. "The whole experience showed me that, had Arthur had the opportunity to study music seriously, he could have been an orchestral composer. He was a natural musician and also a natural thinker. That combination suggests a symphony composer. No one got what he was doing, not even the other rock groups, until later. You can feel his influence today. He also didn't have a musical education which, in itself, isn't vital, but what he lacked was belief in his capacity to be a composer. And, of course, being drugged a lot kept his thinking from going from A to B. It would go from A to Z and back. He didn't have what you would call logic, but he had an instinct for deep thinking that didn't get straightened out. It was the power of his focus and willingness to repeat things that impressed me, to replay the same song, day after day, for me. He had that dedication and ability to stay with it, without being distracted."

Prior to commencing the *Forever Changes* recording sessions, Neil Young had been mooted as a potential producer. Having quit Buffalo Springfield at the end of May over issues about control of the band, Neil was at a loose end. He had been pulling away from the group for some time and had already recorded tracks on his own under the aegis of former Phil Spector arranger Jack Nitzsche. By the end of May, he felt confident enough to quit the band and launch a solo career (which initially failed to ignite, leading him to return in August, tail between legs). Sunset Sound was Neil's studio of choice and one of his collaborations with Nitzsche, the lushly produced ballad "Expecting To Fly," had been engineered by Bruce Botnick.

"I had just recorded with Neil and had developed a deep relationship with him," recalls Bruce. "I was talking with him, and he said he hadn't settled on what he wanted to do as a solo artist, although he really *did* know. So I said to him, 'Do you want to produce a record?' and Neil said, 'Yeah!' So I suggested it to Jac and he loved the idea. Neil already knew Arthur; the two of them sat down together and Arthur ran over some of the songs for him. We were just getting ready to go when Neil came to the studio and said, 'Man, I can't do it. I'm hearing too much in my own head for me to immerse myself in someone else's music.'"

Johnny recalls Neil Young showing up but suspects it would never have worked out with him in the producer's chair. "We were contemporaries and very good friends with the guys in Buffalo Springfield. If we were playing a club and Neil came in, he'd jump up on stage and play with us. Bruce said he had a friend who needed some money and would come in and maybe produce a few of the songs on *Forever Changes*. He didn't tell us it was Neil. I guess Neil told Bruce not to tell us it was him.

"When he showed up," Johnny continues, "we all started laughing and said, 'Come on, this won't work. We're not going to listen to Neil.' We did maybe one song together ["The Daily Planet," reportedly arranged by Neil] and that was it. He got some money for that day because he desperately needed it." In the end, production was left to Bruce and Arthur. "We said goodbye to Neil," recalls Bruce. "I called Jac and told him I was ready to make the record, and he said, 'Go for it.' Arthur was OK with that."

Almost a month after signing the May 9 agreement, Love entered Sunset Sound to begin recording their third album. They ran into difficulties from the outset, and therein lies the greatest of all Love-related myths.

When it was time to do the Forever Changes album, I had all my songs together but my band was not all together. I didn't understand at first, but then it hit me hard. Their habits had gotten the better of them. My band was so strung out on heroin, they couldn't function. I thought I had my own habit under control. Just for the record, I've never been strung out on heroin, not for one day in my life. I don't even like heroin. Just ask any of the people who really know me.

Arthur's memory of the first day of the sessions chimes with the widely propagated and perpetuated legend: that his bandmates were too wasted on drugs to perform and thus he replaced them with session musicians. "If you say something long enough it becomes fact," says Bruce of the popular myth. Certainly there were problems on the first day of the sessions, but no band-member has ever attributed those difficulties to heroin use. No one denies that harder drugs had pervaded the group, and Arthur was certainly no exception, although his preferred stimulant would be cocaine rather than heroin. Later, the band's drug use would become an insuperable problem, but at this point their narcotic predilections were yet to become debilitating.

"Drugs weren't a factor in the band during *Forever Changes*," insists Johnny. "It was after that that Kenny and I both become totally involved in heroin." As Bryan related to Neal Skok: "It seems to me I was chipping [using heroin infrequently and in low doses] by then but I'm not sure. It seems to me that during that time drug use was pretty acceptable everywhere. When I got involved in the Beverly Hills set there was just a higher quality of drugs." Michael Stuart admits his own involvement with heroin did not begin until 1968, during the dog days of the original Love line-up.

"The heroin wasn't around during my time with the band," emphasizes Bruce Botnick. "Not during *Forever Changes*. They were smoking a lot of pot and hashish and that's why they couldn't do the sessions initially. Acid really wasn't a big deal, by that time. It wasn't around during the *Forever Changes* sessions. When I was working with them they were just kids, as I was. They were smoking pot and things like that. But they never did it in the studio. It was still very illegal then, and smoking pot was *verboten* in the studio. They came in fairly focused."

That such a remarkably cohesive and inspired body of music as *Forever Changes* could have been recorded in an atmosphere charged with turbulence and divisiveness seems astonishing. With the clock ticking and tapes set to roll, Bryan,

Johnny, and Kenny dragged their feet, tuning up interminably and generally failing to take the session seriously. "Bryan was holding out," says Johnny. "He wanted more songs on the album. *Forever Changes* was supposed to be a double album, so I had written some songs, Bryan had a whole bunch of songs, and Arthur had songs. But then Elektra told us they didn't have the money to do the double set and so it would be a single album." Jac Holzman maintains a slightly different view. "We never conceived or planned *Forever Changes* as a double album. That would be asking too much of the artists by way of excellence and too much commitment on the part of record fans. Elektra did very few double albums." Johnny remembers there being enough material for a double set. "There were a lot of Bryan's songs and all my songs. None of them got recorded except for one jazz song that we did but which didn't make it onto the album. Bryan and Kenny had worked it out that they would just lay back on Arthur's stuff, hoping that the record company would want more of Bryan's songs. That's why Bryan was being stubborn and boycotting things."

Frustration mounted on both sides of the studio glass. That the band had not been given sufficient time to learn the intricate song arrangements added to the problems. As so much of the orchestration had already been predetermined and charted, there was little scope for improvising parts. "Initially, I took the band into the studio and they were literally incapable and disinterested," confirms Bruce. "It wasn't the drugs. I think their confidence had been shaken somehow, and they just weren't up to the level of this music. It was very sophisticated and I think they were frightened of it. So it was a mess, that first session."

Michael Stuart has a similar memory of the session. "Once we got the guitars tuned, the moment we started playing you could hear it was uneven. It was awful. Johnny, Kenny, Bryan, and I hadn't spent enough time going over our parts individually. We were all relying on the time we spent at group rehearsals to get to where we needed to be, musically, in order to record the album. There just wasn't a sense of urgency at those rehearsals. We got high too much. We simply figured that when we got into the studio it would all come together. We were wrong."

Arthur grew increasingly impatient with his colleagues and the tone of his communications over the studio talkback reflected his mood. "Sarcastic chit-chat" Michael calls it. "Arthur was yammering over the booth microphone, engaging in what was supposed to be 'humorous interplay,' but it wasn't making it. The verbal barbs were mean-spirited and inappropriate and they made the others in the studio uncomfortable." The forced banter only worsened the atmosphere of tension and none of the musicians could relax enough to perform. "At that point, our interpersonal relationships were contentious at best," Michael admits. "I think Arthur was of a mind to do what was best for his own interests. I understood that, from Arthur's position."

After several exasperating hours with little to show, and very conscious of the money coming out of his own pocket, Arthur conferred with Bruce in the control booth. They announced the outcome of their deliberations: the band would be replaced by studio musicians who would complete the basic tracks. The members of Love would contribute to any overdubs as required and would sing backing vocals on the album.

When I tried to use my band in the studio, they were nodding and farting more than playing. It was funny, at first. I thought they would at least snap out of it for the album. I can safely say that not all of them were wiped [stoned], but you see, I don't read or write music on paper. I wrote the songs on Forever Changes *while playing my acoustic guitar and either humming or singing the parts I wanted them to play. Doing it this way required undivided attention from all that were participating. They should have been rehearsing the songs long before coming to the studio but, as it was, they just couldn't seem to concentrate. They missed chord changes. They came in at the wrong times. They weren't concentrating on what they were doing.*

When you show your new songs to people the way I do, it has to be a group effort, so that each person not only learns the song but also makes himself or his instrument a part of that song. This way you get that special feeling in the music. So there I was, with my band and some extraordinary faith, but, in this case, faith without action just didn't make it. I tried it with them until I'd spent thousands of dollars, then I finally had to tell them it wasn't going to work.

After a break to cool down and gain some focus, the band again tried laying down the backing track for Arthur's song "The Daily Planet," only to stumble once more. "We did maybe seven or eight takes before Arthur said, 'Hold it,'" recalls Michael. "He came out and told us his hair-brained idea that he was going to bring in session guys, The Wrecking Crew, and be like The Beach Boys, with them doing our parts. It was laughably inappropriate. It was obvious what he was trying to do.

He was trying to dump us. It was like, 'Sorry guys, I gave you your chance but time is money. I don't think you're gonna be able to do it.' It was so transparent. Arthur was concerned about racking up a big studio bill with all these delays."

While it has often been assumed that the intention was to lay down all the basic tracks with The Wrecking Crew (drummer Hal Blaine, bassist Carol Kaye, guitarist Billy Strange, and Don Randi on keyboards) – LA's top session players who commanded triple scale fees for their services – in fact, the decision was merely a ploy to shake up the band. "Those guys in The Wrecking Crew would have cost the label more money than us," Michael points out, "because they got paid more than union scale. All we got was scale, so doing an entire album with those guys would have cost much more. The plan wasn't to replace us altogether."

Whatever the expense, The Wrecking Crew duly arrived next day to lay down some basic tracks. They worked on three of Arthur's songs: "The Daily Planet," "Andmoreagain," and one other that no one recalls specifically (Johnny suggests it might have been "The Good Humor Man He Sees Everything Like This"). Jac Holzman was kept fully apprised of the developing situation. Bruce: "I called Jac and told him it wasn't working, that we'd got terrific songs but the band can't play. I said I want to try something: I want to bring in The Wrecking Crew and record a couple of songs with them. I ran this by Arthur, and he agreed. I told him we weren't going to get the album if we carried on this way. We didn't have the time or the money. The other guys were there in the control room sitting on the couch, in tears. Bryan was sobbing. That was true. They realized they were blowing it, big time. So we did three songs [with the session players]; we only put two on the album. I wish we had re-recorded all of them with the band afterwards, but we kept two. When I listen to that album those two tracks sound so different."

Don Randi was a highly respected, veteran session keyboardist, used to all kinds of studio situations. He recalls the *Forever Changes* tracking session. "I guess they were having some problems with the band, and it may have had to do with drugs, but I can't verify that. It was just too out of hand. Out of necessity, they got The Wrecking Crew because that was a hot band. Why not use those guys who were making all the hit records? We were pretty busy. Lots of times when we were brought in we were augmenting what was already going on." Don had been at Sunset Sound with Bruce the month before, recording "Expecting To Fly" with Neil Young. "Sunset Sound was like a second home for us – that and Gold Star Studios. I remember I was playing the Steinway grand piano on the Love session.

YOU SET THE SCENE

It was a great concert piano. I also remember the spontaneity of that whole thing, having to learn the songs on the spot. There were no charts, but I scribbled notes for myself and learned it right there. Love needed someone strong in the studio, like Bruce, to call the shots. Arthur would make suggestions – looking into his eyes, you knew his mind was going a million miles a minute. He was hearing good stuff in his head; he was a very creative guy. He would give us the basic structure of the song and we would give back our interpretation of what we thought he wanted. That's the way it happened in those days, and we ended up making the arrangements ourselves. If the producer liked it, then that's the way it would stay. If not, we'd try something else. It was a joint effort. We got to express ourselves a little bit rather than just sit there and rigidly read notes." Don would return to Sunset Sound in September to overdub piano on the song "Bummer In The Summer" and harpsichord on "The Red Telephone."

Jac Holzman recalls the session musicians being drafted in. "It was Bruce who brought in the studio musicians, and it scared the shit out of Love. He told me he was going to do it. I said, 'Go ahead, we've tried everything else; maybe we can shame them into it.' The plan wasn't to replace them. The plan was to give them their shot. I don't screw around with artists' careers, but sometimes a little tough love is necessary. As the owner of the company, I know I'm going to get another shot, but they may not. So the obligation was to do everything we could, short of driving ourselves nuts."

"At the end of that [Wrecking Crew] session the guys in Love were really beside themselves," says Bruce. "I was sitting up at the console and Arthur was sitting beside me watching the whole thing, too. The guys were in a terrible state. Arthur was aware of their reaction. I was hoping to shake them into getting their act together, and Arthur went along with me. He knew that this album wasn't going to be Love without those guys' participation. It wasn't going to feel right. He knew that The Wrecking Crew could bang it out, but it wouldn't have the same feel. Afterwards, all four of the guys said, 'We can't believe this. We're better than this. We can do this.' They were just shaken, emotionally, by the whole thing. So I looked at Arthur and said, 'We'll stop now. You guys go and rehearse together and, if you're up to it, we'll do it.' Arthur said, 'Great. We'll give it a try. We'll see what happens.' And we did it. We went to Western Recorders two months later and did the tracks. And we did them in a big hurry. We did all those songs in about three or four days. The band was together by then and really knew those songs.

That's the last time I could get away with that [kind of brinkmanship]. They ultimately rose to the challenge and the album is testament to that."

"We were severely disappointed, that's true, but blubbering and crying? Come on!" says Michael, his normally calm demeanor shaken, slightly. He recalls the group's response to bringing in The Wrecking Crew. "We all reacted differently. There were people in the group of a mind to say, 'Fine with us. I'm not interested in being here recording these songs anyway.' Let's just say I was the only one who was outraged by this suggestion."

"Bruce Botnick claims he fired the group, but if he'd tried that he'd still be looking for his teeth," says Johnny. "The session players didn't work because it was immediately evident that it sounded nothing like Love. It would have been a disaster. Bruce and Arthur heard it and realized it didn't sound like us at all. So when we came back, everyone was serious. Bryan realized that lying back on Arthur's songs wasn't going to work, so we came back and played on the rest of the tracks." Johnny's guitar was later overdubbed onto the backing tracks cut with the session players. Kenny Forssi was always proud of the fact that he actually played the bass on "The Daily Planet" after the unquestionably skilled Carol Kaye was unable to handle his challenging part. "Kenny was showing her his part to play and Arthur walked by and said, 'That sounds good, Kenny,'" recalls a smiling Michael. "Arthur said, 'Why don't you just play on the track?' Steam was coming out of her ears."

Despite the May 9 agreement stipulating that sessions were to be completed by June 16, Elektra agreed to postpone the album recording until August to allow the band to pull themselves, and the material, together sufficiently. The label might have insisted on using the session players and banging out the album but, wisely, they chose to back the band. Rather than looking for the quick buck, Elektra were committed to Love.

The band played live only a couple of times over the next two months; they preferred to practice their individual parts in anticipation of resumed album sessions. One gig they passed on was the Monterey International Pop Festival, held June 16 to 18 at the Monterey County Fairgrounds, south of San Francisco. "Love is probably the only band that turned down an invitation to play the Monterey Pop Festival," acknowledges Michael. A strong performance at Monterey could have altered the band's future; however, given the recent studio debacle, it's possible they had more to lose if they'd not been able to pull off a tight set.

Effectively the first rock festival, Monterey serves as an epochal moment in rock music's evolution, bridging, at least temporarily, the widening gulf between the Los Angeles and San Francisco scenes. Many regard the festival as a watershed moment in which the recording industry first grasped that rock'n'roll had evolved from a passing fad into a durable art form. Beyond the aesthetics, Monterey showed record labels that there was big money to be made in signing rock groups. "I think a lot of our interest in bands stemmed from our being at the Monterey Pop Festival and not having an artist on there," notes Jerry Moss, the 'M' in A&M Records, and the nascent label's president. "We really needed to do something."

Harvey Kubernik: "Love was a band widely admired, by fans and musicians alike, in both the LA and Frisco music scenes. They would have slotted in perfectly at the festival and would have most likely secured a plum slot on the closing night. I know for a fact that Love was invited to play Monterey." The band's name remained absent from the festival roster, all the same. They had thrown up the chance of instant immortality bestowed upon all those who did appear. In fact, the festival's choice of acts was skewed slightly in favor of the northern Californian scene, something which helped launch the careers of several, then largely unknown, San Francisco artists including Big Brother & The Holding Company (featuring Janis Joplin), The Grateful Dead, Moby Grape, Country Joe & The Fish, and the Steve Miller Band. It also provided the all-important springboard for Arthur's old friend Jimi Hendrix. "We all know that if The Doors, The Seeds, and Love had been on that bill, we would have had a slightly different pop festival," notes Harvey. Of the aforementioned groups only Love was actually invited to play.

"You would have had to be crazy to turn down Monterey," says Jac Holzman, "but Arthur did. The thing about Monterey was that The Doors weren't invited and Love was, and the reason they were invited was because so many musicians respected their music." One of the principals behind the festival was Dunhill Records president Lou Adler. His involvement would act as a deterrent to Arthur.

I heard about this show called the Monterey Pop Festival. We were invited to play there, but then they said it was a non-profit organization put on by Lou Adler and John Phillips [of The Mamas & The Papas]. Lou Adler was the one with the group called The Grass Roots on his label, Dunhill Records. I had bad thoughts about non-profits and getting my original name stolen, and so I passed. That would have been a great promotional gig for us. They told us we would get lots of exposure but I'm still not sorry that we didn't play that one.

"I've heard all about the animosity Arthur had for Lou Adler," says Harvey Kubernik, "but there's another reason why Arthur passed on the Monterey Pop Festival. He wasn't going to play for free." As Bryan MacLean told Neal Skok, in hindsight, had the group been asked, they would have agreed to play. "That, I believe, was the turning point for us. When we didn't do Monterey that was when we missed the train."

"I was at the Monterey Pop Festival," says Jim Bickhart, "and I think Love would have gone down really well there. Even though they were an LA band, they didn't seem like one; they were viewed differently to other LA artists. They were weird enough that they would have gone over well with the northern California crowd – as they did whenever they played in San Francisco."

The recording of *Forever Changes* reconvened on Friday, August 11, in Studio Two of Western Recorders on Selma Avenue, Hollywood. There would be two tracking sessions, from 2pm to 5pm, followed by a dinner break and another session from 6pm to 9pm. No fewer than four backing tracks were completed in this time. The band returned over the next two days for a further pair of three-hour sessions, this time in the main room, Studio One, where backing tracks for the remaining songs were completed.

The speed at which they were able to lay down the complex tracks was testament not only to the band's talents but to their dedication in learning the complex parts over the previous weeks. "We just took some time off," recalls Michael of their preparations. "I don't remember rehearsing as a group. But we would all woodshed on our individual parts so that when we came back in we were able to knock every song out in a reasonable number of takes. We had given up too quickly on that first session, and that trick of bringing in the session players was totally premature. It was mostly an attitude adjustment that made us able to do these songs. We had rehearsed enough times to get the parts down. It's just that [prior to the earlier session] we didn't go over them as many times as we should have. Even *Da Capo* required learning parts in the studio. We were a minimum rehearsal band."

On Tuesday, August 15 the band assembled at Sunset Sound for an evening session of guitar and vocal overdubs that ran from 8pm to 1am. They returned on August 20 for two more sessions, afternoon and evening, to add further vocal overdubs. They then broke until September 9 when still further vocals were added at Sunset Sound. Overdubs continued on September 14 and 15 at the LA home studio of Leon Russell, the noted session musician, keyboard player, and future Joe Cocker collaborator. The tracks were mixed down during a six-hour stint at Sunset Sound the following day, making room for the orchestral overdubs. "We did two vocal overdubs and maybe a guitar dub at Leon Russell's house," recalls Bruce. "I remember Leon had frozen plates of bacon, hash browns, and scrambled eggs in the freezer. You just took them out and heated them up. Arthur thought that was the funniest thing he'd ever seen."

Johnny recalls how the album's most enduring song achieved its very particular flavor. "Bryan started 'Alone Again Or' as another one of his folk songs. I started playing flamenco licks and flourishes in rehearsal, and it went from being a folk song to a Spanish-influenced song. We changed the cadence of it. I was just noodling around, trying to find different things that would compliment what Bryan was doing. I would always rearrange Bryan's songs, trying to add something so as to pull them away from sounding like show tunes. It had that Spanish feel, to me. There were probably two or three overdubs of mine where I'm playing inside the chords of that song. It ended up probably the best known song on that album."

"Unlike Arthur, Bryan didn't know what to tell me," says David Angel, recalling the skeletal nature of "Alone Again Or," as initially presented to him. "He didn't have any idea what he wanted, so I had to ask him a lot of questions to draw out something that I could hold onto. In the end, I made all the suggestions and he would always say that sounded very cool. With Bryan's songs, the orchestration was completely an interpretation from my point of view. On "Alone Again Or," he just told me to take it where I wanted to take it. I heard this very strong Spanish guitar effect and I went with that feeling, more than the song. The song itself had no Spanish effect at all, but the rhythm of the guitar drew me into that feel and I just reacted to it. I suggested to him, 'What if we have a baroque background with a trumpet doing a kind of Spanish style?' It's not Mariachi. It's not Mexican. What makes it Spanish is that the background is baroque in style, not polka. It's like bullfight music, because that's Spanish music."

Johnny adds another pertinent detail: "Arthur didn't even know how we had arranged 'Alone Again Or.' He wasn't there when we put that together and gave it that Spanish feel." Nonetheless, on the finished track it is Arthur's voice, not Bryan's, that is the more prominently mixed of its twin lead vocals. Bryan's voice becomes the supporting line, something which has often been cited as a bone of contention between the two. "That was because Bryan had a different idea for the way he wanted to sing the song," Johnny explains. "When Arthur's voice was louder than his, Bryan wasn't happy. When they were mixing it, Arthur had his voice louder. But I think it sounds better with Arthur's voice mixed on top, because Bryan's voice tended to break a little bit and was reedy and thin. It didn't have the sweetness Arthur's voice had, and that gave the song a more commercial and a more complete sound."

"Arthur wasn't confident in my singing," Bryan revealed to Neal Skok. "So the harmony is actually the melody you're hearing. You're not really hearing the song the way it's written. I was singing lead but they mixed Arthur's harmony over my vocals. That was Arthur. But I understood that because I knew I wasn't that great a singer at that point. He probably did it out of necessity and I probably knew that in my heart."

"We had a problem with the intro guitar part on that song," says Johnny. "I tried it several times, but because it was Bryan's song he wanted to play it. However, Bryan played with heavy steel fingerpicks that you would use in bluegrass. These were loud, not subtle. He hit the top of the guitar with these picks. They turned his guitar down low at the start to try to minimize the noise of his picks on the strings. Then they turned it up as the other instruments come in, because they kind of drowned out the noise. I played it with my fingers and it sounded fine to me, but he said he wanted to play it."

I've always wanted to remix that album, because Bruce started the build-in too low on "Alone Again Or," and you always have to adjust your set to hear it. Although that was a successful song, one day I would like to go back and mix it all over again. It was Bruce Botnick's idea to start that song soft on the entrance and then gradually build it. I think it would be better if the balance was the same all the way through, and I'd also mix it so that the other instruments sounded brighter. Though it turned out OK, I always thought it could have been done better. Bruce was the co-producer with me on the whole Forever Changes album. Throughout those sessions, we argued about everything. I saw him at the Eric Clapton concert in

1974, and he told me that he was sorry and that he just didn't know what I had been trying to do at that time. He said I was a genius. Now, if he didn't know what was happening, who did? After all, he was the producer, right? I really think we could have done a better job on that album. I thought I was the producer. He thought he was the producer. Jac Holzman gave him that title, not me.

"A House Is Not A Motel" would follow "Alone Again Or" on the finished album. Johnny recalls the song's genesis. "It was about the Vietnam War. We were up in San Francisco, at the Warehouse, with Janis Joplin and Big Brother. She was a very loud singer and the band was drowning out any conversation we were trying to have backstage. So we went on the other side of the partition, where the bar was, to get away from her. There was this AWOL soldier there who was drinking and getting louder. We're at our table, just minding our own business and laughing, when he came over, plopped down, and started saying, 'You guys think you're so great. You should be fighting in the war instead of being here, thinking you're so great.' Whether it was jealousy or something else I'm not sure, but he started telling us what it was like [in Vietnam], about the blood mixing with mud and turning into gray rivulets of blood. We were listening to all this and Arthur took it all in, and later he wrote that song with that line about the blood mixing with the mud." As for the fierce double-tracked lead guitar which segues into the song's coda: "The soloing was supposed to represent war, the chaos on a battlefield, people dying, all the wailing, things blowing up, people's fears ... all that. I've read that people think that it's Arthur and I on guitars, but it's actually just me overdubbed, dueling with myself. Arthur never played lead guitar. There was something wrong with the headphone amplifier at the console, so I was unable to hear the first solo. I could hear the backing musicians but I couldn't hear my solo. Here I was trying to have a duel with myself without being able to hear what I'd played. It came out really great, though, considering I was going by memory. It's one of my favorite things we did."

According to Johnny, the song "Andmoreagain" was about a girl Arthur knew. "The title was simply him going back to the song on the first album, 'And More,' and adding 'again.'" In a 1991 interview with Frank Beeson, Arthur said: "Everybody thought it was Ann Morgan, the actress. Give me some credit, man! And ... more ... again: that's your life story. Everybody's life story is 'Andmoreagain.' What is life? Andmoreagain, and some more, and some more." As for "The Daily

Planet," one of the songs begun by The Wrecking Crew, Johnny recalls: "I played the guitar part that shadows the vocals. The studio guitarist, Billy Strange, also played on it, as did Carol Kaye. I think Kenny Forssi played on it, too. And that's Hal Blaine on drums. Michael insists that it's Jim Gordon, but I knew Hal Blaine and had played with him. That was him. Even though Hal did a beautiful job on that track, I still think Michael Stuart is probably one of the most gifted drummers around. He never got the credit he deserved. When you listen to the totally unexpected things he would do, they're still fantastic."

According to Johnny, Bryan MacLean's other composition on *Forever Changes*, "Old Man," almost didn't make the cut for the album. "Bryan's singing is just a little out of tune and they didn't have Auto-Tune software back then to vary the pitch. I tried singing it in that Johnny Mathis voice, but Bryan wanted to sing it. At Bruce's studio, they only had a four-track machine, so we went over to Western Recorders where they had an eight-track and we switched to that. It's an average song, but the strings really make it, and the cymbals, with reverb on them, give it a kind of eerie sound."

According to writer Ben Edmonds, the song is based on the "Troika" movement from Russian composer Sergei Prokofiev's *Lieutenant Kijé Suite*. It's often been suggested that its lyrics concern Bryan's father, something he denied in his interview with Neil Skok. "It was simply my expression about a guy that had been told some things by this wise old man but he doesn't understand it until he falls in love with somebody." Bryan also revealed that he was not pleased with the final version of his song. "To me, 'Old Man' was over-arranged. It had all this drama. It was meant to be simple and direct, almost a folk song. I remember I insulted David [Angel] for what he was trying to do with my song."

As for Arthur's song "The Red Telephone," Johnny says: "That was totally Arthur. He conceived it and came up with ideas about how he wanted us to play it and how he wanted it to sound. That was one of the few times when he offered suggestions on how he wanted us to interact with each other. That came out in rehearsals before the sessions." The evolution of "Maybe The People Would Be The Times Or Between Clark And Hilldale," a song that started life in the jazz-rock vein, was much more organic, Johnny reveals. "We wanted to continue in the direction we were going with 'Stephanie Knows Who,' instrumentally. When we met to rehearse the song, Arthur said, 'Check this out' and he sang the words. After hearing them a couple of times, everyone agreed this was a cool song. I told him that I would need some time to work out my guitar part, so that it would all come together. At the session, I played him the part you hear on the record, and we decided to go for it. After the tracking session, Arthur wanted to go straight to the vocal overdub. As we came to the end of my solo, Arthur began scat singing along with my guitar. David Angel continued the theme with the brass, pacing, then answering, the lead guitar. The results sound like they were planned that way from the beginning, but now you know the rest of the story."

The song "Live And Let Live" was a leftover from the *Da Capo* sessions. "The instrumental line-up, at the time, was just not right for that particular song," says Johnny. "We couldn't find a way to make the sax, flute, or harpsichord fit. When we started looking over material for *Forever Changes*, Arthur said, 'Echols, you're always bitching about not being able to stretch out. Why don't you take "Live And Let Live" and kick ass with it?' He was right, but this was a tough call; the tune was not intuitive, with no rock or blues changes that I could get behind, and it had that dissonant melody. I was forced by the nature of the song to play the high frets exclusively, so I found it hard to find the tune's personality. I wanted to try more and more takes until finally Arthur said, 'Dude, you nailed it.' I remained uncomfortable about it. When the album was released the critics all loved my guitar solo, but I still think, 'just *one more* take … .'"

According to Johnny "The Good Humor Man He Sees Everything Like This" was one of the songs on which Bryan refused to play the rhythm part with any conviction. "He would add a country flavor that was totally inappropriate for the song. He thought that if Arthur's song didn't cut it there would be an opening for one of his tunes. What Bryan failed to understand was that he just did not have the clout to force that kind of play." The country feel would be more appropriately applied to "Bummer In the Summer," however. "That was a kind of Bo Diddley thing. We wanted to play around with it, so we added a country influence. I wanted to play a steel guitar, but we couldn't get one from the studio rental place and I wasn't going to buy one just for one track. So I'm playing country guitar licks. Everyone thought that country music was going to be the next thing."

Arthur's crowning achievement on the album would be an anthemic song suite, running almost seven minutes in length, entitled "You Set The Scene." The song closes the album, its lyrical theme echoing and encompassing Arthur's current fixation with life and death. Johnny Echols: "That song is the one most people associate with *Forever Changes*. 'You Set the Scene' was originally three separate songs that we worked up before putting them together. It was Kenny who came up with the links to put those together but he never got any credit. He put them in the sequence that became the song and worked out the bass line that married the three pieces together. It wasn't easy to do because they were in different keys." Originally, Arthur had included what, to modern ears, is undeniably a rap over the orchestrated coda. However, in mixing the album, Bruce edited it out, leaving the orchestral crescendo wordless. In Rhino Records' 2001 reissue of *Forever Changes*, the original 'rap' mix is included as a bonus track. Johnny explains: "There was a group called The Young Poets: they were the first rap group, although no one called it that back then. It was called 'talking music.' They don't get any credit for starting rap music. But that's what Arthur was emulating. Because it was so radical, Elektra decided to mix it out."

A further bonus on Rhino's reissue is the finished outtake "Wonder People (I Do Wonder)," complete with orchestration from David Angel. "It didn't fit," says Johnny. "It just felt weaker than the rest of the songs, and it is when you listen to the whole album. I think they made the right choice in leaving that one out."

On September 18, the orchestra – eight string players, including Bruce's father Norman Botnick on viola, and four brass players, all under the direction of David Angel – assembled at Sunset Sound for two sessions, morning and afternoon, to overdub their parts on the tracks. Arthur was present, as was Jac Holzman.

I walked into the studio and took a seat in one of the chairs. I must have been there at least 45 minutes when one of the classical musicians said, "If this guy Arthur Lee doesn't show up soon, I'm leaving." I said, "I'm Arthur." Most of them, if not all of them, couldn't believe their eyes. This black hippie guy is Arthur Lee? They looked at me as if to say, "You wrote the music to the charts we're supposed to play?" I said to myself, "Yep, I sure did." David introduced us and we were on our way. Me, a kid who dropped out of school in South LA, in a recording studio with members of the LA Philharmonic Orchestra! Finally, I was about to be able to show my stuff. There I was, with David Angel, going over the charts with classical musicians, to use on our album. David and I worked real well together and I thank him to this day. I not only wrote the music but I also wrote the solos the trumpets and other instruments played. After we laid out the classical parts, the rest of the album was pretty much smooth sailing.

David Angel recalls the orchestral overdub sessions as a serious business. "Arthur was there and sat quietly in the corner the whole time. He never left his chair except to go for a cup of coffee. He never said a word. I think Arthur realized that he had said everything, in his way, and done everything he could to influence me. At the session, he just let the orchestra play. And I think he liked it. At the end, he walked up to me and gave me a compliment. It made me feel that we'd got what he wanted. String players would talk to me during the break and say, 'You're really doing something very unusual here.' They sensed that this was groundbreaking, and they did sessions every day. I think I was 26, and these were older guys, mostly from Europe, complimenting me. They never did that at other sessions, and that meant a lot to me. Once we finished recording the strings and brass, that was the end of my involvement. Elektra kept my scores. I just left them in the studio; I have no idea what happened to them. Maybe they were thrown away, or kept in Elektra's vaults. I never talked with Arthur again. I knew instinctively we wouldn't talk again, unless we worked together. He wasn't the kind of person to just call you up and say 'How are you doing?'"

Bruce would mix the tracks (in three sessions, from September 19 to 21), with Arthur in attendance. He would submit the completed master tapes to Jac who then sequenced the album. It was Jac's decision to discard "Wonder People (I Do Wonder)" and to bookend the album with "Alone Again Or" and "You Set The Scene." He regards the former as "the Rosetta Stone of that album. I don't think *Forever Changes* would have lasted the way it has if it weren't for 'Alone Again Or' and Bruce suggesting David Angel for the arrangements. Take out those arrangements and you remove the portal which carried you into the album's special dimension. It would not have happened without that gateway. And Bruce Botnick's contribution to that record is enormous. He really is the primary producer of that record."

For all that, the album jacket would credit production to Arthur Lee with Bruce Botnick. "Toward the end of the sessions, I got angry with Arthur and I called Jac and told him I didn't want my name on that album," reveals Bruce. "It got very intense. I don't remember what the argument was over but I think my pride got the best of me, because I produced that album, period. I did it and Jac can verify that. But I wanted my name off the album. Arthur had tried hustling me one too many times, and I'd had enough. On the credits, Jac put 'Produced by Arthur Lee with Bruce Botnick.' I lived with it. I'm very proud of that album. It's right up there in terms of my career, even though, as a staff engineer at Sunset Sound, I never saw a dime from it, and still don't. Maybe that album cost $20,000 to make, because I had strings and horns on there, but it's more than paid for itself."

Bryan was disappointed with the sound of the album. "I thought it was a totally prosaic mix." He said later: "There was no punch or power. I didn't like the bass sound, I didn't like the guitar sound. I guess that's the way they wanted it." Michael was initially dismayed with the finished album. "When I heard it for the first time, I cringed. Part of it was the mix. I didn't think the drums were mixed up enough. But that was out of my hands. I told Arthur, during the sessions, that he wasn't putting the drums where they needed to be, and I got an ass-chewing. He said, 'You're worrying about the drums; Kenny's worried about his bass; everyone's looking out for himself. That's what's wrong with this band.' So I said OK, but it didn't sound like the drums were up loud enough. All the drums were put on one track, often along with another instrument, so remixing would be extremely difficult."

Rhino Records' 2008 deluxe reissue of *Forever Changes* boasts an alternative mix of the album that places the vocals and some instruments more prominently than in the better known version. "Where Rhino got that alternate mix on this new release, I don't know," admits Bruce. "I suspect it was probably a rough mix that I made. We've been trying to find the original masters, but they're gone. I wanted to remix it in surround sound, but Jac and I have been looking for those original tapes for 15 years and not been able to find them."

Johnny remembers seeing the master tape boxes in the early 70s. "I was in New York and had come by to see Jac without realizing they [Elektra] were packing up to move to Los Angeles. There were boxes everywhere, including the original masters to *Forever Changes*. I could have just walked out with them. There was no guard or anything; they were just waiting for the moving company to pick up all these boxes. Nobody knows where they are now."

Annette Ferrel recalls hearing the album at Arthur's house. "He invited me to hear *Forever Changes* and I remember "You Set The Scene" – it was dramatic, with all the trumpets and strings. Arthur stood up and started waving his hands in the air, as if he was conducting the music. He was very proud of that album and wanted me to hear it."

For David Angel, *Forever Changes* represents Arthur's creative zenith, although there might have been greater achievements, he believes. "Arthur needed the orchestra. It was in his soul somewhere to have one. If he had been given the opportunity to work with an orchestra more and more, he would have grown into it and he would have had a chance to refine this attitude toward his work. But he wasn't given another chance. He should have been given more opportunities to do this type of work. I think he needed it and wanted it. Maybe going the other way, back to a small group and more aggressive music, was partly because he didn't have the chance to go on in this direction. I had the feeling that this was his real destiny, his real life's worth, making rock music a higher art form."

With the tracks mixed, all that remained was the selection of a jacket design and an album title. Provisionally known as *The Third Coming Of Love*, the album's iconic title would be arrived at after a casual, valedictory remark of Arthur's. "The real story behind the title *Forever Changes* wasn't all this peace-and-love New Age mantra stuff," explains David Fairweather. "Arthur told me he was breaking up with this girl, at the time, and she said, 'But you told me you'd love me forever?' and he replied, 'Yeah well, you know, forever changes.' So the full title is really *Love Forever Changes*."

As for the jacket, Elektra art director William Harvey commissioned Bob Pepper to create the striking kaleidoscopic collage of the five band-members' images arranged in the rough shape of a heart (or, as some fans believe, a graphic rendering of the African continent). Ronnie Haran took the somewhat provocative back-cover photograph. "We were all inside Arthur's house and we'd just had one of the few rehearsals for *Forever Changes*," Michael Stuart explains. "This was at *The Trip* house, with the indoor/outdoor pool. We were out on the patio and there was a railing all around. Ronnie said, 'All you guys get down at that end,' and as I stepped back I knocked that vase over and broke it. Arthur looked at it, reached down, and picked it up. Then he said, 'OK, take it.' Everybody thinks it's something symbolic. Maybe it was, in *his* mind. Johnny's wearing this Cossack hat and holding a reefer in his hands. He had started wearing a hat because he was already losing his hair. Bryan looked like Errol Flynn in the photo. Kenny is just exhaling a cigarette. He always used aqua filters. I had just got a haircut that day and I was always sorry I did that. Never get a picture taken the day you get a haircut."

I've been told that me holding the broken flower pot with dead flowers in it, on the Forever Changes album back cover, symbolized the death of flower power. But it just happened to be there on the ground and I picked it up and did it, that's all. There was no reason. Half the pot is at the bottom of my stomach and the other half is at the top, so my stomach's 'in' the pot.

From the mixing and sequencing of the tracks emerged a cohesive album that transcends its individual songs. Although not conceived as a concept album, *Forever Changes* holds together from track to track as if that were the case. It offers a consistency and continuity rare in albums by Love's contemporaries, with the exception, perhaps, of The Beatles' *Sgt. Pepper's Lonely Hearts Club Band*. As brilliant as Buffalo Springfield, The Byrds, The Doors, and even Arthur's buddy Jimi Hendrix were, none created such a consistently strong and unified album, track for track, from beginning to end. *Forever Changes* boasts no filler, no weak moments, no throwaways, and is the kind of album best appreciated as a whole rather than by sampling specific songs. "It's a fully realized concept from start to finish," acknowledges Bruce Botnick, "a complete piece of music. It's a long album and a very deep album, and was it an intense experience [to record it]." The album continues to resonate with each new generation.

The album was OK. I sure paid enough, but to this day, I'm still not satisfied with the end result. Every time I considered doing it again, I remembered all the trouble I had getting down what I'd recorded and it was just too overwhelming for me.

Jim Bickhart reviewed the album for the fledgling *Rolling Stone* magazine. "I thought *Forever Changes* was better, off the bat, than *Da Capo* because it didn't have a throwaway side on it. I was impressed with the album. I knew it was a substantial piece of work. I had heard orchestration in rock before but it had never been incorporated into the arrangements like this. In Los Angeles, we had a slightly warped impression of the record because 'Alone Again Or' was treated as a hit single here. So we had this impression that they were doing well and the album was doing well, too."

Released in November 1967, *Forever Changes* in fact made barely a ripple on the album charts, posting a disheartening #154, and with its lead single, "Alone Again Or," failing to even breach the coveted Hot 100. Ironically, when released in the UK in early 1968, the album was heralded by critics and fans alike and reached #24 on the charts there. Perhaps, as with *Da Capo,* Arthur had exceeded his fans' ability to grasp what he was attempting. "I think it was a little too sophisticated for its time," suggests Bruce. "When you're in the middle of something you're not necessarily aware that what you're doing is groundbreaking; but I was totally aware that this was different, bringing all these other influences in. *Forever Changes* wouldn't have worked if the personalities – Arthur, David Angel, and I – hadn't clicked, if we hadn't been able to speak the same musical language. But it did work."

"The timing of *Forever Changes* was probably wrong," admits Jac. "Thinking about it today, I wouldn't have released that album in November. I would have waited and released it in January. It's a crowded marketplace going into December. If *Forever Changes* had come out earlier, the result might have been a bit better. But if you don't support the record by performance, and the band isn't available, you lose your audience. You're then relying on the record to be like a seed which will sprout something over time. It happens, but that's the hard way of doing it."

Critics certainly loved *Forever Changes*. In a February 25 1968 *Los Angeles Times* review, Pete Johnson described the album in awed tones: "Melodies ripple across each other, embedded with symphonic parts, doses of hard rock, a few volts worth of electronic effects and interesting stray elements such as the plaintive bullfight-like cry of a horn. The tasty diversity is matched by the words to the songs, dovetailing almost randomly inside the tunes, sentences ending freely in mid line for the enlightened impact of unexpected structures. Parts of the album are beautiful; others are disturbingly ugly, reflections of the pop movement towards realism. All of it says something, drawing power from insanity and beauty of individuals and the society which feeds and kills them. The LP is their best so far, one which can survive endless listening with no diminishing either of power or of freshness."

Variety, in its December 27 1967 review, declared that the group had "produced their most sophisticated album yet." Gene Youngblood, writing in *The LA Free Press,* May 10 1968, gushed that the album "shimmers like a precious stone" and dubbed it "one of the finest collections of the New Music." His lavish description would not abate: "Soft, subtle. Forever changing in tonal color, rhythm patterns, vocal nuances, lyric substance. Exquisite musicianship. Flawless arrangement by Arthur Lee. Smoothest integration of brass I've yet heard. *Forever Changes* is melancholy iconoclasm and tasteful romanticism. It speaks more for me – for the world I see – than any other music I know. Compare [The Moody Blues' heavily orchestrated and then recently released] *Days Of Future Past* with *Forever Changes* and you'll see how shallow the Moody Blues really is: ersatz Mantovani; some of the most vulgar and overwrought pompous orchestration I've ever heard. Ah but Love knows how to use strings; the softness of their integration with acoustic and electric guitars and vocalized choruses. Arthur Lee belongs in the same league as Dylan, Lennon and McCartney."

The album would beguile critics far and wide. The *Sunday Post Crescent*, in Appleton, Wisconsin, reviewed it early in 1968 and observed that: "They seem to be picking up the pieces of what used to be called folk rock and are trying to move on to something else, though they aren't sure what. Love has come a considerable distance and still seems to have a lot of mileage left." The reviewer cited "You Set The Scene" as the standout track.

And yet, despite these accolades, the album sold poorly and was out of step with its times. Perhaps it was the use of strings and horns that left the hippies scratching their heads. "There were a lot of musical gymnastics going on in the songs on that album: tempo and time changes in the middle of songs, and all that," reflects Jim Bickhart. "Your typical pop music listener of that era, or any era for that matter, has trouble with that kind of stuff."

"The *Forever Changes* album coming out locally in LA was like people in Liverpool and London hearing *Sgt. Pepper* for the first time," suggests Harvey Kubernik. "Partly because the band was based here, we were waiting for the next thing from Love. LA people understood Love. It meant a tad more for us."

"I was actually surprised it was released," says David Angel. "I thought it was too good for the pop idiom. It was bordering on classical music. But every few years, someone would come up to me and ask me to sign their copy of the album. So I began to get the notion that there were people who did get the idea of what this album was all about, and understood that it was superior and not just disposable pop music."

The album's timelessness is rooted in the fact that it eschews almost all the trappings of its era. There are no backwards tapes, Indian flavored ragas, or sitars. There are no meandering fuzz-toned guitar excursions, and no trippy poetry. Indeed, the album's lyrical themes offer a stark audit of the underbelly of 1967, not its hazy veneer. Though it was made by rock music's first integrated band, *Forever Changes* remains racially neutral; there are none of the stylistic markers

YOU SET THE SCENE

of stereotypical black or white music from that period. Arthur's voice has no overt inflection, one way or the other. Love had created music that defied labels and typecasting. Perhaps that's why it went over the heads of its peers and has instead connected with later generations.

British singer-songwriter, former Soft Boy, and dedicated Love fan Robyn Hitchcock still finds *Forever Changes* unique and inspiring: "It's romantic, in an angry, bittersweet way: a fruit hanging from a branch that dared you to bite into it. Life is impossible, but beautiful. "Live And Let Live" is a sublime protest song against the human condition and "The Red Telephone" sums up life in the ominous vegetation of LA. Frustration filtered through bliss. It's a mood, as well as being a strong collection of songs – two by Bryan MacLean which add a melancholy sweetness to Arthur's feistiness. Pop songwriting flowered at that time and turned into rock. Almost everyone peaked in '67, and Love were no exception."

Jim Bickhart believes it is Arthur's audacity as an artist, unafraid to stretch boundaries and break rules, that characterizes *Forever Changes*. "On the first three Love albums you had this audacious artist who was basically fearless and willing to take these recognizable musical forms and do different things with them. He started off saying, 'OK, we're going to be the new Byrds, but we're going to do it our way,' then said, 'Well, we did that, now we're going to do something else that'll sound real different,' and that was *Da Capo*. After that, he basically did an art cantata which was *Forever Changes*. As an artist, Arthur was fearless until he sank under the weight of it all. Maybe he could be fearless for only so long, especially as he was not getting the recognition he thought he deserved."

Arthur and his bandmates had certainly created a unique, eerily insightful symphonic statement that was unlike any other album at that time. The question inevitably arose: what next? *Forever Changes* was the third act in a musical play that had been evolving and altering expectations and perceptions. How could Arthur ever top it? "I really think the tragedy of Arthur's life was that he wasn't given a chance to do more of the same," reflects David Angel. "If someone had supported him in this direction I think he would have been more fulfilled in his life. That energy and discipline would have produced more albums like *Forever Changes*. He was just beginning. Beethoven got to write nine symphonies; Arthur Lee only got to write one."

"True, Arthur only created one masterpiece," concurs Jim Bickhart, "but by his own choice. He had time to write more; Beethoven didn't. Arthur chose not to do any more. That's the saddest part of it all. The whole thing about people reaching their peak, and then never being able to match it, let alone top it, happens to rock artists, too. Brian Wilson may have done some good things after *Smile*, but nothing as consistent. Another artist on top of his game for two years, and never again, was [The Lovin' Spoonful's] John Sebastian. He was brilliant and then it just stopped. It's like he lost the page, although he didn't have the kind of issues Arthur had."

"*Forever Changes* contains fascinating yet contrasting moods and lyrics, from utopian visions to almost ominous, existential observations which only add to its timelessness," observes Kara Wright, a 20-something LA music-publishing worker and, like a surprising number of her generation, a devoted Love fan. "I believe the album still resonates with generations four decades on because it is an album of alternate realities, and a reflection of our everyday lives. *Forever Changes* continues to win new converts because of the powerful psychological subject matter accompanied by varying degrees of folk, rock, pop, progressive, psychedelic, classical, and Latin influences. There is something for everyone on this album. It is a Technicolor tapestry of musical explorations, evoking the everyday sounds of life, which truly transcends time."

For Jac Holzman, it's no surprise that *Forever Changes* continues to resound decades after it was recorded. "That record just gets more legendary as time goes on. It's so rare that an artist gets connected to a piece of music that lasts a long, long time. It's very special. And for all the problems that went into making that album, it sounds effortless. That's one of the most amazing things about the record: it just floats into your psyche. I remember the session where we all sat around listening to the finished album. Arthur was there along with some of the band-members. At one point, I turned and caught a momentary glimpse of Arthur, and I got a sense that he knew he had transcended himself and that he might not get back there again – that feeling of, 'Wow, I'm involved with *this*! I'm the cause of *this*.' I think it scared the shit out of him."

CHAPTER 6

ONCE I HAD A SINGING GROUP

The Four Sail / Out Here Love – left to right:
Jay Donnellan, Frank Fayad, George Suranovich, Arthur Lee

Forever Changes got lost amidst all the other records released during the pre-Christmas rush. As brilliant as it was, the album was nonetheless overlooked in what was a golden era for so many bands. Nobody really got it. That was frustrating and demoralizing for Arthur and contributed to his negative opinion of the album in later years – that and the fact that he was never able to top it. To have put his heart and soul into something only to have it fall on deaf ears was crushing and a factor in Arthur's subsequent decline, not to mention the demise of the original Love line-up. At the time Forever Changes was released, Love's national presence was marginal at best and the record did little to change that. They had released three albums but rarely ventured beyond Southern California. In hindsight, it's clear Forever Changes was a construction that was way ahead of its time. But even if he could have known that, it would have been cold comfort for its principal architect.

Never wishing to repeat himself, Arthur had covered so much ground over Love's three albums that, to him, it seemed there was nowhere left to go other than in a hard-rock direction. The tide was with him. By 1968, rock music was moving away from psychedelic experimentation and toward a grittier, blues-rock sound. Could the existing line-up of Love make the transition?

Love closed out 1967 with a three-night stand (December 15 to 17) at the new Blue Law club in Torrance, California, before a return stint at the Whisky after Christmas. Reviewing the band's Blue Law appearance, The Los Angeles Times' Pete Johnson noted that Love played "a stunningly good set of old and new material." He went on: "The group is polished and tight despite the knottiness of their music, which wanders from straight blues and ballads to hard rock and jazz with flamenco overtones, sometimes all within a given number. Lee's singing is explosive, though he can decelerate to savor the sadness of a song such as 'Signed D.C.' which he wrote."

DJ Rick Williams caught the slimmed-down Forever Changes line-up in concert. "Obviously, they couldn't do many of the songs live, without the orchestration. The string arrangements were too vital to most of those songs. I clearly remember them doing 'A House Is Not A Motel' and nailing it, though. They were really stretching it out in the end, with Johnny's guitar solo."

In an agreement between the band and Elektra, dated January 11 1968, it was arranged that all correspondence, statements, notifications, and, more significantly, royalties due to the band would be sent to Arthur Lee, care of

Schlesinger and Tabor, attorneys at law. Arthur, Johnny, Kenny, and Bryan all signed this agreement – in effect, relinquishing control of the disbursement of money and the information supporting it, in the form of sales statements, exclusively to Arthur. This would become a bone of contention in later years, with band members insisting that they were never adequately compensated.

On January 30 and 31 1968, Love returned to Sunset Sound to cut a new single, this time with John Haeny engineering (after fighting with Arthur during the completion of *Forever Changes*, Bruce Botnick would no longer work with him). While "Alone Again Or" had been a hit in and around LA, the song had failed to chart nationally and it was hoped that a new single might do the trick. Arthur was producing and had come up with two of the hardest-rocking songs in the Love canon to date: "Your Mind And We Belong Together" and "Laughing Stock."

Those were the last songs we ever recorded [with the original Love line-up]. Out of all the songs I ever did with the first Love band, "Your Mind" is one of my favorites. I remember when we did "Laughing Stock" and what Jac Holzman said about it: "Well, what are you guys going to do next?" as if to say, "You've just about covered everything, musically." At least I thought that's what he meant.

For Michael Stuart, who remained skeptical about *Forever Changes*, these two songs represented a robust return to form. "When we went back into the studio to record 'Your Mind And We Belong Together,' I thought, 'Finally, we're recording some cooking music.' We were on the right track. The mix was good and everyone was together with their instruments." In an interview with *Crawdaddy* magazine, Elektra executive David Anderle recalled the sessions. "I was having my head blown sitting there," he told writer Paul Williams, "watching Love really getting it together, sounding better than they had ever sounded and happier than I'd seen them in a recording studio."

Johnny Echols remembers that "Your Mind And We Belong Together" was one of the few songs that was 'finished' when the band first heard it. "It had a beginning, middle, and an end. It tells a story in itself: where the group was and where it was going. The song required only an hour or so for each of us to decide what we would play. Arthur listened to us run through it a few times, declared it ready to 'burn,' and offered no suggestions, at that point. But what started out so smooth and easy turned out to be anything but. From the first take, I knew this was going to be a trip! Mike Stuart counted off the beat but Arthur stopped him, saying, 'it's too slow.' Mike counted again, 'too fast.' That's how the first ten takes went. Next it was Bryan's turn. He was too loud, too soft, playing too much rhythm, or not enough. … Then Kenny's bass didn't sound heavy enough, he wasn't driving the beat; maybe he should pay more attention to Mike and match his groove. Arthur would say, 'Echols, I dug your solo when you guys were rehearsing it, do it like that.' Ten takes later it was, 'Echols, I don't understand your trip, man. You're playing too much on the low notes; you're not playing the high notes!' We did about five more takes and then I heard, 'Echols, that was smoking, man.'"

"Your Mind" may have been a complete composition the first time the band heard it, but "Laughing Stock," according to Johnny, was a different matter. "There was no beginning, no middle, and no end. There were no chords, no words, and no song structure at all. Bryan started playing folk chords, just sort of tripping on the guitar. Mike joined in on drums, followed by Kenny. I listened for a while, watching Bryan's fingers, noting which chords he was playing, and, after a bit, I found my part. Soon after, Arthur started singing and scribbling down words as we went along. After about an hour or so, we went into the studio and cut the instrumental track. We had been smoking herb and Arthur started laughing. His laugh was so infectious it started me going, and neither of us could stop. After at least another hour of false starts and laughter we managed to finish the track – on the record you can hear my voice on the right channel and Arthur's on the left. 'Laughing Stock' was the right title."

Love lore has it that the two songs were to be the first tracks on a putative fourth Love album entitled *Gethsemane*. Johnny scotches the rumor. "I came up with the name *Gethsemane*, which was the working title for the three or four songs I was going to do on *Forever Changes*. These were jazzy songs. I chose that name because we had been lied to by the record company about us doing a two-album set. Jesus was betrayed by Judas in the Garden of Gethsemane, so that was my way of expressing my feelings about Elektra. There were a few songs that were written during that period, a couple of them with Arthur. We never went in and recorded a whole other album, though. There aren't any lost Love tapes. That's all myth. There are maybe three or four songs that people haven't heard that are somewhere, but maybe they were lost with the masters. There's no finished album that Arthur destroyed." (Since 2005, Johnny has been working with Vince Flaherty on his *Gethsemane* tracks, with the goal of releasing them to a public still eager for anything Love-related.)

There is no such thing as an album called Gethsemane. I don't even know what that word means. After "Your Mind And We Belong Together" and the song "Laughing Stock," that was it as far as the original Love group recordings are concerned. Sorry folks, but that was it.

By early 1968, Love gigs were becoming few and far between. Even their loyal LA fanbase saw them infrequently. "We weren't playing at that time," acknowledges Michael. "I couldn't help but wonder why we weren't playing more concerts around LA, let alone going to England, or to the East Coast. I was getting calls to book the band at the Santa Monica Civic Center, but when I'd tell Arthur he'd say, 'I look after the bookings; you just play the drums.' We used to play every weekend, then it was every second weekend, then it got to be once a month. Arthur had a nice house and a Porsche and seemed to have lots of money, but the rest of us needed to work. We needed the money. At first, we each got a weekly paycheck from the group's attorneys, Schlesinger and Tabor. They even paid our rent and utilities. But as musicians, we wanted to play; I didn't join Love to sit at home and watch television. After *Da Capo,* Love only worked occasionally, then less and less so. We had been doing so much sitting around, and the drugs were just waiting. The drugs didn't break up our group: inactivity broke us up."

Despite the inactivity, Michael wasn't ready to quit. "I didn't leave and play with another band, because Love was *the* band. It was my band as much as it was anybody's who was in it. So I wasn't going to bail out. But it was like a Mexican standoff. Arthur didn't really want to work very much, but the rest of us said, 'Let's work. We're sitting by the phone waiting.' We figured that, eventually, Arthur would book a gig, or a series of gigs, that would start us on the road to playing more often, and doing another album. We thought that – right up to the end. There never really was an end. Months went by with no activity. I never spoke to those guys when we weren't playing. Kenny and I were living in a house on Kirkwood. He had a gorgeous Jaguar. He had it fixed up beautifully and it looked like a showpiece. But he still owed money on it, and when we weren't working, it finally caught up with him. He couldn't make the payments. So he had to find another pad, a garage. He could park his car, sleep beside it, and make sure the repossession people couldn't find him. By then, none of us were living together or in contact with each other. We should have put our personal differences aside and played music. Arthur didn't want to do that. That was hard on all of us."

The idleness only deepened the divisiveness between band members and accelerated the descent into harder drugs. "At the point when everybody started using [heroin], we were self-medicating," Johnny admits. "That might sound strange when you consider the lifestyles that we had come to enjoy and the adulation surrounding us, but everything was changing. The Hollywood scene was changing; the police were becoming hard on the kids on the Strip. And we were changing."

By this point, the relationship between Arthur and Bryan had reached its lowest ebb. They were finding it difficult to exist in the same band together. The episode with Stephanie Buffington had created an irreconcilable rift between the pair. Elektra's decision to release "Alone Again Or" as a single had widened the chasm. "Bryan had lots of great songs but he wasn't allowed to put many of them on the albums," says Michael. "Having one of those songs picked as the single from *Forever Changes* is what did it for Arthur. That tore it apart. He figured he couldn't go on being in the band with Bryan if they're going to pick Bryan's songs over his. Arthur thought, and rightly so, that he could make music with other musicians."

By 1968, Arthur was willing to cut Bryan loose. As Michael recalls: "When we recorded 'Your Mind And We Belong Together' and 'Laughing Stock,' those were supposed to be the first of many songs for a fourth album we owed Elektra. We met up at Arthur's house, where we'd worked up the songs for the previous albums. We were all there, except Bryan. Arthur said to me, Kenny, and Johnny, 'I'm thinking we don't need Bryan. I think we should eliminate him from the group. Are you guys with me on this?' We all kind of said, 'Bryan's hard to be around sometimes, but we wouldn't want to see him leave the group.' We still thought Bryan was an integral part of the band. So we said, 'No, we don't want to kick him out.' The combination of Arthur and Bryan was necessary to making Love what it was. And Johnny was a part of that, too. I always believed it was in Arthur's best interests to keep Bryan in the band. Arthur didn't like that and grew angry. At that point, he began to see the future without any of us. He saw it as his group, and it was his group to break up, if he chose to. That's what I surmised. Bryan was just as special as Arthur, and that's what made Arthur nervous."

In 1968, we filmed the documentary that would eventually come out in 1995 [when it was released alongside Rhino Records' Love Story CD boxed set. It was later used in Start Productions' Love documentary, also called Love Story]. Although it was made in '68, I didn't see it until the mid 90s. One of the things that shocked me, besides memories of those days, was seeing Bryan standing beside me. I tell you the truth, if I had seen what he was doing behind my back, making those faces and carrying on, that would have been it for his part in the group, right then and there. You have to see the video for yourself to know what I mean. I try not to give it a second thought, but even now it sort of reminds me of Judas.

To confound the issue, Bryan had progressed into hard drug use. "He was into needles and heroin," admits Elizabeth McKee. "They all were. It was around. I was in denial; I didn't want to believe Bryan was doing it. I knew something was up but I didn't want to go there and I didn't know enough to ever try to get him to stop."

Johnny and Kenny were also shooting heroin by this point. "I went into it with my eyes wide open," says Johnny. "It wasn't that I was surprised by what happened. I knew what would happen. But reality just didn't set in. I just decided I was going to do it, and when I did, I didn't stop. This was only maybe a six or seven-month period in my life. To be defined by that short period of time is kind of tough. Kenny used it a little longer and Bryan maybe not quite as long. We were trying to cope with what was happening in our lives, and heroin made it easier to forget, to nod out, and not deal with the responsibilities. We weren't touring or playing as much; we needed money – we had creditors at our door. Then, Jimi Hendrix was stealing our thunder. It was all slipping away, and instead of fighting to keep it, we just kind of lulled ourselves to sleep with the drugs. It seemed like we were into hard drugs a long time, but that's all myth. I even heard that I died of a heroin overdose."

We were in New York, once. Part of my routine was to see if everyone was ready to go to a soundcheck. I went to check on Bryan. When I walked into the room, he was sitting in a chair with his head against the wall. He was a deep blue color, almost purple. It freaked me out, so I went and got Johnny. He walked into the room, grabbed Bryan by his hair, and slammed his head up against the wall a couple of times. Bryan's eyes opened up and Johnny said, "He'll be all right." I said to myself, "He may be awake, but what about the concussion?" To say that my band was slowly disintegrating was an understatement, but I still thought that it was going to be OK.

To further complicate the situation, there was intrigue over the prospect of Bryan making a solo album for Elektra. He had been talking with the label and had received tacit agreement to back his sessions. "Unbeknown to us, Jac promised Bryan that he would allow him to make a solo album of the songs that he'd wanted to put on *Forever Changes*," Johnny maintains. "Arthur and I were at Bryan's house when he said to us, 'Oh, I talked with Jac and he's going to let me do a solo album.' Arthur and I did a double take, and Arthur said, 'No, you're not. You're either part of Love or you're alone.' Bryan agreed and said he wasn't going to do it. A few months later, we found out that he was making arrangements to go into the studio and record his songs. We decided that just wasn't going to happen. Behind our backs, Jac was trying to manipulate Bryan."

Arthur had finally acquiesced to manager Mike Gruber's urging and agreed to tour the East Coast, opening with a two-night stand at New York's New Generation Club, beginning May 8 (an outrageously discriminatory reference to their performance in *Variety* referred to Arthur as a "Negro lead singer" and Johnny as "second Negro"). Despite arriving too late for one college date in upstate New York, by all accounts Love performed and behaved admirably enough on the tour; that is until they were scheduled to appear at the Miami Pop Festival on May 18. With a layover of several days prior to the show, the band remained in Florida while Arthur flew back to LA, claiming he had pressing business to attend to. In fact, he had grown anxious about leaving his girlfriend, Suzanne Hausner, alone.

I had become acquainted with a guy that I found to be quite amusing, and also a good friend, as I got to know him. His name was Neil Rappaport. I would see him around the canyons in Hollywood, walking his dog. I had a black Labrador retriever with a personality that wouldn't quit, named Self. Although the two dogs weren't allowed to be together, I became friends with Neil because of things we had in common. It wasn't only dogs; we liked doing a lot of the same things, and shared a lot of the same friends. I don't know anyone in that band that didn't

*think Neil was cool. So when it came time to go to New York, and since we didn't
have a road manager, Neil seemed to be the man for the job.*

*After we touched down in New York, we walked out of the airport and a
long, white limousine was there to meet us. This was our first time on the East
Coast. When we arrived in Manhattan and got to our hotel, we were assigned to
our double rooms. Before one guy had even turned the key to his door he was on
the floor shooting heroin. Mike Gruber and I thought the same thing at the same
time, just when we thought we had seen it all. … Anyway, everyone finally settled
in and we all just wanted to get some rest before the soundcheck, which was to be
held later that evening. In fact, we never did a soundcheck because no one was
satisfied with the instrument they had or their amplifiers. The band persuaded me
to call the record company and see if they could get new ones. I phoned Elektra
and they said "OK" and called some music store and told them my band was en
route. Bryan wanted a Gibson Byrdland guitar, Johnny wanted a Les Paul. I don't
remember if Kenny got a violin-shaped bass or not. Michael wanted a brand new
set of drums. And me, I didn't even get a harmonica out of the deal. All I know is
that the money was an advance toward my next royalty statement. After
everything was cleared at the store by the record company, they were off.*

*I guess I figured, since I wasn't getting anything, there was no need for me to
go, and since Neil was acting road manager, he could take them. All they had to
do was rent a van and get the things they needed. I remember asking Neil before
they left if he thought he could handle it and, as always, he said, "Sure,
Meeaaannn" – he always said that in New York Jewish fashion – and they were
off. After a long wait, someone finally turned the knob, opened the door, and there
they were. I asked Neil if everything was all right and he said, "Sure, Meeaaannn."
I asked where the instruments were and he said they were downstairs, in the van.
Then, he started feeling around in his pockets, finally saying, 'I think I left the
keys down in the van!' He ran downstairs and in a minute came back up with this
surprised look on his face. Someone had stolen the van with all the instruments in
it! I felt very let down, to say the least, but show time was getting near, so I called
the record company and re-ordered everything all over again. This time, there
were to be no mistakes. So they were off again. When they returned they came
back with everything. We had a successful show that night at the New Generation
and it seemed like everyone liked the show but me.*

Our next concert was to be at a college in New York, called Stony Brook. We had the next day off and, never having been in New York before, we decided to go up Broadway. Now, at that time, the movie 2001: A Space Odyssey was premiering at some theatre on Broadway and we all decided to go and check it out. While I went to get some popcorn, a couple of the guys were smoking, and when I came back one of them had nodded out with his cigarette in the arm of the seat. Smoke was coming from it. Another guy had nodded out with his cigarette in a lady's hat in front of him and the hat was on fire. These were just a few of the things that made me think about calling it a day with these guys.

From New York, we were supposed to go to Florida and play this festival with Jimi Hendrix, Albert King, and some other bands of the day, but the gig wasn't going to be until a week later. I decided to fly back to LA, and then meet the band in Miami in time for the show. The band drove from New York to Florida, and when they got there, Neil called me, in Hollywood. It was about three in the morning and I can remember what he said as is if it were right now. He said, "Hey, man, I called to tell you that Johnny and I just threw our outfits [needles] in the Atlantic Ocean."

"Kenny and I had both become totally involved in heroin," Johnny admits. "Even if Bryan hadn't done that thing with Jac Holzman, the band probably wasn't going to be around much longer. Arthur's girlfriend, Suzanne, was probably one of the stronger influences on him. She was constantly trying to get him to pull away from the group or to get more money. We were in Miami, but Arthur decided he was going back to LA because he heard that Scotty [Arthur's friend James Scott] was over at his house with Suzanne. That was total nonsense, but he never trusted any of his girlfriends. He didn't want to come to Miami because he had become really, really in love with Suzanne, and she didn't want him to be with the group as much as he wanted. She thought that if he went out on his own he would be this big huge star, without realizing there were five people responsible for our success. So she was pulling at Arthur, there was Bryan's solo thing, the heroin, and Arthur also becoming involved in cocaine. Four of us were heroin addicts – Bryan and Michael, too – and Arthur was shooting cocaine. We had to cancel the Miami gig and come home."

"There were only four or five days before we were supposed to play," recalls Michael. "Then I got the call from Arthur saying, 'I just saw the bill and we don't get top billing like they promised me. So we're not going to play. You guys come on back home. Ronnie [Haran] is going to be there with the tickets and you guys fly back to LA. Michael, you tell the other guys.' I was shocked and disappointed that we weren't going to play again."

Left to cool their heels in Miami, their supply of heroin (previously stashed inside their guitars) now exhausted, some band members managed to kick what was still the early stages of addiction. Road manager Neil Rappaport was also now clean. However, his return to LA would prove fateful. "That was sad about Neil," reflects Johnny. "He died of a drug overdose. We were on tour and were away about six weeks. We were in New York and he couldn't score any drugs because he didn't know anyone there. During that time, we all kicked the habit. So we came back to LA and Neil saw his drug connection, who lived a couple of doors down from him. She saw Neil and handed him a freebie. Now, he hadn't had drugs in his system for a while and he couldn't tolerate the amount he would normally use, and so he died. Nobody was assassinated. We didn't murder our road manager, as the rumors had it. It was an unfortunate accident."

The band arrived back in LA a few days later, a Sunday, I think, and Suzanne and I went over to Neil's to welcome them back. He lived on Franklin and La Brea. We got out of the car and walked inside. I was just getting ready to go upstairs when the manager stopped me and said, "Neil's dead!" It felt like pins and needles all over my body. To this day, I still don't know what happened to him. I do know that the band asked me if I'd got the money that he was supposed to be carrying, and I said "no." So ended the life of the guy I invited to be road manager. After that, I wrote two songs about him, one called "Neil's Song" and the other about us both called "I'm With You."

Over a decade later, I got a phone call from Johnny. He told me that he's going under the knife and that there was a fifty-fifty chance he would survive. He started telling me how they had ripped me off all those years ago. He said, "You remember that time in New York, when Neil said he left the keys in the van full of new equipment, and when he went downstairs someone had taken everything? Well, no one took that stuff. We sold it. Neil, me, and the guys in the band sold all that stuff." Sorrow, heartaches, gloom, and two songs to boot about a guy who I'm later told not only lied, but who also ripped me off, in New York. God rest his soul. The van incident was a wake-up call too late, but what a learning experience about people.

I remember once, we went to this motel place to score. On one side were weed and psychedelics, and on the other side was heroin. Two of the band members went to the heroin side. It was like the parting of the Red Sea. After that, things just started to get worse and worse. I went over to Kenny's place in Laurel Canyon. He lived in a garage that was under a second floor house. It was actually pretty decent for one person, the way it was fixed up, but what was a trip about it was that the inside was painted black. I mean the whole place was black, the windows and everything. There was one candle lit, in the middle of the room, which he used to cook up dope. He had been in there, in the dark, for quite a while. I asked him what was going on and he said I wouldn't want to see. I didn't have to guess where that was going.

Doing drugs was one thing, but when the drugs were doing you, that was a whole other story. It wasn't just any drugs. Who didn't smoke pot in the 60s? The thing that wrecked the band was heroin.

Johnny Echols: "All this was happening simultaneously: Suzanne, Bryan, the drugs, Neil's death, and the changes on Sunset Strip. Together, they were enough to pull the group apart." Despite the rampant drug use, Love stumbled on, gigging sporadically around southern California (with one road trip to Salt Lake City, Utah, on July 18). They were merely going through the motions, however. "Everyone was on heroin and no one could hold up their end," Kenny Forssi later recalled. "We were all shot. The drugs started taking over around 1968."

Reviewing a June 18 show at LA's Hullabaloo club, Pete Johnson, a *Los Angeles Times* music critic and, by now, proven Love aficionado, found the band underwhelming, despite drawing lines of fans "half a block long." He found their sound to be "a fragmented, dense mixture of hard rock, blues, jazz and flamenco music surmounted by linear and non-linear lyrics." It seemed only Arthur still impressed him. "Lee is incredibly good. The rest of Love can be good, but Friday night they did not seem to be able to match the demands of their music."

No meeting was called to formally dissolve the group. Arthur simply stopped calling the others about gigs. In August, Michael heard, via Bryan, that Arthur had assembled a new Love line-up and was already gigging, as he recalls. "Arthur was of a mind to do what was best for his own interests. From his position, he wanted a hired group, employees that he had control over. I think he needed us to keep him in line. Heroin was a component in the breakup and it got worse for some of us. I really got into it at the very end, after the group fell apart. My regret is that we didn't get our priorities straight."

"We just couldn't trust each other and so we weren't going to play together as a group," Johnny explains. "We decided that Bryan would leave and we tried rehearsing as a four-piece, but it didn't feel the same without him. Bryan was a part of Love. So it just kind of atrophied to the point that it never could be put back together. We talked about going back into the studio but it never happened. There was never any big meeting where the band folded."

In his 1993 interview with Neal Skok, Bryan was candid about Elektra's interest in his putative solo album being tied to the imminent demise of Love. "It was facilitated by Jac Holzman. He's actually responsible for the end of Love. I might not have quit, but when they offered me a way out I started thinking, 'Maybe I'm unhappy here.'"

Although there were tragedies in the band, I can't help but think of all the good times we shared. We were as carefree as they come, and when things were going half way right, we had a bond unlike any I've ever shared with any other group of fellows. We were a part of one of the greatest periods in the history of mankind: the 60s. It didn't matter what race, color, creed, or culture you were, we just all seemed to get along. One thing I can also say about my band members is that they came on this Earth and left a mark and were a part of the greatest name of any time period, and that was Love. Though things may not have gone exactly the way I wanted them to, I can honestly say that each and every one of my band members was a pathfinder for us all. It was more than a pleasure sharing my life with Johnny Echols, Bryan MacLean, Kenny Forssi, Snoopy, Michael Stuart, Tjay Cantrelli, John Fleckenstein, and Don Conka, the first successfully integrated rock band in the world. Thank you!

There is little doubt that the original line-up forever defined both the sound and image of Love. The three albums the group recorded – in spite of their diversity of styles – remain the band's apex, their best-known and best-loved output, even though there are fans of the later Love recordings. For the next three decades, every version of Love which Arthur assembled would be measured against the original band and their masterpiece, *Forever Changes*. "I think, in the beginning, they were the same, Arthur Lee and the band," reflects Jac Holzman.

"But by *Forever Changes,* it was Arthur and a bunch of supportive guardian angels that came to give him a hand. After that, there was no Love."

"If you think about those first three Love albums, it's a prodigious output," acknowledges Bruce Botnick. "Arthur was evolving, and these albums were a product of their times. If your creativity doesn't evolve it just withers and dies. By that point, he had expended every bit of creativity he could get out of that line-up."

In later years, Arthur would insist that *Forever Changes* was a work of singular genius, minimizing the contributions of his bandmates. "Arthur would continually say 'I' as in 'I did this' and 'I did that' when clearly it was really 'we' or 'us,'" insists Johnny. "Success didn't spoil Arthur; it was the adulation that changed him. Arthur always wanted to be somebody."

"Arthur had a lot of respect for Johnny Echols," notes the singer's friend Herbie Worthington. "He told me time and time again that there was no other guitar player that was like Johnny. But he cut off his nose to spite his face when he let that original band fall apart. He didn't support the people who were supporting him. I'm not sure he knew how. He was his own worst enemy. Arthur did it to himself because he wouldn't play the game. He wouldn't tour and he didn't trust anybody."

Elektra followed through with an offer to record a Bryan MacLean solo album, and sent him a ticket for a cooling-out trip to Hawaii immediately following the dissolution of the band. Bryan did not use the ticket. "They said they didn't mind losing Love but they didn't want to lose me," he told Neal Skok. After kicking his addiction, Bryan presented a demo tape of his post-Love songs to Jac, who was unimpressed. Elektra passed on the solo album. "His best stuff turned out to be the songs he recorded with Love," says Jac. Bryan's Elektra demos would finally be released, by Sundazed Records, in 1997, as the album *ifyoubelievein.*

"Bryan called me up a year or so after *Forever Changes,* and we met," recalls orchestrator David Angel. "He said he'd written some songs and was thinking of making a recording, but he wanted to have the strings and horns involved, like they were on *Forever Changes.* I told him I would be very happy to work with him as we had done before. So we met twice and I took notes on his songs for the orchestration. He said he'd call me, but he never did and I never heard from him again. We had been very seriously working through his songs. I felt he had separated himself from the gothic starkness of 'Alone Again Or,' or from Arthur's music. His songs had become more folk-like and poetic. I felt they needed some color and orchestral depth."

Bryan washed up in New York City, ostensibly to cut music for a John G. Avildsen movie soundtrack. He then tried recording for Capitol Records but that, too, came to nothing. "At that point, I was starting to drink and was drunk quite a bit," Bryan later recalled. "I lost confidence in what I was doing. I walked away from the music business until around 1979 or so." Returning to LA, Bryan dabbled in real estate and stocks, among other vocations, before becoming involved with a Christian organization and eventually turning his life around. He died of a heart attack in LA on Christmas day 1998.

"You have to understand something about Arthur and me," said Bryan in 1993. "He was one of the most clever and humorous people I'd ever met. We were like instantaneous friends. We were very close and hung out together the whole time. I'd get up and go over to his place, and we'd sit and talk and laugh. My memories of Arthur, even though there was conflict, are mostly good ones. If I could have beaten him up, I would have been the leader. If I'd been the leader the band would have been a success."

After Love, Michael Stuart worked with a number of other artists, including Danny O'Keefe and Neil Diamond, before giving up music and moving to the South Lake Tahoe vicinity to settle down and raise a family. In 1971, he sued Arthur for royalties owing from the two Love albums he'd played on. "He had promised me one per cent and we signed contracts," Michael explains. "I just never got a copy of the contract. He told us again and again that we'd get royalties. I tried to get the others together to go after him in the final days of the band, but they'd just say, 'He'll give us our royalties.' I was the only guy asking him. He said, 'Look man, we have a recording debt. That album [*Forever Changes*] cost $20,000 to make. It hasn't sold that well. Once that's paid off, you'll get your royalties.' In the end I won. I got a $10,000 settlement. The album still sells but I got what I wanted. I just wanted to win."

Kenny and Johnny were the band-members most adversely affected by drugs immediately following the dissolution of the band. For decades it was rumored that the pair had become notorious donut-shop bandits, robbing several LA eateries to supply their heroin habits before being arrested and sent to prison. Johnny vehemently denies the story. "That donut-shop thing is total nonsense. Kenny and I were drug addicts. We were waiting for our connection outside the donut shop. He would sometimes show up a couple of hours late. So we're hanging around outside this person's place of business, just waiting. We didn't have cell phones in those days, so we kept going inside to use the payphone. We were waiting at this guy's donut shop for six or seven hours. Obviously we drew attention, a black guy and a white guy together, looking scruffy. He didn't know if we we're there to rip him off, set him up, or what. He was getting ready to close and we were still there, so he called the police. They came and took us downtown. We couldn't tell them we were drug addicts waiting for our connection, so we told them our car wouldn't start. They bought that, took us back to the shop, and we drove away. That's the whole donut caper: just us being outside a coffee shop for eight hours. Snoopy has turned that into a whole story about us robbing donut shops and being sent to San Quentin. They keep records of who was in that jail, so you can try and find my name on the roster. It isn't there."

Johnny would virtually disappear for the best part of the next two decades, fueling rumors of a debilitating condition. Johnny refutes these. "I went to New York City. Don Randi, of The Wrecking Crew, hooked me up to be a kind of liaison with musicians who came from LA to play in New York. He would do the same with New York musicians going to LA. I also did a lot of studio work and taught guitar at a school. My wife worked as a jazz dancer. I lived in New York until the mid 80s and then moved to Arizona. I talked to Arthur on and off during that time but I wasn't that into music. That part of my life went by the wayside. I left the drugs decades ago, when I left LA. New York was a new start for me. I met with Jac Holzman about doing some producing but nothing came of that. Arthur tried, periodically, to get back together to play, but I was reticent." As for the enduring stories about members of Love being busted for drugs and going to prison, Johnny is insistent. "I was never in prison. I went to a rehab by my own choice. Kenny went to a county jail but never to prison."

Kenny's addiction lasted longer and did, indeed, land him in the California Rehabilitation Center, in Corona, a facility whose stated goal is "to successfully treat and return all civil addict commitments to a useful and productive lifestyle." His brother, Charles, explains what happened to Kenny. "He was hung up on drugs for a long time and was in the rehabilitation facility for a couple of years. Then he moved to Sarasota, Florida, where he dabbled in a few local bands for several years, but nothing that ever lasted very long. After he came home, in 1971, he was a nightmare for my parents. He came back with a suitcase full of pills. He would nod off every night at their house. He didn't want anything to do with Arthur Lee. Arthur would call him up to see if he'd do a reunion, but Kenny wouldn't talk to him. He never got any money from Love and said he was ripped off by Arthur." Kenny died in hospital, of cancer of the brain, in Tallahassee, Florida, on January 5 1998.

"I think Kenny just grieved and worried himself to death," suggests Johnny. "He'd gotten onto the internet and he would see stuff about himself and the band, and he would take it to heart. He'd worry about it and he'd call me up and say, 'Did you see that, man? They said this and they said that,' and I'd tell him, 'There's nothing you can do about it. Whatever's going to happen is going to happen.' But he was really affected by it, and I think it's sad that it took its toll on him."

By late summer 1968, Arthur had assembled his new version of Love. He unveiled this line-up at the Whisky from August 29 to September 2. He'd found his new bandmates at a club called the Brass Ring on Ventura Boulevard, in Sherman Oaks, a few blocks east of Sepulveda. It was a popular hangout for musicians and Valley criminals.

After my original band and I split up, it was time to look for some new Love members. I went to see Nooney Rickett's band at the Brass Ring. I had seen Nooney play at Ciro's in '66. The band was called the Nooney Rickett IV. Nooney sang and played guitar, and was, to say the least, a natural on stage. He was funny, charismatic, and very entertaining; Nooney could really turn it on. His bass player, Frank Fayad, was a guy I knew back in the California Club days. These guys could really play and were very versatile. In my opinion, they were just what the doctor ordered. I saw right away that if I could get these guys, my mind would definitely be opened up to new and different styles of writing. In other words, to keep up with them and their group, I would have to change what I was doing to a heavier, jazzier, rock-funk type of thing. That was what I did before the first Love group. If I could get them, it was going to be a lot of fun.

I told Frank about my situation, and after showing him what I had been doing with my life, musically, he thought there might be a chance to try out this Love thing. I had a bass player. Now I needed to see if Nooney's drummer would go for the idea. His name was George Suranovich and, man, could he play! He was one of the best jazz-rock drummers I had ever seen. The only thing was, he was doing well with Nooney, and he was recording a song with a guy named Joe

South, it was called "The Games People Play." It hadn't come out yet, and he didn't know whether to go on the road with that guy, stay with Nooney, or to join up with me. I wanted George for my drummer and I made up my mind I was going to get him. I invited him up to my place in Studio City and told him about my idea for the band, and how I didn't think that song he was working on expressed the drummer enough. I said he would stand out in my band. At the time, I had two houses on the lot in Studio City, and I told George he could rent one and rehearse there. George went for the idea and, besides his drumming, we became really good friends. George was from Pittsburgh and had played with a group called The Skyliners who'd recorded a song, "Since I Don't Have You," which was one of my favorites of all time.

All I needed was a lead guitar player and I was on my way. I got a guy named Jay Donnellan who, like George, could play just about any style of music that I was familiar with. We also became real close and hung out together a lot. We were one big happy family, playing and sharing. Jay and I even wrote a song together: "Singing Cowboy."

I had gigs to do. I was lucky to get these guys, but I had to whip the group into shape as quickly as possible. As fast as they would learn an old Love song for the set, I would be writing a new one for the band. I was really having a ball. I liked these guys. They always thought they could outplay whoever we were playing on the bill with. It was really a competition thing and they really cared about how they sounded. Whoever it was, George always thought he could play better. Cream's drummer, Ginger Baker, had these double bass drums. George just had to get some and play better than Ginger.

The version of the Nooney Rickett IV that Arthur had caught at the Brass Ring featured a guitarist called Gary Rowles. However, when Arthur appropriated Nooney's band to be the new-look Love, Gary initially chose not to join, having already committed to play in ex-Buffalo Springfield drummer Dewey Martin's recently formed band, New Buffalo. "Arthur had a reputation, back then, for being hard to work with," says Gary. "Instead, I did the New Buffalo thing, but that was a mess. As soon as I found out that Dewey was trying to pass the band off as Buffalo Springfield, I was out of there. By that point, Arthur had already picked Frank and George from Nooney's band to be the new Love."

James 'Jay' Donnellan (alias Jay Lewis) was playing in a band with Snoopy and Tjay Cantrelli, at a Beverly Hills hotspot, the Factory. Snoopy told Jay that Arthur was looking for a guitar player and arranged for Jay to audition at Arthur's house. A native Angelino and a guitarist since the age of ten, Jay had been playing in clubs with The Coachmen and doing sessions before forming a band called Moorpark Intersection who recorded a single, released in February 1968 on Capitol Records. Jay was familiar with Arthur and Love, having seen the band on the Sunset Strip. When he arrived for the audition, he expected Arthur to be in subtle, acoustic, *Forever Changes* mode, but discovered he had taken a hard-rock direction. "I had my electric guitars in the car, but I walked in with a Martin acoustic and started tuning it up. Then I looked at George's double bass drum set up and Frank's amps. Arthur said, 'We're not doing that shit anymore. We're doing something else.' So they dove into [one of Arthur's new songs] "August" because he, Frank, and George already had a couple of weeks of rehearsals as a trio and had that song formulated. I went back to my car and got my electric guitar and amp, set up, and started working on that song. In about an hour, we had it worked out and I got the gig."

Jay was impressed with Arthur. "He had a real presence. Arthur was this handsome, exotic, half-black, half-white guy in colorful hippie clothes. He had an attitude as well as a real chip on his shoulder and a lot of charisma. He had his clothes custom made, drove a Porsche, and had the best hashish to give to all his friends. He would say he was half-black and half-Russian. Who knew if that was true or not? It was all part of his mystique."

With a new line-up hired, Arthur could exert full control over the new version of Love. No more dealing with personality conflicts, clashing egos, jealousies, or challenges to his authority. He could hire and fire at will. He would control the songwriting, recording contracts, album production, and advances, as well as gigs. In effect, Love became a vehicle for Arthur Lee, who would now act as manager (having secured a release from Mike Gruber on September 17), booking agent, and producer. In every respect, Arthur Lee was Love and Love was Arthur Lee.

Arthur's new songs eschewed orchestration, harpsichords, and flutes, and were instead inspired by Jimi Hendrix, Cream, and the other heavy riff-rockers of the era, while retaining something of a jazz-rock feel. Although it's not entirely inconceivable that his former band could have played these songs, the new players came from a heavier blues-rock background and, just as their predecessors had done, they injected their own skills and personalities into the songs to make them their own. "If Arthur showed me ten percent I'd be amazed," Jay reflects, on the myth that the musicians were told what to play. "I can remember that for 'August' Arthur sang the melody part to me but that was it. I was left to conceive the riff, based on what he sang to me and everything else that was on that song. I put that riff where he wanted it, and probably started it the way he wanted it, but after that it was all me. As for the rest of it, it was more or less a free-for-all. Arthur had a good feel for his vocals, and good hands on his acoustic guitar. He could sit down and play us the song, and by doing that imply what the song was supposed to do without giving it licks or saying, 'Here's the solo.'"

Jay suggests that Arthur changed musical direction for practical reasons. "Maybe he realized that to take *Forever Changes* into a concert venue was going to be too difficult to do. He needed extra players and a good sound system. The Moody Blues had to use a Mellotron to get that orchestral sound. So Arthur probably figured it was a huge roadblock for live performances. That could really cause a change in him. It was, 'Let's get back to the roots, the four-piece; let's make some money.' He'd made this great album and now he couldn't go out and perform it. We would get people calling for *Forever Changes* songs at our shows and we would do the ones we could as a four-piece band. He wasn't disgruntled in that way. He loved the pats on the back and the kudos he got for that album. Part of the problem was Bryan MacLean leaving, not to mention the other studio players involved. Maybe he felt like he wasn't in control of the final product. Also, how was he going to follow it? If you try to do the same thing again, or you try something different, either way you're screwed. Arthur was never one for explanations. He was more about deeds. Arthur kind of steered his own car off a lot of cliffs."

We became close friends, but the new band didn't like the Forever Changes bit. They weren't into that. That's one of the reasons why I shied away from it. It didn't sell that great when it started. Besides, these guys were more into rhythm & blues, jazz, and stuff like that.

Of his new bandmates, Jay notes: "Frank was always nice. Definitely the real soul brothers were George, Frank, and Gary Rowles. I'm sure there was a little bit of resentment that I joined the band and not Gary, in the beginning. But George was a lot more open to it than Frank, so George and I became closer friends.

Frank would start taking his drugs, mostly acid, generally right after his morning coffee. He would do these drawings on big paper with a detail that should be put on the head of a pin. It was all really great art, very psychedelic, overlapping, and intricate. Occasionally he was brilliant on bass. George practiced the hardest: he was a really fine drummer. But he tended to be dictatorial in the manner in which he treated a song: the whole song had to come to him. It was hard for him just to play a simple backbeat every four bars or something. It was kind of like asking [Miles Davis drummer] Tony Williams to play surf music. But in his way of playing, George was really brilliant. And Frank would just get high and follow everything. He was a little more of a yes-man to Arthur."

When Jay came to audition, Arthur was still living high up on Kirkwood, in *The Trip* house, with his girlfriend Suzanne and his dog, Self. "The dog would come wagging his tail and put his head in your lap," remembers Jay. "You would start to pat his head but if you got to talking and forgot to pat him he'd growl at you and get ready to bite you. And, in fact, he did bite some people. I always thought that the dog, with that name, kind of personified Arthur and his personality." Annette Ferrel agrees: "Self was like Arthur's alter ego."

Self would often go missing and Arthur would search Laurel Canyon. "I lived in the last house up at the top of Ridpath, and Arthur lived directly across the canyon," recalls one-time Byrds bassist John York. "Self would stray from home quite often. Sometimes, usually late at night, we neighbors would hear Arthur calling out, 'Self, Self ... Self,' into the hills of Laurel Canyon. It was pretty eerie." Ria Berkus once witnessed Arthur blowing hash smoke into Self's nose to make the dog high.

The following year, Arthur sold *The Trip* house and purchased a more secluded luxury estate at 3580 Avenida Del Sol, near Coldwater Canyon, in Studio City. Perched high on a hill, it was protected by an electronic iron gate (installed by Arthur's stepfather, C.L.) at the end of a long, winding driveway that shielded the main house from the street. The isolated property, whose previous owner was television actor Wally 'Mr. Peepers' Cox, was built on several acres overlooking a ravine. It included a servant quarters suite and a separate guest house to the side of the long main dwelling. Here, Arthur resided with Suzanne. It would remain his home until 1975.

I was taken around by a realtor to look at different houses in the area. We went over Mulholland Drive, in Studio City, where we found a lot at the very top of

Avenida Del Sol. It was all leveled-off on top with two houses on it – a main house and a guest house. The guest house had two bedrooms and the main house was fairly large, with bachelor or servants' quarters that had a small living room, bath, bedroom, and a fireplace. I remember taking Self to see the new house and he went missing right after that.

When I lost Self, I felt so bad, I decided not to get another single dog. Instead, I would get a few, so I wouldn't get so attached. Suzanne's dog, Mam Saub, who was an Afghan, had puppies. I took two males and a female. I named the two males Noshita and Bare; the female was Dancer. I also had a Russian wolfhound and an Irish wolfhound. The first was named Tuna and the second I named Screwbop, after this guy who went to high school with me, this big guy who was a quiet type but you knew not to fuck with him. [The dog] Screwbop's father, named Maui or Vindicator, was supposedly the biggest dog in the United States. I had three-and-a-half acres and a large part was fenced off for the dogs. I never taught my dogs any tricks or gave them any rules or regulations to follow. For once, I wanted to see something grow up naturally.

At one time, I had 5 dogs, 11 cats, about 120 pigeons, and a canary named Gary who was the best musician I ever heard in my life. He would get in the same key as the guy on the radio playing a solo, and he would take that solo and blow circles around it. He blew rings around anyone I ever heard take any kind of solo.

One of the strangest, or most beautiful, things that ever happened to me was one night when I got so high that I passed out in the area where the dogs were. It was the same night I was supposed to play with [The Jimi Hendrix Experience rhythm section] Mitch Mitchell and Noel Redding at a club in Hollywood. When I woke up, I was on the ground, surrounded by hair. I couldn't figure it out, but when I did, I saw the dogs had made a tight circle around me. I woke up in the middle of five dogs that had united to keep me warm, protecting me from whatever. Although they didn't get along, when they saw me on the ground, they made peace with each other. They came together as one to protect me. When I got up from the ground, they went right back to growling and barking like nothing had ever happened.

"Arthur had that big dog, Screwbop, an Irish wolfhound," recalls his childhood friend Azell Taylor. "That wasn't a dog; it was more like a horse. Arthur had a party one night, up in the Hollywood Hills, and people were scared to leave because that dog was sitting by the door." Meanwhile, Arthur still owed Elektra one more album according to the terms of Love's original 1966 contract. However, knowing that he would shortly be a free agent, he went in search of a new record deal. Despite the critical acclaim bestowed on *Forever Changes*, Love's record sales had actually been on a steady decline since their debut album, two years earlier. As a result, major labels were less inclined to take a gamble, even on a refreshed line-up of the band, with a more contemporary sound. Arthur's reputation as a difficult artist was another impediment. Nonetheless, a recently launched label, Blue Thumb, was keen to attract a living legend and its president, Bob Krasnow, formerly with Warner Brothers, duly signed Arthur in early 1969. However, before he could release a planned double album on Blue Thumb, there was still the Elektra agreement to satisfy. The label held an option for an extension to the contract, but Arthur was eager to be released.

"*Forever Changes* was never going to be topped," Jac Holzman maintains. "It would have been great but I didn't see it happening. When I saw the nowhere direction of [Love's subsequent album] *Four Sail*, I recognized we'd had the moment, and it was gone. When he asked to be released I said 'OK.' It was tough, because The Doors' success kept staring Arthur in the face. Arthur said he had Blue Thumb talking to him and I said, 'fine, go with Blue Thumb.' I always thought Bob Krasnow was a terrific guy. He later ended up running Elektra and doing it very well. So I let Arthur out of the contract. Then I got a call from Krasnow asking about using Love's logo on Arthur's record. I said, 'We own all the logos but you can have it. You can use it on this record.' All the stuff Arthur did after that was just awful. I would listen to a cut or two, but that was it. I never bought any of it. No, Elektra had the best from Arthur Lee. I still consider him an Elektra artist, but I never knew him in his harder drugs phase. He was already in bad shape on *Four Sail* but I wasn't sure what the mix of drugs was at that time."

Marathon sessions were held for *Four Sail* (and, as it transpired, tracks for Love's post-Elektra album, *Out Here*, also), not in a formal recording environment, but in a house converted into a studio. "Here we were, learning 25 songs more or less all in one go," remembers Jay, "and a few weeks later we were in a little dumpy studio recording all these songs. That was the mysterious interaction of Arthur and business. Out of that, Elektra got their pick of whichever songs they wanted. The rest were the seeds for the first Blue Thumb album, *Out Here*, for which we went into another studio later and finalized the tracks. The studio was in a residential area in the heart of Hollywood. It was definitely a house like any other, but the owners had put in a window between one bedroom and the living room. The living room was where we played. Arthur rented an 8-track, or maybe a 16-track, but they had the console and the other stuff already there. So it was a studio in the making. The luxury of it was that the album was rehearsed, so all we had to do was play it. There were no overdubs, no fixes, nothing. Sure, I think a vocal or a second guitar part might have been added, but even my part on 'August' was a live take with no opportunity to repair or fix it. I think I got one overdubbed solo [on the song 'You Are Something,' released on *Out Here*] because I wanted to make it stupid and it required slowing the recording machine down. The rest of it was pretty much live. Time really was money, and that meant Arthur's money."

The session was very interesting. I recorded those two albums in what was more or less a garage, or a house. I rented equipment at Wally Heider and the guy with the house charged me eight bucks an hour. So I rented all the equipment out of my own pocket and it was all right. The energy the musicians put into it, you couldn't ask for more than that. I was at the end of my Elektra contract.

The title Four Sail means like a sign on a lawn, as in 'for sale.' It was actually 'Love for sale,' because I'd had it with Elektra. I had Bob Krasnow at Blue Thumb waiting and a double album was going to him. Jac Holzman said I owed him and those were the ten songs he took. The others went to Blue Thumb but it was originally supposed to be a 26-song double album.

Love's new, harder edge took fans expecting another *Forever Changes* by surprise. Not everyone appreciated the new direction. "The *Four Sail* line-up was a major contrast to the Love bands I had seen before," says Rick Williams. "That was the first version of Love that made my ears ring afterwards – and the original Love had been a pretty loud band. The new guys were all great players, but the songs and arrangements were so radically different from what Love had been like before. Much of the intricacy was gone. There were some songs that could have almost fit the earlier albums, but the way they were performed, live, was very heavy-handed. It was as if you were being punched in the chest, especially the kick drum and bass. The drum solos were way longer than necessary. I saw that line-up later at the Hullabaloo: they had these huge Marshall stacks and it was painful."

Jim Bickhart witnessed the new-look Love on July 17 1969. "I remember seeing the *Four Sail* band at the Aquarius Theatre in LA, the old Hullabaloo. They were solid, I remember, and were a good, hard-rock band, but kind of undistinguished. Before he died, Arthur admitted that what he did with the reconstructed Love was partly adapting to the new musicians' dislike for *Forever Changes*. While it still had some of his distinctive lyrical and melodic sensibilities, it was a retreat from the adventurous frontier of Love's third album. I only saw them once, but what I remember about the performance is how competent yet unremarkable it was. It sounded like the records: melodic hard-rock played by relatively faceless musicians, fronted by someone who was anything but faceless. It was still a little unique – a hard-rock band fronted by a black man with eclectic abilities – but the music didn't stick in my head."

Longtime Love fan, and Arthur's friend, Dennis Kelley, in LA on shore leave from the navy, was unaware that the band's line-up had changed when he attended a show at the Shrine Auditorium. He was impressed, nonetheless. "I went expecting to see them playing the *Forever Changes* album, with that line-up. When they walked out on stage I remember thinking, 'Who are these guys?' That was only the third time I had seen Love, and each time it was a different line-up. They were amazing, that night. They played the entire *Four Sail* album and George Suranovich was just a monster on the drums. It wasn't what I anticipated, or was hoping for, but, again, Arthur blew me away."

Reviewing a performance at the Pasadena Rose Palace in June 1969, *Los Angeles Times* critic John Mendelsohn declared the new Love to be "better than ever." He, for one, didn't miss the old personnel. "A gang of surly egotists no more, the group was propelled by founder and only remaining original member Arthur Lee's clear and controlled voice. His new sidemen, particularly the lead guitarist (whose playing betrays some jazz experience) are more than competent and play together (which the old group seldom did). The only thing one could complain about was that a few of the old Love favorites lacked instrumentation and voicing. 'Orange Skies,' for instance, just wasn't right without that lovely flute line behind Lee's vocals."

Jay Donellan remembers wanting to outdo the previous incarnation of the band: "We all felt a real need to play good and perform well following the previous line-up of Love. Not to just go through the motions. Arthur was really putting a lot of energy into his performances and so were the other guys in the band. It was kind of a high energy deal, and that's what won over the people who were expecting the *Forever Changes* Love."

The band continued to work Love's familiar Southern California turf, where they remained a major draw. "There were never any really long tours," Jay recalls. "I don't think Arthur liked airplanes very much. Also, with the redneck condition of the United States at that time, he didn't like to get involved in all of that. I'm sure that was part of it. I don't think he thought there was much money to be made out on the road. And there were so many great gigs in and around Southern California. All he had to do was get in his car and drive to the show." Jay remembers one particular offer which Arthur turned down flat. "I was at his house and an agent phoned him. I remember hearing Arthur say, 'Naw, fuck it. I don't want to go to New York for one gig!' I later found out that the 'one gig' was Woodstock."

After some additional studio sweetening, Elektra released *Four Sail* in August 1969. Despite besting *Forever Changes* on the *Billboard* album charts by reaching #102, creatively and critically, the record compared poorly with its predecessor. In truth, few albums in 1969 could stand up against *Forever Changes* and, indeed, such comparisons are perhaps unfair. The only song on *Four Sail* that is remotely similar in style to that of Love's magnum opus is the elegant closing track, "Always See Your Face," with its subtle use of French horn. There is much to recommend *Four Sail* in its own right, however, and it certainly deserves its place in the Love canon. Arthur's songwriting remains expressive if not as insightful or as dark as on *Forever Changes*. In fact, the overall mood is generally more upbeat, optimistic, and positive than on any previous Love album. Each of the players holds his end up well, notably Jay, with his fluid, jazz and country-infused guitar work, which was more free-form and experimental than other heavy-rock guitarists of that period. And the drumming is outstanding. "George Suranovich could blow me off the stage with one hand tied behind his back," admits Michael Stuart – himself no slouch behind the kit. Certainly the album's opening track, the complex, jazzy, heavy-rock flavored "August," sent a clear signal that this was a whole new Love. None of the band's albums ever sounded like its predecessor, so in that sense *Four Sail* is consistent with the group's oeuvre. "One thing Arthur told me about writing songs was, 'Don't ever backtrack, look for something new and fresh,'" recalls his friend, Riley Racer.

Several cuts on the album would go on to become Arthur Lee mainstays for a number of years thereafter: songs such as such "Good Times," "August," and the Arthur Lee/Jay Donnellan collaboration "Singing Cowboy." Two other album tracks, "Your Friend And Mine – Neil's Song," and "I'm With You," were inspired by the recent death of road manager Neil Rappaport, while "Robert Montgomery" was based on a character Arthur knew (actually named *Jerry* Montgomery).

I remember, in 1966, when I was playing at Bido Lito's, a lot of the black guys from my old neighborhood had, at first, put me down. Now, when I looked out into the audience, I would see some of them. They were wearing their hair long and some of them even had wigs. It used to crack me up. One night, I looked out into the audience and saw this black guy who must have been over six feet tall and was the shape of a football fullback. He was black and his face almost resembled King Kong, with a gap between his teeth. To boot, he was wearing a blond wig, beating a tambourine, looking straight at me on stage, and laughing. This was Jerry Montgomery. The way he introduced himself was with the tambourine: he threw it directly at me while I was singing. I stopped doing what I was doing, picked up the tambourine, and threw it back at him, hitting him right on the top of his head.

Former Crazy World Of Arthur Brown drummer, Drachen Theaker, appears on three tracks on *Four Sail* (and one on the follow-up album *Out Here*). "Originally, I heard that Arthur thought Drachen might have a better feel for those songs than George," says Jay, "but I also heard that George had a disagreement with Arthur over money and said, 'Fuck you, I'm not going to play until you straighten this out.' I don't know which version is true, but Drachen was a good guy, I liked him a lot. He came in like a session musician, played his part, and was gone." George and Arthur subsequently resolved their differences and the drummer returned to the fold.

Jay's time with Love came to an abrupt end one year after joining, following an altercation with Arthur over a missed gig on August 2. "I got along with Arthur, but I was always a thorn in his side because it's my nature not to take any shit. One of the reasons he kicked me out of the band was to do with a big outdoor gig we had, in Oakland. We were all excited and flew up there. When we arrived, it seemed Arthur hadn't arranged a truck to meet us and collect the gear. It was a holiday and we couldn't get transport. By the time we got to the gig, we were over an hour late and were told we couldn't go on because the closing act, Blood Sweat & Tears, had it in their contract that they would close the show. The promoter said we couldn't go on. Arthur started in on him saying, 'Fuck you! You don't know what you're missing, you fuckin' stupid ... .' So George and I went and talked with the managers of Blood Sweat & Tears and told them what had happened. They said, 'No problem. You can go on after us.' We went back and told Arthur, but he said, 'No, man. Fuck 'em! Just get in the car. Let's go.' Everyone turned quiet, did what they were told, and got in the car. I spoke up and told Arthur that it was a real shitty thing to do. We had resolved it, and Arthur was the one who stopped it from working. That led to a brawl between him and me, with George and Frank hiding behind the amplifiers. It ended up with no words being said all the way back to LA. Not long after that, I showed up at the studio and found a locked door. Arthur poked his head out the door and said, 'We don't need you today, man.' I got this telegram later the same day from the manager. It said: 'Pursuant to your desires and wishes you are no longer a member of the group Love.' That was the end of the story. It read like it was my decision to leave the group. What a legal spin that was. No one had the balls to sit down and talk to me about it."

This presented Frank and George with an opportunity to get their friend, Gary Rowles, into the band. "They were finishing up the double album at the time, so Gary completed the tracks," says Jay. "He was a good player and good for the band, but there is a way to do things that's in the best interests of everyone concerned. In Arthur's mind it was *his* band. He was the one constant. It was Self again, the big dog with a bad habit of biting people who didn't pat him."

"Arthur called me up and asked me to come over to the studio and record a solo on a song on *Out Here*," explains Gary Rowles. "He said there was one song that has to have a long, extended guitar solo on it. So I came over and played on 'Love Is More Than Words.' After that, Arthur asked me to join the band. He said they were going to New York to play the Fillmore East, to Europe, to tour, then back to make a record. I wasn't doing anything at the time and I missed playing with Frank and George, so I agreed. We had something really special together."

Gary was the son of noted jazz pianist Jimmy Rowles, LA born and raised, and from a tender age had been exposed to a lot of high level musicians and music business people. "It was always assumed that I would have something to do with music," he says. Self-taught, he had played in a high school surf band that was a contemporary of the early Beach Boys. He later backed "Mission Bells" singer Donnie Brooks and did a stint in Las Vegas. On joining Love, Gary moved into the servants' quarters in Arthur's house. The band would jam in the guest house where George now resided.

For all the new activity, the legacy of *Forever Changes* still clung to the band and clouded the public's expectations of them. "We were a psychedelic band and that's what Arthur wanted," says Gary. "He wanted to move on. He didn't want to be stuck in that other stuff." He agrees, however, that the post-*Forever Changes* bands never earned the same respect as the earlier incarnation of Love. "The stuff they did on *Forever Changes* was amazing music. I would say it was Arthur's swansong. I don't think he could ever get back to that. I think his attitude was, 'I've been there and done that.' Ours was a whole different thing. We were a rock band. Unfortunately, he didn't quite have it together enough to get it off the ground at a self-sustaining level. It kept crashing and burning. Every band became a trimmed down version, because it took more effort to get it off the ground."

Despite the reconstituted line-up, Blue Thumb, then preparing to release their first Love album, still had the *Forever Changes* band in mind. The failure of *Four Sail* had made Bob Krasnow apprehensive about the viability of the new Love. He convinced Arthur to be reconciled with his former bandmates and to play a high-profile gig – at the Santa Monica Civic Center – in the hope that it might be enough to persuade them to stay together. Everyone agreed to perform, although Bryan MacLean was not invited.

This was supposed to be a big thing: the return of Love. I don't know how much promotion was done but I do know that, like before, I had to rent instruments and amplifiers. The guys all promised that they had changed and everything was going to be different. It was different all right. When we got out to Santa Monica that afternoon, there was an airplane flying over the ocean and the city with a banner behind it that read 'LOVE at the Santa Monica Civic tonight.' That really made me feel good.

The curtain opened and we started out with "7 & 7 Is," but in a way I had never heard it before. Johnny sounded like he was playing a ukulele and the rest of the music was just as soft. I screamed, "What are you doing?" and Johnny said something like, "It's too loud." I flipped out. "It's supposed to be loud, man. What's the matter with you?" That turned me off so bad I can't remember playing anything else after that. Where we used to get standing ovations, all I heard from the crowd now was a little courtesy clapping. I was mad. After the gig, I went looking for the equipment I had rented and it was gone. I looked everywhere for the guitars. I found them, later, in a pawnshop in the old neighborhood where Johnny and I grew up. I felt like a fool. Worse than that, my hopes and dreams were let down once again.

"It just didn't feel right," says Johnny of the underwhelming reformation show. "This was before I went into rehab and I was just miserable. I didn't play worth a damn and nor did Kenny. Michael Stuart and Arthur, they were always on, but the two of us were just not playing well. Then we started bickering and so we decided we just couldn't do it. Yeah, Arthur did try to get us back together, but we weren't ready. We were still chasing the dragon, so to speak. We maybe thought that if we rehearsed and did a European tour it might work, but then Arthur got together with this management company and changed the ground rules about how we were going to be paid. It wasn't an equal split any more. Kenny and Michael would have gone for it but I wouldn't. So we decided we wouldn't do it. I went to New York."

A UK tour was mooted, to commence on November 17. However, with the old guard unable to pull it together, Arthur postponed the overseas visit until the following year and hooked up once again with Fayad, Suranovich, and Rowles. In December, Blue Thumb released the double album *Out Here*.

While Love's fifth album is not without merit, offering a lighter touch than *Four Sail*, it seems evident that Elektra, not Blue Thumb, had got the best of Arthur's recent songs. "Listening to those two records, it's like one triple album, because they were all recorded together," says Jay Donnellan. "I can't separate the two. I think *Four Sail* got some of the better songs but *Out Here* has a few good moments." Had there been some outside influence culling the herd, *Out Here* might have made for a more consistent single album; Arthur was determined to release a double set, however. Eclectic is certainly an apt description of its 18 tracks, which range from country picking (the throwaway numbers "Abalony" and "Car Lights On In The Day Time Blues") to pop-rock ("Willow Willow"), exquisite baroque-folk ("Listen To My Song"), Crosby, Stills & Nash-like soft rock ("I Still Wonder," co-written with Jay), jazz ("Nice To Be"), and psychedelic guitar explorations ("Love Is More Than Words Or Better Late Than Never").

Despite George Suranovich's stunning technique, the extended drum solo on "Doggone" is overly indulgent. "George thought of the drums as a melodic instrument and played them as such," notes Riley Racer. "Gather Round" recalls the earlier Love sound, while an ungainly remake of enduring live favorite "Signed D.C." (featuring Drachen Theaker on drums) pales by comparison with the haunting original.

The cover art for *Out Here* features a striking, gatefold-size psychedelic image by painter Burt Shonfeld which had caught Arthur's attention (he would ultimately buy the original painting). The inside photo finds the four band members cavorting with guns in a park. "We were at the merry-go-round in Griffith Park, having some fun with cap guns and acting like kids," explains Jay. "I never put the two together, Arthur and guns, until much later. He probably always had guns, but they weren't sitting out on the coffee table or anything. I think the more paranoid and reclusive he got, the more the guns became of value to him."

One curiosity on the sleeve was Arthur's chosen credit, production and songwriting being ascribed to 'Arthurly.' "That was, as I recall, a very stoned moment," explains Jay. "Arthur had some kind of gigantic hash pipe in his hand and said, 'I'm going to change my name to *Arthurly*.' It may have been a very clever move on his part, legally, because of the switch in labels, the commitment to material, credits, and all that. But who knows what he was thinking?" Jim Bickhart: "I remember one of my former colleagues remarking, after seeing the *Out Here* album credits, that Arthur Lee was the only guy who's ever turned his name into an adverb. That was another example of the audacity of Arthur. At that particular time in his career, that was how the audacity manifested itself."

Out Here fared worse than *Four Sail* on the *Billboard* album charts, peaking at #176, although it fared much better in the UK, reaching #29 (having been released on EMI's progressive Harvest imprint). Over the years, the album has come in for reappraisal from fans who find redeeming qualities in its odd assortment of tracks. However, at the time of its release, concerns were widely aired about Arthur having lost his muse. The specter of *Forever Changes* continued to hover over anything with Love's name attached to it. Critics pointed to the absence of Bryan, Johnny, Kenny, and Michael as the reason for the absence of Love's old magic. "A lot of people respond very favorably when they hear I was in Love," says Gary Rowles. "When they find out it wasn't the *Forever Changes* line-up they say, 'Oh, you were in that *next* version.' I can understand why people feel that way."

News of a long-awaited UK tour (followed by dates in Sweden and Denmark) may have spurred sales on that side of the Atlantic. The tour was to commence on February 19 at London's infamous club for musicians, the Speakeasy (with the first full concert date the following night, at Goldsmiths College, New Cross). Riley Racer accompanied the band on their European jaunt as Arthur's assistant. "I think Arthur liked having me around. Friendship was important to him. We did some warm-up gigs in the States, at the Fillmore West and Fillmore East, and from there went to Europe. Arthur flew out a day or two ahead of us to do interviews. We stayed at a flat [Gary Rowles claims it was Keith Richards' apartment in Belgravia] and it was such a thrill for all of us to be in London, and to see the way people responded to the name Love. It was a real eye-opener, just how much they loved Love. I remember, in London, I was walking through a doorway heading backstage and some guy hollered out, 'Can I get your autograph?' He must have mistaken me for Arthur – I was the only black guy there. I said, 'No, no. I'm not Arthur. He's backstage.' And he replied, 'Oh but you *know* him!' Just knowing the guy as justification for an autograph is pretty good." The tour would prove a major event for Love-starved UK fans.

We went to a club in England called the Speakeasy, and George thought he saw Ginger Baker there, so he went over to the guy, cursed him out, and told him how much better a drummer he was. Of course, it wasn't actually Ginger Baker. George used to crack me up. But talk about showmanship: this guy used to take solos you wouldn't believe and he was always a crowd pleaser. He would get ovations even before the band would. That would make us play even better toward our final encore. We'd get at least two, three, or more standing ovations, every time. We could really turn it on. Everywhere we played it was the same thing.

Gary Rowles played lead guitar. He was one of the best guitar players around. Gary was a perfectionist and he had every gadget for every sound that you would want to hear: wah-wah pedals, Echoplex, phase shifters ... you name it. It was always: "Arthur, listen to this, listen to that." The man was very interested in what he was doing.

"On that 1970 tour, Arthur didn't do a lot of his older songs," notes Riley Racer. "The one song he would do from *Forever Changes* was 'Andmoreagain,' because it had the least frills. Audiences always wanted to hear the *Forever Changes* songs. In 1970, he had a reputation that was still growing. People weren't writing about him in magazines every day, but places would be packed and people were really digging it."

In fact the band did pull out "My Little Red Book," "Bummer In The Summer," and "Orange Skies" on occasion during the tour. The UK leg wrapped up in Birmingham on March 10, after which the band crossed the North Sea to play a memorable show at the Tivoli Gardens, Copenhagen on March 12 (video of which still exists). Following a show in Stockholm, Love returned to Copenhagen for a final show on March 14 before landing back in London for a few days prior to the flight home. Brief as it was, that first European tour did much to solidify Arthur's fanbase and support there. The UK would remain his principal market for the next 35 years, even as his currency plunged drastically in the USA.

CHAPTER 7

LOVE JUMPED
THROUGH MY
WINDOW

Arthur Lee, 1971

During their UK visit, Love found time to enter Olympic Studios in Barnes, South West London, for a now legendary jam with Arthur's old acquaintance, Jimi Hendrix. The session would yield the opening track of the band's next album and rekindle a relationship, dating back to the early 60s, between rock music's premier 'psychedelic black men.' "It was truly overwhelming," recalls Gary Rowles of the session. "No matter who you talk to, when you tell them you played with Jimi Hendrix they pay attention."

When I said I knew Jimi it was like I'd told Gary that it was the millennium and he was going to meet Jesus Christ. I told them I was gonna try to get Jimi to do an album with me. When I introduced Jimi to the band it was as if they had all turned to stone. I never saw anything like it. I couldn't believe Jimi had such an impact on people. Boy, did we have fun at the Olympic recording studio. The band and Jimi all took mescaline. Although they didn't know it, I was as straight as Cochise's arrow. Somebody had to steer the ship.

By the close of the 60s, Seattle-born Jimi Hendrix was the brightest star in rock music's firmament. He achieved godlike status among fans and fellow musicians for an incendiary mastery of the electric guitar. He was the most successful and most recognized black musician in America. Those close to Arthur claim he had a conflicted relationship with the guitar icon. While he applauded Jimi's success as a black man in a white rock milieu – and even sought to bask in the reflected glow of the Hendrix aura – he also resented what he considered Jimi's appropriating of his image and disliked Jimi's acclaim outweighing his own. "In an interview, Jimi once said how much he loved Arthur," says Herbie Worthington, a close friend of both men. "I read that to Arthur, and he went really quiet. He was very jealous of Jimi and yet he loved him. And Jimi looked upon Arthur as an equal."

A disproportionate amount of space in Arthur's own memoirs is devoted to recounting his times in the company of Jimi Hendrix. Arthur idolized Jimi the way fans idolized Arthur in the 60s. "Often, when Arthur felt he was in competition with somebody, he would take on this very standoffish, negative attitude," notes his friend Len Fagan. "He didn't like the fact that someone was way up there above him in popularity. It was a continuation of that competitive streak he'd had since childhood. I'm sure he felt in competition with Jimi Hendrix. I heard him say that Jimi got his whole image from Arthur."

Gary Rowles saw in Jimi qualities which Arthur palpably lacked. "Jimi really loved people. He had the ability to communicate with people beyond just being an incredible guitar player. It was part of who he was, that ability to love and connect with others. Arthur recognized that and wanted to attach himself to it, or wanted to present it along with what he was doing. But Arthur wasn't a people person. He didn't even want to tour. He just wanted to control a bunch of people, make records, and have a place where he could do whatever it was he wanted to do."

When I heard that Jimi was playing the Whisky, my friend David Biali and I went down there. I was walking across the street to the club and this black dude came walking out, looking just like me in '66. It tripped me out. As I got closer, the guy became more familiar. I said to David, "That's Jimi Hendrix." It was the guy that played on "My Diary." Jimi also remembered me. All of a sudden, a crowd of people started following us. Seeing the pair of us must have flipped those people out. I said, "Hey, man, why don't we drive up to my house? It's cool there. If you wanted to just sort of get away, it's cool for that." I was living in the house with the swimming pool in the middle. Also, I had just what we needed for the head, so we went there. I couldn't help but notice how shy Jimi was. At the time, I didn't know if he was just trying to be polite. Anyway, we had a good time.

I don't know if Jimi was my best friend, but I sure tried to be his best friend. I could see, on the outside looking in, how people were ripping him off, left and right, and I wanted to make sure that I wasn't one of them. The crowd he was hanging spent his money as fast as he got it, and he was just giving it away to others. I made sure that whatever we did, or wherever we went, I never let him spend a penny. Besides the love and respect we had for each other, that was one way of showing him that I was a true friend.

In 2002, Jimi's brother, Leon, told me that before Jimi had the hippie look, he'd picked up the first Love album and said, "I think I'll try it this way," meaning the way I looked on my first album cover. That might've been one reason why he seemed so shy around me. Jimi was one of my closest friends, and one of the best guitar players I ever heard, but he was another example of staying too long at the fair. It seemed to me, he didn't know the party was over and it was time to go home.

During that first UK tour, Jimi visited Arthur in the London flat he was renting. The two decided to book studio time to record a song Arthur had written.

"Arthur introducing me to Jimi was a highlight of my musical history," says Riley Racer, recalling the March 17 Olympic recording session that followed. "I had seen Jimi in concert at UCLA, less than a year before; now I was meeting him. That was pretty cool. Arthur had never really talked about knowing people like Jimi Hendrix. He wasn't like that. Jimi was just one of his peers. They were like two casual friends meeting up and talking over old times. I don't know if the session was planned; I don't think Jimi came over [specifically] to play; it just happened. They cut that song 'The Everlasting First.' Hendrix had that short solo and, from what I've read of Jimi, he was quite a perfectionist and would have happily sat there and played it over 30 times. Arthur said, 'No, it's great!' Sometimes, the first take is the best, however many times you replay it. I remember them doing the song "E-Z Rider," too."

In fact, Love cut three songs at Olympic with Jimi, the third being a long jam given the title "Loon." Gary Rowles has vivid memories of the London sojourn. "When I was in England, I came back from one of my walks and there was Jimi Hendrix, sitting on the couch in our apartment. I just thought, 'Man, how cool is this?' I told him I loved what he did and what a pleasure it was to meet him. We talked, and I showed him my Fender Strat, which was a '54, serial number seven. He got excited about that. He played it a bit, then Arthur said, 'Hey, maybe we can get together and go down and play some music?' Everyone thought that was a cool idea. Our English roadie, known simply as 'H,' who looked like a Member of Parliament, only with a little ponytail, called up Olympic studio and it was available. So we went down there and ended up playing for over 12 hours."

While I was in New York, playing at the Fillmore East, I met a girl who looked just like Brigitte Bardot. Her name was Dessa and she told me she was from Finland. It was sort of like love at first sight. Although I was living with Suzanne, in LA, we weren't married and I just had to see Dessa again. I told her I was going on tour in the UK and asked how she would like it if I sent for her when I got there. She said she would like that very much and so, after I had been in London a few days, she arrived.

When we got to the flat, we headed straight for the bedroom. I must have lost ten pounds! For some reason, I just didn't take Dessa out much. I still wanted to see if the grass was greener on the other side of London, with another chick. One night, I told her I was going to a club to meet Jimi. I don't know why, but I asked her if she knew Jimi. I remember saying to myself, "Don't let it be so." She smiled at me and said, "Yes, but Jimi's like my brother. You're my lover." Well, that did it. Jimi and I had a lot in common, especially with the groupies. It seemed that almost every chick I'd get with had been with Jimi, and every chick he'd been with had been with me. The next morning, I told Dessa that I was married, had four kids, and was sorry but I had to get back to LA to see them. I would pay her way back to Finland and give her whatever she needed to make it. I must have tipped the cab driver $100 !

After she left, this song came to me called "Flying." I wrote it about Jimi and me. It's on False Start. It goes: "He flew in and I flew out, yeah / Flying's a wonderful thing / He sat in and I sat out / Flying's a wonderful thing / And if you find someone that you think you can love and you find out she's in love with your big brother / Yeah, flying's a wonderful thing." I think I was in tears as I was writing the song.

You're probably thinking that I sure was unfaithful to Suzanne, and I was. But she was unfaithful to me, too, and with some of my closest friends, among them James Scott, for whom I wrote the song "He Knows A Lot of Good Women (When Their Husband's Not At Home)" [sic].

One of the ways I got Jimi to do the session in the first place – or how I got his attention, anyway – happened one night at the Speakeasy. He and I arrived together. The guy at the front door told me I could come in but Jimi couldn't. When I asked him why, he said that Jimi had been fighting in the club on an earlier occasion and they didn't want that happening again. So I told him that Jimi was cool, the entourage that was with us was cool, and I didn't think any fighting would be going on that night. He finally agreed. I said to Jimi, "Look, man, neither one of us is going to be around much longer, anyway; so while we're here, we might as well do something together." When I said that, whatever we were talking about, or he was thinking about, just seemed to stop and I had his full attention. He really went into some deep thought as he looked at me from across the table. He was looking into my eyes and I knew he could only be thinking about our early deaths.

The session went completely differently from the way I was used to recording. I thought it was to be a private session. I don't remember telling anyone to come, except the band; but, to my surprise, there were people all over the place. There were girls I'd never seen before and faces popping out from where you would least expect a person to be. I was in a state of shock, but Jimi said, "It's OK, let them stay." More than once, Jimi thought we were done and went to pack everything up. Then he would come back into the studio while we were playing and say, "What key?" Once, when we were learning a song I wrote, called "Ride That Vibration," Jimi came walking back in during the middle of it. He asked me, "What did you just say in that song?" I said, "Ride the vibration down like a six foot grave / Don't let it get you down." Then he said, "I gotta go; it's getting too heavy." He called a cab, took George's girlfriend, and was out the door. George just looked at me as if to say, "That's Jimi." After a while, Jimi came back and suggested that everyone jam, and were my band-members ever happy!

On that session in London, we managed to lay down a few tracks, among them "E-Z Rider," "The Everlasting First," and a jam that I would later add lyrics to. Jimi sang on "E-Z Rider." I gave the master reel to Bob Krasnow. He never gave it back. At the time, I wondered if someone was filming us, although I never saw a camera. I found out, in the early 90s, they had been.

Back in the studio, it was almost daylight, so I signaled to H to start wrapping it up. I don't think Jimi was ready to quit, but it had been a long night for me. The tour we were doing was over with; I just wanted to go back to Studio City in California. As we were walking out of the building, Jimi asked, "Where are you going?" I said, "Man, I gotta get back to LA; to my woman, dogs, and pigeons." Jimi said, "Come here, I want to show you something." We walked back inside the studio. He pointed to his guitar case on the floor. Then he opened it up. I thought he had a stash in there, but as he stood up, he pointed to it again and said, "This is all I have." I couldn't figure it out at first, but then it hit me. He was telling me that the white Stratocaster guitar in the case were his only possessions. I felt kind of sad for him.

Jimi said something similar to me when he first came up to my place in Studio City. I had this land on the top of the hill: a main house, guest house, and servants' quarters. Jimi said, "You know, I have enough money to buy five houses like this. Why am I living in a motel?" I didn't answer him. Who could answer that but him?

Returning to LA in June, the band resumed recording, this time at the Record Plant. They were cutting tracks for what would become Love's next album, *False Start*. When Blue Thumb's Bob Krasnow learned that Love had recorded a session with Jimi Hendrix, he was beside himself. A Love album boasting a guest appearance from Jimi was a potential hit.

At Olympic, we had recorded a song I wrote about the both of us called "The Everlasting First." Bob Krasnow wanted to see if I could get Jimi to do the song again. He was a huge Jimi Hendrix fan and he wanted to meet him in person, just like everyone else, it seemed. I called Jimi and told him. He was skeptical about the idea at first but then I said, "Aw, come on down to the studio. I'll hold your hand." So we both showed up at the Record Plant studio, on Beverly, where, in fact, Jimi had cut some of Electric Ladyland [the third and final Jimi Hendrix Experience album]. It was owned by a good friend of mine, Gary Kellgren. Bob Krasnow was such a Hendrix fan that he had a portrait made of him. It was a picture with stars and planets in space, with Jimi's face as the center of the universe. Bob gave me the picture and told me to be sure that I got it to Jimi.

When Jimi and I showed up at the studio, there was Bob with a few of his friends. Nooney Rickett was there, too. I can still see the smile on Bob's face. He was getting to meet his hero for the first time. I said, "Jimi, this is Bob Krasnow, president of Blue Thumb records." Jimi never even looked at the guy, although he must have been standing five feet away. Then Nooney says to Jimi, "Hey man, did anybody ever tell you that you sound a lot like B.B. King?" That did it! If looks could kill, I think Nooney would have died on the spot. Jimi gave him a look I didn't know he had in him. After that, I wasn't really up for doing the song with all these vibes going on.

There would be no further Lee/Hendrix collaborations, but when *False Start* was released, in December 1970, promotional ads trumpeted Jimi's presence on the album.

"The Everlasting First" was even released as a single, although it failed to chart. Nonetheless, Arthur continued to cultivate the friendship in the months following their session. Jimi visited Arthur's house on several occasions, and jammed with him, Gary, and George, in the guest house. Gary Rowles recalls the occasion when a certain guitarist came to call. "I was asleep in the little apartment, off the kitchen. There was a knock on the door. It was about 5am. I got up, and there was Jimi Hendrix standing at my door. He said, 'Hey man, you got any guitar strings?' I said, 'Yeah, sure.' I went over to the house with him but he didn't really play. That afternoon, we went over to the guest house where George lived; he had his drums set up, so we did some jamming: George, Jimi, and me. That was fun."

I'll never forget the time I invited Jimi Hendrix over for dinner and he wound up staying two or three weeks. I remember Jimi calling up on the phone and telling me he didn't think he'd be able to make it. He told me that there was a time to stay and a time to go. I was a vegetarian, then. I said, "My old lady cooked all this food, and you're telling me there's a time to go and a time to stay? Say, brother, I don't know what you're talking about, but you'd better get your little butt over here or, better yet, I'll come and get you. Where are you staying?" He said, "I'm at the Beverly Rodeo Hotel, in Beverly Hills," so I went to pick him up. When I arrived, to my surprise, who was there but one of the girls I used to fool around with, Devon Wilson. Actually, we did more than fool around. We were lovers, too, and good friends. There was another girl there, too; her name was Collette. Man, she was pretty. Now, Jimi had just finished Electric Ladyland and he played one of the cuts for me, it was "Cross Town Traffic." I remember him being excited to see what I thought about it. All the time, Collette was giving me the googly eyes. Trying to be polite, I told him the record sounded fine. Later, that song became one of my favorites. After that, I went right into the room where Collette was, past the beads hanging from the top of the doorway, and into the bedroom. I don't think I even told her my name. I remember turning around and seeing Devon and Jimi standing in the doorway, looking at us.

I had a Bentley at the time, and we all got in and I drove over the hills of Coldwater to my place. I remember Suzanne Hausner's face when I introduced her to Jimi Hendrix. She seemed to be as much of a groupie as everyone else. I don't think Jimi had introduced me to Devon until we walked outside at my place. When he did, he looked at me, then looked at her, and said, "Do you two know each other?" Devon signaled me to say "no." We shook hands and I said, "Glad to meet you." I don't think we fooled Jimi for a minute.

Even though we had done a session together in England, the guys in the band were still star-struck about Jimi. They just seemed to idolize him and were anxious to know if he would jam with them in the guest house. So I took him over there and I remember them asking him if he'd brought his guitar. He said "yes." I thought I should go to the store to get some more liquor and stuff. At that time, this new drug called MDA had just come out. A couple of my band-members had some and they gave a handful to Jimi. I didn't know if he was showing off, or what, but, like in London, if he was going to take a flight, I wasn't. I wanted to make sure that nothing went wrong. Anyway, I went to the store. When I came back, Jimi was lying over in the corner, with this strange look on his face. I found out that MDA wasn't a visual type drug; it was more like a hearing type thing. Jimi was doing all he could to look straight.

I had never seen Jimi, Mitch Mitchell, and Noel Redding – The Jimi Hendrix Experience – play before; I'd just seen Jimi. They were playing San Diego and Jimi called me up and asked if I would like to come down there to see the show. I thought that it would be a trip. Jimi was staying at the Hilton. My hair was fairly long and I had on this brown leather vest with fringes hanging down and maybe a few beads on it. After landing in San Diego, we took a cab to the Hilton. When the cab pulled up in front of the hotel and I got out, people started screaming and throwing paper out of the windows. They thought I was Jimi. When we went inside the hotel room, Jimi was being sort of shy around me. One of the first things I said was, "Jimi, I almost got a ticker tape parade when I got out of the car; the people thought I was you."

For a change, I was going to see someone else play; and play he did! I had never seen anyone attack the guitar like that. Jimi playing left-handed was weird enough, but there were two people standing in back of him with guitars as well. They were there in case his guitar went out of tune. He would press down on a pedal and sustain the note while the people behind him slipped another, ready-tuned, guitar over his head. Without having to stop and tune up, he just went right on with the song. Jimi used to tune down to D, instead of E, which meant that he could bend the strings easier, or at least that was one way he did it. When he played a solo and turned the guitar up, the people seemed to fall back like bowling pins. He was quite a crowd pleaser. Everyone seemed to love his show and I was quite impressed.

After the show, Jimi gave me some acid. I didn't know it, but he didn't take any. What they say about payback is true, I guess. Twice, he dropped and I didn't, and now I was on and he wasn't. Jimi invited me to go on to the next city with him, but I declined. Then he said, "Well, you've got to come up to Seattle with me and have some of my grandmother's cooking." I said that maybe I would, someday. Little did I know that would be the last time I would ever see Jimi alive. Next time I heard about him was when my former manager, Forest Hamilton, called me on the phone and told me that Jimi was dead.

Before he died, Jimi and I talked about putting a group together. He thought that it should be called Band Aid. He suggested Stevie Winwood, Remi Kabaka, and me as the band-members. I don't remember who the bass player was going to *be. When I did my first solo album for A&M Records, I called the group Band Aid in memory of what Jimi had said.*

Jimi Hendrix died in his sleep, of asphyxiation caused by excessive drug ingestion, on September 18 1970. "Arthur once said that Jimi was 'Clark Kent until he put his guitar on. Then he became Superman,'" says Herbie Worthington. "That was so true of Jimi, and very astute of Arthur. Off stage, Jimi was so soft spoken, but on stage he was a monster."

Compared to the less than flattering critiques that had greeted the previous two Love albums, *False Start* earned decent notices. The presence of Jimi Hendrix on the opening track, so soon after his death, was enough to draw media attention. It was a more consistent album than *Out Here*, and the Hendrix connection on several tracks bore his influence in style and execution. The guitar-heavy sound was boosted by the presence of Nooney Rickett, who played second guitar and sang on the album (he would feature in the group cover photo, although he didn't tour with the band). In addition to the studio tracks, the song "Stand Out" was recorded live, on the UK tour, at Waltham Forest Technical College.

In *Rolling Stone* magazine, the foremost music publication at that time, Mike Saunders lavished praise on the album, paying particular attention to Arthur's singing and writing, admitting that he could "rave on all day saying wonderful things about it." *The Washington Post*, in a favorable December 13 review, noted that there had been something of a hiatus since the last Love release but concluded: "This fast-paced, tightly assembled record makes the wait worthwhile." As with most reviews of the album, Jimi Hendrix's guest appearance was acknowledged as the highlight.

Unfortunately, the positive notices did not translate into substantial sales and *False Start* stalled at #184. Bob Krasnow had high hopes for the album and confidently boasted that if it wasn't a hit he would release Arthur from his contract. Arthur had him put his money where he his mouth was and sign a restaurant napkin promising to do just that. "After the *False Start* album had come out and not done well, Arthur had me drive him up to the Blue Thumb offices in Beverly Hills," recalls Len Fagan. "He went up there and Krasnow honored his word and let Arthur go."

Jim Bickhart: "Of the three albums Arthur did in the early 70s as Love, the one thing that stood out, not because it was a great song but because it was a pretty intense performance, was "The Everlasting First." It had Hendrix on it, and it didn't sound like the other stuff the band had been recording. When you listen to those three albums, you can't help but think Arthur was selling himself short, especially given his history on the earlier Love albums, which were never predictable. Even in that earlier era, there were people doing really good hard-rock. Arthur wasn't one of them. Knowing what I do about him, now, I think Arthur was carrying a burden of his own manufacture. That really got in the way of him being the artist he could have been, and that's a shame."

"Arthur was a wonderful wordsmith and a good singer who wrote timely stuff but who just had to be in control of everything," concedes Gary Rowles. "It ultimately led to his downfall. He just didn't know that the people who were really successful, where he wanted to be, had to work at it. I never saw Arthur work hard, ever. He expected everything to come to him. Maybe *Forever Changes* was when he was allowing the muse to direct his communication, instead of allowing the frustration of who he was, and who he wanted to be, to direct him. Maybe that's why he was so apathetic after that, because he couldn't top it. I think his life was based on frustration. When I knew him, nothing ever satisfied him, yet he never really knew what he wanted. He had a lot of unresolved conflict. That certainly made him an enigmatic person, and hard to read."

Ronnie Haran has another explanation for Arthur's dwindling creative stock. "There is something I learned long ago, and it applies to Arthur. When a musician can do his music, that's all he should do. When he gets involved in business, the music suffers. After I was no longer involved with the band, there was basically no one who controlled Arthur or advised him. Arthur started doing his own business. The brilliant, inspirational expression disappears when an artist takes over his own management; the only two exceptions are Mick Jagger and Paul Simon. That's what happened with Arthur: he tried running his own ship."

Following late November shows at the Fillmore West, George Suranovich quit again (over issues concerning Arthur and money, inevitably). Don Poncher, Gary's former New Buffalo bandmate, stepped in, playing at December 4 and 5 Fillmore East shows. George returned to the band in late December only to depart again in the New Year. Michael Stuart even filled in on a couple of gigs.

Gary Rowles was next to exit. "Arthur started really getting out of it with substances. He would stay up for several days until finally having hallucinations of paranoia, and would then show up completely wasted. I couldn't be around that any more. Arthur had become unreasonable and unrecognizable and his direction had ceased to exist. I would get a buzz on once in a while, sure, but nothing like what Arthur was doing. It wasn't any incident in particular, it was just the way I felt after playing the music. Every time we got done with a song, Arthur always acted like he didn't enjoy what had happened. It was evidence of his manipulation and that really showed me what his reason for doing it was, which was basically to present himself, not something for the people. It was a hedonistic presentation. The name of the group was Love but it was all about loving Arthur. It was all about Arthur."

George briefly joined Blues Image before becoming a member of Eric Burdon's backing band, while Gary worked with John Mayall and Flo & Eddie, among others. By early 1971, Love consisted of Arthur, Frank Fayad, and Don Poncher, with John Sterling on guitar, the latter soon replaced by ex-Sons Of Adam and Daily Flash guitarist Craig Tarwater. Arthur was tipped off about Craig by a mutual friend, David Biali. "Craig was a mechanic as well as a musician," says Len Fagan. "You'd see him in the early afternoon with his overalls on, bending over his Porsche, tools flying in the air behind him. This was a man who truly loved the inner workings of an automobile. Arthur was afraid to rile Craig because he tuned Arthur's car."

The band then undertook a short, flying tour, starting in Vancouver, Canada, and finishing in St. Joseph, Missouri. On the final leg, part of the aircraft's wing skin came adrift and was held on by just a handful of rivets. Considerable onboard anxiety resulted. "It was like the plane had been hit by a giant sledgehammer," Craig Tarwater recalls. "The guy in the window seat looked out and fainted. Arthur looked out and began laughing like a crazy person. He was ordered to sit down because he was freaking people out. The pilot told us to remain calm." In the end, they were able to get the wheels down and land without further incident.

In December, the band embarked on a major East Coast tour, beginning at the Milwaukee Arena. Dates at Cobo Hall in Detroit, with Alice Cooper and the Stooges, and at the Boston Tea Party followed, before they headed south to the Miami Beach Marine Stadium. "We played well every night," remembers Craig. "We were a good band. I remember Milwaukee Arena was the biggest audience I had ever played for over 10,000 people. We were opening for Grand Funk. After we were done, there was this deafening roar and all these lighters held in the air. When we came off stage, someone delivered us a case of beer from the Schlitz

Brewing Company of Milwaukee. Then a dealer came through and cocaine was distributed discreetly."

According to Don Poncher, although the crowds yelled for the old songs, Arthur remained obdurate and refused to play them. "He made it quite clear that he wasn't doing the old songs. It was often dependent on his mood, or the mood of the crowd. He'd either explain it to them, or we'd just blast into the new stuff and win them over. It was powerful music, pretty intense. When we played in Florida, Arthur was really uncomfortable; this was still a very bigoted country at that time. We had a few days beforehand and someone gave us a car, so we went out driving around. If any white guys pulled up beside us, Arthur would duck down and tell us, 'Don't say anything. Pretend I'm not here.' He knew what bigotry was all about, in the South."

"We played hard and people liked it, especially on the East Coast where Love weren't that well known and hadn't toured much," recalls Craig. "I thought it was among the best work I ever did, and Arthur gave me the freedom to play full out and be creative. He didn't try to hold me back and tell me what to play. He would give you a basic idea of what the song was, but then let you put your own parts in. Don Poncher was a monster drummer. His timing was impeccable, and he had a lot of chops and color. He was really into tuning his kit; the consummate professional."

As for his own contributions, Craig demurs: "I felt that I didn't contribute as much because I was busy learning, whereas the others were busy implementing. But I had a great time, despite the fact that it only lasted a while. I always wished Arthur had been more into the guitar than he was. But he could never tune it. He would walk over, on stage, and have me tune it. Arthur always looked good. He had lost his hair, but always wore a hat. He was kind of lofty in the way he carried himself."

Now that Gary and George had moved on, Riley Racer moved into the servants' quarters on Arthur's property. Craig Tarwater took up residence in the guest house. "Arthur was into vegetarianism, then," says Craig. "He had an expression, 'Death under the golden arches' [directed at the McDonald's hamburger chain]. His song 'Ol' Morgue Mouth' was coined during that time. He was an activist vegetarian. He fed all his dogs this food he bought, frozen, all vegetarian. The dogs were all thin but they were happy."

Arthur had become a vegetarian in 1970 (allegedly after seeing *Satyricon*, Frederico Fellini's bacchanalian 1969 movie) and embraced his new lifestyle with the zeal of an evangelical preacher. He would hector all his friends about the evils of consuming meat products. And it didn't stop with his intimates. "One time, he went down to the Mayfair Market with a cattle prod under his coat," remembers Arthur's friend Herbie Worthington. "He stood by the meat counter and would jolt people with the cattle prod if they tried to buy meat. 'Don't eat the dead,' he'd say to them. He got arrested for that. Arthur was driving once with [later bandmates] David Hull and Charlie Karp, and maybe Riley, too, and David and Charlie went into a hamburger place and got food. As they drove down the street, Arthur reached over and grabbed the hamburger out of David's mouth and threw it out the window saying, 'I don't ride with the dead.'"

Don Poncher remembers Arthur being the first person to warn him about the dangers of eating red meat: "This was before the whole vegan thing. He was really tough on McDonald's and all that." According to Diane Lee, C.L. used to ask Arthur: "Boy, are you still a *vegenarian?*"

When I was vegetarian, no one around me could eat meat. I didn't even let my dogs eat meat. I really went on that whole veggie trip. I didn't eat meat, fish, or fowl; no flesh at all for five years. I used to pay this company called Consolidated Pets to make up their food, consisting of vegetables, eggs, soy beans, and some other protein supplements, for my dogs.

Besides fulfilling his duties for Arthur, Riley Racer was also responsible for his dogs. "When I was living up there [with Arthur], one of my chores was to scoop poop from five big dogs," he recalls. "Not too many people would go in the yard with these dogs, but they trusted me. They were not house-trained. His house was all glass on two sides, facing the backyard. One day, Arthur had to go and play a show; when he came back, the dogs had mounted a rebellion. They had busted through the glass windows and had chewed up rugs, chairs, sofas, and beds. They had a field day. Arthur was really bummed out by that. That's the problem with not training dogs. He wanted them to be free, but that's what happens."

In February 1971, Craig moved out of the guest house and Herbie Worthington moved in. Herbie would soon become renowned as a rock photographer (the jacket picture on Fleetwood Mac's *Rumours* is his work). He had met Arthur through a mutual associate, James 'Scotty' Scott, as Herbie recalls. "Scotty brought Arthur to my house. About two weeks later, Arthur called me and asked if I wanted to move into his guest house. It was a completely unselfish act on his part. He could be that way when he didn't have that demon in him. I really loved my guest house." He and Arthur would develop a close friendship. "Arthur once said to me, 'Herbie, you're a nice guy. There's just no call for nice guys.' That was saying he liked me. It was a compliment. Arthur didn't like many people. He didn't trust them. I went out of my way for him to trust me. After I moved into his house, I didn't do drugs with him because most people around him would use him for his drugs. I didn't want him to think that's why I was there. That impressed him. I didn't want him to associate me with cocaine. We smoked pot together." Living adjacent to Arthur, Herbie was often witness to his changeable personality. "Arthur was a walking contradiction. He could be the sweetest person one minute and then his mind would click and he could be an asshole. You had to walk softly around him."

Following his departure from Blue Thumb, Arthur signed a solo recording contract with Columbia Records (then known as CBS) and began new sessions on May 5 1971, at the label's studio on Sunset Boulevard. He would continue for a total of 13 sessions until CBS finally pulled the plug on July 15. With him were Frank Fayad, Don Poncher, and Craig Tarwater. The studio dates were characterized by a loose, party atmosphere, fueled by copious quantities of drugs. "I was there for a few of those sessions at Columbia," remembers Len Fagan, "and there was no music being made. Arthur had me come down without my drums, but he made me sign in, so I got session money. It was just chaos."

Herbie Worthington remembers Arthur being reprimanded for his indolence. "One of the Columbia executives, this guy with one arm, called Arthur into his office and really ripped him a new asshole. He told Arthur how much he was wasting their time and their money, and asked whether or not he was going to record. He wasn't afraid to tell Arthur off. When we got back to the house, Arthur said to me, 'This guy just fuckin' reamed me,' and then he said, 'You know, Herbie, sometimes I need that.' The fact that he admitted that really knocked me on the ground. He would never usually show a weak side or any vulnerability. I think something happened in his childhood that threw him off-kilter, because he had all these idiosyncrasies about not trusting anyone and having to be in control all the time. If you didn't play his game, you didn't play. And he treated his band-members that way, too." The abandoned CBS tracks, most still in demo form, were finally released in 2009 as the album *Love Lost*, courtesy of reissue specialists Sundazed Records (and the diligence of Arthur's sometime manager, Mark Linn)

"There was too much ingestion of inebriating substances," says Len, recalling the sessions. "I sure didn't hear any music going on when I was there. Maybe they did when I wasn't around, but all I saw was a whole bunch of craziness. I felt so sorry, seeing Arthur go from being a big star, the biggest in LA, to this. No wonder Columbia dropped him."

Arthur's drug habits were beginning to spin out of control. Always a serious hash smoker, he was also using needles to shoot up cocaine. His career was becoming secondary to his preoccupation with coke and getting high. Len Fagan: "Arthur had a big problem with cocaine. When you do too much of it, you become very paranoid. You keep looking out the window thinking the cops are coming. Arthur would come out of the bathroom, after shooting up, and he wouldn't say a word. He'd go lie on the sofa. He had a bunch of stand-up mirrors in the living room that he had adjusted so that, if he lay down on the sofa, he could see in every direction. All he had to do was lie there and he could see everything that was going on. We spent too much time getting high, me snorting and him shooting."

"I'm surprised Arthur and Frank [Fayad] survived that period and that Frank is still alive," says Don Poncher. "Those were some serious users. There was never enough. They were right on the edge; they couldn't stop."

Arthur's friend Annette Ferrel recalls the long shadow cast by drug dependence. "I saw Arthur when he was living on Avenida Del Sol, in the early 70s. He'd become very guarded. We were all doing a lot of drugs. It wasn't like they were new any more, but now we were all getting strung out. Arthur was kind of spooky, then. Those were the cocaine days. Shooting coke just made you absolutely nuts. You didn't want to do it, yet you couldn't get enough of it."

While his own narcotic intake remained prodigious, Arthur steered clear of heroin. He also saw fit to dispense anti-drug advice to others, as Len Fagan remembers. "There were all these rumors that Arthur was a junkie, a heroin addict. I never saw that, ever. In fact, when I got into it, years later, he really tried to get me to stop. I said to him, 'What's the problem with me doing a little heroin once in a while?' He replied, 'Because you're a punk.' Arthur didn't like that word 'punk.' When anybody gave him credit for being the first punk-rocker he wouldn't accept it or be flattered. In his neighborhood, growing up 'a punk' meant being somebody's bitch or something like that."

"We all have our demons, and Arthur was no exception," contends Riley

Racer. "But it wasn't just Arthur. Birds of a feather flock together. There were quite a few people into that [drug scene] at the time. There was this young girl we knew; she was living with a guy who ran a store called Head East, on Sunset. One night, Arthur and I were at the Whisky and ran into her. She ended up coming back to the house. It turned out she knew someone, a pharmacist, and she had sheets and sheets of pharmaceutical LSD. For a while, it became our daily repast. I was as much a participant as anyone else. It's not something you can stay on, constantly. It loses its effect after you use so much of it. You still feel a tingling but it's not like the first times you take it. Those were pretty heady days. Everybody was in a state of bliss. It eventually got to the point where I couldn't deal with it all any more, so I had to get out."

Arthur's behavior was becoming increasingly unpredictable. Gary Rowles remembers Arthur injuring himself while tripping on acid. "He was hallucinating. He got up on the roof of his house and jumped. He landed badly and really messed up his foot. He ended up on crutches. That was the direct result of all that excess." Others had to be on their guard when around him, remembers Herbie Worthington. "One night, Suzanne called me in the guest house saying, 'Herbie, you have to come over here. Arthur's gone crazy.' Arthur thought there was a prowler outside. He was so paranoid on coke that he had called the police. I found him standing there, staring at his own reflection in a mirror. He kept saying, 'I see you.' The police came and he got his senses back real fast. He told them it was all a mistake. But he was flipping out."

Robert Rozelle, Arthur's friend from the heyday of the Strip and a future Love bass player, recalls having a gun pulled on him. "I came to Avenida Del Sol to get some money Arthur owed me. We had a fight and he threw the money on the floor. I picked it up and he jumped on my back. I told [later Love guitarist] Melvan [Whittington] to hold him down on the floor while I ran outside to my car. But Arthur got up and ran at me with a gun and then put it to the windshield of my car." Robert reversed at speed, but it had been raining and he lost control, sending the car off the road and down the hill, where it kept rolling: "Melvan was at the top of the hill yelling, but there was no way I could stop. Arthur thought he'd killed me and went back into the house to wait for the police to arrive. He was sweeping the floor and cleaning up, getting ready for the cops. Finally, I stopped rolling. I hollered up to Melvan, 'I'm here.' Arthur heard that, came running down to the car, and carried me back up the hill to his house. I had a cut on my nose and was bleeding. Arthur felt so bad. He was crying and holding me. He kept saying over and over, 'Why'd you make me do that?' The car ended up in somebody's backyard in Coldwater Canyon."

For all his misadventures, Arthur's doting parents continued to look after him as best they could. C.L. handled maintenance of the property on Avenida Del Sol, including cutting the lawn and gardening. He installing iron entrance gates and built Arthur a coop for his pigeons as well as a pen for his dogs. Meanwhile, Agnes would attend to Arthur's laundry and other household chores. "I always objected to them doing that," insists Arthur's girlfriend Gaye Blair, "but he was OK with his mother and his step dad doing all that work." C.L. would also check on Arthur's house when he was on the road. "Arthur's stepfather had worked hard all his life," says his cousin, Joe Joyner, "and here was this kid with a guitar in his hand making all this money and living in this fancy house."

"C.L. loved Arthur," says Robert Rozelle, "and Arthur loved him, too. But Mr. Lee knew about Arthur messing around with drugs. He'd say to him, 'Boy, you leave that dope alone.' He was concerned about what Arthur was doing but he didn't try to interfere with his lifestyle. That was Arthur, and he accepted him the way he was."

It's often said that genius walks a fine line between sanity and insanity. His close friend, Ria Berkus, believes that Arthur suffered from a borderline disorder. "He had that from the time he was a little boy. His mother knew that he was very mentally unstable, at times. He told me his mother believed that. He once said to me, 'I love my mom so much. When I was shooting drugs, I would bring my shirts home to her to wash. She would see the bloodstains on the sleeves but would never ask me any questions about them.' That must have broken her heart. He was her only child and he was very possessive of her. I felt very sad when he told me that. Whatever their relationship was, she let him be himself." Herbie Worthington once asked Arthur's mother why her son's behavior was so erratic. "Agnes said to me, 'Herbie, Arthur just has a demon in him and, one way or another, it's gonna come out.' She was the sweetest lady you could ever find."

Arthur's inconsistent behavior also impacted on his dealings with Suzanne. While their relationship was best described as volatile, Arthur clearly loved Suzanne. However, as with all his girlfriends, he never trusted her, nor was he faithful to her. Suzanne could also be manipulative. "She broke Arthur's heart," suggests Riley Racer.

Arthur always believed that his friend James 'Scotty' Scott was out to steal his girlfriends. "Scotty used to sleep with other people's women," confirms Herbie. "He did that to Arthur, with Suzanne." Friends recall Suzanne and Arthur's arguing turning violent. Snoopy Pfisterer: "Suzanne would come over to our house when he would be abusive and domineering. Every once in a while, she would give him shit and he wouldn't take it. He would get physical with her. I couldn't stand that. He could have a real violent temperament, actually."

"Suzanne was certainly a prima donna," says Jay Donnellan. "She was very intelligent, sexy, slinky, and beautiful, but also very conniving. I heard a few arguments from the other room, so I knew she could hold her own. I know Arthur cared about her a lot. I would guess she was a real love, not a trophy girlfriend. She was with him for quite a while, but as he disintegrated, she bailed out."

Gaye Blair remained close to Arthur throughout his relationship with Suzanne. "Suzanne was just out for what she could get," she asserts. "The day after Suzanne left him, I left my boyfriend – I was back with Arthur. We had been talking on the phone. He was really upset because she had taken some money. Arthur always thought everyone was stealing from him. He was embittered because he gave and got taken advantage of. That's exactly what he'd done to everyone else, of course. I said to him, 'Now, how does it feel?' There was a turning point when Agnes was up at the house, once. We were doing laundry or something and we heard this big thud. We went into the bedroom and Arthur was on the floor having this grand mal seizure. We just started screaming. Agnes started praying. I said, 'Quit praying. We've got to do something!' I put a spoon in his mouth to keep him from swallowing his tongue, but it was the most violent, horrible seizure. When he came out of it, I told him, 'OK, that's it. You're done with the drugs.' He did stop for a while, but then he turned to alcohol and replaced the one with the other. We tried to get him into rehab programs but it just wouldn't work. He wouldn't go. I said to him, 'Jimi, Janis, and Jim are gone. Do you want to be the fourth?'"

During the period when he was still living with Suzanne, Arthur would cross paths with another woman, Diane Diaz. It was a propitious meeting and theirs would not be a fleeting relationship. Born and raised in LA, Diane Diaz (née Bardizian) was divorced from her first husband by the time she encountered Arthur. Although she had met him briefly some months earlier, Diane entered Arthur's life on New Year's Eve 1970, via his bedroom window – an incident that would inspire the song "Love Jumped Through My Window." She recalls: "Arthur and I met when my friend Samantha Hearn [daughter of famed sportscaster Chick Hearn] wanted to meet Arthur Lee. I had been married but had split with my husband, and my daughter and I had gone back to live with my mother, who looked after the child. For a while, I was living in an apartment with this other girl. One day, this friend of hers came over, and he knew Arthur. Samantha asked him to introduce her to Arthur. She asked me to come along, so I did.

"Arthur always had his door open and people would just walk in," Diane continues. "Samantha met him and I was just floating around. She was gaga over Arthur. I met him and I thought he was pretty cool, but I wasn't gaga. I was in love with Gary Hearn, Samantha's brother. Then, it was New Year's Eve and we went up to Arthur's. We'd been there a couple of times since that first meeting. It was the middle of the night, so we knocked on his bedroom window and he let us in through the window. Arthur stayed in the bedroom and I went and sat in the living room. Before long, I just walked back into the bedroom and that was that. He was a wonderful lover. But we didn't develop a relationship right then. We just became buddies."

It was the beginning of an on-again-off-again relationship that would last for the next 30 years. What began as a friendship would develop into love, but the road to that end would be a bumpy one. "There were lots of women in Arthur's life, but we really bonded," says Diane. "He was 'Arthur Lee,' so it wasn't easy."

"Diane was probably the most stabilizing force in Arthur's life," says Robert Rozelle. "He was kind of loose and wild. She was the anchor and showed him reality."

After the CBS deal was cancelled, Arthur gigged even less frequently. According to Craig Tarwater, the band was supposed to have played a string of gigs in Europe. "That would have been huge, but the band kind of ground to a halt before that. When the European tour didn't materialize, we did these sessions at CBS, but no record deal came out of those. After that, we just didn't do anything any more."

Arthur did appear at the Whisky on January 6 and 7, billed under his own name. There, he was spotted by longtime fan Allan McDougall, by then an A&R man and producer with A&M Records. The label was fast becoming a major player in the international music scene with a roster of stellar acts such as Joe Cocker, Humble Pie, Bread, and The Carpenters. Allan was surprised that a legendary figure like Arthur Lee was without a recording contract and promptly offered to sign him to the label for a solo album.

Don Poncher was still in tow, but Arthur needed a band. Herbie Worthington recommended two young players from the East Coast, guitarist Charles Karp and bass player David Hull. Both had joined Buddy Miles's band in their teens and had spent two years on the road with the Band Of Gypsys drummer – a musician whose excesses and career trip-ups were a match for Arthur's. "I had the feeling that I had to move on," says Charles of his time with Miles. "I knew I couldn't build anything working with Buddy. David and I had already been playing together for years and were tight. We came as a package. When we added Don Poncher, we had a smoking little group. We gelled instantly." Nonetheless, before pressing ahead, A&M insisted that Arthur's new band had to audition. "I remember going over to Arthur's place, David and I," Charles recalls. "When you walked into the house, he had a kind of big living room and it was full of these chicks, the GTOs [notorious LA groupie gang Girls Together Outrageously], throwing light bulbs the length of the living room, and exploding them. I looked at Arthur as if to say, 'What the fuck are you doing?' And Arthur says, 'Check this out. It sounds so great when they explode!' Then Arthur says to me, 'Charlie, you want to dig some hot wax?' I go into the kitchen and he's got vinyl albums burning on the stove. Half of me was horrified, the other half was thinking, 'Wow, this is great!' It was like some Hollywood movie. He had a TV in the living room and there was a video camera, which, in those days, were huge things, crushed into the screen. Arthur said, 'Hey Charlie, what do you think of that? I did that last night. I call it *Close-up*.' He was a real character."

At the house, Arthur had a small rehearsal room filled with semi-wrecked instruments and amplifiers. "It looked like a frustration room, where you go and break things," remembers Charles. "We had these funky amplifiers and remnants of stuff all over. I can't remember if the drummer brought his own drums or adjusted what was there. The guys from A&M arrived and Arthur said, 'Let's do this one,' and I had no idea what song he was referring to, but we all just followed along. Arthur had this little Wollensak tape recorder, like they used at school. He was using the microphone in it. It couldn't have had more than a two-inch speaker, and his voice was sounding all garbled. I was horrified as we launched into this song and all you could hear is this roar coming from Arthur. You couldn't make out any words. These were serious record people. I couldn't even look at them; I was afraid they might be responding badly. We played two or three songs, then one of the A&M guys says, 'Great, Arthur. That's enough.' I didn't know whether to be embarrassed or not, but they signed him up right there. I didn't realize that he was already a star and what they were signing was 'Arthur Lee,' the legend."

Sessions for what would become *Vindicator* – Arthur's debut solo album – took place in March and early April 1972. Like many of Arthur's previous recordings, it was done quickly and simply – an approach which came as a surprise to the musicians. Charles Karp: "It was like, let's go down to A&M and make these demos in the afternoon, and the demos then became the album. I was really sore about that for ten years. I thought I could do a better solo if we'd done it again, but we just played through the songs and Arthur said, 'That's the album.' I was very young and idealistic at the time. Then I realized, after listening to it, years later, that it's pretty good. The looseness is what's good about it, and Arthur knew what he was doing, even if we didn't. We just let it rip."

Certainly, Charles was the right choice for the batch of Hendrix-inspired songs Arthur presented. His rapid-fire blues-rock style was reminiscent of the best Jimi had to offer. "*Rolling Stone* magazine said something to the effect that Lee and Karp were very good Hendrix mimics," remembers Charles. "I thought Hendrix was God back then, and being accused of being a mimic pissed me off. But in hindsight, I realize it's the ultimate compliment. On that project, Arthur was my boss. If that's where he wanted to go, then I went with him, especially since they were one-take things. It was a demo that became an album."

Don Poncher: "When we went to record *Vindicator*, that's all we had rehearsed. Arthur would present a tune and we'd work on it. We worked for weeks on those things. Arthur would come in with the songs and we'd put the parts together. Arthur played rhythm guitar on the album but he had a lot of trouble keeping in tune. He also played with a really distorted sound. You can hear that on a lot of the tracks. He'd play so hard the guitar would go out of tune all the time."

Several songs originally demoed for the aborted CBS album the previous year were re-recorded for *Vindicator*, including "He Said She Said," "He Knows A Lot Of Good Woman (Or Scotty's Song)," "Love Jumped Through My Window," "Sad Song," and "Everybody's Gotta Live." Arthur's new vegetarian philosophy was unambiguously promulgated on "Hamburger Breath Stinkfinger" and "Ol' Morgue Mouth." "I remember, in the studio, some A&M executive brought in a bag of fried chicken," laughs Charles Karp. "Arthur grabbed this guy's lunch and said, 'I don't hang out with no corpses.' He opened the door to the parking lot and threw this bag of chicken out. I figured we'd be off the label after that. He became a militant anti-meat guy." Arthur had not lost his wry sense of humor, however, and produced several witty, if baffling song titles, not least, "You Can Save Up To 50% But You're Still A Long Ways From Home."

Arthur's Jimi Hendrix fixation was best exemplified on "Love Jumped Through My Window," "Find Somebody," "Every Time I Look Up I'm Down Or White Dog (I Don't Know What That Means)" – a poke at Led Zeppelin's "Black Dog," according to one Arthur associate – and most overtly "Busted Feet" (co-written with Charles Karp). Critical accusations about pinching his pal Jimi's style stung Arthur, however. "That was just how Arthur played," says Don Poncher in his defense. "People criticized him for copying Hendrix, and it hurt him. For years after that, he wouldn't play those songs because of the criticism. Arthur was reinventing himself. He just never got the respect he deserved for his music after *Forever Changes*."

Riley Racer goes further. "Arthur was exploring different songs and styles on *Vindicator*. That just wasn't what his audience expected. He was a completely different artist on that album."

Vindicator was released in August, its jacket bearing wacky front and back cover photos depicting a pair of Arthurs: a bizarre, bewigged prize fighter and his shaven-headed, janitorial alter ego. The jacket credit said 'Arthur Lee with the group Band Aid. A Dr. Hyde World Wide Production,' just to muddy the waters further. "I think he called the album *Vindicator* because it was supposed to be a vindication regarding his career," maintains Riley. "And 'Clean Sweep Janitor Co.' [as written on the back of Arthur's janitorial overalls, on the cover shot] is about that, too; making a clean sweep in terms of his career. We talked about that and had some laughs about it. It meant coming up from the bottom. The Mr. Hyde reference was to do with the chemicals of the day: the author of *Dr. Jekyll And Mr. Hyde* [Robert Louis Stevenson] used to use cocaine. It was about the schizophrenic lifestyle. It was a very chemical time."

For all that, reviews of *Vindicator* were generally scathing. Even the usually sympathetic and loyal UK press savaged the album. Although a more consistent effort than its immediate predecessors, for die-hard Love/Lee fans, Arthur's work was still too far removed from *Forever Changes*. Few wanted to accept Arthur Lee as an alternative Jimi Hendrix or Led Zeppelin. The critical mauling wasn't quite universal, however. Writing in Canada's *Winnipeg Free Press*, critic Andy Mellen, who had previously declared *Forever Changes* to be among the ten greatest albums of all time, found room to accommodate *Vindicator* in Arthur's canon, declaring it "one of this year's few truly outstanding albums" and praising the music for its "strength and confidence." He likened "Everybody's Gotta Live" to Love's earlier heyday, called Arthur "an out and out genius," and concluded that "the entire album is a pleasure." His pay-off line was telling, however: "Buy it and keep Arthur from completely wigging out."

Jac Holzman's opinion of *Vindicator* was more typical. "I don't know how A&M could release that. I would have said, 'It's not good enough, Arthur.' I wouldn't have released it."

"I'm very proud now to have been on that album," concedes Charles. "This was like Led Zeppelin meets rauncho. There was Black Sabbath in it, too. Arthur stepped out from the Love mold and kicked ass. He had a great rock'n'roll voice. I thought that cover was a fucking riot. He didn't care what anyone thought." Arthur was still the risk-taker. Like all his 70s output, *Vindicator* has come in for re-appraisal and, with hindsight, is now generally regarded as a bold and consistently confident effort.

Jim Bickhart was freelancing for A&M Records' publicity department at the time. He was tasked with writing the official press biography to accompany *Vindicator*'s release. "I was surprised they could get Arthur to show up at the A&M office at 11am, but he did. He seemed stoned but was talkative. He wasn't loquacious and didn't say anything particularly remarkable, but he answered all my questions. I was there to write a positive bio of the guy, not a psychological exploration, although I'm sure there would have been plenty to deal with. This was hardly a high point in either his life or career. I remember he wanted to sit on the floor, so we both sat on the carpet of this unused office. There was some of that 'legend' thing surrounding Arthur at A&M, but not a feeling that it was going to translate into commercial success. Bob Garcia [A&M's head of publicity] liked the album, and tried to treat it with respect. Bob had dealt with Gram Parsons and then Joe Cocker, who had gone through a bad period, so when Arthur came to A&M they knew what dissolute was all about and just tried to take it in their stride."

The issue of money would, predictably, hasten the break up of Arthur's latest band. "We knew in our hearts that those demos only became the album for monetary reasons," admits Charles. "We realized he was the star and it was his group. I knew I was a sideman. I knew it was Arthur's show. But when we raised money matters with him he just made these negative comments. He may have been too high at the time but that's what happened. By no means were we demanding exorbitant amounts of money, but we were freelance musicians and we were working for a living. Whenever the subject of money was raised Arthur would go into a tirade. You couldn't talk to him about money."

"We got paid session fees," confirms Don Poncher, "but it was Arthur's deal. He was signed to the label and so he got paid. We didn't get royalties. Arthur always took care of Arthur and you had to look after yourself. It wasn't going anywhere, so I left." But not before receiving a helping hand from Arthur. Friendships were still important. "Arthur helped me out with a personal dilemma. He saved my ass or I would have been in prison. Arthur put up his house for my bail. That was really something. He got his money back because the case was thrown out, but he was there for me. Nobody else would have done that. He had a heart."

By 1972, it had become a crap shoot whether Arthur would be on his game or not. Rather than keep a steady band together, he began relying on a floating pool of players, calling them up on the increasingly rare occasions when he did take a gig. Len Fagan deputized several times when Arthur found himself short of a drummer. "Don Poncher had left him and Arthur didn't want to go looking for another drummer," recalls Len, who had recently toured Japan with The 1910 Fruitgum Company. "He asked me to play with the band, and I was honored. We played under both Love and just Arthur Lee. Rehearsals were really kind of a sham. Arthur didn't like rehearsing much. We'd set up our gear and smoke a lot of pot or hash, among other things, maybe drink some wine, then play a couple of songs. Arthur would say, 'OK, that sounds great,' and that was it. On the first few gigs, I didn't feel completely confident of the material. I did well enough, apparently, and he kept me with him for a while. I used to go to his house and he'd play me the new songs he was writing and ask my opinion. I could tell him, 'This is OK but that other part sucks,' and he'd never get mad. Arthur and I never bullshitted each other. That's why our relationship lasted so long. I used to be the only one who called him 'Art' or 'Artie' and he used to call me 'Lenny.' Nobody else called me that. One time, Arthur and I were watching this dance program on television and the kids were dancing something called the Philly Dog. We thought that was hilarious, so we kind of adopted it and would say that to one another, and know exactly what we were talking about. He'd call me up and say, 'Philly bucks,' and I knew he'd gotten a new deal and an advance. So 'Philly' or 'Philly Dog' often preceded things we'd say to each other. We used to laugh a lot. That's what I miss most about Arthur. Arthur and I used to love to parody Amos & Andy. We'd do all the accents."

Len recalls Arthur's behavior being characteristically inconsistent: "We did a gig once, at the Whisky, and Arthur played almost nothing," remembers Len. "He was just babbling. He would start a song, then stop and begin disparaging everyone in the audience. I hid behind my drum riser, it was so shameful." Len also remembers a gig in San Diego where the band played without a lead guitarist. "Arthur wouldn't let Craig [Tarwater] drive his own car down to San Diego, so Craig didn't play. We went on as a three-piece. The first set was a disaster, but he managed to pull it together for the second show that night. We did a beautiful version of 'She's Not There' by The Zombies. We were just following him. We wouldn't finish a song. He'd do a crescendo and get applause ... then he'd turn around to Frank and me and lead us into the next song, without stopping the previous one. It was one of the best sets I ever played."

"Arthur would do a gig when he needed the money, but he was unreliable," says Robert Rozelle. "He got to a point where people didn't want to hire him because of his attitude and how he behaved. They'd give him a deposit but he might not show up. When the time came to perform, he would be so incapacitated he couldn't play. He would be so high that you looked in his eyes and there was nothing there, just null and void. That was in the 70s. He would get high and then get paranoid and not leave the house. Arthur just wanted to make enough money to be able to kick back at home."

Still able to draw on his legend, in mid 1973, Arthur inked a deal with an upstart independent label, Buffalo Records, owned by impresario Michael Butler, producer of the hit musical *Hair*. Paul Rothchild was also involved with the label and assumed production duties. Arthur put a backing band together drawing on friends from his past, including Robert Rozelle. When Arthur asked Robert to join the band, the bass player greeted the opportunity with some trepidation. "I was shaking in my boots when he called me up to his place to jam. He told me he needed to get a band together so I called [guitarist] Melvan Whittington and [drummer] Joe Blocker. Melvan and I had played in a band together called The Young Hearts." The guitarist had recently been working with Little Richard. "When I met Arthur, all his furniture was gone," Melvan recalls. "There he was in this big, redwood house, with no furniture. I had my guitar and we got to talking and I made Arthur laugh. He liked that. The people he hired in his bands were his friends. We would all hang out together. We were all together for a whole year. That's how we put together the *Black Beauty* album. We'd be rehearsing all the time. The second gig I played with Arthur was at the KROC concert at the Coliseum. We opened the show. It was Stevie Wonder, Sly & The Family Stone, Sha Na Na, Merry Clayton, and Love. We get out there and we hadn't had a soundcheck. We're blasting out of these amplifiers. It was overwhelming. Arthur had this Zorro cape, with pink lining, and he came out wearing it. I looked at him and he took the cape off, smiled at the audience, pulled his teeth out, and took off his wig. I just thought to myself, 'Yeah, I like this dude!'"

Joe Blocker came from the same neighborhood as Arthur. "I first knew Arthur through my older cousin. They went to Dorsey High together. As Arthur started performing, my cousin went to some of his shows and I sometimes went along. I didn't really know him, then, because I was 10 or 12 years younger than Arthur. I played with Johnny 'Guitar' Watson and worked with Ike & Tina Turner and Little Richard. Robert brought me in to work with Arthur but I knew guys he played with, like George Suranovich. When I was about 18, Melvan and I rented Arthur's guest house from him. The thing about that particular group – me, Arthur, Melvan, and Robert, before John Sterling joined the band – was that we got along very well. It was always fun. There were no conflicts with Arthur."

Under the aegis of producer Paul Rothchild, whose reputation had been built on his work with The Doors (and, to a lesser extent, Love's *Da Capo*), Arthur and the band cut ten tracks at Wally Heider's studio in LA for what was to be a follow-up solo album, in a similar hard rock vein to *False Start* and *Vindicator*. Arthur resurrected several songs from the CBS sessions, including "Good & Evil," "Midnight Sun," and "Product Of the Times." "Skid" was a song by Riley Racer while "Beep Beep" proffered Arthur's first, but by no means last, venture into reggae music. "Walk Right In" was a clever, hard-rocking cover version of a 1963 folk hit by The Rooftop Singers, itself an update of a popular blues song dating back to the 20s.

"*Black Beauty* was more eclectic than *Vindicator*," reflects Robert. "It had a little bit of everything. The band was really tight and the tracks sounded good." The album also featured stronger supporting vocals than had been the case on Arthur's previous releases. "There was an Australian band called The Brothers recording in another room when we were doing the *Black Beauty* sessions," remembers Robert. "Arthur got them to sing on a couple of the tracks. They had the sweetest harmonies."

As solid a recording performance as *Black Beauty* undoubtedly was, before it could be completed it had to be shelved – Buffalo Records had gone bust. Bootleg copies have circulated for years. At the time of writing, Diane Lee is trying to secure an official release for the album. Arthur Lee fans will not be disappointed.

Despite the negative reviews of his recent albums and the collapse of two other recorded efforts, Arthur still had fans in his corner, some in very exalted places in the rock music pantheon, as his soon-to-be producer, Skip Taylor, explains. "Eric Clapton was a fan of Arthur's. Bill Oakes, who was running RSO Records, told me that because of Clapton, who was an RSO artist at the time, they were interested in signing Arthur. Clapton put pressure on Robert Stigwood, owner of RSO, to sign Arthur Lee because of Arthur's notoriety in England. The *Forever Changes* album had been voted the #1 album for 12 years in England. Another guy who talked to Stigwood was [Led Zeppelin singer] Robert Plant. He idolized Arthur."

A veteran band manager, Skip had also produced albums for the likes of Canned Heat, John Lee Hooker, Harvey Mandel, and The Who's Keith Moon. He met with Arthur and they discussed making an album together. "I had known Arthur, on and off, for many years while living in LA and being in the music business," he explains. "I talked with him, and we had a great meeting. I told him that my production ideas were probably different to anything he had done before and that I was a firm believer in getting involved in the early songwriting, arranging, and rehearsing of the songs for the studio. The studio is a place where you record, not rehearse. I've always believed in the power of the song and of the vocal. And those were two areas where Arthur always shone. It wasn't about the arrangements or the band. It was about hearing the lyrics and having a distinctive vocal sound. No one that I worked with was ever a better performer and singer, in the studio, than Arthur Lee."

Taking on Arthur was still a gamble. However, RSO had faith and stumped up a $100,000 budget for an album. "Arthur didn't trust a living soul," acknowledges Skip. "That made him unmanageable. But when I negotiated the record deal with RSO and put the check in his hand, I remember the look on his face. It was like, 'Holy shit! This is pretty amazing.' And I said, 'Arthur, as far as I know, this is the last big record contract you're going to get. If you blow this I don't know who's going to be in your corner, but it won't be me, it won't be Robert Stigwood, Bill Oakes, or Eric Clapton. Right now, you have a lot of people rooting for you and trying to help you have another shot. I don't know how many more shots you've got.' That was a lot of money at that time and, of course, Arthur said to me, 'Let's go make a $10,000 album and you and I can pocket the rest.' I said to him, 'That's not what we're going to do, Arthur. We're going to make a $100,000 album. If it only takes $90,000 in the long run, fine, there's $10,000 left over for you. I don't need a dime out of this. I want to make a good record.' They gave me $10,000 up front and I had a three per cent deal as a producer, so I was fine. I told Arthur that I wanted to put in the time and energy to make a great album. What I didn't tell Arthur was that I had a major ace in the hole. Stigwood told me that, if the timing worked out when we delivered the album, he would put Arthur on Clapton's world tour."

The record that would emerge from this collaboration, *Reel To Real*, would be unlike anything else Arthur had recorded. Steeped in rhythm & blues and funk, this was Arthur Lee's black roots album. Robert Rozelle: "That was the time of black awareness and black pride. That was the thing, then: 'I'm black and I'm proud,' and Arthur got into all that. He was divorcing himself from the white sound and getting into soul. He felt that's what he needed to do, and he'd never done it before. Love always sounded white. Now, he was into that Black Panthers thing and being more soulful, getting more into the funk sound. He was a really good blues singer. He was going back to his roots."

Arthur took to spouting black pride rhetoric, but for some it rang hollow. "I got a little bit miffed at this guy finger-pointing at Whitey," says longtime Arthur observer Harvey Kubernik. "That bothered me. Arthur was about unity and harmony on record. I believe all the record company advances and royalties had pretty much always come from white people, so I don't quite understand this 'ripped off by Whitey' thing. And Arthur was one of the few people of color who retained his publishing, unlike most artists, black or white, in the 60s. White people like Al Schlesinger cautioned and instructed Arthur on the importance of keeping your publishing. There have been 100 instances where white people helped set things up for Arthur, only to have him dismantle them. I was heartbroken when I would read him saying that stuff, because nothing could be further from the truth."

Skip Taylor echoes those sentiments. "Nobody wanted to know about Arthur because he was, unfortunately, one of these guys who had the white chip on his shoulder. It seemed Whitey had stolen everything from him and never given him his due. But Arthur was the whitest black guy I knew. He didn't live the black lifestyle, always liked the white way of life, and liked white girls." For all that, Skip and Arthur got along with one another. "He knew that I already had money and I wasn't out to rob him. He was gonna have to find some other reason to dislike me. But there was so much more to him once you got through the veneer that he encased himself in. There was a good human being, inside. There were so many who saw the talent in Arthur, tried to help him, and put themselves out for him, and he never repaid it with kindness or with a thank you. So you had to know that's what you were getting into if you dealt with Arthur."

Racial rhetoric notwithstanding, there was a palpable black roots feel to the sessions and the songs Arthur was coming in with. Having an all-black backing band reinforced that flavor. Arthur's recordings always reflected his players' tastes and experience, whether folk-rock, hard-rock, or funk. "Arthur had these songs that were sort of R&B, and we were an R&B kind of band, so he had us record with him," says Melvan.

Joe Blocker: "Arthur the black man grew up in Memphis and the black area of LA. What's he supposed to grow up to be like, David Crosby? He was who he was. Arthur was a hustler. No question about it, a street hustler. He came right off the streets. If people wanted to see him as the great flower power genius of the Sunset Strip, well, he was that too. But to us, he was just a homeboy who figured something out." Arthur's stylistic changes shouldn't have been a problem, Joe believes: "Look at David Bowie's career. He's made a lot of different kinds of records. Arthur always wondered why people didn't want him to do that, too, why they just wanted him to play *Forever Changes*. He used to say, 'I'm not into that any more. I was, but I'm not any longer.' He was into singing R&B, being funky, and having horns."

Robert Rozelle: "It was so much fun doing that album. We recorded that at the Record Plant, and John Lennon was in the studio next door. All these different musicians were coming and going. I remember Keith Moon coming into our sessions and wanting to join in. 'Aw, that guy can't play,' Arthur said."

"We made a hell of an album," says Skip. "We worked hard on it. Arthur was sober during the recording, didn't do too many drugs, and was on time every day. He really put in his all for this album, and we had a ball making it. It's a real solid record and still holds up today." Skip was not averse to supplementing Arthur's core group of musicians with noteworthy guests. "There were some places where

I thought using outside people was advantageous, although that wasn't always agreeable with Melvan. I remember bringing in [ex-Paul Butterfield Blues Band guitarist] Howard 'Buzzy' Feiten to do a solo and Melvan going, 'Why's he coming in? I'm the guitar player … .' He'd already had his shot and it didn't do a thing for me or Arthur. So Buzzy came in and Melvan went up to Arthur and said, 'Arthur, this just isn't fair,' and Arthur replied, 'Fair? I'll give you bus fare! Get outta here and let this guy play!' That, to me, is one of the all time great Arthurisms."

Besides the new songs, Arthur chose to re-record "Singing Cowboy" (with John Sterling on slide guitar) as well as "Busted Feet" and "Everybody's Gotta Live" from *Vindicator*. According to Skip, the latter song began when Arthur was fooling around in the studio after a session, singing a cappella. Prudently, Skip kept the tape running. "Arthur said, 'Ah, get rid of it,' and I said, 'Nah, we'll save it.' We ended up mixing it and getting a great vocal sound, and I thought it was one of the best songs he did. It's the perfect closing track for the album. It really makes a statement and shows his personality."

The album also included a cover of a recent rhythm & blues hit by William DeVaughn called "Be Thankful For What You Got." Skip thought it "the strongest song on the album" and it would go on to garner considerable airplay in a number of cities. "That's the one that RSO wanted out as a single," the producer recalls. " It was smooth and, even though it was similar to the original, it had a different vibe. It was reminiscent of the old Arthur. He sang the hell out of it."

Indeed, the whole album showed Arthur to be a fine rhythm & blues singer. The use of horns on several tracks, notably "Stop the Music" and "Good Old Fashion Dream," lent further credibility to the style. Elsewhere, "Which Witch Is Which?" had a palpable Sly Stone quality, while the slick funk song "Who Are You" sounds like an Earth Wind & Fire track. Although apparently prophetic, the use of gunshots on "You Said You Would" was, according to Skip, probably down to engineer John Stronach, not Arthur.

Robert Rozelle left part way through the *Reel To Real* sessions. "I played on that album, but I needed to get away from the madness around Arthur. He was still being Arthur, still getting high. That's when Sherwood Akuna came in and played on the album. In the 70s, everybody was doing drugs. But Arthur would do more than everybody else. I got myself clean and I tried to tell him that it wasn't going to be easy, but he needed to play naturally and not use the drugs. I told him to play some gigs [straight] and that it would be great. He did it for about a month, but then he said, 'Robert, I don't know what to play when I'm not high.'"

The album jacket featured impressive original artwork from painter Ron Durr, as well as two startling photos of Arthur. On the back he is pictured along with his band members, bald-headed and sporting a kaftan that resembles a granny dress, while the inside photo, taken at his new home at 14818 Round Valley Drive, finds Arthur seated in an ornate shower stall. "If you look real closely, there's a joint in one of the corners," Skip reveals. "That was Arthur's idea. I thought it was a cool photo. He was shaving his head at that time. I thought he looked good."

RSO released *Reel To Real*, to much fanfare, in December 1974. Reviews were encouraging, although the new rhythm & blues Arthur Lee was a surprise to many critics and fans. Whether you liked Arthur's new guise or not, it was hard to knock the production quality of the album, which was consistent from start to finish. All things pointed to major comeback potential after several years in the hard-rock wilderness, something which the upcoming Eric Clapton tour would surely enhance. In the event, Clapton was thrilled to have Arthur opening for him and the high profile which Slowhand commanded brought Arthur before tens of thousands of fans, many eager to hear what had become of the once mighty Love legend.

"Not only was it his last shot, it was his biggest shot ever," says Skip of *Reel To Reel*. "Neither Elektra nor Blue Thumb ever put that kind of money behind Arthur. The first show we did was in England, with me standing in the wings, right beside Robert Stigwood and Bill Oakes. Arthur went out to open the show and got a standing ovation from the entire audience. And then he said, 'Yeah, I'm back, but things aren't a whole lot different than they were. Now, I'm just a slave to a new owner, Robert Stigwood.' And there I was, with Stigwood. He grabbed me by the shoulder and said, 'Let's go in the back, right now.' He said to me, 'We'll buy you out of the deal and I never want to see that man again.' That's why it ended up a one-album deal. We were doing 60 dates with Clapton and he was paying Arthur well, paying for hotels and promotion all the way. It would have broken Arthur open, worldwide, again. I just remember standing on that stage and having my heart broken. It was really sad."

For Skip, it was another example of Arthur torpedoing his own career. "I told him, 'I can't believe you said what you said. At the very least I want you to call Stigwood and apologize,' and he said, 'I'm not calling that motherfucker. That's the way I feel.' It was one of the most devastating moments of my career. I walked away from him right there. After that, nobody would take a chance on Arthur."

Joe Blocker recalls the Clapton tour being a major event. "There were big crowds, but Arthur wasn't in the best of shape, because he had too much money. Any time Arthur got too much money, he got really weird. Sure, he insulted Robert Stigwood. Arthur didn't give a fuck. When Led Zeppelin came up to meet him he didn't even come out of his house. I said, 'Robert Plant and Jimmy Page are out in the yard. They're cool.' He says, 'Who? Fuck them dudes, man.' Arthur didn't give a fuck. On the Clapton tour I remember, as clear as a bell, Eric Clapton on the side of the stage watching Melvan. He said that Melvan reminded him of Jimi Hendrix. That Clapton tour was a fantastic opportunity, but Arthur wasn't going to take advantage of it. By the time the tour was over, I knew I was done."

"I had sold Arthur this Cadillac limousine I owned," says Skip, "and the next thing I heard he had put a rod inside to hang his clothes and was living in the back of this car, with one of his buddies driving him up and down Sunset Boulevard. Then I heard he was being sentenced for firing a gun. I tried with a number of other people and attorneys to get another hearing for him, because I didn't think he deserved to be sitting in prison for that. He called me after he got out and thanked me for the efforts on his behalf. He asked me if I wanted to manage him again and I told him, 'I don't think so, Arthur,' and I wished him luck. Then, a year or so later, he called me and told me he was playing at Club Lingerie in Hollywood. So I went down there and watched his show. I thought it was fantastic. Arthur sounded better than I'd ever heard him sound, and he was straight, too. I went backstage and he started into all the 'white man' bullshit again, and I told him, 'Arthur, isn't that water under the bridge now? Don't include me in all this "motherfucker" stuff. I was, perhaps, the truest friend you ever had.' He grabbed me and hugged me, and said, 'You're right, man. I'm sorry.'"

Despite the way their relationship ended, Skip retains warm feelings about his experiences with Arthur: "He was who he was. I never worked with a more talented singer. Beneath that veneer, deep down, he was a good guy and had a lot of heart. With a guy like that, you're never surprised. He was always living on the edge and pushing the envelope."

Skip's earlier prediction proved prophetic. Arthur never again had a major label recording contract.

CHAPTER 8

FEEL LIKE I'VE BEEN THROUGH HELL, BUT YOU TELL ME I HAVEN'T EVEN STARTED YET

Arthur Lee at Entourage Studio,
North Hollywood, February 1994

*L*ike Jimi Hendrix used to say, "You can't believe everything you see and hear, now can you?" I remember telling Robert Plant, "When you start believing you're that person they're writing about, you're in real trouble."

In the latter 60s, Arthur Lee was prince of the Sunset Strip, idolized by fans and peers. By the mid 70s, he had become a recluse, living in an isolated hillside estate, cut off from the public by electric security gates. Plagued by his own insecurities and a pathological distrust for everyone other than his cadre of old neighborhood buddies, Arthur increasingly retreated into a drug-induced haze, safe in his cosseted environment. Public appearances became less and less frequent. Between the latter 70s and early 90s there would still be occasional flashes of his former brilliance, but those would be few and far between and tempered by erratic behavior and a reputation for being difficult and unstable. "Arthur's bandmate became drugs," observes Bruce Botnick, "and that, basically, destroyed him. He was making records, not out of creative desire but as a vehicle to get money for drugs." Arthur was further hampered by the inexorable weight of *Forever Changes*. "He never topped it," says Bruce, "but Arthur would never admit that."

Len Fagan: "Arthur would record or do a show every once in a while but he no longer had the muse or the ambition. The things that he really thought he wanted in life, like a Porsche and a big house, he found didn't make him feel better or make him happy. He loved the fact that, up on Avenida Del Sol, with a private gate and a big yard overlooking the city, he could walk around and not worry about the police. He was never very materialistic but he was also never satisfied."

Ria Berkus lost touch with Arthur during this period. "I didn't hear from him for maybe four years. He was a huge part of my youth and my soul, but I couldn't handle all the drugs. He was out there all the time. I remember we got together in the 80s and he was in a dark place. He was very reclusive." Johnny Echols believes Arthur found it difficult to maintain his status in later years and that living as a mere 'mortal' was always problematic. "That's what caused Arthur to continue with drugs long after it was fashionable, or after anybody who had any sense would have continued using them. They were his security blanket. He needed those drugs because reality had finally caught up with the myth. He was very, very insecure. He needed to be loved and lionized. And he hated to be alone."

While friendships remained important to Arthur, he was also wary of other people. "Arthur could, with the right people, be very affectionate and could let them know how he felt about them," says Len Fagan. "He still had lots of friends from his childhood who were a part of his life. But he was very suspicious of everyone he came in contact with. It was imperative that he did not feel that you were using him because of his status and prestige. If you were trying to use him or rip him off, he wouldn't have anything to do with you."

In late 1975, Arthur moved to 14818 Round Valley Drive, in Sherman Oaks. The house was a former hunting lodge that had been extensively renovated. "Arthur figured he would sell his Avenida estate and buy a cheaper place. He needed the money," says Len. "He just wasn't making money and didn't seem to aspire to work. He finally found a property south of Ventura Boulevard, up in the hills. I didn't think it was a good house for Arthur to buy. It was very odd and had a lot of rooms added on. I think he bought it because it had a bathroom with a glass wall and he liked the fact that the place was secluded."

Arthur had sold the Avenida Del Sol property to actor Max Julien, star of several 70s blaxploitation movies. Max had written, produced, and starred, with Vonetta McGee, in the 1974 movie *Thomasine & Bushrod*, for which Arthur contributed a folksy song that played over the film's closing credits (the remainder of the score was composed by Coleridge-Taylor Perkinson). Arthur did not stay long on Round Valley Drive (actor Judd Hirsch would later purchase the house). When his stepfather was stricken with colon cancer, Arthur moved back to 27th Street to help look after him. In a very selfless act – uncharacteristic for those who only knew his tough guy public persona, yet a side of Arthur those closest to him knew well – he set his career aside to provide primary home care for C.L. until his death in August 1978.

Diane Lee: "Arthur told me his mother was having a difficult time dealing with C.L.'s illness. She went back to Tennessee for a while and Arthur stayed and did all of the care-giving for his father. He never referred to him as his stepfather; he said 'my father.' C.L. raised him like a father. Arthur also referred to Chester Taylor as 'my father' when he spoke of him."

His stepfather never gave up worrying about Arthur's livelihood. "C.L. taught Arthur many things and tried to teach him even more with regards to learning a trade as a means of earning a living," says Diane. "But as we all know, Arthur was the dreamer and his world was completely different to his stepfather's. C.L. was the practical man, the family provider. He only knew one way."

Rumor has it that Arthur became a house painter, alongside his stepfather, during this period. "That is ridiculous," counters Gaye Blair. "There's another story where people claimed they saw him panhandling on Sunset Boulevard. Arthur would never do that. He didn't need to. He could con somebody out of their money in two seconds. Why would he panhandle?"

"After he sold that house on Round Valley, Arthur was going from apartment to apartment, before living with his parents for a while," Len Fagan remembers. "One time, I called him up there and asked if he wanted to hang out. Arthur replied, 'I'd love to, but my mom and I are watching [television variety entertainment] *The Carol Burnett Show* right now. It's kind of a tradition in this house for us all to sit down after dinner to watch Carol Burnett.' Arthur liked to project a dark image and he liked the fact that people were afraid of him, and yet here was Arthur Lee – with his hip, psychedelic, underground world and taste for all things odd – a fan of Carol Burnett. You wouldn't have guessed that. I got the impression that he did not do a lot of drugs when he was living with his mother. He may have been drinking a little wine, but there is no way he could consume the substances he would otherwise do and still behave acceptably around his mother." After C.L.'s death, Agnes sold the house on 27th Street and moved to a spacious apartment on Don Lorenzo Drive, in Baldwin Hills. Arthur would stay there from time to time.

In the fall of 1978, Arthur surprised Love fans by playing at the Whisky with Bryan MacLean. At the shows, on October 20 and 21, they were backed by drummer George Suranovich, John Sterling on guitar, and Kim Kesterson on bass. They played several classic Love songs including "Alone Again Or," "Andmoreagain," "7 & 7 Is," "Signed D.C.," and "Old Man," alongside songs from Arthur's later Love incarnations. Those in attendance, expecting a return to former glories, would be disappointed. In the event, Bryan was relegated to a minor onstage role and complained that he was not paid by Arthur. "There was always tension between the two of them," says Len Fagan, who attended the shows. "Bryan had a lot of fans of his own. When Bryan walked into the dressing room, before the initial show, the first thing he said was, 'Where are all the groupies?' It had been ten years since he was in Love. Things had changed; there were no groupies. I was not impressed with what was going on. I did not like the other musicians Arthur had surrounded himself with. They may have been better players than the original musicians in Love, but they didn't have the magic. So I was disappointed in the show." A bootleg of the gig made the rounds until 1982 when Rhino (and Line Records in Germany) released an official version (which still sounds like a bootleg recording). The erstwhile bandmates played together again, sharing a Whisky bill as separate acts, but that would also fall short of the Love-in fans were still hoping for, as Arthur badmouthed Bryan from the stage and allegedly threw a cup of coffee at him.

In 1980, Rhino Records issued *The Best Of Love*, pulling together 16 of the better known tracks from the band's Elektra albums (the label had already mined Love's back catalog with two best-of packages – *Love Revisited* and *Love Masters* – in the 70s). Rhino's efforts did much to revive the Love name at a time when it was largely forgotten everywhere beyond their dedicated fanbase. "We just thought it was good music and should be out there," says Rhino's founding partner Harold Bronson, a longtime Love fan. Rhino's ethos wasn't only about record sales: it was also about releasing music which deserved to be heard. "We wanted to turn people on to good music. We put a lot of quality into it. For the first album, we tracked down William Harvey, Elektra's original art director, and he had some unseen band photos that we used for the cover. The idea was to try and find things that hadn't been seen before, along with informative liner notes, and information that people didn't know. Also, we had the disc mastered at Elektra, thus avoiding one more generation of tape, because we wanted the best possible sound."

The effort would pay off and also bring Harold in direct contact with Arthur. "As a fan, I had seen Arthur but never spoken to him. Bruce Gary [drummer with The Knack and a friend of Arthur's] gave me Arthur's number, so I called him to get some comments for the liner notes. Arthur being Arthur, he was a bit vague. I asked him about 'Signed D.C.' because I'd heard it was about Don Conka, and he said, 'Oh no, man. It's about Washington, D.C.' Here we were, putting out this album, and he's kind of jiving me. That didn't sit well with me. But I developed a good relationship with him and, on more than one occasion, he referred to me as 'the most honest man in the record business,' which was nice to hear. Then, there would be moments when I would get the opposite: Arthur calling me and being incoherent and claiming he never gave me permission to release the *Love Live* album. So I had to Xerox the contract and send it over to him to show him that he'd signed, not to mention the fact that we'd given him an advance on that album. So, in dealing with Arthur, you always had some bumps in the road. One good thing I can say about him was that he had long-enduring friendships. Those are a good barometer of someone's character, and Arthur still had guys from high school, or thereafter, still in his life, 30 or 40 years later." Rhino's interest in Love did not extend exclusively to Arthur Lee. "I also tried to do some things for Bryan MacLean," says Harold. "At the time, it was hard for Bryan to make decisions and he ended up doing nothing. One of the things I tried to do was to locate those tapes he recorded for Capitol Records in New York, but there was no record of any Bryan MacLean tapes in Capitol's vaults."

In 1979, Diane Lee left her second husband, Jeff Skorman, to move in with Arthur. "Arthur and I didn't get together romantically again for a while after we met in 1970. But we saw each other occasionally. I saw Arthur's name in the paper, it must have been in 1978, and went to see him performing at Madame Wong's. I was married and he was living with another woman, but we would get together in his big green limousine. Finally, my husband realized something was going on and we ultimately separated. I went to Arthur's."

Diane moved into Arthur's rented house at 6301 Morella Avenue in North Hollywood. She says: "Arthur didn't want me to work when we were together. I didn't work for many years of my life: I always had someone taking care of me. My mother looked after me for years and my daughter after I was divorced. In 1978, I got a job at a hospital in the Valley. It was like I was growing up and learning to look after myself. I didn't want to be dependent on anyone, even when Arthur and I were together. Later, in 1983, I took a job at the LA Children's Hospital. He always called it my little chicken-shit job. He'd say, 'Why don't you quit that little chicken-shit job?' I always kept that job. That was my security – and it turned out to be very important for Arthur, later on."

For a time, Diane's daughter lived with the two of them, moving out when she turned 18. In 1981, Diane required surgery. "Arthur took very good care of me. He made the bed, changed the sheets, straightened up, and looked after me. He was very sweet that way." Despite his problems, Arthur continued to impress Diane. "One of the very important things about my relationship with Arthur was that I always had respect for him, as a man. I did not always agree with everything he did or said, but I still respected him. He was my hero, not for the man on stage, but for the man he really was. It was his philosophy, broad understanding of life, and spirituality. It was the way he saw life and people; watching him with an animal, watching him relate to his friends. Then again, that was all in his music, too. We had our ups and downs, to be sure. We were together, we were apart, he was involved with other women, but there was always a bond between us. I knew him and he knew me. He would say to me, 'You don't know who I am,' but I did, and he understood that I did."

Meanwhile, Arthur's career was in limbo. When he did perform, the shows were loose and under-rehearsed, utilizing whichever of his cadre of musical associates was available – the quality of the performances dependent on his state of mind. Payment was always in cash, in advance, or Arthur wouldn't play. David Fairweather was a novice booking agent who was assigned Arthur's account. As a musician, some years earlier, his band had played on the same bill as Arthur. Now, he found himself booking a legend. "I remember that, back in the 70s, Arthur was a bald-headed, scary guy who didn't seem to like me very much. I didn't meet him again until around 1980. I was a lawyer by then. I had been practicing law but I decided, at that time, that I wanted to be an agent. I was working with an agent named Al Becker, and he said to me, 'Have we got a client for you!' They gave me Arthur as my assignment, for one summer. I booked him into various gigs around town, like Madame Wong's. It was my job to go and collect the money, give Arthur his share at the end, and make sure we got our cut. That, of course, led to innumerable arguments with Arthur. The job lasted for one summer and then I went back to law. I maintained my friendship with Arthur and it actually got much stronger once there wasn't money to argue about. He was playing, off and on, with Melvan Whittington, John Sterling on guitar, Sherwood Akuna or Robert Rozelle on bass, and Joe Blocker on drums. If you could get all these guys altogether, and sober, at the same time, it was OK, but that wasn't always the case." David became Arthur's confidante. "He'd phone me and we'd talk about his problems, or all sorts of other things, so we became close. Arthur was a big fight fan and he'd get pay-per-view TV of the big fights. He would invite me to his house and we'd watch the fights together. It was always fun."

With the major record labels wary of Arthur's reputation, his only recording outlets would be smaller independent labels, offering low budget, one-album deals. One such label was E.X. Pression, owned by Jeff Gruber, who signed Arthur in 1977. The plan was for Arthur to record some tracks for an album to be called *More Changes*; however, the album was never officially released. Rhino, still an independent label at the time, specializing in reissues, later acquired seven of the tracks and used them as the basis for a self-titled Arthur Lee solo album, released in 1981. "It was nice to give Arthur an opportunity to release new recordings and not just reissue previous material," says Harold Bronson. "Because we had those [E.X. Pression] tracks – for which Arthur claimed he received no money – we decided to use them, and record some new ones to make it long enough to issue as an LP. We were able to get Herbie Worthington to do the cover – he was riding high at the time having worked for Fleetwood Mac."

Arthur Lee was another album recorded on the cheap, using Arthur's floating stable of players, augmented by George Suranovich on three tracks and Azell Taylor, Arthur's neighborhood friend, singing on a cover of a 1957 song by The Bobbettes called, what else, "Mr. Lee." The real surprise was the addition of the unknown Velvert Turner on lead guitar on three tracks. Joe Blocker explains: "Velvert was a good friend of mine. I met him in '71 or '72, when he was into imitating Jimi Hendrix, who was apparently his mentor [Turner was indeed a Hendrix acolyte]. He played some California gigs with us in the late 70s and was fun on stage, but he and Arthur had that love/hate thing that Arthur seemed to have had with lots of people."

Another musical highlight was Arthur's wailing harmonica playing, something at which he excelled but essayed only rarely. His recent penchant for reggae and funk found plenty of room on the album, too. "Arthur was fascinated with Bob Marley and listened to reggae all the time," confirms Diane Lee. "It's not easy to play but he did it. He was into it."

Elsewhere, a prettified re-arrangement of "7 & 7 Is" failed to improve on the dynamic original, and Arthur pulled out "I Do Wonder" from his back catalog (the song, given its full, parenthetical title, had yet to see the light of day on *Forever Changes* reissues). Undoubtedly the high point of the album, however, was Arthur's poignant cover of Jimmy Cliff's "Many Rivers To Cross," although "Stay Away From Evil" ran it close. Arthur's singing was impressive throughout what is ultimately an under-produced album of average songs. Friday Music re-released the album in 2009.

According to Diane, Arthur was always composing new songs. "When Arthur was working on the *Arthur Lee* album he had a keyboard at the house. I can see him sitting there, with a smile on his face, expressing the pleasure he got from the music. His mind was always going and the songs would come into his head. He would wake up in the morning and go into a room by himself. He heard songs in his sleep and he wanted to get them down before he forgot them. He liked to write in private."

There were other facets of Arthur Lee that few got to witness, like the tenderness and generosity he would show to loved ones. "He was wonderfully romantic," says Diane. "I remember when he and I were alone, at home, with an old R&B song playing and he held me close and we danced. One Christmas, he had gifts for me arranged by the fireplace so that I would walk in and be surprised to see them. He always gave people gifts. His pleasure came from the happiness he might give. Another time, he carried me, in the rain, for two blocks up Arlington Street, where there is a steep incline. Arthur would go for early morning walks and pick me a bouquet of flowers from people's gardens. On weekends I would go with him and he'd fill my arms with flowers. He was a very romantic man." Arthur's largesse was another virtue. "He would give someone his last $20 and if he didn't have it he'd turn to me and say, 'Diane, you got $20?' His pockets were always open for people. He liked to help. He got Curtis Woods and his band opening one of his shows. He would have some of his relatives working for him." Robert Rozelle remembers an avuncular Arthur. "He loved kids. When my daughter, Nicole, was born, he used to bring her presents. He just loved her to death and she loved her Uncle Arthur."

One of Arthur's favorite Hollywood restaurants was Lucy's El Adobe Café, at 5536 Melrose Avenue, across the street from Paramount Studios. He adored Lucy's tacos. "The first time Arthur took me there, in the early 90s, Lucy pointed out a picture of Arthur with Jimi Hendrix, hanging on the wall by the cash register," says Diane, with a smile. "Arthur had signed it: 'With LOVE to Lucy's.' In another room was the grand piano which Arthur would occasionally sit at and play."

Despite their apparent closeness, in the summer of 1983 Arthur and Diane split up. "We would fight, and it wasn't always Arthur's fault. I was no saint, back then. I had a wild, stubborn streak in me, and I wanted to get my way. How do you do that when you're with Arthur Lee, this huge star? I wasn't one of his fawning fans. You always had to prove yourself to Arthur. He was always testing your loyalty."

Following the split, Arthur ran into some legal trouble. On December 19 1983, he and a companion had gone to a lady friend's second-floor apartment – she apparently owed them $100. When she wouldn't open the door, one of them started a fire. Arthur was later arrested and charged with arson. "His friend, Jimmy, started the fire, but Arthur never told on him," says Diane. "He [Arthur] went to a prison, in Chino, California. Arthur liked the weirdest people."

This was Arthur's first strike. Soon afterwards, he left LA. "He was worried about some potential legal problems, so he high-tailed it out of town and went back to Memphis," explains Diane. His mother, Agnes, had moved back to Memphis in 1985 and was living with her sister, Edwinor Porter. Arthur stayed with them. "He called me every night," Diane recalls. "He sat in his aunt's backyard in Memphis and wrote the song 'Five String Serenade.' The guitar had only five strings and he wrote that song sitting under a tree, alongside a dog that belonged to his cousin, Peaches. He played the song for me over the phone after he wrote it."

While in Memphis, Arthur also composed "You're the Prettiest Song" for Diane, as well as the song "Ninety Miles Away." He laid low in Memphis before returning to LA in 1988. "He was trying to woo me back, but I wasn't ready for his lifestyle," says Diane. "I still had my job and, for the first time in my life, I wanted to establish my own identity. But he hounded me. He'd phone me at home or at work. I'd pick up the phone and he'd be crooning like Sam Cooke. He even followed me around."

Arthur incurred more legal problems after a fan charged him with car theft. "He was playing at the Universal Amphitheatre and this nutcase managed to get backstage, posing as a journalist, and knocked on his door," Diane explains. "He took her back to a friend's place. She was a real crazed fan but he let her in the door. His mother always used to say, 'Why'd you let the devil in the door?' After that, this fan kept calling Arthur. She even called me, crying over Arthur. He did see her again but she ended up putting Arthur in jail. She had rented a car and let Arthur use it, but his cousin stole it. Arthur kind of took advantage of her, and when she didn't get the car back she called the police on Arthur. They arrested him and I think he did some time for that."

Arthur was fortunate that both arrests went under the media radar, sparing him public humiliation. Meanwhile, he had resumed gigging around LA under the Love moniker, although his reputation continued to make him a liability for most club owners. "By that point, he had done so many lousy shows, no decent club would book him," says a sighing Len Fagan. "He tried to intimidate promoters and didn't trust them. Back in the 80s and 90s, I was the booking director for a club on the Sunset Strip called the Coconut Teaszer. Arthur called me up and wanted to do a show there. I was hesitant. He called me, as a friend, to help him out. Then his drummer, Joe Blocker, didn't show up, so Arthur said to me, 'You're playing drums tonight.' I hadn't played for him in years. He wasn't nasty, just really fucked up. People still wanted to see the great Arthur Lee, not the fucked up Arthur Lee. He was babbling on and on. At one point, I leaned over to Sherwood Akuna and said, 'I'll give you $20 if you start "Orange Skies" and Arthur stops talking and starts singing.' He said 'OK' and we started the song. Sure enough, Arthur stopped babbling and joined in, singing and playing. Then, halfway through, he stopped and began to babble again. I did the same thing with 'My Little Red Book.' I don't think we finished one song all night. You would think people would be booing and walking out, but the crowd would accept anything Arthur did. They'd be going, 'Yeah, Arthur Lee! Arthur Lee!' He was this legend, but it was shameful. If it was me, I'd have wanted my money back. His audience was so grateful just to see him there, they would accept anything."

In the fall of 1989, Diane and Arthur reconnected, and Arthur moved in to Diane's rented apartment at 5222 Wilkinson Avenue, in Valley Village. "He called me to pick him up," says Diane, "put his things in my car, got in, and said let's go to your place. That was it – he'd moved in." From there, they moved to a third floor apartment at 4912 Kester Street, Sherman Oaks. "He cleaned up for one year," she maintains, "but Arthur was always Arthur."

With his career trajectory on a downward spin, Arthur thought it might be worthwhile getting the original Love back together. "He had reconnected with Johnny," confirms Diane, "but the early 90s were a bad time for Arthur." Kenny Forssi would not take Arthur's calls and it wasn't likely Bryan would have agreed to a reunion. The idea fell through, but Arthur did not abandon it completely. At this point, he was pulling in between $300 and $500 a night for a gig, an embarrassingly paltry figure for an artist of his former stature. On one occasion he even opened for a Doors tribute band.

To acquire some ready cash, in March 1991 Arthur sold 50 per cent of his song publishing to Leiber & Stoller's Trio Music, on the advice of a confidante, George St. John. George was reputed to have mob connections, something that appealed to Arthur's sense of danger. "George led Arthur to believe he had some unsavory connections," reveals Diane. As Arthur's sometime manager Mark Linn recalls: "George St. John was this scary, *Goodfellas* kind of guy who had somehow been involved with Hendrix. He had gold records on his wall. Arthur had me, this kind of nerdy kid, doing a lot of stuff for him, and he had George, who he trusted, on the big business deals. Somehow, George convinced Arthur to sell his publishing, which he'd clung onto even when his stock was much higher and he might have sold it for a premium. In 1991, he sold half his catalog for $80,000, which meant $40,000 for Arthur and $40,000 for George. They both bought Lincoln Town Cars with car-phones." The catalog was later sold to Windswept Holdings, currently under the umbrella of Bug Music Ltd.

Mark Linn first met Arthur in 1990, when he was working as a booking agent for indie bands. A friend gave him Arthur's phone number. "I called him up and went to see him play a show at the Eye Beam, in San Francisco," Mark recalls. "He knew I was coming and we talked afterwards. I didn't have an agenda, I was just curious. After the show, he played me some songs on acoustic guitar: 'Five String Serenade,' 'You're The Prettiest Song,' and a version of 'Girl On Fire.' I thought they were fantastic. The idea of Arthur doing a solo show seemed exciting. He had Robert Rozelle, Melvan, and a drummer, and they played the typical four or five Love songs. Arthur looked and sounded great, but it wasn't inspired. It all depended on his mood. I just wanted to get him out of that thing because it was going nowhere."

Mark looked to the East Coast, where Arthur's legend had not been diminished by familiarity or notoriety. "It was tougher booking him on the West Coast. He'd just about worn out his welcome everywhere. Every single club had a horror story about him. I wasn't a high-powered manager, I was really just a fan, so it was a learning experience for me and I really enjoyed it."

Rather than fly a band out from LA to back Arthur, Mark chose instead to book local East Coast players who were eager to hook up with the great Arthur Lee. There was no shortage. Among their number were Lyle Hysen, David Motamed, and Alex Totino, former members of New York band Das Damen. "We had little shows where you could have heard a pin drop," Mark recalls. "People couldn't believe they were seeing Arthur Lee. Opportunities started coming his way. But Arthur was so hard to control; I was no match for him. He was his own worst enemy, to a huge extent. It was frustrating because there were moments when he was fantastic. Those were usually the times when he would give up drinking and drugs for a while. Those times, he would be clear about what he wanted to do, and maybe a little scared, too. Then, when opportunities came, he would do something to sabotage them. His demeanor varied wildly. In retrospect, I should have been scared to death. He seemed kind of defeated and was feeling like he should have had more success than he did, without realizing what he needed to do to make it happen." Arthur didn't give up, however. "We traveled the East Coast in a rented Geo Metro car, staying in motels. It was low budget. He didn't pay the band much and they had to find their own accommodation. Arthur would come back from these East Coast tours with money. We started selling t-shirts and things, and it was kind of growing. But it was all word of mouth. We were looking to take it to the next level, but some problem always seemed to arise."

Mark wanted to move Arthur's career forward and believed an album of new material might be the key. "I really wanted him to make a great record. I didn't care if he sang cover songs. In retrospect, I wish he had done that because he could sing anything. I just wanted to get him in a studio." Unable to land a decent US record deal, Mark eventually found an ally in Patrick Mathé, a Frenchman who ran the Parisian record label New Rose. "The label paid Arthur a lot more than anybody else was willing to: $40,000. That was a fortune for Arthur Lee in the 90s. No one else was talking more than $3,000 or $4,000 for an album from him. Patrick flew in to meet Arthur, and Arthur was completely straight and charmed the pants off of him. Patrick and I were excited that this was going to be a major revival for Arthur. But I don't think he completed the record as I was hoping he would. I think it was more of that Jekyll and Hyde thing, where his intention was to do something great but he still had the propensity to hurt himself. He had a couple of good songs like 'Five String Serenade' and 'You're The Prettiest Song' and a couple of others, but I felt like something had changed. It's an OK record but I thought it was going to be a lot better, based on the songs I knew he had. He definitely threw some tracks on it."

The story goes that Arthur spent the bulk of the recording budget on a car and drugs, leaving a small fraction for actual studio costs. Mark does not deny that scenario. In the end the album, entitled *Arthur Lee And Love*, although released in France, remained an import-only item elsewhere. "We tried to get it out in the US but the deals were ridiculously low. We just didn't want to give it away for so little money."

Trust was still an issue for Arthur. "He never trusted anyone, not even me," Mark admits. "I did the New Rose deal and worked really hard on it, and Arthur then decided what he was going to pay me. In the end, he decided to give me seven-and-a-half per cent. He sent me a check for $2,400." Santa Monica alternative rock band Mazzy Star would record Arthur's "Five String Serenade" on their platinum-selling, 1993 album, *So Tonight That I Might See*. "Arthur made some money from that," says Mark, "but he never gave me a dime, even after I'd hustled them the song."

Released in April 1992, *Arthur Lee And Love* was an improvement on *Arthur Lee* in terms of the songwriting, although the production values left much to be desired. Synthesizers and pianos overwhelm some of the songs. For all that, "Five String Serenade" was one of Arthur's best compositions in years, followed closely by "You're The Prettiest Song" and "Somebody's Watchin' You" (once you get past its cheesy circus organ). "Ninety Miles Away" featured old LAGs bandmate Allan Talbert on saxophone. "The Watcher" was a swampy slice of funk, while "Passing By" returned Arthur to the Jimi Hendrix school of electric blues. *Arthur Lee And Love* would be Arthur's final album of new music.

In an effort to promote the record in Europe, Mark arranged for Arthur to do several shows over there, beginning April 27, backed by Liverpool quartet Shack. "I met Arthur at the airport in Paris and I couldn't believe what he looked like," recalls Mark. "He was almost like a homeless person. In the year-and-a-half I'd known him, I had never seen him like this. He looked haggard and like he hadn't slept in weeks. I learned later, he hadn't. Arthur had hooked up with Don Conka and they'd gone on a binge with the money he'd had from those deals. For the first few days [in Europe], he was nodding out at the table. I was nervous that he wouldn't be able to get through the shows with Shack. He didn't look good but his voice was incredible, and I think the band kind of blew his mind. They really had it together and were playing songs from deep into his catalog, many of which he hadn't sung since recording them. He was really knocked out. It kept him on his toes."

Shack guitarist John Head relates how the band came to back their hero: "A friend of ours, a guy who used to come and watch us play in the very early Shack, came to us and said he had Arthur Lee coming over to Paris and asked us if we wanted to back him up. We said, 'Are you joking … definitely!' We didn't need to learn his songs; we already knew pretty much all of them and we sounded like Love. We didn't want it to be all clean and crisp. We wanted it to be raw, with as much energy and passion as Love."

Although only in their twenties, the members of Shack – bassist Martyn Campbell, drummer Johnny Baxter, and brothers John and Michael Head on guitars – were diehard Love fans, in awe of Arthur. "We were completely aware that we didn't want to let him down," remembers John Head. "We wanted to play what he wanted. But I think we knew a lot more songs than he anticipated. When we first rehearsed, in Paris, during the soundcheck – our only rehearsal with Arthur – he kept trying to walk off the stage. We would be saying, 'What about this one?" and start playing another of his songs. He'd say, 'You guys know *that* one?' That happened time after time. He'd be so humble and thank us, then we'd say again, 'Well, how about this one?' and start in on another song and he'd come back and do it with it us. He was just so chuffed that we knew so many of his songs."

Michael and John Head of the band Shack really blew my mind. We had one rehearsal before the show and I thought they learned all of the songs in just about one night. We met in Paris, through Mark Linn and [Shack's manager] Stéphane Bismuth. Musically, it was Love! I couldn't figure it out. I thought these guys must have been playing the songs for 25 years. They came as close to the recordings as they possibly could. John, the lead guitar player, played Johnny Echols solos in songs like "Your Mind And We Belong Together," so well, that a couple of times I had to look to see if it wasn't Johnny himself. I really had a good time with those guys.

"All our friends kept telling us we were going to be disappointed, because your heroes aren't always what you expect them to be," says John, "but we told them, 'No way.' And when we met him, there was this big mutual respect between us. Every show was amazing. You knew everyone there was feeling the same as we were, just seeing Arthur Lee and hearing those songs. Everyone had so much love for Arthur, and he just soaked it up and sang like a bird. We would stand at the edge of the stage every night and watch him." The tour wound up in Shack's home town on May 5. "He really liked Liverpool and said he'd like to live there. I think he felt a real affinity with the place and the people, maybe because of The Beatles, I'm not sure. The next time he came here, Michael took him for fish and chips and Arthur said to Michael, 'It's really nice to be home.'"

When I went to England, back in '92, one of the things that amazed me was Liverpool, the city in which The Beatles wrote "Penny Lane." The band that toured with me in the United Kingdom was Shack, of whom I grew fond almost immediately. They took me all around the town, showing me the different places where The Beatles played, all the different clubs where they started and the Sgt. Pepper posters still on the walls of the club, just like they were, then. But I was looking for the places where they'd written those beautiful songs. I looked and looked ... and finally it hit me: just like me, they must have written them from within.

The show in Liverpool is still one of the most memorable of my life. The warmth and love of the people there is something I will never forget. Not only did they know all my songs, they sang them aloud as we played. They really made me feel welcome. I had no idea that I was so popular, there. After the show, they took me to a restaurant and when I walked in, everybody started singing my songs. I really didn't know what to do. What an honor. The feelings that came from those people were unbelievable – nothing but good vibes. Sometimes, I think I should have stayed there. I do intend on making my home somewhere near there for a while in my life, and not just because of the Arthur Lee onstage trip. For a long time I have known that it's my destiny to live in Europe.

While Europe continued to embrace Arthur, he did not move there. He did, however, consider recording with Shack. He wrote to Stéphane Bismuth in January 1993 and suggested that a four-song EP, including a re-recording of "Your Mind And We Belong Together" (a song on which John Head had played impressively) would "definitely be a good business and fun thing to do for all included." No such recording was undertaken, however, although a live CD of the Liverpool show was released by Viper Records in 2001.

Back home, Arthur continued occasional gigging with his usual pool of support players, appearing at clubs and the odd retro festival. He returned to Europe for a Jimi Hendrix tribute show in November, but, by the beginning of 1993, he was back on the local LA club circuit playing scattered dates, booked by agent Tom Sweeney.

On April 29, Arthur appeared at the Troubadour on Santa Monica Boulevard. The opening act was a young band, Baby Lemonade. Formed the previous autumn by guitarists Mike Randle and David Ramsay (alias 'Rusty Squeezebox') – both employees of Santa Monica secondhand record outlet Moby Disk – drummer David 'Daddyo' Green, from Minneapolis, and bass player Henry Liu, the multi-racial quartet were familiar with the name Arthur Lee. "We had all Arthur's records in the store because Rusty and I were such big fans," says Mike Randle. "One day, this guy comes up to the counter and he's got all Arthur's albums and all the Love albums. I said to him, 'You must be a pretty big Love fan,' and he says, 'Well, I book Arthur around town.' This was about November of 1992. We had just started Baby Lemonade about a month or two before that. I had a five-song demo tape of our original songs and I told him, 'We have a band and people always say we sound like Love.' He said, 'Give me your tape and maybe you can open up for Arthur sometime.' We didn't even want to get paid, just the opportunity was enough. The guy's name was Tom Sweeney. Sure enough, three or four months later he called me and said that Arthur was playing the Troubadour in a couple of days and the band that was supposed to open up couldn't make it, so he asked us if we would do it. I remember we played our set and Arthur was up in the balcony checking us out. Afterwards, I introduced myself to him and talked to him. The next day our manager, Jeff Davis, got a call from Tom Sweeney telling him that Arthur wanted to know if maybe we could back him. We weren't really retro and Arthur, I think, liked that. He wanted us to get together to see if there was any chemistry between us."

The group met Arthur at David Green's home studio in Baldwin Hills. "Arthur walked in wearing his shades," recalls Mike Randle. "He looked around, didn't say much, then called out "7 & 7 Is," and we did it. He called out another song and we did that. This went on for a few songs, then he shook our hands, got in his Lincoln, and left. There wasn't much conversation. He was cool but I also think he was nervous. Arthur then called Tom Sweeney, who called our manager, saying, 'Arthur wants those guys to be his band.' So he came back another day and was more relaxed. We did some more songs, he hung out with us and was completely cool, except that he asked if we had any secret microphones and were bootlegging the session. We weren't."

"It wasn't about the money," stresses David Green of their decision to work with Arthur. "When we met Arthur, he was playing for anyone who would guarantee him $500. We were maybe making $80 each, with Arthur. It was a real pleasure to be working with him. But we were Baby Lemonade and we were serious about our own career. Playing with Arthur was a sideline, just a kick, and, if you stayed on Arthur's good side, a pure pleasure. For a struggling rock band to suddenly have a built-in audience was fun. At that point, with Arthur, it was never that serious a time commitment. All you knew about was the next gig."

On June 2 1993, Baby Lemonade made their debut backing Arthur at a small club called Raji's, in Hollywood. Both sides were pleased with the results, so much so that Arthur made their relationship official. Baby Lemonade was his backing band (although, for economic reasons, he continued to use other musicians on East Coast and European jaunts over the next year). It would prove to be a most fruitful, if sometimes fitful, relationship. In the young members of Baby Lemonade, Arthur had found a solid group of musicians who were dedicated to playing Arthur's music with the respect, reverence, and enthusiasm it deserved. They were not part of Arthur's retinue of hangers-on nor old school buddies seeking to bathe in his fading aura. Most importantly, they were not drugged out. The four players were straight, focused, and dependable, and they came as a tight-knit package. "The one thing we had over previous musicians of Arthur's, was the close relationship between the four of us," confirms David Green. "He couldn't fire one of us and couldn't play one against the other – there could be no divide and conquer. We were very tight as friends, the four of us, and he knew that. But that was also an advantage. Arthur could rely on us."

Nonetheless, bassist Henry Liu would quit the band in the summer of 1994, the result of an altercation with Arthur. "Henry and Arthur got into a fight at a show in San Juan Capistrano," explains Mike. "Henry was a sweet guy and very sensitive. Arthur made a derogatory onstage joke about Asians while some of Henry's family were in the crowd, and it hurt Henry's feelings really badly. Even though Henry came back into the band after that night, it was never the same. Arthur said that if he couldn't be himself around Henry then it just wasn't going to work." According to David Green, Arthur called Henry 'a Chinaman.' "After the gig, Henry went after Arthur. Arthur thought it was funny, Henry didn't." Not long afterward, Dave Chapple joined on bass.

I have not seen as devoted a group of people as my current band, for a long, long time. They used to be called Baby Lemonade and they have CDs that you can buy under that name. Although we have different behavior patterns, musically I couldn't ask for a better group of people. Mike Randle is one of the best guitarists in the business. Rusty Squeezebox plays rhythm guitar and he not only plays the hell out of his instrument but sometimes helps me remember the words to some of the songs I've written over 35 years. As flattering as it is, I sometimes get tired of singing those old songs. Dave Chapple is a very accomplished musician on the bass. So much so, that it's like you show him a new song once and when he feels it, it's all but over with. As far as David 'Daddyo' Green is concerned, he can play anything he wants, and when I give him the nod to take a solo, no matter what part of the song it is this guy is ready for Freddie. He reminds me of the drummer in Led Zeppelin, John Bonham, and he was one of the best rock drummers I ever heard. I've seen musicians come and go, but the band I'm working with now reminds me of my first Love band, only without the drugs. Their dedication to the songs I have written, whether old or new, is tremendous and these people learn and play my songs with their hearts as well as their open minds. I thank the Lord for such a contribution.

Arthur had returned to the East Coast in October 1993, working again with the members of Das Damen. Mark Linn then booked him and Baby Lemonade to play Chicago's Cubby Bear club, on December 4. The trip did not go down well with the band who found themselves whisked from a midnight plane arrival straight into a Chicago recording studio to cut versions of several classic Love songs, plus Arthur's early composition "Feathered Fish." David Green: "We didn't know why we were recording these cover songs. We felt manipulated." Five tracks from this session, including "Feathered Fish" and a new song, "Girl On Fire," were later released as an EP.

"I had some free recording time at a little studio," Mark explains. "I think Baby Lemonade was upset with me because I put them up with a friend as opposed to getting them a hotel. My devotion was to Arthur. I didn't know them that well and they kind of rubbed me the wrong way. I appreciated them and they played well, but I found the guitar player too flashy, playing in a sort of 80s power pop way rather than the way the songs originally were. They seemed like kids with Arthur. They didn't turn me on, even though it was tight."

The managerial relationship with Mark Linn ended not long afterwards, although he did continue to find work for Arthur outside California, backed by other musicians. "We had plenty of ups and downs," says Mark. "There would always be people at shows, whether it was in New York or Europe, who really wanted to party with Arthur Lee. Sometimes, it might be some rich kid with money and drugs, or, in England, it would be these young bands, or the guy from Primal Scream [singer Bobby Gillespie] who followed Arthur around like a little dog. I was always trying to protect him from these kinds of things. But Arthur and I fell out about an argument over money from t-shirt sales."

Arthur played a memorable two-set gig on March 4 1994, at Tramps, a club in New York City. "He did these two fantastic shows, back to back," says Mark.

"I felt really proud at those Tramps shows because there were 500 people there and you could see their jaws dropping as Arthur came out. No one really knew of his whereabouts on the East Coast; he was still this legendary character. There were years where no one heard anything from him. [Renowned journalist] David Fricke was blown away and wrote about him in *Rolling Stone*."

On June 3 1994, Arthur made a return visit to the UK, appearing at a north London club, the Garage, backed by British band The High Llamas. Their leader, Sean O'Hagan, recalls receiving a song list from Arthur in advance of his arrival. "We'd been rehearsing for a week. We had a six-piece band, plus three violin players, a flute, and harpsichord. Arthur finally arrived, walked in, and said, 'Right, what have you got ready?' We said, 'How about "Orange Skies?"' We started the song, he opened his mouth and it was glorious. The songs were pretty complicated, but as soon as he was there it was dead easy, like walking for the first time. We all wanted to fulfill his musical expectations. It was probably the best gig The High Llamas ever played. We knew we were making a little bit of pop music history. It was likely the first time he played those songs with a string section and flutes, and he appreciated it. 'This is the best Love!' he would tell us."

As with all things surrounding Arthur, the event was not without its tribulations. "Before the show, Arthur went missing," recalls Sean. "We had a full house, with everyone on the edge of expectation, but no Arthur. We had to send out a search party down the Holloway Road, not the nicest part of town. He was eventually found in a bar about a mile away, shooting pool with some Irish guys. So we said, 'Arthur, they're ready for you' and he replied, 'Sure. Just let me make this shot.' With that, he bounced on down the road to the gig. He knew no one was going to leave: they were waiting for *him*." Arthur did have one familiar concern, however. "He was worried that he wouldn't get paid. He kept asking, 'Are they gonna pay us?' There was this manic woman hanging around, filming him all the time, and Arthur would be saying, 'I don't know who she is!'" Backing Arthur Lee would have a positive effect on the fortunes of The High Llamas, who duly landed a major recording contract in their own right.

The following night, Arthur made a solo appearance at Kensington's Royal Albert Hall, as part of Creation Records' tenth birthday bash, hosted by LA scene-maker Rodney Bingenheimer. Backing Arthur was Sean O'Hagan on nylon-string guitar for "Signed D.C." and "Alone Again Or." He recalls: "Arthur soundchecked OK, but by show time he was a little bit wired. It was very difficult.

I did the two songs and John Head from Shack was there. I gave him my guitar and said, 'I've done two songs, you can do the last two with him,' and he was thrilled. Arthur was not in the best shape that night. He jumped over a drum kit and started playing it with the palms of his hands, then jumped back to the microphone." Sean was tasked with minding Arthur during the afternoon before the show. "It wasn't easy. After that, I thought I had done something special, but that was it for me. If they'd have asked us to do a whole tour with Arthur, I'd have turned it down. It was so difficult that day. I just thought to myself, 'I don't think I'll do that again.' But I wouldn't have missed it for the world."

Whatever the difficulties, Arthur's mere appearance was enough to elicit a rapturous response and solidify his reputation as a living legend. "He was welcomed at the Royal Albert Hall as a hero," says Harvey Kubernik, "and it seemed to be the only time where expectations were high and he didn't blow it. Primal Scream, Oasis, and all these bands were there to worship him. Following that, there were some nice bookings for him in the UK and Europe."

Later that year, tiny Pennsylvanian indie label Distortion Records released a single, "Girl On Fire," backed by "Midnight Sun," under the name Arthur Lee And Love. The two new compositions were recorded at Entourage studios, North Hollywood, with back up from Baby Lemonade. The single failed to reignite Arthur's career. It seemed that all anyone wanted from him were the oldies.

Arthur's reputation for inconsistent performances had not yet abated. Music journalist Bill Wasserzieher caught one of Arthur's shows around this time and wrote about it in *The Jazz Review*. "There is a grotesque fascination in observing someone go over the edge ... how else to explain crowds gathering to watch suicidal leapers on building ledges or drivers slowing to a crawl to gawk at roadside disasters? Sometimes it's a little like that at an Arthur Lee show. Over the last three years, since Lee started playing around Los Angeles again, he has performed sets as brilliant as fireworks on a festival night and, at other times, he has been so far over the edge that Syd Barrett and Peter Green would probably shake their heads." He went on to describe Arthur's set with Baby Lemonade. "What followed was a mudslide of half-finished songs, broken narratives, jokes without punch-lines, and stories that started over the microphone but became interior monologues that only Lee could hear. In just under an hour of stage time, Lee managed not quite 26 minutes of music, finishing just six of the 11 songs he attempted. The show didn't so much end as fizzle out. Southern Californians are still a fairly laid-back, forgiving lot, and Arthur Lee hobbled off stage to a bit of applause and only a few catcalls. In New York, he probably would have been eaten."

Arthur closed out the year with a disastrous New Year's Eve gig at Hollywood's Hell's Gate club, where Melvan Whittington joined the band on stage. This show would mark the end of Tom Sweeney's relationship with Arthur and Baby Lemonade.

Diane and Arthur split up once again in February 1995. For Diane, Arthur was spiraling out of control. "He saved my life by dumping me. It got me out of a bad situation. I got out of that environment, stood back, and got to grow. I really freed myself. It wasn't easy or pretty. This was part of the dark times with, and for, Arthur. He was not the sweet and loving Arthur I loved. He and I were not getting on too well. I had left and come back twice before, hoping the situation would get back to the good times. Arthur was wanting to 'party,' for lack of a better word, and there were plenty of people, male and female, with their hands out wanting to party with him, as long as he was fronting the party. Then he met Susan Levine, while he was bingeing, shall we say, and wanted to party."

Arthur had been introduced to Susan by a mutual friend, Dave Brown, who looked after the sound at Arthur's shows. Susan had relocated from Chicago to LA with her eight-year-old daughter, and was living next door to the Browns. "I knew who Arthur Lee was when I met him: someone I had heard of many years ago," explains Susan. "But I really didn't know anything about him for all those years. I felt like we did sort of have a connection. Arthur had a presence about him. He needed to be the only one shining if he walked into a room. That was important to him. He was with Diane when I met him. He asked me out but I wasn't interested in him because he was in a relationship. He asked if he could call me and he started doing so, two or three times a day, for months. I dealt with the wild side of Arthur and I spent time with him when he was sober. I saw all of it: the good, the bad, and the ugly." The sober Arthur could still be beguiling. "He was the sweetest, kindest person on Earth: soft-spoken, polite, with an almost Southern gentleman's charm. He would literally give someone the shirt off his back."

Still, the relationship was more typically volatile. So much so that Susan's daughter stayed with grandparents for a year because the situation was just too unstable at home, with Arthur drinking heavily. His personal life was in freefall, without a safety net. At one point, police were summoned over allegations of physical abuse. "Arthur was a dangerous man, then," says Bill Wasserzieher. "I felt the threat every time I was around him. There were stories of him beating up his girlfriend and pulling a gun on a cart-bumper in the grocery store. My wife refused to go to shows with me after a while, although she liked all the guys in Baby Lemonade and loved the music."

Arthur's friend and occasional drummer, Gary Stern, noted, as many had before, a split personality. "There were two Arthurs, as if he was schizophrenic. There was the really nice, mellow Arthur who would go out of his way for you and make you feel like you were his best friend. He got me a job doing sound at the Knitting Factory and stood up for me with his manager, for example. And then there was the other Arthur. He could really be an awful person who you couldn't rely on. He could be unreasonable."

Susan and Arthur's relationship had begun to deteriorate badly. "I had been over to his apartment and it was clear to me that there was some friction between Arthur and Susan," says Len Fagan. "She would stand up to him and talk back to him the way most people would never do with Arthur. He was just too imposing a figure. I remember thinking, 'It must be miserable living here.' Then I heard from Harold Bronson at Rhino Records, and it was confirmed by someone else, that Arthur had been arrested for domestic violence. Harold Bronson was a very good and honorable man and he was now having second thoughts about working with Arthur. Next thing I heard, Arthur was arrested for shooting off a gun on his balcony."

Arthur's business advisor and confidante, George St. John, passed away in October 1994. Ten days later his wife, Ruth, also passed away, leaving their two boys and half-sister, Cory, in the care of their grandmother. Arthur gave Cory money for the cremations. Soon after, Cory came by Arthur's apartment with a box for him, saying George would have wanted his friend to have the contents. She left immediately. When Arthur opened the box he found a computer, a .44 Magnum handgun, and 500 rounds of Teflon-coated bullets. "It was a shock to Arthur when she came over with it, then left right away," says Diane. For a convicted felon, it was a serious offense for Arthur to have a firearm in his possession. Instead of disposing of it immediately, he put the box, containing the handgun and bullets, in his closet. "He brought it out once and showed it to me," says Herbie Worthington. "He came walking out of the bedroom with it and I thought, 'Oh my god, Arthur, that's all you need.'"

On the evening of June 10 1995 (according to official County of Los Angeles court records, and not July 4 as is often stated), Arthur and Susan were entertaining friends from New Zealand, Doug Thomas and his wife, at their third-floor apartment on Kester Street. Sometime during the evening, a gun was discharged on the balcony. A neighbor witnessed Arthur holding a handgun and subsequently called the police. When they arrived, Arthur was arrested and charged with discharging the weapon and being a convicted felon in possession of an illegal firearm. The gun in question was the one given to Arthur by George St. John's stepdaughter.

Doug Thomas was a successful New Zealand businessman who imported electronic equipment. A professional musician in Australasia in the 60s and 70s, Doug was very familiar with Arthur and Love's recordings. "They had spirituality to their music," he says. Through friends, he managed to track down Arthur's phone number and the two hooked up. "The next time I was in LA, I brought a few bottles of good New Zealand wine, and we went back to his apartment in Sherman Oaks. Arthur was on large doses of legal medication, prescribed by a doctor. He had really abused himself in his younger days and it's a wonder the guy hadn't died young. I've never known a man with so much stamina. But, of course, it all takes a toll. While he was taking his medication, we were going out for lunches, breakfasts, and dinners. We were always drinking wine and tequila. We were having a good time, and all the while he was on this ultra-strong medication. I've never seen a person consume so much alcohol, but he was never really drunk. However, the combination of the legal medication and the drinking would spin him out, at times. It would have spun anyone out."

On the night in question, Doug claimed it was he who found the gun in the box inside Arthur's closet and brought it out. In court, he would testify that it was he who fired the gun, not Arthur. "I didn't say I did fire the gun. I said *in court* I fired it," Doug states emphatically when asked whether he was really the one who pulled the trigger. "This is something that Arthur and I would not discuss. They did an examination and did find a tiny fraction of gunfire residue on Arthur, but not the legal amount. What was there could have come from merely handling the gun. It was a set up, I'm sure of it. Nothing made sense or added up."

When asked about the testimony, Susan Levine says: "There was nothing Doug Thomas wouldn't have done for Arthur." Neither Doug nor Susan will go on record to state categorically what, in fact, transpired that evening. "Arthur and

I made a pact not to talk about what went on that night," maintains Doug, who, perhaps contentiously, still regards Arthur's arrest as a positive turn for his career. "Going to jail did generate millions of dollars of free publicity for Arthur. That helped his career after he got out and his concert tours became highly successful."

If Doug Thomas did indeed bring out the gun and fire it, as he testified in court, there has yet to be a clear explanation as to why he did so. As he reiterates: "I fired the gun. They [the court] did not believe me. I was not tested for gunfire residue." Moreover, Doug hints at other possible motivations for Arthur being charged. "The whole thing was very odd. Arthur was the only black man in the room, apart from several police officers. At first, we thought the whole thing was a joke. There was a knock on the door and this loud voice says, 'Come on out. We've got the place surrounded. Come out with your hands above your heads.' Arthur had some crazy mates and we thought it was one of them doing this as a joke. Next, the door was opened and there were half-a-dozen SWAT police, with semi-automatic pistols: the whole shooting box was there. That's when I realized this was no joke. I was worried that my wife was going to panic and start running or something, and they would start shooting. They took Arthur away and my wife and I remained behind with Susan. It was a minor crime. He hurt nobody, he threatened nobody. That night, he was arrested on about seven charges, including being a suspected terrorist, having armor-piercing bullets, being a suspected police killer, and of being in possession of a Class A drug, which wasn't even his. They totally overreacted." The drug charges, and some of the others, were later dropped.

Arthur was ultimately freed on $50,000 bail, pending an arraignment hearing, which occurred on April 18 the following year. He faced Judge Michael Hoff on June 14, and a jury trial was set, commencing three days later. Arthur was represented in court by Attorney Ronald Carpol. Prior to the trial date, Arthur was given permission by the court to leave the country for a nine-date European tour, beginning May 19 in Odense, Denmark. No one on the tour knew of his impending court case.

The tour was booked by Gene Kraut, an ex-pat American residing in Sweden. He would be an almost single-handed catalyst in the reviving of Arthur's career. David Fairweather was the link between Gene and Arthur. He says: "I'm a big Jimi Hendrix fan and a big computer fan, too, and on one of these Hendrix internet mailing lists I mentioned, kind of casually, that I knew Arthur Lee. A guy in Sweden named Gene Kraut responded, saying, 'You know Arthur Lee? We love Arthur Lee over here!' Gene was a promoter and wanted me to ask Arthur if he would come over to play a gig in Sweden. This would have been around 1995. I talked to Arthur about it and he didn't want to go over there by himself and play with pickup bands. He had already hooked up with Baby Lemonade by then. Because it wasn't economically feasible to bring the band over for one concert, Gene said he'd look into booking a whole tour. By this time, Arthur had developed a reputation for being unreliable and this made it difficult for Gene to convince promoters that this was real and that Arthur would show up. I hadn't met Gene. It was all emails back and forth. Then, the airline tickets showed up for Arthur and the band. Arthur asked me what I wanted to get out of this and I said that I wanted to come along. I had to work my keep, so I became Arthur's minder and would stand in for Gene, and collect the money if he couldn't be there." Things got off to a predictably ragged start. "We arrived in Copenhagen and immediately got on a ferry to Odense, Denmark, for the first gig. Everyone was uncertain how it was going to go, including Arthur who had a cold and was a bit insecure about embarking on this tour. Because of his insecurities, he drank too much before the first gig and it was a disaster. The show was also broadcast on Danish public radio, too. I was disappointed with Arthur. I was always the one pushing him to do better. I kind of tore into him. After that, the tour improved. Every night got a little bit better. By the time we got to Malmo, Sweden, it was great."

Arthur initially approached Mark Linn to look after his interests in dealing with Gene Kraut. "I emailed Gene but he declined," Mark recalls. "Gene didn't want anyone else involved. He was going to be the Svengali for Arthur and he had all these big plans. He wanted complete control. It seemed like a good thing for Arthur, so I just stayed out of the way. I'm surprised Arthur lasted that long with Gene. He wasn't easy to manage. But I think Arthur had more respect for Gene than he had for me. I don't know if it was because Gene was older, or Arthur thought he had more money, but Gene was able to tell Arthur 'no' about a lot of stuff. Gene kept things in line, to the point where I heard that Arthur would play his shows then come back to the hotel and go to sleep. With me, he'd disappear all night and come back in the morning. I'd have no idea where he'd been. It was a wild ride."

"Gene took a chance on Arthur when no one else would," insists David Green. "Financially, it was barely worth it for us. It was always a struggle, but we made it work. We were taking trains and we'd have to carry our gear on and off and get to a gig. But the tour went really well and we were really excited about the future." Arthur seemed to enjoy the process, says Dave Chapple: "He was kind of surprised at the response. Arthur hadn't done a lengthy tour in a long time. Gene taking a chance and booking the tour opened the door for more reliability. It was about establishing Arthur's name as a dependable act to book. We knew that if we could just get Arthur in motion and on the tracks, it could work."

David Fairweather remembers Arthur being relatively stable at this point. "We had some great times in those hotels on that tour. After the shows, Arthur would relax. He'd sing songs you'd never hear him do onstage. He loved singing R&B."

Just prior to the tour, Rhino Records had issued *Love Story*, an elaborate, two-CD compilation which drew from the band's four Elektra albums and included a detailed booklet containing photos and a band history. The set was well-received and by 2003 had sold over 32,000 copies. Rhino sent a couple of boxes of the compilation for sale at gigs on the European tour and they proved popular. "By the time we got to Stockholm [the fourth concert date], we had run out," notes David Fairweather, "so I was frantically on the phone to Rhino back in the States to send us more CDs. Arthur got used to keeping the money from the merchandise and that created some problems with Gene." Harold Bronson remembers Arthur cooperating for interviews for the compilation and being supportive of it, before the predictable money issues arose.

Rhino organized a CD launch event at the Coconut Teazser on June 15, with Arthur and Baby Lemonade performing; however, Arthur failed to show up, thanks to his ongoing legal issues, and Rusty Squeezebox had to take the mic. A further promotional gig, at New York City's Bitter End club, also fell through after Arthur failed to make it to the airport for his flight. "He was out of control," observes Mark Linn. "Arthur called the club owner that night and kind of blamed it all on me. The owner called me and suggested I stay away from Arthur. This was just before his trial."

Following completion of the European tour, Arthur's next date would be in a Los Angeles courtroom. On tour, he had never once mentioned his upcoming trial, as David Fairweather recalls. "Arthur knew I was a lawyer, yet never once did he say anything about legal problems throughout that whole tour. I knew he had some legal issues awaiting him back in the States, but I had no idea how serious they were. He probably didn't realize how serious they were, either. Within weeks of getting back, I got a call from Arthur saying, 'I'm being sentenced tomorrow.' I said, 'What? Why didn't you tell me about this before? I could have done something to help you.' He never told me he was on trial. It was too late for me to do anything about it. He had a lawyer, but if he had told me, I could have found him a better one. I know the best in town. The best I could do for him was to secure the best appellant attorney I knew."

David is probably correct in assuming Arthur was unaware of the severity of his situation. "Arthur had skated around the law too many times and they wanted to nail him," suggests Johnny Echols, who had reconnected with Arthur. "His attorney kept telling Arthur that this was serious. Arthur had played so many of his shenanigans and shown so much disrespect for the legal systems and the court. You can be contemptuous all you want when you have control, but they had all the power and they can lock your ass up, which is what they ultimately did. They offered him a plea bargain of a few months but he wouldn't take it."

Susan Levine confirms this. "His attorney tried to get him to accept the plea bargain, but Arthur didn't take it all that seriously. He was convinced he was going to walk out of there." Gary Stern was a friend of the district attorney. "He called me up and said, 'Your friend's in a lot of trouble.' He tried to shuffle the papers so that an inexperienced prosecutor would get Arthur's case, but it didn't work out that way. The woman who got it was really good and never lost a case, so my friend told me to expect the worst. Then Arthur pissed off the judge by telling him, 'Only God is my judge.'"

Although no stranger to guns, Arthur insisted he had not discharged the weapon. Doug Thomas's testimony that *he* had fired the gun cut no ice. "After Doug Thomas flew in to testify that he shot the gun, the prosecution said all it proved was that Arthur had fans all over the world who were willing to lie for him," says Gary Stern. What's more, prosecutor Barbara Burleson was able to bring up Arthur's previous felony conviction for arson and paint him as a danger to society. Arthur's testimony was often flippant and obstructive, which further alienated him from the court. All this was enough to convince the jury to convict Arthur on three counts: illegal possession of a firearm; negligent discharge of a firearm; and being a felon in possession of a firearm. Arthur's predicament was worsened by California's controversial 'three strikes' law which meted out the toughest punish for anyone who was convicted of a third offence, regardless of the circumstances. This was Arthur's third strike.

On June 27 1996, the jury rendered a guilty verdict on all charges. Following a sentencing hearing on July 18, Judge Hoff reprimanded Arthur for his attitude and behavior, and sentenced him to 12 years and 4 months in the state penitentiary. He denied probation, citing Arthur as a dangerous individual. "I was surprised," notes Susan, who was present in court. "I wasn't expecting so many years. He never really expected that, either. Initially, he was offered a plea bargain of one-and-a-half years but he was so sure that he would beat it that he turned it down. We were both stunned by the outcome. I'll always remember when they were taking Arthur away: all he was concerned about was that I was going to be OK. He asked the bailiff if he could give me his check book or some money."

The members of Baby Lemonade attended the sentencing hearing and had earlier written letters to the judge on Arthur's behalf, citing him as a father figure and noting that his career was on an upswing. "We were scared for Arthur," says Dave Chapple. "It all came up so fast, we almost didn't have a chance to react. Then, *boom*, he was gone."

David Green thinks Arthur was entirely unprepared for the severity of the sentence. "What he had done wasn't that serious, but I don't think he understood the three strikes situation or what he was up against. I don't think he understood his lawyer or the fact that the prosecutor and the judge wanted him gone for a long time. It all came crashing down on him."

"The judge basically said that Arthur was a disgrace," says Mike Randle. "He said all this terrible stuff. Arthur was in shock. The judge asked him if he understood what he had told him and he replied that he didn't. Then his lawyer said, 'He does.' But Arthur was totally shocked."

I was sent to the Pleasant Valley State Penitentiary in Coalinga, California. I was sentenced to 12 years for a crime, by law, I did not commit. By law, I mean you are innocent until proven guilty. My case was a simple one. Four people in the suite where I was staying said Doug Thomas fired the shot straight up in the air, including Doug himself. He took the stand three times and each time he said he was the one who fired the shot, yet when the police came, I was the only one taken to jail. I was also the only one in the room who was black. When they took me to jail, they put my hands in two sacks and duck taped them off above my wrists to find out if there was gun powder residue on my person. They also took my shirt. The tests came back negative.

Arthur Lee had finally hit rock bottom.

CHAPTER 9

SERVED MY
TIME, SERVED
IT WELL

Arthur and Baby Lemonade, 2004 – left to right:
Dave Chapple, Arthur, David 'Daddyo' Green,
Mike Randle, Rusty Squeezebox

"**O**nce you're gone you can never come back," sings perennial rock iconoclast Neil Young in his 1979 paean to rock'n'roll survival, "Hey Hey, My My (Into The Black)." The reality is that few rock artists ever come back from the wilderness of artistic bankruptcy or drugged oblivion, let alone a prison cell. Rock fans have short memories. That Arthur Lee could defy such daunting odds to mount a comeback like no other is testament to the enduring quality of his music and the legend surrounding the man. His is rock music's ultimate story of redemption. He enjoyed telling people, "I went from the cage to the stage."

The same day Arthur was sentenced, an appeal was filed on his behalf. Unfortunately, the appellate wheels grind slowly and it would take several years of legal back and forth before the petition could be heard. To exercise the appeal, David Fairweather had secured the services of William Genego, of Santa Monica legal firm Nasatir, Hirsch, Podberesky & Genego. He was one of the finest appeal attorneys around and would pursue Arthur's case for five assiduous years.

Meanwhile, Arthur did his time quietly and anonymously. He wanted no one inside to know he was a rock star. To his fellow inmates, Arthur Lee was just another con. He wanted few visitors, the humiliation of his circumstances more than enough for him alone to bear. "He wrote me pretty regularly from prison," says David Fairweather, "but I never visited him. I would have people calling me wanting to go see him but he didn't want anyone. He didn't even want a guitar. He didn't want anyone to see him in a helpless condition. He used to write about prison life, and what bothered him the most were the noise and the smell. He was a sensitive person and to go through that was difficult. He told me he got beaten up once but he didn't fight back." Doug Thomas makes a similar observation. "Arthur just wanted to stay clean, keep out of trouble, and get the hell out of that place. He wanted to make the most of his time and get on with his life."

"I visited him in the beginning, when he was still downtown," says Susan Levine, "and then at all the different places he was sent. We wrote to each other every day. I have all the letters." Indeed, in spite of his desire to avoid visitations, Arthur corresponded frequently with many of his friends. "We wrote all the time," confirms Diane. "I had power of attorney over his bank accounts and looked after his money because he didn't trust Susan. When he went to jail, she was his girlfriend, but he asked me to watch his money, even though we weren't together. Before he got out, she had washed her hands of him. I got a lot of his business papers in order."

"I was getting frustrated with him about halfway through his time in prison," says Susan. "I hung up on him at one point and just said, 'I'm not going to deal with this any more.' That's when he called Diane. She called me because I wouldn't talk to him. I appreciated the help. She stepped in and we ended up becoming good friends. We had a lot in common. Many people would meet Arthur and run away, but we'd both met him and stayed. I'm just happy that Diane was there for Arthur. She loved him, always cared about him, and was always there for him, no matter what."

Jac Holzman also heard from Arthur. "My history with Arthur didn't end with the music. Suddenly, while he was in prison, Arthur found me again. Out of the blue, a letter came from him. It was very affectionate but also contained a long list of stuff that he needed. It took me two shipments before I figured it out. He wanted cigarettes and various foods. Everything had to come in a clear plastic container and I could send nothing that could be turned into a weapon. Every six months I would get a letter from Arthur, asking for this stuff. There would be things like gym clothes in sizes medium, large, extra-large, and double extra-large. That was the point when I realized I was supplying trade goods. I had become 'Trader Jac,' going up the Zambezi River. I knew I was being had, but I didn't care. Arthur was being the scoundrel again."

Bryan MacLean wrote to Arthur in prison. An article on Love in the June 1997 issue of *Mojo* magazine was less than flattering, playing up the conflict between the two. Bryan had written to the editor, criticizing the piece and its negative slant. He wrote: "Why this onslaught of relentless negativity toward Arthur, as if being in a prison cell is not enough punishment? Prison, after all, is the ultimate rejection, and rejection was what Arthur, in his reclusiveness, was trying to avoid, and Arthur, out of reach, and more or less helpless, is sort of fair game for every vitriolic brand of idle slander." Bryan then wrote to Arthur. In his letter, dated January 12 1998, he asked: "Did you see the letter I wrote to *Mojo* magazine telling them to stop picking on you?" Bryan went on to ask if it was true that Arthur was eschewing visitors while in prison and revealed that he had recently completed an 18-month "intense rehab program." Bryan's letter concludes: "I still believe in you, and I'm praying that this is all working out together for the best (and for your appeal!)."

The hardest thing Arthur had to endure in prison was the death of his beloved mother, Agnes Lee, on February 18 1999; the day after her 96th birthday. She had been bedridden for some time and died of pneumonia at her sister Edwinor's house in Memphis. When their care-giver Margaret was hospitalized, Agnes and Edwinor, age 94, were left on their own. By then, Agnes required round-the-clock attention. Arthur paid for the care even while in prison. "He helped his family all the time and he didn't mind," says Diane. "He also helped the family back in Tennessee. Blood was important to Arthur. He even paid to have Preston Porter's body brought back from Mexico after he drove over a cliff." Agnes died overnight. She was alone in the house as the care-giver was at the hospital with Edwinor. Diane Lee: "Agnes was a huge presence in Arthur's life, so the news of her death was devastating to him. But he was in prison and he had to be strong. He couldn't cry. We took care of the arrangements for him, long distance, with his cousin Bubba, Preston Porter's brother. Arthur wanted Louis Armstrong's "What A Wonderful World" played at his mother's service, even though they wouldn't let him out to attend." Arthur's cousin, Joe Joyner, went to the funeral, in Memphis, on Arthur's behalf.

While I was in prison, I lost my mother, Agnes Lee. That hurt me more than any sentence. I didn't cry. I wasn't going to cry in prison. In there, you can't show weakness. You hear guys crying all the time. I can remember my mother, when someone told her somebody died, she would say, "Well, I'll say." While I was in prison, Kenny Forssi died of a tumor, and Bryan died at Canter's, on Christmas Day. I was very sorry to hear that. I'll never forget seeing and hearing Kenny play. In 1996, I talked with Johnny Echols about maybe putting the original Love back together and doing something musical. With me getting busted around the same time, and us talking about putting the band back together, something just wasn't right.

I would have to say that being in prison is the hardest thing I've had to face, so far. It was really hard not to be able to touch or share in any part of what was happening on the outside.

After several delays, Arthur's appeal was finally heard on December 10 2001. Arthur was granted bail at $25,000 and was released on December 13. The grounds for appeal rested on a claim of prosecutorial misconduct. This centered on two related matters: the moment in the trial when the prosecutor, on cross-examination, had raised details of Arthur's previous convictions, and the failure of Arthur's defense attorney to object to the line of questioning. It was concluded that Arthur had been "deprived of his due process right to a fair trial." The appeal stated: "We have serious doubts whether the jury would have convicted Lee on the shooting charge absent the prosecutor's prejudicial comments" (United States Court of Appeals for the Ninth Circuit). The appeal won Arthur a retrial, slated for March 12 2002. However, the prosecution and defense had worked out a deal whereby two of the charges were vacated, with Arthur pleading guilty to possession of an unlawful firearm as a felon. He was sentenced to time already served. After almost six years, Arthur was a free man again.

The state of California doesn't recognize constitutional issues. When appealing a case, you have to start in the state first, each time. So I went from one state court to another. I was denied all the way to the Supreme Court, where I was also denied. Each time I appealed, it took a year for them to reply. I appealed five times in five years. I didn't get justice until I took my case to the Ninth Circuit Federal Court, which recognizes constitutional issues. By that, I mean, for example, prosecutorial misconduct and ineffective assistance of counsel, which is what the Ninth Circuit said had happened to me. I should have been exonerated the first time.

The two witnesses that the court heard never saw anyone fire a gun up in the air. Only one said he saw me with the gun in my hand. Doug Thomas said it had to have been when I took the gun away from him, on top of that three-storey building. Doug Thomas said he fired it. My attorney failed to act or object on my behalf, or do anything but take my money. I had never been to a trial before and I didn't know much about the law. That's why I hired an attorney to defend me. I might as well have hired a thief who robbed me and left me for dead. I should not have been sent to prison because the prosecutor used improper conduct and my trial lawyer was guilty of not doing his job, something called 'ineffective assistance of counsel.' It took me five-and-half years to prove myself innocent of the crime.

I know that, no matter how dark things are, I will prevail. You have to know there's night and day, and when you're in darkness and you can't find your way, you have to have faith that the sun's gonna shine in the morning. What a treat it is to be like the phoenix rising from the ashes. And when someone asks me, "How are you doing?" I can honestly say, "Fine, thank you. And you?"

Upon his release, Arthur stayed for one month at the Mikado Best Western

Hotel in Valley Village, followed by several temporary hotels, before renting the guest house on the Topanga Canyon property of his friend, Gary Stern, at 20430 Callon Drive. "He kept pretty much to himself and wasn't playing much music when he was alone," observes Gary. "Dewey Martin, from Buffalo Springfield, was living with me in the main house and he would visit with Arthur."

Arthur tried reconnecting with Susan Levine but she rebuffed him. "My family and my daughter suffered a lot through our relationship," she says. "It caused a lot of hurt to a lot of people, to everyone who ever cared about me and loved me. So when Arthur called and said, 'I'm coming home,' I said, 'No, you're not.' It was all unexpected. I wrote him a letter. If it hadn't been for my daughter I would have let him come back, but I had to protect her. He was angry and hurt. It was a difficult thing for me to do. He was just expecting to come home. We actually tried to get married before he was arrested, and again while he was in prison, but it just didn't work out." Susan has no regrets about turning Arthur away. "It was the right decision. If I could have been given a guarantee that he would stay sober, there's no doubt we would have been together. I just thought it was too big a risk, one I wasn't willing to take again. I tried to erase that whole time from my mind, but I'll never completely erase it. There's not a day that goes by that I don't think about him."

"Prison was not easy for him," says Diane. "He didn't want to see anybody while he was there. He just wanted to do his time. He didn't play any music, didn't want a guitar. But he did come out a little changed. Arthur was still Arthur, but he was a little more subdued. I never lost touch with him. He was still with Susan, but I was always there to help him out. It broke my heart. After he came out, he called me. I had visited him in prison and was going to pick him up when he was released. We wrote all the time."

Ria Berkus remembers, years later, after he was out of prison and his career was enjoying a belated revival, hearing Arthur reflect on his prison sentence. "Arthur told me, 'As much as I hated it, if I hadn't gone to prison, I would be dead and I wouldn't have had this rebirth. I would have killed myself and that would have been it.' There was a part of him that understood that. But I don't think that, emotionally, he was ever able to regain his footing after that."

While at Salinas Valley Prison, before being transferred to Coalinga, Arthur had noticed a tremble in his left hand and arm and was diagnosed with traces of Parkinson's disease. He was prescribed medication for his condition. "What I saw in him at first, after he got out, was that he was, naturally, much quieter as he adjusted to his freedom and took stock of his new situation and opportunities," says Diane. "He was outwardly more humble but, then again, Arthur always did have a humble quality, regardless of whether others saw it or not."

During Arthur's absence, Gene Kraut had never lost faith that, one day, he would return to performing. He had a plan to launch Arthur's career comeback by mounting a *Forever Changes* tour, using strings and horns, and performing the entire album from start to finish – something which Arthur had never done. "The *Forever Changes* concert tour was Gene's idea, not Arthur's," acknowledges David Fairweather. "If it wasn't for Gene Kraut showing faith in Arthur Lee, this whole resurgence of interest in him would never have happened. Gene really took a risk and believed in Arthur. He put together the whole *Forever Changes* tour and, as a result, gave Arthur the greatest success and acclaim he had ever enjoyed in his life. All that is directly attributable to Gene Kraut and he deserves to be recognized for his efforts."

As Diane observes, Arthur had to resign himself to performing *Forever Changes*. "That was it. 'I'll do it now.' That's how he felt. But he also believed he would record new music. He had a song that he really had high hopes for, 'My Anthem.' It meant a lot to him." Arthur came out of prison claiming he had 100 songs composed in his head, but only three ever made it to the rehearsal stage. "I think he had lost his muse even before then," suggests David Fairweather. "I always pushed him to pick up a pen and write something. His greatest talent was his songwriting and it seemed to have dried up."

Arthur may now have been a chastened character, but his spirit hadn't entirely left him, says David. "I was expecting to see this shell of a man, but soon after he got out, he started playing again with Baby Lemonade. Gene had already started planning this *Forever Changes* tour. Arthur was a different person in the sense that, for the first time in his life, he admitted to himself that he'd fucked up. Maybe now he'd try to do things your way instead of his way. In that sense, he was willing to go along with Gene's plan." Another factor in Arthur's compliance was that his appeal had cost him roughly $100,000. He also believed that winning audiences over with *Forever Changes* songs would lead to the acceptance of his newer material.

The members of Baby Lemonade had been left hanging when Arthur was imprisoned. "We assumed that Arthur was going to come out and not do music," notes Mike Randle. "Then, lo and behold, on December 21 the phone rings and it's Arthur. 'Hey Mike, I want to get the band back together again.' I had quit my job at the record store back in 1996, because the gig with Arthur was really starting to happen. I had to go back and ask for a job, which was difficult. When Arthur called, the band talked about how we might get the thing back together. We wanted Arthur to agree to some things, some guarantees. We'd given up a lot to be his band and he'd left us in the lurch. It wasn't so much a financial guarantee, it was more about what we were going to focus on. What were we going to commit to? When Gene got involved, in Europe, that was the first time anyone was able to make Arthur focused, and the first time he saw the benefits of focusing. And he liked that. So Gene flew out and we all sketched out a plan, just for the summer. We would do a surprise show in April at a club called Spaceland, and not call the band Love. Arthur was nervous, it was his first show back, but he was really good. We played the Knitting Factory a month later and it was awesome. That was the real comeback show and everyone was there, the media and all the local celebrities. Everybody came to see Arthur. A few weeks later, we went to Europe." Arthur insisted that henceforth the band was to be booked as Arthur Lee And Love. No more billing as Baby Lemonade; they were the new Love.

Reviewing the April 2 Spaceland show, *LA Weekly* critic Jonny Whiteside wrote: "Mere fans' faith did not prepare one for this Arthur Lee, who hit the stage and tore into 'My Little Red Book' with such focus and force he seemed like a different person. The entire set was a dazzling showcase both for Lee's renewed ability and for Love's extraordinary catalog – some of the most complex, idiosyncratic, and artful examples of rock ever created. Lee relished the highly vocal adoration of a sellout crowd and the atmosphere was poignant, verging on the surreal. ... Beyond historic, this was no mere comeback frolic. Arthur Lee still has plenty to tell us."

"I was so proud of him for his comeback," says Ria Berkus. "I took my 16-year-old son, Jordan, to see him perform. I wasn't expecting much, I just wanted him to see a piece of my own history. Everyone was absolutely blown away that night. He looked incredible, he sounded incredible, and the band was great. It literally looked like not a day had passed, and I'm a tough critic. He was so happy. It was never a retro show because his songs never became dated. We went backstage to say hello to him and we struck up our friendship again. When we got together, the two of us, we were driving in my car and I put on 'What A Wonderful World' by Louis

Armstrong and he cried. It was very moving." Arthur later confided to Diane that this was the first time he allowed himself to cry for his mother. "I would go over in the daytime and we would play records, sing, and laugh together," Ria continues, "just reliving the old days, which he really enjoyed doing. But he came out of prison sad. How can you go to prison for six years and not be? He felt very sad that he had missed his mother's funeral, but he was determined to get back on stage and to perform again. His strength was unbelievable."

"He was beaten down, emotionally," says Dave Chapple of Arthur's demeanor upon his release. "He looked tired and hard; he didn't look healthy, more like he needed to be rejuvenated. But he got it together pretty fast. He bought an exercise bike and also walked a lot. He started doing the right things for himself."

"Do you know how much stamina that took, to jump right back to performing?" asks Diane. "He never flinched. He never told anyone what it took. He would walk miles every day to build up his stamina for performing." Mike Randle also noted Arthur's new-found rigor. "Arthur dedicated himself. He went home and practiced those songs. He practiced stage moves, and was serious. He worked on enunciating his words and using his hands, and on how to connect with people. I don't think he had ever been that dedicated for decades."

Since being committed to tape back in 1967, many of the 11 songs of *Forever Changes* had never been performed again. Arthur had to go back and re-learn his own lyrics. Perfecting the songs' complex arrangements would prove challenging for the young players, but they were up for it, recognizing how significant for the fans it would be if they were able to pull off the entire album. "It was a labor of love for us," insists David Green. "On the surface, it sounds so complicated, but once you get into it, and peel away the layers, it makes more and more sense. It's so smart and so well-written. Once you play it, you get it." Dave Chapple adds a caveat: "You have to stay on your toes to play that music, you can't zone out."

Meanwhile, over in Sweden, Gene Kraut had enlisted arranger Gunnar Norden to write out the string and horn arrangements, since no original scores existed. Gunnar and the orchestral players then rehearsed separately. Arthur and the band arrived in Stockholm (having first played several dates without the additional musicians) and a quick run-through in a hotel room was all there was time for, prior to the May 21 2002 appearance at the Södra Teatern. "It was thrilling to see the young players getting so excited about this music," recalls Dave Chapple. "Arthur was unsure about having the orchestra. He wanted to rock. But once the rehearsal got underway, he lowered his sunglasses and mouthed, 'Holy shit!' He realized how incredible it was." The Swedish government had provided some financial support for the young musicians so they could rehearse for the tour. "They were all young and had a great sense of humor," recalls Mike Randle. "They weren't stiff at all and they completely understood and appreciated the music. Each of them was a prodigy in their own right. They brought such energy to the whole show. They also worked with Brian Wilson on his *Smile* tour."

The whole ensemble – band and orchestral players – debuted that night to a resounding response. Initially, the strings and horns came on mid-set to play several *Forever Changes* songs, and then left as the band carried on with a selection of Love's best-known numbers. The repertoire would later be refined to embrace *Forever Changes* in its entirety, performed as a separate, orchestrated mini-set.

On the road, everyone had their job to do. "Rusty was definitely the musical director; he has perfect pitch," notes Mike. "But I was like the leader of the group. I was the one Gene communicated with. David Green was like Arthur's personal manager. He made sure that Arthur was where he was supposed to be at all times, and had his plane ticket, his passport, or a ride arranged. Dave Chapple was the technical guy who ensured all the equipment was working. Rusty made sure Arthur had all the lyrics, because he had forgotten some of them. A lot of times, we'd purchase Arthur's airline tickets so all he had to do was show up at the airport and get on the plane."

David Green kept a close eye on Arthur. "I would watch his receipts and carry his passport so he could relax. He was very nervous going through borders, having been in prison." In the event, Arthur was denied entry into Canada – turned away at the border to British Columbia – and was not allowed to travel to Japan, because of his criminal record. There were no such problems entering the UK or anywhere in Europe. There, Arthur basked in the adoration pouring forth from audiences at every tour stop. This was validation, if any were necessary, that he had created a body of music that was timeless; playing it touched hearts and souls. He had come back from the brink to be embraced by fans, old and new.

He took a break from traveling on June 12, to be feted by no less a prestigious body than the British House of Commons, following a motion tabled by the Hon. Peter Bradley MP, a Labour Party backbencher, recognizing the brilliance of *Forever Changes*. Members from both sides of the House gave Arthur a hearty welcome when he graced Parliament. "That was one of the greatest moments of Arthur's life," says Mike Randle. Even the Mayor of London, Ken Livingstone, weighed in with praise, calling *Forever Changes* "one of the best albums ever recorded."

I was invited to Parliament, in London, and there they passed a motion to declare Forever Changes the greatest rock album of all time. Can you dig it – me, signing autographs and posing for pictures with the Members? The day I was invited to Parliament was a day I'll never forget. Those guys did everything they could to make me feel at home. When my manager said, "You've been invited to Parliament," all I could think was, "I don't have a thing to wear." I had just bought these punk boots, in Manchester. My cowboy boots were done in, so I wore these high top, steel-plated shoes to Parliament.

I want to thank Mr. Peter Bradley and the rest of the Members of Parliament for that invitation. What cracked me up the most was when one of the MPs asked me, "How many times have you been invited to Congress, in the United States?" I almost bit my bottom lip off to keep from laughing. Of course, my answer was "none." Then they told me that they'd taken a vote about whose album was the greatest of all time and it was between me and Van Morrison [for the album Astral Weeks]. I didn't tell them about the acid I think someone slipped Van at the Whisky A Go Go. It was between him and me and they chose me. Thank you, Parliament, for recognizing my existence.

I heard somewhere that Peter Bradley thought inviting me to Parliament might spoil my image. I'd like to say this now. Peter: I didn't even know you guys knew I had an image. What an honor.

It was a Love-fest at every concert. In Manchester the band was unable to carry on until the audience's en masse chanting of "Arthur Lee" finally waned. Newspaper previews and reviews all used the word "legendary" in describing Arthur's return to the stage and tried to outdo each other with superlatives. The spring tour ended on June 29, at the Roskilde Festival, in Denmark, before picking up in San Francisco on July 23 – with a different string/horn section – and then crisscrossing the United States. Arthur's summer European tour began on August 22 in Aberdeen, Scotland – a mere ten days after the US leg had ended – and carried on until September 5 with a show in Athens, Greece. Following more US dates, the ensemble ended 2002 in Anaheim, California, with a December 28 show at the House of Blues. This was the most extensive touring schedule Arthur had ever embarked on and left little doubt that he was back and stronger than ever. After almost six years without singing a note, there was little hint of any loss in his vocal range or strength.

Still, Arthur was Arthur and there was always the fear that he could go off the rails at any moment. "While the traveling was sometimes brutal, the best part of the day was being on stage with Arthur," says Dave Chapple, with a smile. "He had his moments, just like any dysfunctional family member, but there were some sweet times, too. Arthur was the real deal. He was rock'n'roll."

According to Mike Randle, on the road, things were smoother if everyone worked around Arthur. "He could be difficult. He had a lot of inner turmoil that was made worse by being in prison. He was never good with down time, so we'd give him activities, or call his room and tell him to look at something on television. Otherwise, his mind would run wild and he'd call us up and say things like, 'Hey man, are you guys stealing my songs?' Stuff like that."

On November 27, Arthur and Love played B.B. King's club in Universal City, LA, on the occasion of what would have been Jimi Hendrix's 60th birthday. Unfortunately, Arthur's performance descended into a fiasco when, during their set, the group was unceremoniously ushered off stage to make way for Buddy Miles's drums, in anticipation of his ensuing performance. Needless to say, Arthur did not take this well. Enraged, he aimed volleys of abuse at the club manager, bouncers, and at Buddy himself, Arthur's one-time friend. "Fuck Buddy Miles!" he bellowed, "I don't care if his fat ass is in a wheelchair [which it wasn't]. Nobody wants to hear those tired old Band Of Gypsys tunes. Somebody tell Buddy Miles that Jimi Hendrix is dead!" Apparently, Arthur's outburst had been precipitated by a years-old squabble over some money which Buddy allegedly owed Arthur.

Barely pausing for a Christmas break, they were off to the UK and Europe once again early in the New Year, opening the *Forever Changes* tour on Saturday, January 11 in Milton Keynes, England. This time, Arthur would do the album from top to bottom as an exclusive set, book-ended by other Love favorites. Following another sold out show in Bristol, the tour arrived at London's Royal Festival Hall on Wednesday, January 15. Gene Kraut had arranged for video and audio recording of the show, having signed a deal with the independent Snapper Records to release a concert DVD and CD later that year. Despite a case of nerves all around, the set went off well enough. Fans rushed the stage during and after the show. "That first time at the Royal Festival Hall, nothing seemed to be going right with the lights and sound, and we thought it would sound terrible," recalls David Green. "We were relieved when we heard it and it sounded OK. That was only the third show of the tour. We were so upset. We needed some time to get warmed up. Gene Kraut spent all his money on that one recording. It was a one-shot deal. There's no overdubbing."

Mike Randle was also nonplussed by the recordings. "We had asked Gene if we could record our second Royal Festival Hall appearance, on February 3, a lot further into the tour, but he insisted on choosing the third show for whatever reason. It was probably too early in the tour. We actually had to redo 'A House Is Not A Motel,' as Arthur got lost in the moment and completely forgot where he was in the song. He was nervous, which was a very rare occurrence. Mark Linnett and the crew edited the film expertly, but if you watch the DVD, you'll notice Arthur wearing different clothes when he sings that song." Blur guitarist Graham Coxon (introduced by Arthur as "Gram Caxton") joined Arthur and the band for one of the encores, "Singing Cowboy."

Arthur had introduced a new composition on this tour, one he was extremely proud of, "My Anthem." He regarded it as a statement about America at that time – one reviewer tagged it "a love-hate letter to America." The band worked up an arrangement and the song was added to the set-list. At the first Royal Festival Hall date, the song was performed with bagpipe accompaniment, at Arthur's behest. "That guy got paid £100 and he was grossly out of tune," says Mike of the piper. "Arthur had Gene run around London, an hour before show time, to find this guy." Unfortunately, a later concert review singled out the song as being unworthy of inclusion alongside *Forever Changes* material. Personally slighted, Arthur pulled the song from future tours. "He composed that song in his head, in prison, because he didn't have a guitar," says David Green. "But it didn't come out the way it should have."

Reviews of the tour were consistently glowing: "Lee's Love Conquers All," declared the Scottish *Sunday Mail's* headline. *The Daily Telegraph* gushed that Arthur's revitalized presence "was a dream come true."

On February 3, the tour returned to the Royal Festival Hall and, with the cameras absent, the group was able to relax and rock out. "On a good night, Arthur was as great as Mick Jagger," Mike insists. "He gave everything. When he got out of jail, he had a completely different take on things and he could be amazing. Part of that was thanks to us going in earlier in the day and doing the grunt work, getting everything ready. Arthur hardly ever came to soundcheck. It was better for him to stay at the hotel and rest. Then, when he came to the gig, he was dynamite."

English singer-songwriter and lifelong Arthur Lee fan Robyn Hitchcock was in the audience for the second Royal Festival Hall concert. He would join Arthur and the band for the encore. "My first glimpse of Arthur was when he stalked on stage, like a hipster snake in bandana and shades, to sing 'Alone Again Or.' I was magnetized by the whole performance. Arthur was in good voice and, apart from miming firing a gun, seemed steady of mind. The performance was note-for-note from the album, like a classical piece. Occasionally, I would notice my blue guitar on its stand, at the side of the stage. Was I really supposed to get up and join this show? It was like being told I was scheduled to sit in with The Beatles after watching them perform the whole of *Sgt. Pepper* … . Would Arthur mime blowing me away, or worse?"

Robyn might have been forgiven for expecting trouble after penning a song entitled "The Wreck Of The Arthur Lee," in 1991. "I had conceived that song when I was marooned, recording [the Robyn Hitchcock & The Egyptians album] *Perspex Island,* in LA. I was getting migraines and listening to Love. When I got home to the Isle of Wight, I awoke next morning, at 5am, with jetlag, a hangover, and nothing to eat, so I wrote that song. It was essentially a tribute. I had been getting pretty wrecked in LA and could identify with Arthur, as I could with Raymond Chandler: both denizens of this fleshy, claustrophobic world where everything seems too good to be true but isn't, really. In the song, I represent Arthur Lee as a lost ship foundering in the Sargasso Sea, the place where a flight of Grumman Avenger torpedo bombers disappeared in 1947." Arthur hadn't been best pleased when he'd first heard the song. "I'll wreck him" he'd growled to a journalist in the mid 90s. "I was a little edgy when I was invited to join Love at the Festival Hall," admits Robyn. "Arthur didn't do the soundcheck, but Rusty and Mike took me through the chords of '7 & 7 Is.' In the end, Arthur got his own back by calling me up a song early to play on 'Singing Cowboy,' which I hadn't rehearsed, and introducing me as Alfred Hitchcock." Arthur didn't bear a grudge. "He was friendly and hugged me several times. I was exhilarated and loved playing along. My abiding memory is of discussing Syd Barrett with Arthur, backstage at the RFH. 'Yeah' said Arthur, 'what the hell happened to him?' Barrett had been a big fan of Love. It was heartening to see that Arthur Lee was still able to perform and bask in the appreciation of his greatest work, whereas Barrett had utterly distanced himself from his brief career. They died within a month of each other."

The European tour wrapped up on April 4, in Athens, Greece, after triumphant shows in Rotterdam, Glasgow, and Dublin. It had been Arthur's most successful tour, ever. "I thought it was cool that Arthur did the *Forever Changes* album live, years later," says the album's co-producer, Bruce Botnick. "To do that album live is a pretty prodigious effort, especially in England where he had such a huge fan base."

Following a short respite at home, the group was off again, this time to Australia, with shows in Sydney, Byron Bay (for the East Coast Blues & Roots Festival), and Melbourne. Dave Chapple recalls a classic Arthurism from this period. "Arthur was very hard on this tour manager, Bent. Two days before the tour ended, he came to Arthur and said, 'I know we haven't always gotten along but I'd like to give you something to make up for it,' and he handed Arthur a little bag of weed. Arthur just looked at Bent and said, 'Man, why didn't you say goodbye last week.'"

Back in the States, the band was booked at UCLA's prestigious Royce Hall on May 30 for the LA debut of the *Forever Changes* concert. Expectations ran high, only to be dashed when Arthur fell off the wagon and appeared confused and disoriented onstage.

"Somebody gave him something that he thought was something else, so he was really out of it," recalls Ronnie Haran. For his longtime friend and supporter Harvey Kubernik, Arthur's disheveled performance was the final straw. "I always rooted for him but he broke my heart at Royce Hall. It was like the Super Bowl final for him. Here was the triumphant hero at UCLA; it was the return to Westwood, a little orchestra on stage, the best sound system money can buy, the thirty-fifth anniversary of *Forever Changes* ... and he did not deliver. I kept going to the well for this guy but after that, although I was still rooting for him, I was no longer in his fan club. Arthur was his worst enemy. I stopped making excuses for his screw-ups and stopped being forgiving."

Jac Holzman was also let down by Arthur's performance: "I was really disappointed in the show. I really didn't want to go backstage because it was one of those things where you're rooting for the artist but it isn't happening. He was busy, so I promised to call him the next week, but I didn't call him. I think it just slipped my mind."

Johnny Echols and Jay Donnellan joined the group, individually, during the encores – Johnny for "7 & 7 Is" and Jay for "Singing Cowboy." "Royce Hall was not a good gig," recalls David Fairweather. "I was backstage with Arthur and Johnny Echols walks up to him. Arthur didn't recognize him. [In the interim, Johnny had undergone some facial surgery.] He hadn't seen Johnny in years. Not only did Arthur not recognize Johnny, he argued with him, saying, 'You're not Johnny Echols!' Johnny came out on stage and played on one song but Arthur was really out of it." Jay was also disappointed. "I had heard some of the shows they had done in Europe just kicked ass. Arthur was sounding great and the band was spot on. But this was not one of those nights. People say Arthur was fucked up, but I think he was really sick and the medication was causing him problems. We did 'Singing Cowboy' and it was good for me, for closure with Arthur, and for my kids to see me play."

Arthur was hanging out with his old friend Don Conka, again, and the two were on the tear. "I said to Arthur, 'Please don't get involved with Don again,'" sighs Gaye Blair. "I told him, you have the chance to break free of these people. Make new friends, because these guys get you into trouble.'"

Arthur had been clean until reunited with his old friend, remembers Diane Lee. "When Arthur got sick – he had a cyst on his pancreas because of his drinking – the doctor said to him, 'What did you do to yourself?' That was a wake up call. So Arthur didn't drink or do anything for a full year [1990]. It was so nice. Then he ran into Don Conka. Don had been in prison earlier on, for about ten years, and had cleaned up. Arthur always loved Don. Who couldn't love Don? They both got back into mischief again. Arthur loved his friends."

Returning to LA's House of Blues club for its tenth anniversary show, Arthur invited Johnny and Don Conka on stage for the encore, "Smokestack Lightning." Don would pass away on September 24 2004; Arthur was devastated, Diane Lee recalls. "He said to me, 'I have no one to talk to any more.'" Johnny Echols was on his way to LA to join Arthur and Love for a tour when he heard the news. "Arthur called and all he said was, 'Your boy's dead.' He'd often call up and tell me if some old friend or musician we knew had died. Arthur put the phone down and couldn't even say that Don had died. Then Sasha [Matt, Arthur's girlfriend at the time] picked up the phone and told me Don had died. Don was always there for Arthur, even at his lowest point. Very few people would say 'no' to Arthur, but Don could, and Arthur would accept that. He was Arthur's reality check."

Arthur returned to the UK for the 2003 Glastonbury Festival, where he and the band wowed a huge audience with the *Forever Changes* material. US dates, and their third UK trip that same year, followed. But cracks were already starting to show. "Things started to get out of hand after he'd come back from Europe and had played gigs around LA, with the strings," claims David Fairweather. "I would get calls from the band saying, 'Can you talk with Arthur?' because they wanted me to get back into the role of minder. There were times when I would be on the phone pleading with Arthur to straighten up. I tried to guilt him into doing what he needed to do. The band kind of knew that I was one of the only people who could talk to Arthur on that level. He had his health problems, which nobody knew about. Things started going downhill and his behavior became more bizarre."

When Arthur walked out of prison, he was suffering serious health problems, yet he ignored them. Never one to frequent doctors, he believed getting back to a healthier regimen was all he needed. He was still on medication for early Parkinson's disease. "Arthur knew he wasn't right, coming out of prison," Diane insists. "He was self-medicating with drugs and alcohol. Later, around 2004, he became more aware that there was something very wrong with his health. Actually, there were a few things he mentioned to me earlier, in 2002, that I foolishly let pass as symptoms of diabetes. Arthur had become a diabetic in later years. Sometime in 2004 he knew something was seriously wrong. He kept this to himself and became quieter and more introverted." Joe Blocker recalls Arthur mentioning his ill health back in 2003.

In February 2004, Arthur and Love were back in the UK for their fifth tour there in just two years. "He never liked touring the States," says Mike Randle. "He only liked touring Europe because they loved him there." According Len Fagan, Arthur needed to work as much possible. "It was my gut feeling that Arthur was going to take this love the fans were showing for him and do as many shows as possible, while he could. He was going to milk it. I think he was looking to the day when he wasn't going to be able to do it any more. He never told me he was sick, but I think he knew."

This time, the band was minus the mini-orchestra, and they were rocking at every stop. The strings and horns returned for an April 2 appearance staged at the Shepherd's Bush Empire in west London, following which the five-piece version of the band traveled across to the continent for some further dates. Arthur had, by this time, severed his relationship with Gene Kraut, following a financial disagreement, and was being booked by the UK-based Glenn Povey, who had previously worked with Gene.

A quick trip home (where Arthur and Love played a May 6 benefit show at the Knitting Factory for Arthur's friend, James "Scotty" Scott, who sadly died two days later) was followed by a further UK jaunt in June, including another appearance at Glastonbury and a slot at Liverpool's Summer Pops Festival. In early August, Arthur and the band traveled to Lisbon, Portugal for the Festival Sudoeste, and then on to the Benicassim Festival, near Valencia, Spain. Up to that point, Arthur was holding himself together, but the wheels came off in August. Arthur missed the gig in Lisbon after failing to catch his flight. "Glenn paid everyone out of his own credit card, including the Swedes who flew in to play the gig," Mike explains. "He put up with a lot, but he did a lot of things to keep it going that not everyone knows about. He went bankrupt and had to borrow money to keep going."

In Valencia, Arthur was too out of it by the time he took the stage. "I felt so awful in Spain," sighs David Green. "There were 14,000 people crammed into this tent and they were so excited to see Arthur, but he just couldn't do it. He was self-medicating. He didn't even know he had played the show. He got a cab to the venue the next morning because he'd forgotten he'd already played. The audience went from 14,000 to about 100 at the front, laughing. That's how bad it was. We just wanted to crawl under a rock. Rusty did his best to sing for Arthur but it just wasn't enough."

The revivified Arthur continued to be greeted with veneration, however. *Mojo* magazine honored him with their 2004 Hall of Fame award in recognition not only of his lasting achievements but also his remarkable comeback. In the same year, Britain's long-running music weekly, *New Musical Express* (the *NME*), presented Arthur with a Living Legend award.

My band and I were all set to watch the NME awards show on TV, but one of them said they had edited my part out. All I could think was, could it have been because of what I said when I received the award? What I had said was, "I would like to thank God and NME for this award. I never got an award from the 'enemy' before." I thought everyone was going to laugh, although I must say that it was quite an honor and everyone stood up when I walked on stage. Thank you, NME.

Back on the road in the US, on a double bill with Arthur's favorites, The Zombies, Love was joined by Johnny Echols on lead guitar. "I loved having Johnny along," enthuses Mike. "I was happy to play the string and horn parts and let Johnny do the leads because he's amazing. Nothing made me happier than to step aside and let him play the solo to 'Live And Let Live.' There is only one Johnny Echols. No one can sound like him." Dave Chapple: "Johnny was a stabilizing influence on the road. He was very together and I think that helped keep Arthur together." For diehard fans, this was as close to a Love reunion as they would experience, and they relished seeing the two original members, and old friends, on stage together.

Johnny was impressed by Arthur's band. "Before he went to prison, Arthur and I had talked about putting the band back together. After he got out, he called me again. I went to see Baby Lemonade several times and hung out with them to see whether it was just a cartoon of what we had before. I found that they were good musicians and I liked them. They weren't in it for the money, because there wasn't much money. And they were not druggies. They were dependable people and I respected them. It took me a while to fit in, so as not to take anything away from what they were doing. They had actually played with Arthur longer than the original Love played as a group. They couldn't be manipulated by Arthur. In the past, he could hire and fire anyone and he would do so, but he couldn't do that with Baby Lemonade. He tried playing one off against the other but they were a unit and stuck together."

At a gig in Cleveland, Ohio, back in 2002, Arthur had met a 26-year-old girl named Sasha Matt. He would ultimately bring her back to live with him in LA. He and Sasha moved out of Gary Stern's guest house to a spacious home, with a pool, at 5057 Biloxi Avenue, in the Toluca Lake neighborhood. "He called me and told me he had this girlfriend and that she was 26," recalls Diane. "I told him that wasn't a girlfriend, that was a granddaughter! He was lonely. He was still getting his sea legs after being in prison. But I told him that was it; I was going to go my own way. That age difference thing killed me. They would fight a lot and she would go back home to Ohio; then she'd come back. Every so often I'd get a phone call from him and we'd talk. She would break up with him and go back. She was still a young kid. One day, I got a phone message from Arthur and my heart just knew he needed me. I admitted to myself that I really cared about him. But I knew something was wrong with him. I worked at the Children's Hospital in LA, and had seen that same look in kids who were ill and dying. Arthur would say he had pneumonia – he'd had problems with his lungs. He was very susceptible to drafts in his chest and throat, so you'd often see him with scarves on to protect his neck. His mother had TB when she was pregnant with him. In 2004, he was still touring but something wasn't right. I started going back and forth to Arthur's: I knew he needed me. I got a call from him. I answered coyly, saying who is this? His reply was: 'This is your soul mate, fool.' We *were* soul mates, kindred spirits, but we didn't live together. My mother, age 86, was living with me and needed me to care for her."

Arthur's health was declining and he realized something was seriously wrong. However, being Arthur, he refused to get proper medical attention. He didn't know at the time, but what was sapping his energy and strength was leukemia. Years of alcohol and drug abuse were also catching up with him. "By early 2005, Arthur was drinking a lot to mask the way he was feeling, which wasn't good," says Diane. "He probably weighed 135 pounds by then. He was dying but he didn't know it. He thought he had pneumonia. He had a broken rib after he fell and hit the bathtub. By then, his bones were weakened. It was already in his system. He was no longer strong. You don't just suddenly get leukemia and die. I think there was a seed of it there in 1995, before we broke up. His bones were getting brittle, and this was before he was 50. I think it got worse in prison. Had he gone to a doctor, sooner, maybe something could have been done. Arthur was brought up Christian Scientist and it takes a lot to get them to go to a doctor."

In March 2005, Arthur embarked on yet another UK tour, his seventh since his return to performing. This one would again feature Johnny Echols. "He played so many times in England after he came out of prison, two-month tours, which he'd never really done before, that it got to be a bit overdone by 2005," suggests Chris Hall, the UK-based producer/director of the *Love Story* documentary. "When he first came over and did *Forever Changes*, it was quite an event, but the venues were starting to get smaller each time, because they did so many gigs and it became less of an occasion. People still loved him, over here, but they started thinking, 'Oh, Arthur Lee's over here on tour, again.' When he came over, after getting out of prison, it was like a mythical figure returning. 'Bloody hell, it's Arthur Lee!' There was so much legend surrounding him and Love. He adored the adulation he received over here; but I got the impression it became more like work for him by that last tour, in 2005. I think he didn't want to be a nostalgia act. He'd had enough and was tired of playing *Forever Changes* over and over. I know he was keen to do new material but he didn't quite have it any more. I got the impression that he knew people didn't want to hear his new stuff. In hindsight, I think it's so good that Arthur had those last three years and was able to receive that adulation and respect. Prison may have saved his life."

The final six months on the road with Arthur were difficult. He was back to drinking and criticizing the band. It came to a head with two bad shows in San Francisco, in June. "I had never seen him that way, except when we played that gig in Spain," says Mike Randle. "In San Francisco, he stopped the show to berate me for no reason and said some horrible things about me. I have no idea why. The whole year had been like that and it culminated in those shows in San Francisco. Arthur didn't know why he was hurting but he was sick, so he was doing a lot of alcohol and a lot of drugs. I told Arthur that we didn't need to do this upcoming summer tour but he told me he needed the money."

When the band met Arthur at the airport, prior to the March UK tour, they were taken aback by his gaunt, disheveled appearance. He looked like he had been bingeing for weeks. Dave Chapple: "He had actually been wasted for three months straight." Gaye Blair recalls this period. "There was one conversation where he called me saying there were leopards in his house and he'd called the police. I thought, 'I can't deal with this. Arthur, I think you have brain damage from all the drugs you've taken.' He complained for a long time that his ribs were hurting, that he didn't feel good. There was something wrong."

Chris Hall and the UK-based film company Start Productions had determined to make a documentary on Love and had contacted Arthur, through Gene Kraut, back in 2003, during the *Forever Changes* tour. However, it took them two more years before they were able to nail Arthur down for two interviews for the documentary. The first took place during the spring 2005 Love tour, when the band stopped over in Yorkshire. "We spent an afternoon with him in a bar, Mojo's, in Leeds, of all places," recalls Chris. "I had seen him on that tour a couple of times. He wasn't as impressive as he had been. That was the last tour he did. I don't think we had the full picture of what was going on with Arthur, and I don't think we expected to have it, really. There were people around him saying he was in great shape and others saying they didn't think he'd make it through this tour. It was just after Don Conka died, and I think Arthur took Don's death so badly that it kicked him into a downward spiral. Physically, he seemed good. He had a very impressive physical presence. The interview went pretty well, it was early in the tour. With Arthur, you just let the cameras roll and he'd slowly reveal things as he felt more comfortable with you. You couldn't lead him. You just had to let him relax into the situation, because he could be so guarded."

In June, the production company came out to LA to continue with interviews and undertake location shooting. They spent two days with Arthur, who was more receptive this time. The first day's interview was at the Hyatt Hotel (the scenes, in the finished film, in which Arthur is wearing a white shirt) and the next day they drove around with him, visiting points of interest in the Love story, including The Castle. "On the first day, Arthur came in with Crimson Crout," recalls Chris. "He seemed happier doing these interviews on his home turf, when he didn't have to get up the next day and do a gig. I wasn't aware that he was unwell, at that point. He seemed to be looking forward to it. By then, we had earned his trust. Driving around LA, being guided by Arthur Lee, was a bit surreal. Afterwards, he took us to Lucy's El Adobe restaurant and he was in fine form. He may have been struggling a bit, but he kept that hidden from us. By the end of the day, you could tell he was tiring."

The production team also interviewed Johnny Echols, Jac Holzman, Bruce Botnick, John Fleckenstein, The Doors' John Densmore, Michael Stuart, and Baby Lemonade. Crimson Crout and Rosa Lee Brooks ended up on the cutting room floor. Snoopy was tracked down in Washington State and David Angel's interview was conducted in Switzerland. The filmmakers were also fortunate to receive all the footage from a 1998 Bryan Maclean interview about the formation of The Monkees.

Diane had to help Arthur get ready for the *Love Story* filming. "He had no energy. The night before the filming, I shaved his head and his face for him. He couldn't do those things. It was a real effort for him just to drive the car. For him to do that, and to walk through The Castle, was not easy. He knew he was sick but it wasn't diagnosed as leukemia yet. I was so grateful that hey did that film. They sent Arthur a copy of the promo, which was six minutes long, and he was very pleased with it. He never got to see the completed film, though. They did a wonderful job. Arthur really appreciated them doing the film. He wanted to document his life before he died."

Arthur's return to The Castle would be a highlight of the film for many. Chris Hall recalls the visit with mixed emotions. "At one point during filming, Arthur was strutting about in his cowboy boots and the owner says to me, 'I think his boots have marked up the floor.' I turned white. We had insurance worth about

£500 [$970] and the thought of him grumbling about what's happening to his floor scared me. But the guy was a big Hendrix fan and wanted to quiz Arthur about Jimi. They get tons of requests to film in The Castle, but they refuse most of them."

Released in 2008, *Love Story* was well-received by both critics and fans. "It was not the most straightforward subject to tackle," acknowledges Chris, "and I think people understood that." The film follows the original band's history up to 1968, and then picks up the story with Arthur's *Forever Changes* tour in 2003. Although it was ostensibly a band biography, Arthur became the focal point. "It wasn't as if we started out making an Arthur Lee documentary," Chris points out, "but when you talk to people [about Love] the focus always comes back to Arthur. Everyone's dealings with the band were through Arthur: he was the point of contact for Love. He was the lead singer, songwriter, and frontman, so it's natural that it would focus more on him."

A second 2005 UK tour had been booked for the summer, starting on July 1 in Stourbridge, Worcestershire. However, this time Arthur didn't make it. What transpired remains a source of controversy among fans and factions close to Arthur and the band. The outcome was an unpleasant fight that unfortunately played out in public and left bitter feelings on both sides. Arthur was too ill to travel or perform but continued to hide that fact from Baby Lemonade and Johnny Echols as they prepared for the tour. At the last minute, rather than admit he was in rough shape, Arthur simply did not show up at the airport, leaving the group to go on without him, in the hope that he would join them in the following days. When Arthur did not arrive, the group made the decision to try to salvage the tour by performing without him. They issued a statement to the effect that Arthur was in no mental state to perform. Hurt by this, and the fact that the band had chosen to soldier on without him, Arthur lashed out at them, collectively and individually. Arthur and Baby Lemonade never again performed together.

"I had no idea it was a health thing, but he was in a bad way," recalls Mike. "After that gig in San Francisco, we went over to his house, Rusty, Daddyo, and me. We sat Arthur down and said, 'This can't happen again. We don't want to go on this tour if you're gonna keep abusing yourself like this.' We even talked about having an intervention with Diane and Johnny, and maybe bringing in a doctor. We had no idea what was going on with him. He apologized and said it wouldn't happen again. 'I'm all right, man. We're gonna do this.' So we bought the airline tickets and we bought Arthur's ticket, as we often did. We got to the airport on the day and there was no Arthur. We called him at home and he said, 'I'm not going,' but gave no explanation. He then added, 'And you're not going, either.' He'd been drinking. We told him all our guitars and our bags were already on the plane and that it was leaving in 45 minutes. He still said he wasn't going. Johnny Echols was pissed off. We had made a lot of financial commitments for the tour and were personally on the hook for a lot of money. We had signed contracts. We figured we would fly to the UK and arrange for someone to get Arthur to the airport on the next flight. We were booked to do these gigs, so what were we going to do? The venues had by now heard that Arthur would not be performing, so they were looking at giving out full refunds. Glenn [Povey] talked to the venues and they agreed that everyone who came to the door would get a partial refund with the option of a full refund if they chose. What we had to do was to stand outside the club and talk people into staying. We told people that Arthur was ill and that he'd be joining us later in the tour."

In the end, rumors posted on the internet would scupper any lingering hope of Arthur appearing. "Someone blogged about Arthur telling the band he didn't want to go on the tour, and that the band had told him, 'Fuck you; we can do it without you,' which was not true," insists Mike. "Someone also said that we had organized this big coup. Glenn said that the clubs needed something that actually explained the situation, so together we drafted a statement and put it on the website. From our perspective it seemed that Arthur was going through some mental issues, because none of this made sense. Those people who didn't like us anyway told Arthur that the band had signed a contract kicking him out of the band, and that started this whole negative ball rolling. Arthur was at home, calling our wives and threatening them, all this insane stuff. Only now does it make sense, knowing what Arthur was going through, that he was so sick. He didn't mean any of that. But at the time, we didn't know that. It seemed like Arthur was losing it."

Reducing ticket prices meant the band didn't get paid for any of the UK shows, but they at least met their financial obligations, says Mike. "We paid off the tour bus and that was it. That was a very tough thing, but what made it all right were the fans; they were wonderful. They were feeding us and bringing us groceries because we were dirt poor. We would stop the bus by the side of a road and barbecue whatever the fans had given us. Johnny was wonderful. His house was facing foreclosure; I was facing going to court because I was behind in my child support payments. But all we could do was play the music. We did all this because we didn't want to stick anyone with the bills. We talked with Arthur every day, several times a day, asking him to come over, but he wouldn't do it and he wouldn't tell us why. He told us, 'Stop telling people I'm sick. What I'm sick of is you motherfucking monkeys living off my name.'"

Some fans took Mike to task for what happened between the band and Arthur. "These were people who didn't know the real story. None of us would have ever been a part of kicking Arthur out. I regret that the statement got out. But we were up against the wall. Arthur didn't feel well enough but was too proud to say that."

To Arthur, however, all this was nothing short of a personal betrayal and a mutiny. Still, he refused to admit that his health was failing him. That would have been an admission of vulnerability. "Arthur would not show weakness," confirms his friend Len Fagan. "That was one of the pillars of his personality."

Diane remembers the moment illness finally caught up with Arthur. "He was so ill he couldn't even pack. He was supposed to be at the airport and the band were phoning him, but he couldn't even get himself ready. I told him, 'Arthur, if you don't feel well, don't go.' And he didn't go. But he didn't want to tell anyone. 'I can't go, I'm not well.' He told the guys not to get on the plane but they did and they went on without him."

"I talked to Arthur a few days before he was going over to England, and he said he was going," recalls Herbie Worthington. "Then I called him a few days later and he said, 'I'm supposed to be in England but I'm not going.' He'd been drinking for days. He told me the promoter owed him a bunch of money and he said he wasn't going until he'd paid Arthur. He said, 'Those guys are doing shows in my name.' They shouldn't have done that, but, then, Arthur shouldn't have done that to them, either.'"

The band's statement had been excerpted in *Billboard* and had reached a much wider audience. "The band wrote that open letter about Arthur's mental and physical degeneration. I didn't tell Arthur about it but someone else did and it broke his heart," remembers Diane. "He made his peace with them before he died, though. He made peace with everyone and went with no bitterness in his heart. I met with Mike and Rusty a month or so after Arthur died and I told them how I felt what they did was like telling tales out of school. You don't go public with something like that and use words like that. Mike wrote a nice letter and published it on the website apologizing for that first letter."

In his personal note, posted in September 2006, one month after Arthur's death, Mike stated: "Being a strong and proud man, much of Arthur's anger may well have been due to his own failing health and problems associated with the cancer that was beginning to show itself before its actual diagnosis. ... And we all loved him. We thought we could force him to improve when things started to deteriorate, but what we didn't know was that it was too late."

"Despite the way it ended, I feel very privileged and fortunate to have played with Arthur," says David Green. "It's a time in my life that I cherish. Sure, there were ups and downs, but it was still fantastic. It was always exciting with Arthur." Diane confirms that the feeling was mutual. "They were younger and on a different plane to Arthur, but they were a team together and Arthur always knew he could rely on them. He loved and appreciated them. Before he died, Arthur said to me, 'Tell the guys I love them.'"

Arthur's last recording project was one that was unique and special to him. He was invited by legendary jazz drummer Chico Hamilton, father of one-time Love manager Forest Hamilton, to sing on a track on Chico's new album, *Juniflip*. Never known as a jazz vocalist, but a fan of that genre all his life, Arthur offered a superb, breezy, jazz-swing vocal on a version of "What's Your Story Morning Glory" – a song which Jimmie Lunceford's band had once recorded and which Arthur's father would have been familiar with. For Arthur, it was both an honor and a thrill to join Chico in the studio and guest on his album. As his friends always maintain, Arthur could sing anything. He would sing jazz standards around the house.

Scotty Lee, son of Arthur's childhood friend Hank Lee, stayed with Arthur at his rented house on Biloxi Avenue after Sasha left. Arthur never liked to be alone. Later, another friend, Akil, took over from Scotty but would not stay overnight. "I would see Arthur in the evenings," recalls Diane, "not every evening, at first. I was taking this new relationship slowly. I knew he needed me to be there to take care of him, but without seeming to do so. I would stay until he fell asleep, and then go home."

In September 2005, Arthur made the decision to move back to Memphis. His aunt Edwinor's house had been left to him and was free and clear. As he was no longer touring, Arthur had a cash-flow problem. "I went to see Arthur the day that he left LA to go to Memphis," recalls David Fairweather. "That was the last time I saw him. I'm sure he was already sick, but just how sick, I don't think even he knew at the time. Before that, he bought a new car, a Magnum station wagon, on the spur of the moment. I drove him to the dealership and there was Arthur in his full rock star regalia. The people at the dealership thought he must be *somebody* but they had no idea who. He had received some kind of royalty payment and it was burning a hole in his pocket. So we bought the car and we went cruising down Ventura Boulevard. I plugged my iPod into the car stereo and we're listening to an old radio broadcast I had from the 60s, only Arthur didn't know that. What comes on but 'My Little Red Book' – he figured it out after that. Those were good times. We went shopping for clothes down Ventura, going to different stores and singing the old Coasters song 'Shopping For Clothes.' For the first time in a long time, in LA, people were recognizing him. It turned out he's known by name to the salespeople in all these stores because he was such a good customer back in his sartorial days."

Diane drove to Memphis with Arthur and his dog, a pit bull terrier named Fancy, in Arthur's Lincoln Town Car. "There would be times," she recalls, "when he would say to me, 'If anything ever happens to me, would you promise me you'll look after my dogs?' Fancy was like Arthur's baby. And she loved me. So I said, 'sure' but I didn't get the messages at the time. I knew he wasn't well but he often got pneumonia and he thought he had it again. But it was more than pneumonia this time. He wasn't touring, so financially it was better for him to move to Memphis, because he'd have no rent to pay. But I just had this premonition, this awful feeling about it. He intended to come back after a year. I couldn't take care of him 100 per cent because I was looking after my mother. Before Arthur returned to the house in Memphis, he had a neighbor remove everything of his mother's from the place. He didn't want to see anything of hers because it would make him sad. He also never went to her grave, because he couldn't bear to see it. It would hurt him too much."

Diane ended up doing much of the driving, due to Arthur's weakened condition, despite his insistence that he was fine. The car overheated somewhere in Arizona and they spent a couple of days in a one-horse town, awaiting a replacement part. In the end, they abandoned the Lincoln in Winslow, Arizona, and rented a U-Haul truck for the remainder of the cross-country journey. Arriving in Memphis, they discovered the house had neither electricity nor running water. Arthur and Diane slept on air mattresses and cleaned up the house as best they could while waiting for the utilities to be reconnected.

Howard Lyles, Peggy Porter's uncle, moved in with Arthur after Diane returned to LA in early October.

Not long after Diane left, Arthur was feeling strong enough to think about getting back into music again and hooked up with some of the best young players on the Memphis underground scene. The catalyst would be Mark Linn. "Arthur called me from Memphis and he sounded weird," he recalls. "I just didn't want to get involved. I connected him with some guys from a band called The Reigning Sound who were very 60s influenced."

In trying to contact ex-Reigning Sound frontman Greg Cartwright, Mark called the band's former drummer, Greg Roberson, who took the ball and ran with it, recruiting an A-list band to back Arthur. "I thought it was a joke," says Greg. "I just figured someone was calling to put me on. I was a huge fan of Love. 'Who is this, really?' I would say. Then Mark explained he was serious and wanted to know if he could pass along my number to Arthur. Then Arthur called and said, 'Let's hang out.' He asked me if I could make some calls, so I started thinking about who might fit, and then we started rehearsing."

Greg recruited guitarists Alicja Trout and Ron Franklin, keyboard player Adam Woodard, bassist Jack Yarber, and utility player Alex Greene. Rehearsals were held at a classic 100 year-old Southern house on Williford Street that belonged to Greg's friend, Darcie Miller. "All these cats had been around here for years," Greg explains. "Alicja Trout had actually recorded '7 & 7 Is' and 'Bummer In The Summer,' only real punk-rock style. Arthur told me one day, 'Greg, I'm not gonna bother learning any of these motherfuckers' names until you tell me they're in the band.' He called me up one day and said, 'I kind of dug that girl guitar player. I never had a girl in my band except maybe playing violin or something.' Arthur was going back to the garage band days, totally different from the Baby Lemonade thing. I'm just sorry the world never got to hear this band, because they were great. We didn't sound like the Love bands of the 70s and 80s. We were going back to square one and playing rock'n'roll again. We were basically doing the entire first Love album. Johnny Echols was supposed to be a part of this new line-up. Arthur said he wouldn't do it unless Johnny was involved."

Meeting and playing with a living legend was something Alicja Trout will never forget. "He sounded great and he was a stylish rock'n'roll cowboy, before the cancer started to make him too slender. It is one thing to meet someone famous, quite another to meet someone that shaped your understanding of music.

Love is the greatest thing in the world and there is only one Love, and only one Arthur Lee, and I shook his hand and played with him. Wow!"

Arthur's plan was to play a few warm-up gigs in the vicinity before taking the new band, now dubbed The Memphis Love, to Europe. "We were talking about new material, too," notes Greg. "He had some stuff he had recorded before he came to Memphis that he played for me and he talked about writing some songs."

For Greg, hanging out with Arthur Lee was a surreal experience. "He was this larger than life cat, used to a whole different scene. He had that star quality about him. When he left the house, even if it was to go to the local lunch joint for a plate of greens, he would be dressed to the nines. He would walk down the street and all the kids and the old ladies in the neighborhood, who knew his momma, would call out, 'Hey Po.' He'd have a leather jacket with fringes on it and a top hat or a cowboy hat, and they'd say, 'There's that old rocker dude.' Memphis was a slower pace. It's really laid-back. Even though he was still the great Arthur Lee, and dressed and walked like a star, he could be just this ordinary guy. He wasn't the party guy. He'd smoke a little grass and have a glass of wine but nothing more than that. He and I would get together at his house and he'd play me jazz records. He didn't invite many people over to his house, so I felt honored. He would play me Amos & Andy tapes and tell me stories about growing up in LA and going to the same barber shop where all the guys in the Amos & Andy Show got their hair cut, and being in awe of them. He'd call me up just to tell me jokes and hang up. He was a trip, man."

Memphis-based journalist Andria Lisle was a friend of the new Love band members and sought an interview with Arthur. "Arthur was always this mythic person for me. I went over to the rehearsal house and Arthur was an hour late. These players had all been in bands and were well-known on the scene, but when Arthur got to the door I've never seen a group of people become so quiet and reverent. He was wearing jeans and cowboy boots with a couple of t-shirts, a hooded sweatshirt, an Indian leather jacket, a poncho, and maybe a coat over that, plus a hat and layers and layers of scarves wrapped around him. Then he started shedding clothes, like a snake shedding its skin, until slowly you got down to the real Arthur. What I didn't know at the time was that Arthur had these icy hot painkiller patches, like athletes wear, to alleviate aches and pains. Apparently, his legs were just covered in them, so he couldn't even get out of the car and walk in the door. We were supposed to do this big interview but we chatted on the phone a couple of times and I got what I got. I would ask Arthur questions about growing up in Memphis and he would say, 'I don't feel real good. I gotta go to sleep. Call me and we'll do the interview.' I ended up getting it in bits and pieces." Andria went to Arthur's house, but he didn't come to the door. "I didn't know he was so sick, or maybe I was in denial because of his mystique. He could have shown up in a friggin' surgical mask and I would have thought, 'Oh, that's just Arthur.'" Nonetheless, Andria managed to glean enough from Arthur for a two-page feature that would run in the May 2006 issue of *Mojo*. "Being a Memphis girl might have helped get the interview, and having been around people like Ike Turner really prepared me for Arthur Lee."

Superficially, all appeared to be going well but, in reality, Arthur's health was deteriorating. "At that photo shoot for *Mojo*, Arthur was in so much pain," Greg recalls. "He was sitting on the bed and he couldn't get off it without help. But he was still telling jokes. Then he called me in the middle of the night and he was in so much pain." The band had booked a gig at a local venue, the Buccaneer, but cancelled when Arthur's health worsened. "Right before that first gig, which was for $3,500, his doctor told him flat, 'Arthur, if you do this gig, because you've been so sick and because you're so weak, if you catch something it's gonna kill you.'"

Early in 2006, Arthur's weight began falling dramatically. "He dropped about 30 pounds really fast," remembers Greg. "He caught this cold that wouldn't go away and it turned into pneumonia. He'd been hurting a lot – his back, his legs. He called me one evening and he was complaining that he was in pain, so I said, 'Let me take you to the hospital.' He refused. Then he called me at about four in the morning and left a message saying, 'Dude, I can't take this pain any more. You got to come and get me.' In fact, his cousin came and picked him up and took him to Methodist hospital, downtown. When I got there, Arthur was on a stretcher in the hallway in the hospital's ER. So I got a doctor and I told him Arthur had been in the hallway for hours and people were ignoring him. 'Listen,' I said. 'He's a musician. His name is Arthur Lee. That may not mean anything to you.' And he replied, 'Yeah, I know who he is. I'll take care of it.' And he got Arthur moved into a room immediately. Arthur called me later and said, 'They've found some weird stuff, man – cancer.' I just told him, 'Well, you're a tough, mean old bird. You can take care of it. What do you need from me?' I told him we'd keep rehearsing the band, he'd get through it, and we'd be off and running. I was cool about it, but afterwards I cried because, obviously, it was serious."

CHAPTER 10

FOR EVERY HAPPY HELLO, THERE WILL BE GOODBYE

Arthur with Fancy shortly before moving
to Memphis, September 2005

For so long compelled to control everything in his life, Arthur had finally confronted something more powerful than his will. Yet he was always a fighter and, as he had proved time and again, an obdurate survivor. "Arthur didn't go to doctors," observes Herbie Worthington. "He thought he was indestructible." This time, however, Arthur realized he needed proper medical care and would require a stay in hospital. All the same, he remained optimistic that he would beat the leukemia that was ravaging his body.

Others were not so certain. Greg Roberson began to have doubts about Arthur's long-term prognosis. "I knew it wasn't cool when they had him in a cancer ward that was open 24 hours a day for anyone to visit. His room was full of posters, albums, and awards ... I knew it wasn't looking good. He didn't want to be there, and he certainly didn't want anyone to see him. Finally, he asked me to look through his phonebook for Diane's number. 'I need her,' he said, and she came down to Memphis. Diane was a godsend for Arthur, at that point."

Diane flew out in January to be with Arthur after he was released following 12 days in hospital. "Arthur always bounced back from every adversity," she says. "We truly believed he would conquer this disease. Arthur was even planning to play at the Memphis In May music festival with his new band. I would go back every two weeks or so, stay one or two weeks at a time, come back to California to work and tend to things here, then return to Memphis. We had good times together during his illness, a closeness that only two people will have in that situation, and we had hope for his recovery."

The chemotherapy treatments meant hospitalization for three weeks at a time. "They were so intense they also destroyed Arthur's immunity, putting him at risk of infection," says Diane. "He had to be built up again before it was safe for him to leave the secure, germ-free environment of his hospital room with its special air flow system. In Memphis, if he was in the hospital, I was there with him around the clock. It wasn't a dreary, sad time. We smiled and watched movies or regular TV. Arthur talked to friends on the phone when his energy allowed him to do so. But he longed to go home. He once said to me: 'I know every inch of this bed.' Regardless, he was the best patient, did everything he was told to do, and never ever complained about how his body had betrayed him or the pain he must have endured.

On March 30 2006, Diane and Arthur were married in Memphis. "I wasn't sure about doing this marriage thing again," says Diane, who had been wed twice before. "Arthur proposed to me three times over the course of our relationship. The first time was around 1983, but my divorce wasn't then final. He proposed to me again sometime around 1990. He got me an engagement ring. I'm sure I'm not the only one he ever asked to marry him." When Arthur proposed for a third time, Diane accepted.

"If Arthur hadn't been married to her, I don't know what would have happened to him," says Mark Linn. "Diane was someone Arthur could count on. She was a stable influence, very together; she got things organized."

"We didn't have rings when we got married," reveals Diane. "He was ill, he was thin, and had to have a mask on his face because he was having chemotherapy and had to be protected from germs. He put his mother's ring on my finger. The minister came to the house and performed the ceremony. Howard Lyles was the witness and best man. Arthur knew his time was short. The doctor told him his chances were fifty-fifty. We went to get the marriage licence together in Memphis, but he couldn't make it up the stairs to sign, so I asked the clerk if she could bend the rules and come down to the car. Arthur signed the licence there. I found a minister at a Memphis church which I'd passed many times. I just felt that this was the one. I made arrangements for him to marry us."

Greg Roberson kept the news of Arthur's hospitalization quiet, to keep fans at bay. "I knew that if word got out that he was in this 24-hour cancer ward, some of his overzealous fans would come in and try to take pictures of him in that bed. I lied to the fans to protect Arthur's dignity. Diane and I agreed on that but, later, when they found out, some of the fans weren't happy."

In April, it was publicly announced that Arthur was being treated for acute myeloid leukemia. The condition occurs when normal blood cells become replaced by abnormal leukemic cells, resulting in inadequate healthy white-blood-cell production. The symptoms are not easily recognizable but can include fever, fatigue, weight loss, and anemia. A susceptibility to bruising, bleeding, and bone and joint pain are also common, as is an acute vulnerability to infections. Acute myeloid leukemia most commonly affects adults; chances of being diagnosed with the disease increase with age. It is initially treated with chemotherapy or, if that proves ineffective in bringing about remission, a hematopoietic stem cell (or bone marrow) transplant. Arthur was made fully aware of his condition. Ria Berkus remembers him confiding in her about the disease. "He said, 'Ria, a lot of things have turned on me in my life, but I never expected my blood to turn on me.'"

Like far too many of his 60s music contemporaries, Arthur had no health insurance. His hospital bills were mounting and would eventually exceed $170,000. A tribute fund was set up shortly after the announcement of his illness and plans were soon underway for a series of fund-raising concerts. In an unprecedented show of generosity and support, Rhino Records advanced Arthur $75,000 while he was in hospital in Memphis. They also sent him a giant poster signed by everyone in the company, wishing Arthur well. "That was wonderful," says a smiling Diane. "Arthur was blown away that they cared about him. They didn't have to do that. Arthur had an unbelievable amount of medical bills but he didn't want to owe any money after he was gone. In the end, all the bills were paid."

Rhino president Harold Bronson sought to do something more personal for Arthur. "I wanted to get a gold disc of *Forever Changes* for him. We know it didn't sell that well on release, but, over the years, it has sold very well. I just thought it would be a great thing to do for Arthur. It had to have sold enough for a gold disc, by then." In fact, Harold had difficulty getting sales figures from Elektra and eventually had to abandon the project. "It was disappointing that we couldn't get that recognition for Arthur. He deserved it."

Despite an intense series of chemotherapy treatments, Arthur's cancer had not been forced into remission. On May 25, he underwent a stem cell transplant. Three days later, reporter Mary Powers broke the story in Memphis newspaper *The Commercial Appeal*: "Patient Arthur Lee and his doctors hope they will accomplish what three earlier rounds of chemotherapy failed to do – eradicate Lee's leukemia and save his life," she wrote, before going on to give factual details of Arthur's plight. "So about three weeks after doctors identified cord blood cells that were an acceptable genetic match for Lee, the transplant occurred on the fourth floor of Methodist university Hospital cancer wing. On Thursday, Lee, 61, became the first adult in the state of Tennessee to undergo a bone marrow transplant using stem cells from an umbilical cord."

The procedure took less than 30 minutes and required the surgeon, Dr. Rajneesh Nath, to inject the cells into a vein under Arthur's collarbone via an intravenous tube. Arthur had already undergone a severe treatment regimen that included anti-cancer drugs so powerful that, according to Mary Powers, "they killed his own healthy bone marrow." The transplant was intended to help Arthur rebuild his blood and immune system. "It will likely be 35 to 40 days before doctors know whether the new cells have survived and are rebuilding his immune system," Mary's article continued. "The risk of death remains high for the first 100 days after the transplant. Doctors estimate Lee has a ten to 20 per cent chance of long-term survival. 'If we don't do the transplant his chances of survival are zero per cent,' said Dr. Furhan Yunus, cancer institute transplant program director." The report concluded with a touching quote from Arthur: "But for this disease I never would have known I was loved so much."

"During his treatment, I saw Arthur become humbled and softened," says Greg Roberson. "When I first met him, there was still that rock-star bravado about him; but the prince of the Sunset Strip stuff ended when he realized his own mortality. There were times at the hospital when he felt really bad, but he didn't talk about dying. He was always talking about getting through this, and going out on the road. What kept Arthur going was being aware that the band was out there, ready to roll. It gave Arthur a goal, a reason to get better, and beat the cancer."

"The doctor told him that he had this 100 day window," says Diane. "It was the only shot he had. If he passed that hundredth day, his chances of surviving were pretty good. But Arthur didn't quite pass it." Arthur had the transplant on May 25, but by July 25 he was starting to deteriorate.

Meanwhile, plans for a New York City Arthur Lee tribute concert were underway. It would be staged at Manhattan's Beacon Theater and produced by Steve Weitzman of SW Productions, aided by Mark Linn. The show would feature Robert Plant, Ian Hunter, Ryan Adams, Nils Lofgren, Yo La Tengo, Garland Jeffreys, Johnny Echols, and Flashy Python & The Body Snatchers. Long-time Arthur Lee fan Robert Plant, backed by Ian Hunter's band, performed a 12-song set, including several Led Zeppelin numbers and five Love songs from the 60s: "7 & 7 Is," "A House Is Not A Motel," "Bummer In The Summer," "Old Man," and "Hey Joe."

"When I found out Arthur was sick, I thought this was something I could do for him," says Mark Linn. "Steve Weitzman had done those shows with Arthur at Tramps, in New York. He and I just started cold calling people. Robert Plant said 'yes' right away. That really was the clincher. He really put his money where his mouth was. We paid everybody's expenses and air fares but Robert wouldn't take any of that. He flew in, and rehearsed with Ian Hunter's band. He also did a lot of radio interviews to promote the concert."

The date for the show was set for Friday, June 23. Arthur was too ill to leave Memphis but appreciated the gesture of support and sent his thanks, which were read out by Mark during the show: "Thank you for the caring and the prayers. I mean that from the bottom of my heart. I never knew I had such loving and caring friends such as all of you. I hope to see you all real soon and I hope to be back on that stage real soon. Love, Arthur Lee."

The show's starry line-up offered an embarrassment of riches. "The only problem we had was advertising this show, with *all* these big names," says Mark. "I think people thought that, with so many artists, each one was only going to play two or three songs. Late in the day, we heard that Robert Plant intended to play a full set, so we were able to advertise the fact." It would prove to be a memorable show. "It was a really beautiful night and everyone had a wonderful time. It went way past curfew and the venue ended up charging us for overtime, but all that mattered was that Arthur really appreciated it. A couple of weeks later, I came down to Memphis with the check for him. I didn't realize that would be the last time I'd see him."

Mark confirms that similarly stellar tribute shows were also planned for LA and London, but never materialized. In the end, Baby Lemonade organized their own LA show where they were joined by Johnny Echols and Michael Stuart. The June 28 benefit show was staged at the Whisky A Go Go and dubbed A Labor Of Love. Bryan MacLean's mother, Elizabeth McKee, attended the show along with many of Arthur's friends and associates. "It was overwhelming for Arthur to know how much people really cared," Johnny Echols told journalist Andria Lisle. "The only sad thing was that he wanted to be part of the Rock & Roll Hall Of Fame [in Cleveland, Ohio]. He deserves to be there. All the groups that Love influenced have been inducted. It would've made him so happy to have been recognized by his peers."

Mark Linn was able to present Arthur with a check for roughly $50,000, as raised by the New York show. By that point, Arthur had been sent home to rest while the stem cell transplant took effect. "He was just skin and bones, but I joked with him that I'd seen him looking worse," Mark recalls. "He was really weak and not in the happiest mood, but I felt like he was going to survive and the doctors did, too. I thought he was going to get better. Arthur seemed like he was getting stronger every day, then he just completely crashed. He had a good doctor and they were taking good care of him, considering he had no health plan. Finally, Diane was able to get her health insurance to help cover the costs."

Arthur began reaching out by telephone to many of his friends and former colleagues. Even John Fleckenstein got a call from his old band leader. "We talked for a couple of hours, like it was only yesterday that we were together. It was out of the blue; I hadn't heard from him in years. I sensed he wasn't well." David Fairweather often spoke on the phone with Arthur during his hospital stay. "Arthur was a big fight fan, so I would send him video tapes of some of the classic fights and he'd watch them in the hospital. Arthur liked Johnny 'Guitar' Watson, too, so I sent him a videotape of a live concert. All he said afterwards was, 'He ain't shit.' The only musicians he would ever admit he was in awe of were Jimi Hendrix and John Lennon."

Gaye Blair, Arthur's former girlfriend, also received calls from him. "Near the end, I had long conversations with Arthur. I hadn't let him have my phone number but he got it from someone. I hadn't talked to him for a long time because I was trying to make a break. He told me, 'I'm sorry for what I put you through. I just wasn't always able to accept the love you had for me.'"

Johnny Echols came to Memphis to visit Arthur. "Seeing Arthur in the hospital was awful. I had known him since I was a little kid. He's always been a part of my life. No one prepared me for what I saw. He would talk with me on the phone all the time, but he never let on that things were as bad as they were. He would say he was going home, and then a few days later he would say he was staying a little longer. The way he looked was shocking. I didn't recognize him. He was about 70 or 80 pounds. I didn't realize it was him until he sat up and waved me in. It took every ounce of my courage not to show how shocked I was. The moment I saw him, I knew he couldn't survive. People with blood diseases often have a change in skin color. Arthur was always light-skinned, but when I saw him he was dark. He looked African. And he was so thin. Nobody had prepared me. People were trying to make Arthur believe that everything would be all right but it was devastating for me to see him like that. The stem cell transplant hadn't taken. It was just Arthur's time."

Arthur had developed a relationship with the hospital's chaplain, Mike Revord, who counseled him. "Mike drew close to Arthur, as did so many of the hospital staff," remembers Diane. "He would visit Arthur often. Arthur enjoyed their talks." Aside from his pastoral role, Mike was also a poet and musician and wrote some poignant verse about Arthur that was recited at his funeral. He also gave Arthur a 'certificate of re-birth' after the stem cell transplant. Sadly, the transplant would not save Arthur. His end was drawing near. Diane flew to

Memphis on July 28 to be with him. "He took a turn for the worse that weekend and died the following Thursday. He never suffered."

Arthur Lee passed away peacefully on August 3 2006, at Methodist University Hospital in Memphis. Diane was by his side. He was 61. He was, indeed, at peace when he passed away, having accepted his fate without regret or sorrow. "The only regret Arthur ever had was that he couldn't hit the high note that Jackie Wilson could hit," says a smiling Diane. "He loved Jackie Wilson's music and listened to it a lot."

News of Arthur's death hit the internet immediately and had already spread around the globe by the time the mainstream media picked up the story. Friends and associates were saddened to learn of his passing. "It humbles me that Arthur came through my life," says Herbie Worthington. "I have so much respect for him." Gaye Blair got word of Arthur's passing from a niece who had seen the news on the internet: "I'm having trouble just being on Earth, knowing Arthur's not on the planet. He was a good person. He had a lot of love in his heart, even though he may not have always shown it. And he was a true genius. After Arthur died, my mother, who had never accepted my relationship with Arthur, called me and left a message apologizing. She had been listening to the radio and they had two minutes of silence for Arthur Lee. She said, 'Gaye, I had no idea … .'"

"I'm just grateful for what I got, the time I had with Arthur," says Diane Lee. "He was the love of my life."

Tributes poured in from around the globe. Fans and bandmates, old and new, expressed their admiration for Arthur's genius and his legacy. He received more media attention in death than he had ever enjoyed in life and was widely eulogized in the press. "A singer-songwriter capable of both extraordinary sensitivity and untamed ferocity, Lee was at the forefront of the mid 60s Los Angeles rock'n'roll revolution," observed the *LA Weekly*. *Forever Changes* was canonized anew. Typically, *The New York Times* called the album "a milestone of pop ambition" and praised the "studied inscrutability" of its songs. *USA Today*'s salute extolled both Arthur and his magnum opus. "Arthur Lee, with his band Love, was a profound influence on 60s music trends and made one of that decade's crowning artistic landmarks, the 1967 album *Forever Changes*. Lee's musical range was enormous, a rock smorgasbord that encompassed surf, garage, folk, jazz, Latin, R&B, psychedelic, and orchestral pop elements."

Other notices dwelt on Arthur's idiosyncrasy. The *San Francisco Chronicle* referred to him as "one of rock's great visionaries and forbidding eccentrics," while his catalytic importance was recognized by *The Seattle Times*. "Mr. Lee, the first black rock star of the post-Beatles era, fronted Love through astonishing musical changes that have continued to resonate for other rockers and a cult of critics and fans." *Rolling Stone* succinctly dubbed Arthur "one of the key figures in West Coast psychedelia during the 1960s."

In Britain, the BBC brought Arthur's story rather more up to date. "His return to the limelight in recent years drew acclaim and recognition, his live performances of *Forever Changes* receiving glowing reviews." London's *Daily Telegraph* took a wider view: "Perhaps more important than his own success, however, was Lee's influence on other bands. Groups as diverse as Led Zeppelin, Echo & The Bunnymen, and Siouxsie & The Banshees regarded him as their inspiration. Syd Barrett cited Love as a major influence."

Besieged with requests for interviews, Greg Roberson spoke with only one journalist, Andria Lisle. "I knew she would get it right," he says. Other commentators were not so considerate. "There was an interview with one of the guys in the band, in which he implied that Arthur was coming to rehearsals fucked up," recalls Greg. "That was not true. Arthur wasn't coming to rehearsals fucked up; he was coming to rehearsals *dying*. Some days he could barely walk, he was in so much pain."

A small family memorial service was held in Memphis on Tuesday August 8, at N.H. Owen & Sons Funeral Home, 421 Scott Street. Aside from the handful of family members who attended the service, Mark Linn, Greg Roberson, and Andria Lisle were also present, along with Mike Revord, who spoke a few words. Greg, too, spoke at the service: "It was one of the hardest things I've ever had to do. I told everyone that the great thing is that at any moment there's an Arthur Lee song playing somewhere in the world. He'd left us all these great memories but also all this wonderful music. They all nodded in agreement and said 'Amen.' That was Arthur's legacy."

Following the service, the attendees went for lunch. Then Diane returned to the house for her suitcase, said goodbye to Fancy, and went directly to the airport. Arthur's casket was on the same flight. "I couldn't get out of Memphis fast enough," she admits.

Arthur's funeral took place in the Hollywood Hills on Saturday, August 12. The service, at the Church of the Hills, Forest Lawn Memorial Park, 6300 Forest

Lawn Drive, began at 11am. "Brad Colmer presided over the service," recalls Azell Taylor. "Matilda Hayward played piano, Mark Linn's girlfriend played guitar, and Allan Talbert played the sax. I made a speech. Ann Stewart Denard talked about Arthur as a boy. I'd say there were 200 people at the service. They had come from as far away as London. Leon Hendrix, Jimi's brother, came."

Jeff Blum, Arthur's booking agent in the 80s, spoke about the first time he'd met him. Douglas Prince remembered their childhood together. "Arthur was always my buddy when we were kids. He was like a brother to me." Riley Racer recalled Arthur's love of animals and fun times at Arthur's house on 27th Street. Vince Flaherty remembered Arthur letting him sit in with the band, back in the mid 60s. Mark Linn and Melvan Whittington talked about their experiences with Arthur. Melvan then performed "Five String Serenade" and joined Matilda Hayward for a version of "Stormy Monday Blues."

Leon Hendrix gave a short address. "In my lifetime, nobody inspired me more than Arthur," he said. "He found me on Hollywood Boulevard, found out who I was, and brought me back to his house. We had some hard times, but his heart was so golden. Arthur inspired me and made me pick up that guitar. He said, 'I don't care who your brother is. You play guitar for yourself,' and so I did."

Johnny Echols reminded everyone that. "Arthur and I were friends our whole lives; our friendship went back to before we were even born." He talked of Arthur's "chutzpah" and concluded by saying: "Arthur had an overwhelming presence that affected everyone he met. He loved to laugh and his laughter was infectious."

Pallbearers at the funeral were Azell Taylor, Douglas Prince, Robert Rozelle, Herbie Worthington, Melvan Whittington, Jesse Kirkland, and a fan, Thomas Galasso. Following Arthur's interment in the park, everyone was invited to a repast at Lucy's El Adobe restaurant. Lucy and her daughter, Patty, hosted, pronouncing it their gift to Arthur. "After the memorial service and the interment," recalls Allan Talbert, "we were driving home down Hollywood Boulevard, Matilda Hayward and I, and a whole flock of pigeons did a big swoop right over us. I just thought, 'Damn, those are Arthur's birds.'"

Arthur Lee touched so many lives, both through his music and simply by being the man he was. He knew life's ups and downs and met them all on his own terms. Saint or sinner, visionary or villain, Arthur was his own man and made no apologies for that. Far from perfect, he was often his own worst enemy and his career suffered as a result. A sensitive soul and a romantic at heart, Arthur could never reconcile his talent with the adulation and hedonism that surrounded and ultimately engulfed him. He was a product of his times, and perhaps his artistic temperament would have been better served in a different era. Nonetheless, he never relinquished his indomitable spirit or the drive to create. And he left us with a masterpiece that has outlived him and will outlive all of us.

"I knew I loved *Forever Changes* the first time I heard it," acknowledges Elektra Records president and Arthur's friend Jac Holzman. "I knew it was going to be around for a while. There are some things that you get from artists that you know are just intuitive. Arthur certainly left something behind that is truly magical."

In 2008, the National Academy Of Recording Arts & Sciences inducted *Forever Changes* into the Grammy Hall Of Fame, awarding Arthur a posthumous certificate of honor as a songwriter. Finally, Arthur Lee's gifts were being formerly recognized in the land of his birth. However, as Love drummer Michael Stuart points out, Arthur Lee's place in posterity was already secure. "As much as we miss Arthur, he lives on in each of us every time we listen to his music."

Chris Boyle showed me something I said over 30 years ago. I asked him, "Was that before going to the joint?" and he said: "Yes." Check it out! I said the following: "Although I am confined in this body, that doesn't mean I have to act according to being trapped in here. It's not a permanent thing, so I don't worry too much about it."

Everybody makes mistakes. Everybody's gotta live ... to make mistakes. And learn from your living. You thought I was gonna say "mistakes" didn't you? People can lock up your body but only God can take your soul. And people can lock you up for a little while, but God Almighty is where I want to go for eternity. No matter how dark things are, I know that I will prevail with the God I love.

INDEX

PICTURE CREDITS

Other books in this series:

MILLION DOLLAR
BASH: BOB DYLAN,
THE BAND, AND THE
BASEMENT TAPES
by Sid Griffin

HOT BURRITOS:
THH TRUE STORY OF
THE FLYING BURRITO
BROTHERS
by John Einarson with
Chris Hillman

BOWIE IN BERLIN:
A NEW CAREER IN A
NEW TOWN
by Thomas Jerome
Seabrook

THE
AUTOBIOGRAPHY:
YES, KING CRIMSON,
EARTHWORKS, AND
MORE
by Bill Bruford

BEATLES FOR SALE:
HOW EVERYTHING
THEY TOUCHED
TURNED TO GOLD
by John Blaney

TO LIVE IS TO DIE:
THE LIFE AND DEATH
OF METALLICA'S CLIFF
BURTON
by Joel McIver

MILLION DOLLAR
LES PAUL: IN SEARCH
OF THE MOST
VALUABLE GUITAR IN
THE WORLD
by Tony Bacon

THE IMPOSSIBLE
DREAM: THE STORY
OF SCOTT WALKER
AND THE WALKER
BROTHERS
by Anthony Reynolds

JACK BRUCE:
COMPOSING
HIMSELF: THE
AUTHORISED
BIOGRAPHY
by Harry Shapiro

Autumn 2010:

A WIZARD, A TRUE
STAR: TODD
RUNDGREN IN THE
STUDIO
by Paul Myers

RETURN OF THE
KING: ELVIS PRESLEY'S
GREAT COMEBACK
by Gillian G. Gaar

SEASONS THEY
CHANGE: THE STORY
OF ACID AND
PSYCHEDELIC FOLK
by Jeanette Leech

SHELTER FROM THE
STORM: BOB DYLAN'S
ROLLING THUNDER
YEARS
by Sid Griffin